6

F

CHILDREN IN NEED OF PARENTS

CHILDREN
IN NEED OF
PARENTS

BY *Henry S. Maas* AND *Richard E. Engler, Jr.*

IN COLLABORATION WITH

Zelma J. Felten AND *Margaret Purvine*

RECOMMENDATIONS BY *Joseph H. Reid*

1959

COLUMBIA UNIVERSITY PRESS, NEW YORK

A project of the Child Welfare League of America
financed by the Field Foundation, Inc., of New York
and Chicago

For

DANIEL

ELIZABETH

JOHN

and their young agemates

everywhere

ACKNOWLEDGMENTS

This story about children whose own parents were unable to care for them and about the communities in which they lived could not have been written as it is without:

a generous grant from the Field Foundation, which saw us through two years of inquiry in nine communities, following a year of pilot studies in the San Francisco Bay Area and in a New England city, the latter made by Bernice Boehm and published by the Child Welfare League of America as *Deterrents to the Adoption of Children in Foster Care;*

sponsorship by the Child Welfare League of America, Inc., under whose administrative auspices this study was launched, carried on, and completed;

the field work of Meredith Luther Friedman, sociologist, and Margaret Purvine, social worker, who gathered our facts on the children's cases, the social agencies, and the other facets of community life in our two rural counties, Granger and Norden, and in the three metropolitan areas, Centralia, Jamestown, and Brighton, in the sequence given;

the field investigations of Arnold L. Lyslo, child welfare worker, and Richard E. Engler, Jr., sociologist, who collected the information we have about the children's cases, the social agencies, and other aspects of life in our two small urban communities, Summit and La Paz, and in our two big cities, King City and Westport;

the collaboration of social agency boards and personnel—executives, staff members, and administrative and clerical assistants—in sixty child welfare agencies and in some twenty additional related health and welfare organizations serving the nine communities in which we worked;

the interviews we recorded with 178 persons outside the welfare field —judges, ministers and priests, labor union officials, school counselors, physicians and nurses, industrialists and tradesmen, lawyers, and others in position to know about children and their problems in each of the nine communities;

periodic consultation with key persons in the field of child welfare, especially Helen R. Hagan and other members of the staff of the Child Welfare League of America, mostly during the early phase of the study, when decisions had to be made about the kinds of facts we needed to answer the questions we were asking, and the schedules for the collection of data had to be jelled;

periodic consultation on some of the technical research components of the investigation, especially with Martin Wolins (the League's first Director of Research) and Martin B. Loeb (School of Social Welfare, University of California, Los Angeles), on the multi-community plan for study; with Robert R. Bush (Department of Psychology, University of Pennsylvania), concerning the sampling of cases for intensive study; and with Hanan C. Selvin (Department of Sociology and Social Institutions, University of California, Berkeley), concerning some of the technical aspects of processing and analyzing our quantitative data;

the observations of Joseph H. Reid (Executive Director, Child Welfare League of America), whose Chapter 24 of this book presents his own thoughts on the implications for community action in what we have found and reported;

the pioneer efforts of the study's associate director, Zelma J. Felten, in each of the nine communities we selected for our field studies, where she laid the groundwork for an investigation which none of these communities had asked for, and where she returned with findings and guides to action based on them—which takes us much beyond the story we have to tell in this book;

the over-all design and direction of the study by Henry S. Maas (School of Social Welfare, University of California, Berkeley);

the support of his colleagues at the School of Social Welfare, University of California, Berkeley, who, by their sharing in the assumption of some of his responsibilities at the School, enabled him to have the year-and-a-half's leave needed to complete the study;

the productive efforts of graduate students in two research seminars at the School, the first of which helped in the San Francisco Bay Area pilot project for this study to develop a schedule for gathering data on the children, as reported in the group thesis, "Factors Associated with the Disposition of Children in Foster Care," and the second of which produced "Barriers to Adoption: a Study of Physical and Psychological Handicaps, Ethnicity, and Adoptive Parents' Expectations," containing a copy of the final case schedule and presenting findings, some of which are included in Chapters 21 and 23 of this book;

the essential research assistance, particularly in coding, processing, and basic analyses of the quantitative data on the children, of Hanna Pitkin, James M. Kilker, and, most of all, our staff secretary, Wilhelmina Santos Telmo;

and the patient editorial help of Dorothy M. Swart, of Columbia University Press.

All of these persons and organizations contributed to our story. Responsibility for its telling rests completely, however, with the book's two authors.

H. S. M.

R. E. E., Jr.

School of Social Welfare
University of California, Berkeley
May, 1959

CONTENTS

FIGURES

TABLES

CHILDREN IN NEED OF PARENTS

I. THE PROBLEM AND AN APPROACH TO IT

1. The Children and How We Studied Them

In the United States today there are approximately one quarter million children who are without homes of their own. They are children who are living in foster care—that is, in foster families and in large groups in institutions—under the supervision of social agencies in various communities throughout this country. Some of these children will grow to majority age in foster care. Some will return to their parents or to relatives, and many of these children will then return to foster care again. Only a few will be adopted. For most, the foster care experience will stretch across months, even years, of a crucial period in their lives. This is a book about some of these children. It is a story of children in America for whom the problems of consistent personality development have been greatly multiplied and for whom a sense of worth and identity is difficult to acquire and even more difficult to retain.

For some time there has been concern expressed by persons in public life and specialized professional circles about these children living away from their own families. There is a conviction among most professional child welfare workers that every child has a right to his own parents, and that if his own parents have proved inadequate he should, if possible, be provided with permanent substitute parents—ideally, through adoption. However, in agency and community planning for children, a variety of conditions has been thought to prevent many children from attaining the goal of a permanent family. Some, among the general public, have accused agencies of holding children who might be placed for adoption in order to keep the numbers of those in agency care at a high level.

Others have blamed inadequate and antiquated legislation for keeping children legally tied to indifferent and incompetent parents or for otherwise deterring the movement of children into permanent homes. No one is clear about the extent of the discrepancy which exists, country-wide, between the great demand among the adopting public for infants who are physically and psychologically perfect and the oversupply of somewhat less than perfect children who are older than two years of age. Social agencies have found these children hard to place in adoptive homes. But some such adoptive placements are being made—though the conditions under which they occur, like so much of the complex world of children in need of parents, have not been studied and described in any systematic and comprehensive way.[1] This book is an effort to report what we have seen and learned about many hundreds of children in need of parents in nine different communities. Upon the workings of cultural, legal, welfare, and related forces in these communities many of the major meanings of these children's growing-up years, and thus their later lives, depend.

This study was begun with one major concern and with two major objectives:

Our concern was for children. This, we feel, was merely an open expression of a conscience which lies implicit in American life. That distinctive way of life has developed, traditionally, around certain human values. The great democratic experiment of which we are a part is primarily an experiment in the hoped-for realization of these values. They are the values which inhere in the personality as a thing of dignity and intrinsic worth, possessing certain potentials for development within the human community. Our study is one expression of the quest which is this democratic experiment.

Our major objectives were: (1) to secure information about children in foster care in a variety of American communities; and (2)

---

[1] Published works on the many problems of dependent children which have been most helpful to us in the formulation and completion of this study are listed in the Bibliography. Included are references to research reports and the astute observations of experienced child welfare workers which are given insufficient credit elsewhere in this book.

to make this information available both to the general public and to participating and related communities to stimulate thought and action toward modifying or changing conditions as indicated. The nature of these objectives did much to dictate the approach which we utilized. We wished to gather information in a systematic manner that would do some justice to the wide variety of the situations of the quarter million children in foster care country-wide; and we wished to organize our findings in a way that would be most useful to all American communities, which we see as units through which the core values of our larger culture are uniquely expressed.

Consequently, this study took its researchers into nine selected communities in America, varying in size from rural counties to big cities of close to a million, and in location from Atlantic to Pacific shores and from the Gulf to the Great Lakes, with way stations in between. From October, 1957, to August, 1958, two research teams, each composed of one child welfare worker and one sociologist, studied these nine counties and, simultaneously, the children in care in each of them. Information about the children and their families was gathered from all sixty agencies serving the communities at the time of our study. Key persons were interviewed in each of the communities which produced these dependent children and/or offered placement resources. The legal systems through which many of these children came into care, or which influenced their destinies in care, were studied. And the networks of agencies serving these children and families were also examined.[2]

Seen and described in these social contexts, the dependent children remain the central figures in our story. It is their characteristics, and those of their parents, and their placement experiences which are the heart of our report. Who were these children? How did they come into care? Where were they placed? How long had they been in care? How often were they moved about? Were psychological and other problems prevalent among them? Most of all, what chances of gaining a permanent home, given their current situations, did they have? Our approach enabled us

[2] Some details of the study procedures we used—for example, how a case for study was defined and the techniques employed in selecting cases for intensive examination—are contained in Appendix A.

to see the many community variations which such questions entailed within the larger cultural stream in this country.

Thus we were interested in the ethnic, physical, psychological,
and legal statuses of the children. These are factors which, in
certain degrees and combinations, are alleged to keep dependent
children in limbo—for example, the half-Indian or Spanish-American child, the child with a turned foot, the child who is confused
about his identity, the child who is of dull-normal intelligence, or
the child whose legal relationship to sporadically appearing and
disappearing parents is uncertain. But is the outcome different
when such children are seen in a community where a child's ethnic
background is less important than his basic humanness and his need
for parents, or where a Spanish-American child is a member of a
numerical majority instead of a minority? Are physical anomalies
in a child as much a problem for parents who live in a rural county
as for parents who reside in a highly urbanized metropolitan area?
In regions of the United States where who you are seems less important than what you may become, does a child of less than average intelligence still have value to adoptive parents? Is the suburbia fringing a bustling, ethnically heterogeneous, economically
inflated big city the most likely locale in which to find parents
who can offer an emotionally upset youngster a new chance? Or
is the ethnically homogeneous, and perhaps more individualistic,
small urban community the place where adoptive parents have the
personal courage and the necessary social supports to give a home
to a child who is different? These were the kinds of unanswered
questions, linking children in need of parents and their broad social environs, which we chose to pursue with a wide-angled camera.
Refined questions emerge from cores of cumulative knowledge, but
the unknowns regarding children in general, and specifically those
in need of parents, far outweigh our best hunches and tested hypotheses.

With our major assumptions clear and our questions in focus,
we set out to get pictures of the children—pictures which portrayed
them in the field of forces operating in foster care and adoption in
each community. And as we moved from the smallest to the largest

county, everywhere we heard a theme and variations upon it—a concern for children in America and variety in the ways this concern was expressed in diverse settings.   In reporting these phenomena, we have employed certain key concepts—our generalized ways of looking at the particular things we observed.   We have tried to keep these concepts to a minimum, and hope that any reader who chooses to follow our story through to its conclusions will be able, in the process, to acquire an ever clearer understanding of our conceptual frames of reference.   The test of their utility, of course, is the extent to which they help us understand the complex situations of children in foster care.[3]

The communities of our study were legally defined both geographically and by specific county boundaries.   The areas varied in size and in population; they had different histories of growth; and they showed different rates of population change indicating different paces of life going on within them.   From these basic observed realities we attempted to infer underlying forms and processes that would help us to interpret the significance and the interrelatedness of the phenomena of foster care and adoption.   Each community, therefore, was viewed as having a distinctive way of life, meaningful to those who participated in it and shared its values.   In a word, each was a separate *culture*,[4] and the phenomena of foster care and adoption had particular meanings for participants within each culture.   Each community was also seen as a *social system* in which the participating persons and groups were interrelated.   Thus, the "character" of the whole community—some-

[3] Appendix B is the repository of a rudimentary outline of the concepts put to work in this study.

[4] The following statement (from Edward C. Tolman in *Toward a General Theory of Action,* Talcott Parsons and Edward A. Shils, eds., p. 345) about "culture" may serve as an introduction to our approach which attempts to get at the defined meanings of objects, events, and relationships in a community: ". . . culture has 'names.'   It has, that is, symbolic ways of focusing the attention of its participants upon the particular discrimination and generalization units and beliefs that it favors.   The result of such names is to point out to the actor repeatedly 'what' he is to perceive and conceive, 'how' he is to differentiate it from other 'what's,' and what further 'what's' it will lead to."   It was the "names" and the "whats" of dependency, foster care, and adoption as they appeared in nine American communities that we attempted to discern, plus the conditions of their systematic interrelatedness.

what analogous to the predispositions of a personality—could be partly determined when light was cast on patterns of interrelatedness of the parts, and a community's predominant tendencies in reacting to the phenomena of dependency were one expression of its "character." Moreover, throughout our orientation to communities as sociocultural stages upon which the drama of foster care and adoption was enacted, the basic unit of our analysis was the *role* of the participants. We attempted to infer, in all our interviewing, what the expected and actual behaviors and attitudes were for persons and groups located in different positions in the community system and involved differently in its drama of dependency.[5]

Our analysis of the legal systems as they related to dependency in each community took note of the codes and statutes first. However, we attempted to locate within the system the position of the juvenile judge, and those who dealt with him on dependency matters, so that we could make some approach to determining his role, too, in this story of children without permanent homes. From our analysis of this legal aspect we inferred whether the emphasis in a given community was more toward protection of *parents' rights* or more toward protection of *children's rights*. These were not mutually exclusive tendencies; however, through legal interpretation, communities in our study could be said to be inclined more toward one than the other, and this was likely to have consequences for the placement and movement of children in foster care.

The placement services, administered through the local agencies, were also analyzed on a broad basis that seemed most likely further to complement total community configurations. We focused upon the interagency network in each setting. We avoided an intensive,

---

[5] Thus, Judge X, in community A, and Mrs. Y., in community B, for example, were seen merely as role-players involved in the drama we were describing. They appear in our story as abstractions from the real persons who were living out the multiple aspects of their total lives in their respective settings. No effort was made to describe their total personalities, but only those parts related to children in foster care and adoption. Such a context provided some clues as to the field of forces operating in an aspect of their lives to shape some of their attitudes, at the same time that their attitudes, as they are presented in the pages of our text, are also elements in those same fields of forces.

or critical, analysis of any particular agency and concentrated upon locating each agency in a network of agencies serving children. We plotted the patterns of positive and/or negative relationships between agencies, or noted the absence of such relationships. From these observations we inferred whether a given network tended to be a *collaborative* one or a *noncollaborative* one. With these tendencies as guides we were able to describe our networks of services also in terms that both flowed from, and contributed to, our total pictures.[6]

Viewed on cultural, legal, interagency, and personal levels, the situations of the children we studied became multidimensional. We found differences in the way dependent families were defined and reacted to in each community. We saw differences in the practices of judges in removing children from neglectful parents. We found differences in the availability of foster homes and of adoptive homes and in the use of such homes for placement and in the use of institutions for placement. We found differences in the degrees of cooperation between groups charged with caring for children in the communities. Finally, we attempted to discern differences in the degree to which we Americans accepted the dependent child (depending upon who he was, who his family was, and what background he had) as "our" child, one of the larger family which includes us all.

These variations are the essence of our report. We have tried to present them in a way that makes each variation understandable. We are not presenting our pictures of child welfare placements in nine communities in relation to, or as models for, any scale of values. Rather they represent a spectrum of values all sharing in, and contributing to, the luster of our larger culture. However, it is our conviction that the children who have inspired this study have a right to some initial reference points and to at least the rudiments of a compass as they seek to know their worth, their direction, and their responsibilities in life. For children without homes of their own are in danger of being cast adrift in a culture

[6] Appendix B includes some details of four factors which we think contributed to collaborativeness or its relative absence in the networks of agency services we studied.

which requires creative acts of every individual in his quest for identity and personal integration. Without homes and parents they will have lacked the warmth of parental love and guidance which must accompany life's early challenges. They will have been deprived of adequate parental figures as models for their own development. They will have great difficulties in making the positive linkages to life which grow from one's sense of being a part of the web of human relationships—all with their beginnings in the family circle.

Everywhere that our research took us we found a feeling for children. We would have been surprised if we had not, for certainly it is not the conscience of America that negates the human values we profess. There may be confusion as to means and a lack of clear definition of ends that lead to neglect of our human resources, but the latent sentiments remain to be quickened, utilized, and organized into action in every community. We hope that our presentation will help to broaden the perspective of all of us so that in every American community any child can eventually be encompassed by that circle of concern that makes him a part of the "we" who are considered of intrinsic worth and enduring human value.

II. TWO RURAL COMMUNITIES:
NORDEN AND GRANGER

2. Child Placement and Rural Community Life

Broad pasture lands in the farm belt just west of the Mississippi mark this section of the North Central plains as rich dairy country. Here the railroads that radiate from Chicago pass through the countryside and bring dairy markets close to the creameries for which Norden County is famous. And it was in this county, in Abbotsford, the county seat, that we spent a month and a half studying the situations of seventy-eight children who were in care and living, for the most part, in the local children's institution. This is a peaceful and prosperous farm area. Many of the people who live here have local family roots that predate the Civil War. Yet changes are taking place that quicken the tempo of the way of life. For in Norden industry has begun to absorb a working force that the land can no longer support.

Just 527 highway miles to the north and west, across two state lines, is another rural community, which we call Granger County. There, on the broad prairie between the Bearpaw River Valley and the Missouri Plateau, the black soil yields the finest grains in the country. On this site, in Daleville, the county seat, we spent another six weeks studying the situations of an additional thirty-two children in care—most of them living with foster families in the community and its environs. This too is a quiet area. The winding Comanche River, controlled by a new Federal dam some fifteen miles upstream, now flows placidly through Daleville. And its placidity is in harmony with the pace of local life. In Granger, people who still live close to the land find a place to work, to plant, to watch the seasons changing, and to raise their children.

In these two communities, most of the 110 children under study were without homes of their own, and only a few were moving into adoptive families or back to their own parents. How did these two rural communities care for children in need of parents? What were the situations of children in foster family and institutional care? Who, by comparison, were the children in adoptive homes? One way to begin to answer these questions is to introduce three of the children, two of whom were in foster care placements and one in an adoptive home. Let Karl Bayer represent [1] the children in institutionl care in Norden County. Like Karl, almost all of these children came from outside the county's boundaries to the Lutheran church-sponsored residential center in Abbotsford.

Karl Bayer, thirteen years old, lived with about fifty other boys and girls in the Abbotsford Home for Children. Abbotsford is the county seat of Norden County, with a population of about five thousand. Like most other thirteen-year-old boys and girls in Abbotsford, Karl attended the eighth grade class at the public school and every Sunday morning went to St. John's Lutheran Church. But the other children and their parents and just about everyone in town knew that Karl was "different," for he was from the Home.

About two years ago, Karl arrived at the Home from a county across the state after he had succeeded in "exploding" two prior foster placements. His first had been in a large private institution for dependent children outside Walloon, where he lived for a year and a half following his eighth birthday. Karl's second placement was with a foster family in Walloon for almost twelve painful months. Increasingly during these years Karl's vacillating demands for attention were followed by violently distrustful responses to any and all adults who thought they were giving

[1] We say a child is "representative" of others when what characterizes him and his situation also either characterizes the largest number of other children in his group or illustrates a central tendency of the group of children as measured in some other way.

Also, see Appendix A-1 for our definition of a case for study. Note that no child in care for less than thirty days was included in this inquiry, since the transient, emergency case was no concern to us at this time. Moreover, children classified, like Karl Bayer, as being in foster care must not only have been in foster care on April 1 but must have still been in a foster family or institution on June 30, three months later, for inclusion in this study as a child in foster care. If moved into an adoptive home or returned home by June 30, he would have been classified as an adoption or as a return home case. Appendix A-1 clarifies details on case selection and categorization.

him what he wanted. It became very clear he needed the special care that, in this state, only the Abbotsford Home for Children could give.

Karl had not lived with his parents since his eighth birthday. His mother's attitude toward him and his three sisters was labeled "markedly ambivalent." In effect, Karl's mother, thirty-nine and remarried, seemed almost as erratic as Mr. Bayer. From Karl's birth on, Mr. Bayer was in and out of the household and could never be counted on to assume any obligation to the family. Like Karl's mother, he had completed a tenth-grade education, but, an unskilled carpenter, he had never managed to work at more than odd jobs. Now, at age forty-seven, he was thought to be remarried, but his whereabouts were uncertain.

Understandably, Karl's feelings about his parents were not warm or friendly, nor did he show affection for any of his three sisters, two of whom still lived in a state institution for dependent children and one with a distant relative. None of the three had apparently wanted to see much of him in the past five years. The last brief effort at a visit ended violently with Karl's distant relative swearing she would never again allow the boy in her house. Now, about the only persons in whom Karl showed any interest were a cottage father at Abbotsford Home, the caseworker he saw there regularly twice a week, and a few of the children at the Home.

According to his caseworker, Karl seemed quite confused about himself. Certainly, the flat facts about him did not help him to establish his identity. He was white, Lutheran, of average intelligence, free from physical disability or disease. His last permanent residence was Berlin, a city at the other end of the state. The court had by now deprived his parents of the right to determine where Karl should live, although he doubtless wondered less and less whether either of them really cared. Karl's emotional remoteness from his parents had developed as self-protection many years before his mother volunteered, in her childlike way, that she just could not take care of him any longer. But then, by this time in Karl's life, neither could any of the substitute parents who tried.

One wonders what Karl might be like if efforts had been made to remove him from his immature and completely self-centered parents many years earlier. Would he have been different if the law and legal agents had supported his removal long before his mother voluntarily gave him up at the age of eight? One wonders how the year and a half he spent then in the large impersonal institution for children outside Walloon affected Karl's unstable bases for becoming more grown-up than either of his parents. Presently, institutional care at the Abbostford Home for Children seemed to give him the only kind of setting in which he was able to live—with its skilled adults better able than any foster family member to keep as distant from Karl as he needed them to be without his feeling they were disowning him.

Gary Olsen, to whose situation we now turn, speaks for twenty Granger County children in foster families. While Gary, of Granger, and Karl Bayer, of Norden, had many similar personal and familial characteristics, community responses to these two boys were somewhat different. It should be noted, of course, that Karl was not a product of Norden but arrived there after placement in two other counties in the state. Still, there did seem to be some unity of reaction throughout this state to situations like Karl's. Its long history of institutional care for children included the continued use of two large state-supported institutions for dependent children. Although the state's mode of financing and its segmented organization of children's welfare services nominally offered counties much local freedom, in effect they appeared to prescribe institutions as the preferred homes for children like Karl and his sisters. And children might travel far from home for institutional care. By contrast, Gary Olsen's birthplace, home, and foster family placements were all in Granger County—a setting in which the social convictions and personal energies of Mrs. Camilla Jones, Granger County's director of public welfare, seemed to have ample space for expression.

Gary Olsen was twelve and a half years old and lived with the Meads, just outside Daleville. Like Karl, in Norden County, Gary was white, Lutheran, of average intelligence, and free from physical disability or disease. Like Karl, Gary was one of four children of parents who no longer lived together. Again, Gary's father was in his late forties and earned his living by unskilled work, in this case farm labor; Gary's mother, in her late thirties, was thought to be remarried. These were the similarities. But community reactions differentiated the situations of the two boys.

Mrs. Jones placed Gary and his three brothers in two different foster families when Judge Swanson removed them from their father for "neglect." This was almost three years ago. Actually, Mrs. Jones had known about, and kept a watchful eye on, the Olsen family ever since, a year before, Gary's mother had deserted the family and Mr. Olsen's drinking had become worse. Farm neighbors—mostly the families for whom Mr. Olsen had worked—were able to help on an informal basis just so long. Judge Swanson removed the children until, he said, Mr. Olsen could give evidence that he had mended his ways. While Judge Swanson's assumption may have been that this would not be too long a period, Mrs. Jones seemed quite clear that without appropriate treatment—and none was available locally—Mr. Olsen was unlikely, barring a miracle, ever again to establish a household for his sons.

At first, three years ago, Gary was placed with the Heidts so that he could continue at the same school and be with his best friend, Ted Heidt, and thus experience a minimum of disruption in his daily living. (He had practically been boarding with the Heidts for some time before his official foster care placement with them.) Since the older Olsen boys were in high school and the youngest was just beginning at school, they went to live with a family on the outskirts of town.

Apparently, all went well at the Heidts until ten months ago. Then Gary was accused of being involved in sex play with some other boys; the word got around very quickly, and Mrs. Heidt definitely thought that Gary should be moved to another family, some distance away. Mrs. Jones arranged for this transfer quite quickly, feeling there was a strong bond among the Olsen boys and glad now to have an opportunity to place them closer together.

Currently, Gary's adjustment was a good one. Though Gary's feelings for his father were not strongly affectionate, Mr. Olsen visited occasionally with him and the other boys. The foster parents were not especially disapproving of Mr. Olsen. And Mrs. Jones knew that Judge Swanson was not averse to letting temporary separations for parental neglect gradually become permanent ones if the conditions which initiated the separations did not improve.

Children who found their way into adoptive homes in our Norden and Granger populations were very much alike in background and personal characteristics. But they were quite different, for the most part, from children in foster care in both these counties. Thus, although Sharon Rilke was in an adoptive home in Abbotsford, we need present no separate portrait of a Granger County child placed in adoption. (Such differences as did appear between them, as well as the cases of three somewhat unusual adoptive placements in Norden and Granger, are presented in Chapter 5.)

Sharon Rilke was a year old and had been in the Weber home for ten months. In accordance with her previous plan with the adoption agency worker, the little girl's mother relinquished Sharon at her birth. As soon as the slight physical complications attendant on Sharon's birth were cleared up and the pediatrician seemed certain that Sharon was "a normal healthy baby," the Webers took her home.

Like most of the mothers of the Norden and Granger children in adoptive placements, Mrs. Rilke, as Sharon's mother calls herself, had never been married. Now in her mid-twenties, Mrs. Rilke was a waitress in the hotel in Pearl City before Sharon's birth. Prior to that she had worked as a waitress in Walloon, where she came from her downstate home to live for a while with George, a boy with whom she had fallen in love in high school. The child born of this relationship was being brought up by George's mother. Moved to Pearl City, Mrs. Rilke met Sharon's father, more than ten years her senior, a married man with two teen-age children, living on a marginal income earned as an electrician's helper. Both he and Mrs. Rilke readily approved of Sharon's being placed for adoption.

With slight variations, with either more or less known about the permanence or transience of the relationship between the child's mother and father, and with some changes in the urban or rural areas involved, the story of Sharon and her parents was repeated in essence in nine of the twelve cases of children in adoptive placement in Norden and Granger counties. The children concerned were as likely to be boys as girls, and in Norden they were as likely to be Catholic as Lutheran. Certain other characteristics of most of the adoptive children in these two rural counties were also similar—apparently normal infants, relinquished by their own parents in the first few months of life, going to an adoptive home in a second or at most a third move.

Differences between Norden and Granger, however, began to show up in the adoptive picture too, for the very few children in adoptive homes followed opposite pathways in the two communities. In Norden none of these children was a local child. Rather, a few couples were adopting children who were brought to Norden from outside the county. In Granger, local women had borne five of the six children we found in adoptive placements, although only one couple, a professional man and his wife living in Daleville, provided a child with a Granger adoptive home.

In addition, the representative cases of Karl and Gary suggest that the placement histories of children in foster care in these two counties reflect markedly different community ways of life. For, generally, Norden and Granger—though superficially similar as economically comfortable, rural, North Central Plains counties, populated predominantly by Lutherans of Northern European origin—were serving children in need of parental care in quite different ways. Norden provided primarily institutional care to children like Karl Bayer, from outside Norden County, who first came into care in his school-age years and stayed in care longer than the Granger children. In Granger, proportionately more neighbors voluntarily served as foster parents for local children, and proportionately more of all the children under study were brought into care earlier in their lives and their stay in care was, on the average, shorter. Some of these key details are compared for the counties in Table 1.

Table 1

PLACEMENT, LENGTH OF CARE, AND SEPARATION AGES OF
CHILDREN IN NORDEN AND GRANGER COUNTIES

	Norden County (Abbotsford)	Granger County (Daleville)
Type of placement, by percentage of children in care on April 1, 1957		
In foster family care	25	67
In institutional care	67	17
In adoptive homes	8	17
Average (median) number of years since first separation from parents, for all children under study	5	2½
Age at which children first entered care, by percentage of all children under study [a]		
As preschoolers (0–5 years)	19	40
As school-aged children (6–10 years)	44	16

[a] Because of the nature of the grid used for recording placement history data, length of time in total care had to be computed in "years of life" while date of current separation could be compared with birth date to arrive at child's age at "current separation." Thus different intervals account for small but apparently inconsistent variations which may appear between "total" and "current" separation data.

By comparison with Granger, services for children in need of parents were given to few of Norden's own children—in fact, only seven children, compared with twenty-six of Granger's own. Instead, foster care in Norden was for children who were outsiders—a condition of special import, as we shall shortly make clearer, in a county as ethnically homogeneous and essentially self-contained as Norden. Granger, on the other hand, responded primarily to its own children in need of substitute parents. And within Granger

County there were relatively more families who opened their doors to children seeking a foster home—though only to one child for an adoptive and therefore legally enduring relationship.

What were the forces in each of these rural communities making for their quite different patterns of child placement?

THE TWO RURAL CULTURES

Norden County

Norden is located in a state which calls itself the "richest agricultural area in the world." [2] But this rich agricultural area was rapidly changing, and the change could be seen in the redefinition which it sought for its economy. For the same brochures which declared this to be "the richest agricultural area" went on to invite "industry, science, and commerce" to communities where people who "know how to work" would be awaiting them.

Here, in a region central to avenues that carry core-cultural values [3] across the farm lands, the problem of securing industry which could absorb the growing town populations being surplused off the farms was being faced directly. Still, the concern was with adjusting the economy in the interests of those who, having grown up in the small communities of the state, had a pride in their local areas and wished to continue to live, work, and raise their families there. Thus Norden was not in the market for new people; rather, it sought industry to better the life of those who already were in and of the county.[4]

[2] Norden County is in a somewhat more urbanized state than is Granger, although the 1950 census still listed more rural than urban residents in the state. Better than 70 percent of Norden County's 19,000 people lived in rural homes— that is, all but about 5,000 people listed for the county seat of Abbotsford itself. (Note that all data in this book drawn from the U.S. Census reports are for 1950. More recent estimates were not uniformly available.)

[3] This term is used throughout this book to indicate those beliefs, values, and attitudes which, to a degree, all Americans share in common, but which some share more than others. By it we hope to strengthen the impression that our communities are sociocultural systems which are a part of a larger American culture and are differently located within it.

[4] But farm life was changing. A board member of the Abbotsford Children's Home described this change. Mrs. Fred Lange lived in a house in one of the newer residential areas of town while her sister and brother lived on farms.

What had economic changes meant to Norden and its people? The predominant German Lutheran stock, whose ancestors pre-dated the Civil War, still were anchored to the milk herds and creameries that make Norden the dairy spot of the state. And even the appearance of agriculturally oriented industries, like the large farm machinery plant, had not changed its ethnic make-up. The visitor immediately felt the homogeneity of these people, of whom one resident said, "Here one is either Lutheran or German or both, or an outsider." Even new occupations had tended to spring from grass-roots beginnings so that the industry one saw in Norden was not so much outside industry but, as it were, "inside industry." Still, and this is in contrast to Granger, the total Norden County population had increased, particularly in the decade and a half since the Second World War.[5] But the evidence indicated that the newcomers too, coming mostly from neighboring rural counties, tended also to be "either Lutheran or German or both." Coupled with this is another contrast to Granger County; in Norden only about one in thirty-five of the local inhabitants was listed as foreign born (almost all of these, by the way, were either German or Danish).[6]

These facts indicate something about Norden as a community which contrasts it with Granger. Norden had felt itself to be progressing steadily for a hundred years. It had been relatively closed to any but people much like those who had grown up there in the

But, she said, "They both have much nicer homes than I do. And my brother's eldest boy, who is thirteen, has a 4H project, but if he didn't have this steer to raise his life would be no different from living in town. He plays basketball and is in the high school band."

Mrs. Lange also noted that young people were tending more to stay in the community for their higher schooling. Half of the preceding year's high school graduating class went to the local Lutheran college, whereas it used to be the exception, said Mrs. Lange, to go there. And many youth who went away to college came back to Norden to live.

[5] Norden County's population increased by 5.3 percent from 1940 to 1950, and the population of Abbotsford increased 23.3 percent (*vs.* 15.8 percent for Daleville) in that period.

[6] Evidence of the way in which Norden's reference groups tended to overlap can be seen in the statement of the local Catholic priest that his parishioners were largely Germans and their predominant occupation was dairy farming. So even this small religious minority tended to blend, in the things which it shared in common, with the larger homogeneous in-group of the community.

past several generations. Yet it had continued to grow and to thrive, with the pattern of its growth being largely conditioned by social dynamisms which not only affected internal conditions but deflected and modified the influences toward change which came from without. New residential areas had grown up on the periphery of Abbotsford, and commercial and industrial concerns had added office buildings and factory additions.[7] And the evidence indicated, as we have noted before, that Norden, unlike Granger, was tending to hold its young people.

Granger County

The daily happenings in and around Granger County are in some ways not very different from happenings in other parts of rural America today. Still remote from the main lines of commerce and communication, Granger's rural ways changed slowly. The Big Missouri, scene of an expanding network of Federal engineering projects, is more than a hundred miles west of Daleville. And the new interstate highway, linking the state capital to the east with the state's largest retail and wholesale center to the west, would by-pass Daleville and barely permit the traveler a glimpse of the city's tree-lined streets and stone churches.

The people who settled Granger County were like many of those one finds sprinkled westward across the Northern United States. They raised livestock, and grain from the rich soil of the river valleys, and congregated for their worship and their social and commercial activities in the towns which dot the right of ways of the Northern Pacific—one of the proud empire-building railroads of an earlier era. They were largely Scandinavian and other Northern European folk—Norwegians and Swedes, with a sizable proportion of Germans and Danes interspersed among them. But in Granger County, we found enough Southern and Eastern European stock —Russian, Austrian, Hungarian, Czech, and Polish—and enough Catholicism alongside the predominant Lutheranism for this to be

---

[7] Nearly one in five persons working in Abbotsford was employed in manufacturing—a low figure compared to large industrial centers but almost four times as high as the figure for Daleville.

an area in which differences among people were visible and accepted. Significant too for this feeling of openness to difference in such a relatively small community was the fact that one out of fourteen of Granger's inhabitants was still counted by the U.S. census-takers as foreign born. For the child in need of substitute parents, also in his own way different, Granger's air of acceptance of difference was relevant.

The children of Granger have grown up in this social setting amidst an agricultural economy. But there is a breadth to the horizons of the Granger countryside which makes it difficult for local youths to keep the locus of their life ambitions within the county's boundaries. There is a challenge in a landscape of level fields that invites exploration of what lies beyond them. And just as the whistle of the Northern Pacific once lured away young men during the drought and depression days of the thirties, so the flow of traffic along the east-west artery now takes with it an increasing number of Granger County youth, as often as not in cars which prosperous postwar years have enabled them to purchase for themselves.[8] It was a tribute to the agricultural wealth of Granger County that it had prospered so well in the postwar years and had held many of its human resources close to the soil. Still, with the consolidation of farms and with the advent of more machines that replaced farm hands, agricultural employment was shrinking. And with this dwindling of opportunity in agriculture came a declining population in Granger County.[9]

But Granger was not a poor community or a backward one when

[8] A Granger school official described this change quite dramatically. He said that in the thirties farm children never got into town. The school district sponsored spelling contests and athletic tournaments to get the children into the county seat, took them around to visit local facilities, and treated them to a movie. Now, with two or three cars around a farm, they come to town all the time. The schools once planned tournaments in which every boy would play at least two games on two different days so that he would be in town at least two days a year. Now there is no need for such a program.

[9] According to the 1950 census, Granger County lost 5.2 percent from its total 1940 population of nearly 18,000. The county seat of Daleville gained in population during the same period by nearly 16 percent, indicating the greater loss in rural-farm population for the county. Daleville's growth had been accounted for mostly, the census showed, by older people who retired in town from the farms.

we studied it. The community still saw itself as an agricultural center and foresaw its future prosperity along agricultural lines.[10] In this small community, too, people still tended to meet face-to-face each day with many individuals with whom they personally shared many values—and a nod and a greeting, a chat on the day's activities or on those of the coming weekend, gossip about illness or good fortune befalling one's friends, and talk about family troubles. This was a setting in which the things around which people shared common values tended to overshadow those around which clusters of individuals had unique views. It was here that we observed children like Gary Olsen, children who had been deprived of homes of their own and for whom the community assumed the responsibility of foster parenthood.

Now, we are ready to relate the facts of child dependency and foster care, as we observed them, to the varying contexts provided by these two areas of rural America.

Social Form and Process in the Cultures

Certain tendencies in social form and process may be inferred from the population composition, the rates of change, and the histories of growth of Norden and Granger which we have just sketched. The relevance of these tendencies to patterns of child placement in our two rural communities is a major focus of our study.

First, both Norden and Granger, being small, tended to be relatively homogeneous, although Norden was ethnically more homogeneous than Granger while Granger was economically less stable and prosperous than Norden. We also noted that neither community had a visibly segmented population, nor was class stratification implied to any degree in the social differentiation that was observable. In the historical growth of Norden and Granger we did not see the dramatization of stigmatizing class or caste names which might separate group from group and person from person. A tour of Abbotsford and Daleville revealed that, in living arrange-

10 Only about one in twenty of Daleville's employed population was working in any form of manufacturing.

ments, any objective bases for class distinctions were very subtle. As we were conducted through Daleville by a local minister the sameness of the descriptive words, ranging from "less nice" to "very nice," suggested the slight degrees of variation in streets and housing we observed.   In Abbotsford only two small "lower class" religious sects could be identified by a local Lutheran minister, and, he said, few families knew of the existence of one of these sects until recently.

This kind of social sameness, to which these cues point, emphasizes the importance of the relative visibility of difference of the dependent child as he is cared for in such rural settings.   For in Norden and Granger the prevalence of dependency, the conditions contributing to it, and the recognition and social definition of those conditions appeared quite dissimilar, as did the methods of acting upon dependency and caring for the dependent child.   For example, in Norden, fewer local dependent children were visible; in Granger, more foster families were available.

Secondly, both Norden and Granger tended to manifest social processes in which the symbols of people's assigned or ascribed status took precedence over the symbols of their acquired or achieved status.   By this we mean that both these two small rural areas apparently favored a view of life which placed greater emphasis on a person's family name and place in the community than upon changes in his social position associated with educational, occupational, or economic achievement.   Of course, both communities evinced the physical movement from farm to town that is common in America today.   However, Granger County was losing its young people to surrounding, achievement-conscious urban centers, while Norden County was actually growing—drawing more people into a way of life that was also subtly changing—but was still anchored in a rural matrix.   Both counties continued to provide, however, highly personalized settings for the give and take of community life.   They were small enough for social relationships to be, preponderantly, on a face-to-face and individual-to-individual basis.

We propose that where the values of achieved status are low in a community's hierarchy of values, and where personalization of relationships obtains, adoption through an agency will be an infrequent practice. For the statuses of an adoptive child and his adoptive parents are themselves achieved statuses, and agency adoptions are apt to be formal, contractual relationships rather than highly personalized ones.

Also, Norden and Granger differed in the degree to which each community was inclined to emphasize either separateness or interdependence of groups and individuals. Norden seemed to stress independence of the individual, while Granger had had more growth experience that stressed the importance of interdependence. Wounds of the great depression were recalled as much more painful in Granger than in Norden. And Granger seemed more receptive to visible ethnic differences within the community, having had a wider range of social experience in its history.

Finally, in terms of orientation to the dependent child and his family, Granger seemed to accept the children of our study more into the larger "we," while Norden relegated them more to a "they." If the depression of the thirties brought crises to a larger number of people in Granger than in Norden, dependency conditions were thus more normal to Granger than to Norden. But most of all, the dependent child in Granger was initially one of the community's own, while most dependent children in institutional treatment in Norden came there from outside the community, often after many other foster care experiences. Thus the dependent child in Norden, being seen as different, was in a situation that tended to consign him to a "they" position in this homogeneous, independence-oriented, and highly personalized community. Consequently, his social and psychological problems of personal identity—knowing his worth, place, and direction—seemed greatly enhanced.

CHILD PLACEMENT

Foster Care in the Two Cultures

In attempting to account for the placements of children like Karl and Gary we must keep in mind these major tendencies which, we believe, help to represent the situations and give meaning to the social facts of foster care in each community. In part, they explain the varying definitions of dependency, in these two personalized communities, which we have expressed as differences in the degree to which the dependent person is considered a part of the "we" or more as one of the "they." Some facts bearing upon this issue may now be reviewed.

First, most of Norden's dependent children came from urban homes outside the county, while most of Granger's dependent children were from rural homes within Granger County. Secondly, most of the Granger children in care on April 1—about two out of every three—were in foster families. One might argue that the foster family program in Granger reflected a greater acceptance of dependent children than did the institutional pattern in Norden. It is to be noted that the Abbotsford Home for Children in Norden had clearly changed its purposes from those of its orphanage days. We saw it as an institution for housing and treating dependent children too disturbed to live for any time in a family unit. Still, with a history that dated back to Civil War days, in a state where institutional care still is prevalent, the Home continued to reflect a definition of the dependent child as quite different from his peers. It separated him from the local citizenry somewhat more than did the foster family program in Granger. In fact, and in effect, the dependent child in Norden was an outsider.

It must be remembered, too, that Norden had only seven local children in care at the time of our study, compared to twenty-six in Granger. Thus it seemed that, granted some differences in socioeconomic conditions between the communities, Norden was much less prone to perceive dependency and act upon it on the local scene even though at the county seat was an institution which cared for a large group of children who were highly visible in this ethnically homogeneous and essentially self-contained society. The strongest impression which we gained in exploring the Norden community was that "we just don't have dependent families or children here." [11] The idea arose that, whatever the reason for a

11 While the relative unemployment figures for the two county seats showed only (for 1950) 1.5 percent unemployed in Abbotsford and 3.6 percent unem-

reluctance to take action on dependency, this proud German Lutheran community simply did not define its own families as neglectful, except in extreme circumstances. Many of the people we
interviewed in Norden recounted the very same story of a dependent situation. It was one that illustrated Norden's reluctance
to recognize a dependency problem as such:

> John Wagner's family was known in the community. The father drank,
> and the mother had lived at times with another man. The boy was left
> very much to fend for himself. The county attorney remarked that he
> had never taken a case like this into court unless there was some delin-
> quency involved. While neighbors might be willing to say, informally,
> that a child's home life was not satisfactory, they would never so testify in
> court. Consequently, John never appeared in court until his own delin-
> quent actions—shooting up some unoccupied cabins down by the lake—
> brought him forcefully to the attention of the community. The shots
> which John Wagner fired were his signals to the community, saying, in
> effect, "Here I am—take notice of me and do something about me." At
> least, they had that result.

The children whose cases we came to know at the Abbotsford
Home were probably more definitely separated out from the rest
of the Norden community, as children with problems of emotional
and social adjustment, than their orphan predecessors in this private institution had ever been.   For Mrs. Fred Lange, a local trades-
man's wife and a board member of the Abbotsford Home for Children, recalled that taking children from the Home into one's own
house was once accepted practice.   That was when the Home was
operated as an orphanage and children were temporarily accommodated by local families as a charitable gesture at vacation and
Christmas times.[12]   In those years the children were an even more
highly visible group, wearing prescribed uniforms, toward whom
the community conscience could express itself. Obviously, chil-

---

ployed in Daleville, the number of our "in-county" dependent children in
Granger County outnumbered those in Norden by almost four to one. Median
incomes of families and unrelated individuals were $2,277 for Norden County
and $2,071 for Granger County.

[12] In the case of the Breit family, presented at the end of Chapter 5, a request
for a child for a Christmas visit first brought Roger Wild, a child with many
problems, to their home. Over five years later they adopted him.

dren living at the Home then were not seen in any abiding sense as a part of the "we" in the community but were "different" in being orphans. Still, those children may have served a legitimate function as a "they" toward whom the community could respond with some favor, but now the disturbed children of the treatment setting seemed a more remote and disturbing "they," toward whom the local culture had difficulty adapting itself. As John Lindquist, a local school official, said, "When the Orphan's Home just had normal children everybody automatically had a soft spot in his heart for children without a home. Today, it takes an effort to like the children. They are naturally in various scrapes." He added that "the community could stand a continued explanation of the Home because the current explanation does not seem to be working successfully."

However, the Reverend Emil Schubert, a professor at the local Lutheran college, believed that the "thinking element" in the community accepted the Abbotsford Home and its children. His son, a student in the local high school, remarked that the children from the Home were nice when one came to know them, but the recent ones he had met at public school were harder to know. It seemed to him that some of these children tended to be more delinquent than the orphans had been, and some prided themselves on looking delinquent. For example, a few of the boys from the Home had adopted the newest symbols of rebellious youth—the long haircut and the black leather jacket, certainly more alien and disturbing to Abbotsford citizens than was the formerly prescribed orphan's uniform.

In Granger the situation was somewhat different. Mrs. Camilla Jones considered her "active" cases to be those in which she was working to keep children in their own families before their problems had to be heard in court. To her, the situations calling for placement were usually the "more hopeless" ones. In many of these cases, parents were absent and often had compounded their own delinquencies with neglect of their children. But Mrs. Jones did initiate placement away from home when it seemed necessary, and court action often helped her effect such placement. At the same time, the doors of homes in Granger seemed open to these children, and this seemed in accord with the informal neighborliness of the community. Indications were that in such foster families children were not considered commodities although they might be used as extra "hands" on the farms. As the county auditor put it, "an extra person on the farm is an extra hand, but not so much an extra mouth to feed," since food is usually plentiful and its provision does not depend on a pay check. In this setting there was room for a child. In rural life, a child's value may not be so dependent on how his achievements reflect on his parents, who are not in competition with other parents. This kind of rivalry seems more associated with certain urban settings where the proximity of families to one another and the desire for upward social mobility may inflict greater social pressures on the child.

Other attitudes in Granger supported the impression that Granger children who came into foster care were not, in the process, separated out too far from more fortunate children or from members of normal families. Nor were they deprived of the emotional reinforcements which accrue to those who are a personalized part of the "we" in a rural community. For example, Mrs. Ruth Hardy, the public health nurse in Granger, used the term "community mothers" for those women in rural areas of the county whom she had seeking for "down-and-out" families. Sometimes, she said, these ladies would personally take such families under their wing; at other times they would refer them to her for help. Often people in the county would care for relatives' children.

Even in rural Granger, however, the informal and open acceptance of children in foster families was changing. Mrs. Camilla Jones remarked that her welfare department had received no requests for foster children in some time, and fewer people wanted their homes licensed for foster home care. We can only speculate about the reasons for these changes. For example, while Granger had weathered rough depression days, it currently was enjoying a degree of prosperity. Not only were problems of dependency less acute, but the slight financial remuneration given the foster parent was less attractive now. The foster family program was under-taken in the thirties by Lutheran groups who felt a responsibility to the community's children. The minister at Trinity Lutheran Church estimated that nearly half the dependent children in the state were cared for in this manner, with the others cared for by relatives, mostly on farms. At the time of our study, however, since problems of dependency stemmed mainly from the towns, it was harder to find homes for children. Even where farm homes wanted adolescent boys (and with mechanized farming they were less desired than in the past), a town boy was reluctant to go to a farm. Girls from the farms who got into "trouble" in town were usually cared for in urban centers where maternity homes pro-vided a degree of anonymity for both them and their babies. So even Granger's children might be pushed, increasingly, farther toward the frontier of the "they."

Our picture takes into account how children leave foster care. In Granger only one child and in Norden only three returned to the home of relatives between January 1 and June 30, too few cases for us to generalize about. Moreover, considered against the total number of children in care in these communities, these were the smallest proportions of returns in our study of nine com-munities. Thus, the children in these two rural counties, once they entered care, seemed to stay on—unless they were adopted. What were the facts on movement into adoption in these two com-munities?

Adoption in Norden and Granger

In neither of our rural communities did agency-supervised adop-tion appear to have "caught on" to any great extent, and espe-cially not with farm families. In our total population of 110 chil-dren under study in Norden and in Granger, there were only twelve —six in each community—in adoptive homes. Five of Granger's six adoptive placements were outside the county, four of these five were in urban families, and the one in Granger was with the fam-ily of a Daleville teacher. Since there seemed to be a small amount of adoption taking place through agencies in these two counties, how did these facts square with what else we knew about these two communities?

In Norden, which was still drawing people into its way of life and was holding its young people, we expected to find some local modification of the core-cultural drive toward achievement. The people we interviewed gave slightly conflicting views, but the consensus seemed to be that there were families in Norden definitely interested in adoption. The county extension director felt that there were relatively few adoptions through agencies because "most German families have children" and Norden families tended to be larger than the national average. A pediatrician at the local clinic said that there just was no supply of adoptable children. He accounted for this partly through the low rate of illegitimacy in this county where shotgun marriages, he said, were not infrequent. The public health nurse, too, thought that there was little illegitimacy in the county. Where it did occur, she believed that parents consulted with the family doctor and he then arranged the adoptive placements.

Despite the short supply of adoptable babies, Norden seemed to have a larger potential adopting public than did Granger. The pastor of one Lutheran church said that Norden people liked to adopt children and that he usually referred them to the Lutheran agency in the urban center of an adjacent county. The local Catholic priest knew of eight adoptions among his parishioners in three or four years. Most of the children came from the big cities of the state. The clinic pediatrician stated that he could place twenty-five babies immediately if they were available. And the public health nurse was sure that most people without children in the community would rather adopt children than take them in foster family care.

In a community like Norden where everyone tended to be "middle class" and there were so few obvious symbols of higher or lower status the value of social mobility seemed lessened. Thus the importance of achieved parenthood was probably less dominant here than it might be, say, in the suburban residential areas of a metropolis where everyone is a newcomer and achieved symbols are so highly esteemed. Still, prosperous young families in Norden seemed to desire children to help fulfill their own lives. What is clear is that none of the adoption agencies serving Norden County—neither the Catholic nor the Lutheran nor the nonsectarian agency—thought of Norden County as a particularly useful resource for adoptive families.

Granger's six adoptive placements were mostly outside the county. Within the community itself the pattern of providing foster family care and of accommodating another child much like one's own in a temporary living arrangement was much more frequent. This pattern involved little perception of social mobility, since placement in a foster family does not usually imply social betterment, nor did it seem to evoke any stigma in this community. On the other hand, the process of legal adoption often involves a bettering of a child's status, and perhaps of the parents' status too in having achieved parenthood; and it also usually involves a contractual relationship with an agency. This achievement-oriented process and these contractual relationships were still confined, in Granger, to the near-by urban center of Bearpaw, through which children were now being placed in adoption.

Granger's public health nurse, Mrs. Hardy, who had many contacts in the rural areas of Granger County, could recall no farm family who had adopted a child. The pastor of the Daleville Episcopal Church knew of no requests for adoption among his parishioners since he had been pastor, although one communicant had completed an adoption from a private agency in Bearpaw. The pastor of the largest local Lutheran church could think of only one family in his congregation interested in adoption. But, he said, he sensed little need for adoption in the community. The young couples, who, if childless, might be most interested in adoption, were inclined to move away from Granger to the larger urban centers like Bearpaw. And although Mrs. Jones had referred a few requests to the private agencies in Bearpaw, she thought there were not many adoptions, even on a nonagency basis, in Granger County. She had been asked to make, at most, one or two adoptive visits a year.

The adoption data square, then, with our impression of Granger as a community in which the values of the core-cultural achievement orientation applied mainly to those who had been drained off by urban centers. A school administrator in Daleville remarked that half of the young people now go on to college, and most of this group do not return to the community. "They have the idea," he noted, "that to be a success they must go away from here." An agency executive in near-by Bearpaw quoted Margaret Mead as saying that "the tools for making a livelihood, except with inheritance, are too expensive now for the young." And the tools and the symbols of the achievement complex in American life were increasingly, for these young people, those things like the automobile which carried them away from what seemed to them the more static opportunities of Granger and toward the more bustling centers of urban population. It was in these centers that, when childless, they would probably adopt children.

3. The Legal Systems

The values of a culture are not merely implicit in the behavior of participants at a given moment in time. Predominant values may be expressed explicitly in the formal laws which define the rights and responsibilities of citizens in the political community. Thus, in any study of dependency, the law and its interpreters must also be considered.

LEGAL ROLES IN NORDEN COUNTY

The Judge

Judge Farnham Walker, a man in his early fifties, lived in a town somewhat smaller than Abbotsford and in a county adjacent to Norden. His home was a wooden structure, comfortably and attractively furnished. The melting snow still muddied the unpaved street in front of the house one winter evening as we looked in upon the judge to get his views on child dependency and parental neglect. He talked in an easy, pleasant manner which gave one the impression that he was expressing personal convictions rather than delivering a cut-and-dried judicial lecture.

"God gave the parents children; it would take something very strong to take them away," said Judge Walker, and one felt immediately that this man would not wish to challenge the Almighty on matters so grave. "Yes," he said, "I am quite reluctant to set myself up as judge of someone's fitness to raise children." Then he described the case which seemed to have set a precedent in this rural state on matters of the removal of children from their own parents for neglect. This case occurred some years ago and involved the removal of a group of children from their parents in a county farther west. These children were placed for adoption after the rights of their parents had been terminated, but the State Supreme Court reversed the decision on removal for neglect and returned the children to their parents.[1] Judge Walker felt that this decision made judges in the state reluctant to remove children from parents unless delinquency was involved, and his own practices reflected this situation. "In my three years on the bench," he said, "there have been no cases brought before me of children where the grounds were strictly neglect and dependency." There had been complaints not based on delinquency, he explained, but these were over feeble-minded children who were only technically neglected and dependent and were in court actually because of their mental condition.

Judge Walker was hard pressed to think of any situation which he would include in the "neglect" category. He felt that, perhaps,

[1] The case mentioned is referred to in the annotated code of the state. It occurred in 1951 and involved, first, a temporary removal and, later, a permanent removal of eleven out of thirteen children from a mother who was sickly and a father whose job necessitated his traveling. In the first decision—in February of 1951—the Supreme Court reversed the earlier removal by a lower court (in which some of the children were placed for adoption), and ordered all the children back to their parents. The case was brought before the Supreme Court again in June of 1951, and at that time the children in adoptive homes were left in these homes. Whatever the legal merits of the case, the decisions involved apparently had a marked influence on the decisions of lower courts in neglect cases in this state—or at least support was given to existent values and practices.

someone incompetent to earn a living and care for children might be called unfit—but Norden County did not have many, if any, such people. Once in a while there were situations of immorality or drunkenness arising in other types of cases, and the judge had felt at times that the children involved might be better off in another home. But these cases came to him for other kinds of decisions and presented no issue of "neglect" to be acted upon.

Our visit with Judge Walker left us with a clearer understanding, from a different vantage point, of the Norden community, in which, to our questions, local residents repeatedly replied, "We just don't have dependent families or children here." This key judicial personage was part of a system whose values had best been expressed in the previously cited State Supreme Court decision against releasing children for adoption solely on the grounds of parental neglect. Thus the judge was a part of a judicial process which, for our purpose, was more theoretical than actual. Of the seven children in our study who came from within Norden County, none had been removed by Norden County's court on the grounds of neglect. It was within this judicial climate that other key people, also involved with the legal codes and the court, operated.

Other Legal Figures

Our intent in each community was to be able to describe what happened to a neglected child as he moved through the local legal processes. Since neglect cases were almost unheard of in the court in Norden, we were really inquiring about what might have happened to a neglected child on the local scene if he *had* been recognized as neglected.

One of the influential legal figures in a position to hasten or block a child's entry into foster care was the county attorney, Archie Crane, an elected official whose position permitted him to practice law privately. The combination of public and private duties kept him busy, and possible cases of neglect were a small part of his personal concern and responsibility. Once in a while Mr. Crane saw an extreme case which he would consider one of "neglect." Such a case might involve the children of alcoholic or very disturbed parents. But in effect, the citizens of Abbotsford (and

Norden County) were reluctant to inform their county attorney about instances of neglect and were even more reluctant to be witnesses in court. At the same time, Mr. Crane was well aware of Judge Walker's unwillingness to remove children because of neglect and therefore was not encouraged, even if community witnesses were available, to take such cases into court. With this set of conditions obtaining, it was not surprising to learn that there had been no neglect cases in court during Mr. Crane's two-year tenure and that he knew of no cases having come up for some time prior to that period.

It should be noted that in some communities it would have been the welfare department which learned of families who might be considered neglectful, worked with them, and, if necessary, referred them for court action. This is a frequent procedure where the local welfare department has a protective services program in operation. In Norden County, however, the welfare department had no part, official or unofficial, in the legal system, and the department's social worker had had no occasion to attempt to use the court in a neglect case. Actually, the worker knew of few such cases, and his procedure was to try to help these few families or refer them elsewhere for aid. In any event, he avoided court involvement and efforts to have children removed from parental custody. Consequently, cases involving neglect situations in Norden had to wait until they might finally be handled as cases of delinquency.

LEGAL ROLES IN GRANGER COUNTY

The Judge

Judge Will Swanson seemed close to the local scene in Granger. We walked up the three flights of stairs to the top floor of the county courthouse to meet him in his office on an afternoon when he could spare some time from court duties. The judge greeted us cordially, settled back somewhat expectantly in his swivel chair, and awaited our questions. He was a small man, with tanned and rather leathery skin which gave him the look of one who spent a good deal of time out-of-doors. He spoke softly. There was nothing dogmatic or defensive in his manner. It was soon obvious that he too, like Judge Walker, was more attuned to delinquency cases than to dependency situations. It was difficult for him to keep the two separate, but at least the dependent child was a part of his experience and not a completely alien figure.

"The major problems," remarked Judge Swanson, "are those involving children being out on their own at night. If parents are out in the tavern while the kids are on the streets at eleven, twelve, or one o'clock at night, then I consider the children are being neglected. And it's that kind of neglect that leads directly into delinquency." He paused, then plunged into a discussion of the type of youth problem that seemed closest to his heart. "You may have heard about that big fight in the meadow in which thirty-seven boys were involved. I put all thirty-seven of those boys on a ten o'clock curfew. If we can get the kids *home* at ten," and he slapped his desk for emphasis, "we'd be rid of juvenile delinquency."

We brought the discussion back to the dependent child, for we knew that of the twenty-six local Granger County children in our study well over half had gone through court procedures which resulted in a modification or termination of parental rights. The judge corroborated our impressions. "The younger kids, maybe six or seven years old, would be removed temporarily if parents leave them late at night and go running around," he said. "But I give parents a warning first. And sometimes when parents lose control of their children I place the children with relatives for a while."

Judge Swanson was a key person in the determination of placement for Granger County children. He emphasized his reluctance to remove children from parents, and this reluctance became even stronger, he said, where he was asked to remove children permanently. In such a situation there was no further chance for the parents to come back into the picture, and Judge Swanson, like his counterpart in Norden, was not anxious to sever ties of kinship in a court of human law. Still, there were dependent children in Granger County, children who had been so defined by the community culture and by its welfare agents, and he was called upon to make grave decisions.

Most of Granger's dependent children, it will be recalled, were living in foster families. In many such cases the children were in a legal situation wherein their parents' rights had been modified but not permanently terminated. Since the judge ordinarily had no further contact with these children, there being no provision for periodic review of their cases, they remained in a rather indeterminate status in which their parents retained some but not complete legal control. This seemed to be the situation with about one out of every three Granger County children—a situation probably frustrating to social workers in their efforts to make permanent plans for children like Gary Olsen once they had left their own homes, yet still reflecting an atmosphere in which dependent families were really "not too different from the rest of us." As Judge Swanson so clearly said: "These families whose kids appear before me are really not very different from any other families. All families have problems. It's just that some families let things slide rather than making the kids toe the line. Then someone has to step in to do something about it." At such times Judge Swanson felt it was his duty to move in, reluctantly, to arrange legally for substitute parental care for some of the community's children.

Other Legal Figures

Before a child's case reached Judge Swanson there was a preparatory hearing before Frank Keim, the court's referee, who made recommendations to the judge. Recommendations to higher authority are, of course, never final. Mr. Keim came from Bearpaw and traveled around the judicial district acting as referee whenever a local judge wanted such time-saving help in delinquency and neglect cases. A forceful young attorney, Mr. Keim was deeply concerned about the causes of the situations he saw in court. To him, parents and children were troubled people who needed the kind of help that a brief hearing and an admonition could not provide.[2] He saw many parents he would consider unfit because

2 At Mr. Keim's invitation we were observers at a juvenile court hearing at which he made a sincere effort to get at the causes of a child's behavior. The child had been caught stealing, and the young attorney tried in a sympathetic, but admittedly frustrated, way to find out why the child had been stealing and

of drinking, poor morals, or physical abuse of children, but when it came to removing the children, he could only recommend—and often his recommendations were turned down by the judge. A man of legal training and experience, Mr. Keim expressed a child welfare philosophy closer to the viewpoint of professional welfare people than to that of most spokesmen for the legal profession.

Phil Ross, a local attorney, was another person whose name often appeared in connection with juvenile court matters. He stood ready to give legal counsel to parents who were called in for hearings on neglect charges. As a lifetime resident of Granger, Mr. Ross often knew his clients personally from school days and was equally likely to know personally the children involved in a case. He was concerned about the proper care of children as well as the protection of their rights, but he was not so sure that parents were as unfit as social workers might think them to be. He did not necessarily disagree that parents might be rightly called "unfit," but in any case parents needed legal counsel, and this he was ready to give whatever the shortcomings of his clients. His approach and philosophy were legal, reflecting a definite "human touch." He stood ready to balance the rights of the child with the legal rights of the parents before the law.

In Granger, unlike Norden, the county welfare department stood in the fore of the legal picture. Mrs. Camilla Jones, as director, had contact with the children before they ever got to court or even into an attorney's office. The community's children were her primary concern, and it was a local custom to call her whenever someone thought a child might be living in a harmful situation. Such a call always elicited personal involvement and interest from Mrs. Jones. She was willing to go to great lengths to help a family care for its own, but once she had done this and parents continued their immoral or intemperate ways, she then saw them as subjects for court rather than welfare help. But many times the legal process seemed a frustrating one to Mrs. Jones, particularly when her idea

---

to discover a means for keeping him from stealing again. Thus, the "diagnostic approach" was known to this community, but its application was confined, for the most part, to individual efforts on the part of persons who felt constrained to do something more than merely control and punish offenders of the local mores.

of a neglected child did not coincide with that of Judge Will Swanson. She felt especially thwarted when she tried to plan beyond the temporary placement of a neglected child in foster care. She could not agree to returning such a child to an "unfit" home, but because of the judge's philosophy she found it almost impossible to have a child removed permanently from his parents. And even where she hoped for temporary removal, there could be disagreement between "welfare" and "the court." This conflict was exemplified in her account of the Rickert family.

"The Rickert case," said Mrs. Jones, "was one of utter neglect, although the parents didn't abuse the children physically and loved them the best they could love anybody. Still, the children just ate from meal to meal, and the place was as filthy as a pigpen—and I don't mean a well-kept pigpen." She sighed as she recalled the hearing. "But you know, the Rickerts came in to the judge right after a bath, and their children behaved better than my grandchildren." She paused to let the irony of the situation sink in. "Neglect should include the immorality of parents. As it is now, children have to be practically beaten to death before they are removed from their parents." Then, as if aware that perhaps she was overstating a situation from her own standpoint, she added, "Still, just because we've worked hard on a case, the judge shouldn't take children if he doesn't feel he should."

Mrs. Jones's final statement seemed in tune with Granger's situation as we saw it. For although the legal world of Judge Swanson and Phil Ross, and the welfare world, represented by Mrs. Jones and, in part, by Frank Keim, were not necessarily in agreement on values and procedures, they were in frequent contact. Out of these personal as well as formal contacts it seemed that a feeling of mutual knowledge and a respect for the need for the two points of view had developed.

THE CODES AND STATUTES AND THEIR USE

The preceding sketches of the legal routes into foster care in our two rural communities suggest that the laws governing such movement might be quite different. Actually, a comparison of the pertinent legal sections for Norden and Granger [3] did not show the same degree of variation that a comparison of the children's pathways did.

While most of the differences were matters of interpretation and use rather than of legal provisions, there were a few important distinctions between the two sets of laws. In Norden various sections of the law relating to the temporary or permanent removal of children were not coordinated to the degree that they were in Granger and thus lent themselves to more individual interpretation. Another distinction concerned provisions regarding finances. In Norden's state, the legal requirement that different kinds of placement be paid for from different funds, each with its own regulations, probably encouraged the counties to place children in the state-supported institutions. Granger's freedom to use funds for any kind of placement permitted placement based on the requirements of the child's situation rather than on the type of fund which could be used.

Adoption procedures in the two communities were also somewhat different. In Norden the law permitted voluntary relinquishment to an agency without court action, while Granger statutes had no provision for such relinquishment except in connection with a court proceeding to terminate parental rights. The Norden law seemed to prohibit adoptions except through agency placement or court commitment, but this provision, which would be expected to raise the proportion of agency adoptions, was apparently not used or enforced. This variance between law and its use is similar to the situation in regard to the state institutions for dependent children: by law, placement in such an institution terminated the control of parent or court; in practice, children were placed or committed there on a "temporary" basis without modification of parental rights. Finally, probably most influential on the proportion of agency adoptions in the two communities were the different legal provisions for unmarried mothers, which helped make it

[3] In Appendix D-1 is a condensation of comparable sections from the laws we considered most likely to influence movement into or out of foster care in Norden and Granger.

easier for unwed mothers to use agency services for adoption in
Granger.[4]

In summary, however, it seemed not so much the laws as their
use and interpretation which distinguished Norden and Granger.
Nor was either community using the relevant laws to their limits,
and the gap between the laws and the testing of them was much
more apparent in Norden than in Granger.

The testing of laws involves a community's extralegal values. In
each community we saw dissimilarity in the delicate balance that
always obtains between legal and welfare philosophy. Of the elements making up these philosophies the most important difference
in Norden and Granger pertained to that in emphasis between a
parents' rights approach and a child's rights approach.

If we think of the parents' rights–child's rights philosophies as
lying in a continuous line rather than in two divided segments,
Judge Farnham Walker in Norden appeared to function considerably farther toward the parents' rights end of the continuum, both
in his own philosophy and in others' perceptions of his philosophy,
than did Judge Will Swanson in Granger. In this respect each
judge seemed to represent not only his legal world of statutes but
the social world of his state and its local communities. In each of
these worlds, though more so in Norden, there was a desire to
move slowly on procedures for modifying God-given parental rights.
In addition, in Norden, with the kinds of cases which children like
Karl Bayer represented at the Abbotsford Home, local social workers probably saw little purpose in pushing toward termination of
parental rights at the point in a child's placement history at which
they were caring for him.

[4] The laws on service provided for unmarried mothers were different in these
two communities. In the laws of Norden's state, there was no special provision
for financial assistance for unmarried mothers, and the general residence and
public assistance laws made mobility, and therefore anonymity, difficult to attain.
Medical care was provided at the state university hospital; eligibility included
county residence and financial need, though not on the same strict basis as for
county financial assistance in general. In Granger's state, hospitals were required to report to the state or local welfare department the birth of a child by
an unmarried woman, and there was a special financial assistance program for
medical care for the mother and foster care for the child, given on a state-wide
basis not limited by county residence.

However, variations in the degree of communication and mutual understanding between the legal and welfare worlds in Norden and Granger helped explain the differences observed in their legal pictures. In Norden there seemed to be a mutual lack of knowledge of the other's field in both the legal and the welfare world. These worlds rarely touched, and when they did the contact tended to be tentative and uncertain. The agencies varied in their answers to such legal questions as: "Does the Juvenile Court have jurisdiction over children in private institutions?" "Is an agency required to consider a child's religion in placing him for adoption?" Legal figures in Norden were similarly unclear about the functions and philosophy of welfare agencies. Since agency workers had little place in the legal process involving children, it was the legally oriented people who took the responsibility for these procedures. As individuals, such figures could be quite concerned about children, but as holders of certain legal positions they were governed by the limitations they saw as inherent in their positions. Legal issues were seldom a major consideration in the day-to-day operations of Norden agency workers, and the separateness of legal and welfare worlds precluded the formation of pressures to change approaches and definitions relative to the legal status of children.

Our discussion of Granger, on the other hand, has already pointed out how, in the majority of cases in that community, legal issues were a major element in the daily procedure of welfare people. Such a situation almost dictated that there be communication between the legal and welfare worlds. The evidence we gathered suggests that in the Granger context this communication tended to proceed on a basis of mutual knowledge.

LEGAL ISSUES AND PLACEMENT PATTERN

Knowing this much about the legal situations in the two rural communities, we anticipated differences in certain aspects of their placement of dependent children—in the conditions surrounding separation of child and parent, in the timing of placement, and in the routes out of foster care. We must, of course, remind ourselves that the Norden children, coming mostly from outside Norden County, reflected also the influences of legal systems in other counties of the state. But certain uniformities tended to cover the state, just as its two state-supported institutions for dependent children served children from all over the state. What were the facts on some aspects of placement which, theoretically at least, the Norden and Granger legal systems might affect?

To the extent that Granger seemed more a "child's rights" community than did Norden we would expect to find more involuntary placements in Granger. There was no difference, however—31 percent involuntary separations in both communities—though enforced separations [5] were 2 percent in Norden and 9 percent in Granger.

Similar parental conditions prevailed at separation of parents and child in both communities—primarily conditions involving physical and social deprivation—for about half of all the children. However, marital conflict and other psychological crises in the family appeared as precipitating conditions at separation in 23 percent of Norden's cases, while such conditions appeared as primary in only 12 percent of Granger's cases. This variance doubtless reflected the greater tensions manifested in the backgrounds of more of Norden's "treatment" cases, most of whom came to the local institution through voluntary referrals. Out-of-wedlock birth was a more prevalent factor in Granger, where it appeared as a precipitating condition at removal in 19 percent of the cases. In Norden, out-of-wedlock birth was recorded at time of separation in only 5 percent of the cases. We have seen that there seemed to be less legal provision for services to unwed mothers in Norden than in Granger.

Timing of first separation appeared as a major difference in the cases in the two communities. In Norden, only 19 percent of the children studied were first separated from parents as preschoolers,

[5] A voluntary placement is one made by parents themselves through a direct application to an agency. Involuntary placement is one made through the court process, usually because of neglect or abandonment and, many times, over the objection of parents. Enforced separation is a placement made because of such conditions as death or institutionalization of the parent.

while in Granger the proportion of preschool separations was 40 percent. Percentages separated between ages six to ten showed a similar difference—44 percent separated at these ages in Norden, 16 percent so separated in Granger. The earlier separations in Granger could be logically associated with a greater emphasis on children's rather than parents' rights. In effect, there was then less time for problems to become so serious. By the time children had reached the ages of six to ten, what were once problems of parental neglect could become highly visible as children's behavior problems.

In comparing lengths of time in care, a longer median time was demonstrable in "parents' rights" Norden. The medians for all placement categories combined were five years in Norden and two and a half years in Granger. This could be associated with the maintenance of parents' rights and reluctance to permit legal release of children for permanent planning, such as adoption. However, one could also envision a parents' rights setting, as we found later, in which the parental tie to children is maintained to hasten return of children to their parents, thus shortening time in care.

We hypothesized, generally, that a parents' rights emphasis would probably be associated with fewer agency adoptions and more returns home. This was only partly consistent with the Norden-Granger comparison since both communities had very little return home traffic. However, adoption was proportionately more prevalent in Granger agency operations—17 percent of cases studied in adoptive care on April 1—than in Norden—only 8 percent of cases studied in adoptive care on April 1.

All these facts on placement suggest the interrelatedness of the phenomena we studied. When and how a child comes into care has a relationship to how long he stays and where he moves. The legal systems in these two rural communities seemed to affect when children were first separated from their parents and, subsequently, the kinds of placement, including adoption, likely to be most available. At the time of our study, the two foster care situations obtaining, partly reinforced by, and reflected through, the two legal systems, presented a contrast of relatively long-term institutional care in Norden and shorter term foster family care in Granger.

4. The Agency Networks Serving the Two Communities

To understand some of the why's behind child placement, as well as how long children stay in care in these two rural counties, we turn to a description of the constellation of agencies serving the Norden and Granger children.

THE NETWORK OF AGENCIES AND CHILD WELFARE SERVICES IN NORDEN

Abbotsford Avenue, heading north, becomes highway 23A, and pastures dotted with barns and silos replace the snug little frame houses and small stores as one heads out from town. Just where the grassland begins to take hold, the discerning eye catches a glimpse of a group of buildings that seem, at first, a last challenge by the town to the countryside. This is the Abbotsford Home for Children, its red brick structures surrounded by trees on a slight rise. Occupying this site since 1900, the Home was organized in 1863. In years past, as an orphanage, it was a part neither of the town nor of the country but was really a place unto itself, set down as if by chance on someone's meadow. Now the town's postwar housing growth has reached out to surround the Home and soften its somewhat austere appearance in the landscape. Yet it still remains, relatively, a place apart. It is a residential treatment center receiving children from all parts of the state. It cared for nine out of every ten of the Norden children we studied. It was the central focus of our analysis of the interagency network in the Norden situation. That network, with five child-placing agencies, three of them outside Norden County, is diagrammed in Figure 1.

Over all, the Norden configuration of agencies was a noncollaborative and insular one. Out of a possible ten interrelationships among these five agencies there seemed to be a total of only two collaborative links and one clearly noncollaborative relationship. The collaborative relationship between the Abbotsford Home for

Children and the public welfare department in Norden County was based primarily on the fact that the Community Child Guidance Clinic, located at the Abbotsford Home, was supported mutually by these two agencies and the half-time child welfare worker for the welfare department spent the other half of his time at this clinic. The relationship was maintained primarily through contacts around cases, for the welfare department worker would refer to the Child Guidance Clinic, if this seemed appropriate, and the clinic might, as well, refer a child to the Department of Public Welfare.   The other collaborative relationship was between the Caldwell County

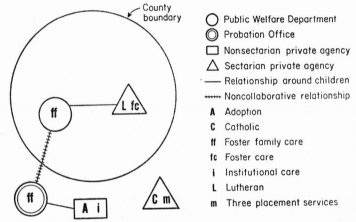

Figure 1. NORDEN COUNTY AGENCY NETWORK

Probation Office and the Valley Dell Infants' Home. This relationship between two agencies which were both outside the county involved the Probation Office's occasional use of the Home for temporary institutional care for children it could not place with a family.   The openly noncollaborative relationship between the Norden County Department of Public Welfare and the Probation Office in Caldwell County revolved around a reluctance on the part of the former agency to pay as much for services for certain children as the latter agency deemed necessary. The Norden interagency network was thus characterized by a minimum of collaborative relationships and by a relative insularity of the individual agencies in their care of children.

We propose that collaborative relationships among agencies may connote an easy flow of interagency referrals, subject to the checks of joint agency planning in each case. We hypothesize that collaborative agency relationships facilitate the movement of children, as needed, and especially toward permanent placement. Such movement is particularly important where agencies individually offer only one or at most two types of placement service and progressive plans for children require the use of resources outside the agency itself. Thus a collaborative pattern of interagency relationships should lead more frequently to children's movement out of care and into permanent home situations.

Peripheral to the diagrammed network, but not included in Figure 1 because they did not offer placement services, were other agencies which had a direct bearing on placement in Norden. The Child Guidance Clinic located at Abbotsford Children's Home offered counseling service both to parents and to children. This agency may have acted as a preventive to family breakdown in the community and helped to account for the small number of children who left local families to go into foster care. The Department of Public Welfare also offered service to children in their own homes. Most of the referrals it received were reported to come from the schools, not bcause of physical neglect of children but because of emotional and behavior problems exhibited in school. Also, in Norden County there were no direct services to unmarried mothers except the medical care that was available to legal residents who were "medically indigent." However, the two private agencies in one-hundred-mile-distant River City did offer services to unmarried mothers, including housing, medical care, and casework. Thus the bulk of services for Norden's adoptions was outside the local area, and, accordingly, all four of the local adoptive families dealt with two agencies outside the county, neither of which was in any active way related to the two child-placing agencies within Norden County.

Agency Antecedents and Present Bases in Norden

Our analysis of services as involving a network of child-placing agencies emphasizes four factors: the history of services in the state; the types of services offered and the persons served by them; the variations in professionalization among agencies; and the spatial location of agencies and their geographical areas served. These factors are used in Table 2 to organize the characteristics of the agencies giving child placement services to the Norden children under study.

Our task now is to elaborate the factors which underlie our de-

Table 2

CHARACTERISTICS OF AGENCIES IN THE NORDEN COUNTY NETWORK

Agency (According to percentage of children under study served)	History	Services	Extent of Professional Education [a] of Staff	Spatial Factors
Abbotsford Home for Children (90%)	Organized 1863; auspices private	Institutional and foster family care,[b] for children, Lutheran preferred, 6–15 years of age	75% of staff (12 members)	Located at Abbotsford; serves the state
Caldwell County Probation Office (2.5%)	Organized 1922; auspices public	Foster family care, for children 0–18 years of age	0% of staff (2 members)	Located at Pearl City, in neighboring Caldwell County; serves that county
Catholic Social Service Center (2.5%)	Organized 1931; auspices private	Foster family and institutional care, adoption, for Catholic children 0–18 years af age	50% of staff (6 members)	Located at River City (100 miles from Abbotsford); serves 31 counties
Norden County Department of Public Welfare (2.5%)	Organized 1925; auspices public	Foster family care, for children 0–18 years of age	100% of staff (1 member)	Located at Abbotsford; serves the county
Valley Dell Infants' Home (2.5%)	Organized 1914; auspices private	Adoption and institutional care, for children 0–4, occasionally up to 10, years of age	0% of staff (3 members)	Located at River City; serves northern half of state

[a] One year or more of graduate study in social work.
[b] Adoption service available for those children admitted initially for treatment.

scription of Norden's relatively noncollaborative network of agencies. We should bear in mind our hypothesis that a major tendency toward collaboration and/or the inclusion of most children in care in multiple-service agencies will facilitate the movement of children in foster care, while noncollaboration coupled with the inclusion of most children in care in single-service agencies will deter the movement of children in foster care.

History. As we see in Table 2, Norden County and the state within which it is located were an example of an area with a long tradition of offering one particular kind of care. Long before the State Department of Public Welfare was organized in the early 1930s, with the passage of the Social Security Act, the state had established child care institutions. The Abbotsford Home for Children was organized in 1863 under private auspices. The first institution under state auspices was opened in 1865. Shortly after these early beginnings, fraternal groups and other associations built and sponsored institutions to care for dependent children all over the state.

It is also important to remember that this was a state where independence, or "rugged individualism" and local county autonomy, had been considered extremely important. Thus, when the Federal Social Security Act was passed and a specific administrative pattern was required in order for a state to receive Federal funds, this state, rather than change its total pattern of administering public aid, superimposed an additional administrative structure on the then-existent welfare organization in the counties. This resulted in one county officer's handling one portion of public aid and another county employee's being responsible for the remaining portion. Later, some counties combined the two positions in one person, as in Norden, but the two separate administrative structures remained.

In addition, two funds, the Poor Fund and the Institution Fund, were established to care for dependent children. Since these funds were handled quite separately, the financing of a child's placement was very important in determining the kind of care he would receive. The Poor Fund was used to pay for the care of children who were in foster homes or in private institutions. The fund from which this money came was subject to many requests, and an accounting of its expenditures had to be published in the newspaper. This meant, at times, that a child might be refused care because the care was considered costly. If a child was placed in a state institution, the state paid one half of the cost of care while the county Institution Fund financed the other half. It should be noted that, although some state funds were available for institutional placements, no state funds were provided for foster family care. The Institution Fund was established specifically to pay for care in public institutions and required no publication of expenditures. Thus, additional weight was given the historically based practice of providing primarily institutional care for children.

The two means of providing care for dependent children was separated not only at the county level but also at the state level. The state institutions, in existence early and well established by the time the social security programs came into being, continued to be administered by the Board of Control. The Department of Public Welfare, with its responsibility for helping local counties develop child welfare programs and for state-wide planning of child welfare services, remained completely separate in its administration. And while this department had responsibility for licensing facilities for the care of children, it had no responsibility for the programs or operations of the state institutions. Such a pattern of welfare organization did not centralize responsibility for services available to children. This background helps to explain the fact that institutional care, even aside from, and prior to, the children's institutional placements at the Abbotsford Home as of the time of our study, was by far the most frequent type of placement the Norden children under study had experienced.

Services.—Considering only the kinds and division of services offered by the five agencies of the Norden network, we should expect extensive interagency communication and collaboration. Here we found that mostly specialized services were available to the general public. The two public agencies offered only foster family placements to all children. One private agency provided primarily institutional care; another, primarily adoption. As the situations of children change, we should expect their referral to the appropriate agencies for other types of care. The panoply of types of place-ment seemed complete when viewed against the kinds of clients served, except that age stipulations at Valley Dell Infants' Home might limit the adoptive placement of non-Catholic older children. Thus, viewing only the pattern of services and the public served in Norden did not help us to understand the limited nature of inter-agency collaboration in this network.

On the other hand, the Catholic Social Service Center and Valley Dell Infants' Home entered Norden County only to supervise the four adoptive placements within the county, and on these occasions communicated only with the adoptive families and not with each other or with either of the two child-placing agencies in the county. The Abbotsford Home operated a relatively self-contained program, focused on children who had apparently reached the "end of the line" in foster care placement and for whom few referrals were considered. And the two public agencies, serving neighboring counties, were likely to communicate only when a child's legal resi-dence involved matters of financial payment across county bounda-ries—a precipitant, as we have noted, of some friction.[1]

Extent of professionalization of agency.—Still further intensify-ing the lack of communication in the Norden interagency network was the wide range of professional education found among different agency staffs. Within the county the two agencies were highly pro-fessional in their programs and in the staff they employed. In con-trast, however, two of the three out-of-county agencies had no pro-fessionally trained staff—the Probation Office in neighboring Cald-well County and the Valley Dell Infants' Home in River City. Between these extremes the Catholic agency, also in River City, employed some trained staff and placed a growing emphasis on professional services to children. Some recent revisions in this agency's program were in line with professional practice in child welfare, as, for example, the removal of preschool children from in-

[1] Agencies in the Norden network were formally related on issues through a state-wide professional association of child care agencies, but this organization did not bring them into frequent or, apparently (from their own reports), very close relationship.

stitutional care.   On the other hand, the Valley Dell Infants' Home
offered as a major resource for preschool children a group or institutional care program.   The two collaborative relationships diagrammed in Figure 1 indicate that only the two least professional
agencies tended to communicate regularly with one another while
the two most professional agencies likewise had a collaborative relationship.

Spatial factors.—Physical distance, moreover, compounded the social distances between Norden agencies.   The Probation Office,
which was not actually on the local scene, had problems in caring
for children from Norden County who were placed with them and
whose expenses were paid by the Norden welfare department.   The
three dual-service and multiple-service agencies had large areas to
serve.   Two of these agencies were located in an urban center over
a hundred miles from the Abbotsford residential center.   And we
must not underplay the fact that the urban location of the three
out-of-county agencies further removed them from the world of the
two rural, in-county agencies.

This, then, was the Norden interagency situation.   Here was a
network highlighted by insularity and lack of collaboration, in
which very little planning for children was shared among agencies,
either on a case-by-case or on a more general basis.

THE NETWORK OF AGENCIES AND CHILD WELFARE SERVICES IN
GRANGER COUNTY

In Granger County one looked in vain for obvious indications of
the children's foster care programs.   There was no institution in
Daleville to which one could point and say, "That is the local orphanage."   The dependent child either blended into the landscape
—in local foster families—or was completely out of sight locally—
under the care of an agency in urban Bearpaw sixty miles away.
In order to understand the child welfare services in their entirety
we sought out a key person in the field.   At the time of our study
this person was Mrs. Camilla Jones, a Daleville resident of some
twelve years, plump, energetic, and intelligent.   Her office on the
third floor of the county courthouse, not far from Judge Swanson's,

was as inconspicuous as the program she operated. Yet the agency she directed, the Department of Public Welfare, was involved in seven out of ten of the cases of Granger County children we studied and was still providing the primary service in four out of ten of all our Granger County cases. It was from her vantage point that the interagency network serving Granger County children came into focus.

The interagency network for Granger, represented in Figure 2,

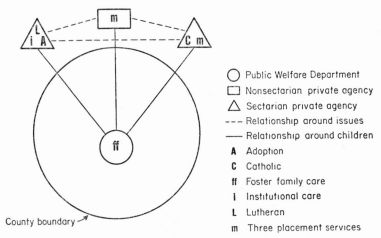

○ Public Welfare Department
▢ Nonsectarian private agency
△ Sectarian private agency
- - - Relationship around issues
—— Relationship around children
A Adoption
C Catholic
ff Foster family care
i Institutional care
L Lutheran
m Three placement services

Figure 2. GRANGER COUNTY AGENCY NETWORK

includes the four agencies that were involved in our study. As the diagram indicates, three of these agencies were located outside Granger County, in Bearpaw, and one was located within the county. This was the central agency, the public welfare department, providing the single type of placement of foster family care. And, as indicated on the diagram, all six relationships among the four agencies appeared essentially collaborative. Moreover, the basic relationship between the Granger welfare department and each of the other agencies was around the care of individual children, while relationships among the three out-of-county agencies, from the perspective of Granger County, were around more general issues in the larger field of child welfare.

The major emphasis of services issuing from this interagency net could be seen in the local operations of Mrs. Jones in Granger.

She stressed services to the child in his own home. As noted previously, she considered her active cases to be those children who were still with their own families and who had not reached the point of placement. She looked upon placement as a last resort, undertaken only after considerable effort and many hours had gone into mobilizing community resources for keeping the child and his family together. At the same time, once placement did occur, Mrs. Jones was aware of other resources outside her local foster family program to which she might turn. In fact, all institutional and adoption services were located outside Granger county. Her own agency, like all other public welfare agencies in the state, was not licensed to carry on adoptions. Children who, she thought, required institutional care or who might be made available for adoption had to leave the local community for agency care. Mrs. Jones would send most of them off to Bearpaw, feeling that at this stage in their placement histories the agencies in that city could better serve them. Essentially collaborative relations around cases between the Granger County Department of Public Welfare and the three private agencies in Bearpaw, two of which sponsored multiple-service programs, were apparent.

Unmarried mothers in Granger County had casework services available to them in each of the three private agencies in Bearpaw, where there were also two independently operated maternity homes. Moreover, unlike the situation in Norden, financial support could be obtained by unmarried mothers during their prenatal and postnatal periods, regardless of their county of residence. Mrs. Jones would quickly refer to the Bearpaw agencies any unmarried mothers who came to her attention.

This introduction to the Granger interagency network has suggested its collaborative nature. Again, a more detailed description of the underlying basis of this network, suggested in Table 3, seems appropriate.

Agency Antecedents and Present Bases in Granger

History.—Granger County is located in a state which, until the Social Security Act of the 1930s, had only one child care agency within its boundaries—the nonsectarian Children's Center, organized just before the turn of the century in Bearpaw. The state was settled comparatively recently and remains one of the most sparsely populated of all the North Central Plains states. In the early days of the Federal assistance programs this state was noted as one that

Table 3

CHARACTERISTICS OF AGENCIES IN THE
GRANGER COUNTY NETWORK

Agency (According to percentage of children under study served)	History	Services	Extent of Professional Education [a] of Staff	Spatial Factors
Granger County Public Welfare Department (41%)	Organized 1935; auspices public	Foster family care, for children 0–21 years of age	0% of staff (1 member)	Located at Daleville; serves the county
Children's Center (28%)	Organized 1897; auspices private	Institutional and foster family care, adoption for children 0–18 years of age	0% of staff (4½ members)	Located at Bearpaw (60 miles from Daleville); serves the state
Lutheran Foster Care Service (25%)	Organized 1936; auspices private	Institutional care, for Lutheran children 8–15 years of age; adoption for those 0–8 years of age	55% of staff (10 members; 2 part-time)	Located at Bearpaw; serves the state
Diocesan Children's Services (6%)	Organized 1926; auspices private	Foster family and institutional care, adoption, for Catholic children 0–18 years of age	0% of staff (5 members)	Located at Bearpaw; serves the state

[a] One year or more of graduate study in social work.

offered leadership in the public welfare field. It was known for its liberal public programs, for placing emphasis on securing professionally trained workers, and for urging county welfare departments to establish service programs.

In this state, too, county autonomy was considered important, and public welfare was state supervised but county administered. The pattern of administrative organization, unchallenged by antecedent programs, had grown with public welfare itself. The State Welfare Department was the only state agency responsible for services to dependent children. In accordance with the best thinking in welfare circles at the time the public program unfolded, foster family care was emphasized, and counties were encouraged to develop their own foster family programs. The county welfare departments handled all the funds providing care for children, and the state department participated in the financing of placement services so that the county welfare departments were financed by Federal, state, and county funds. This fact of financial participation on the part of state and county services had resulted in somewhat closer relationships between county and state offices. Relationships were primarily on a supervisory basis, providing a medium for setting standards of care for children and also calling for continued communication between state and local levels. The State Welfare Department was also responsible for the licensing of private child care agencies.

Of added significance was the fact that at about the time the public agency services were established both the Catholic and the Lutheran private agencies in Bearpaw were being organized, all within a decade of each other. These agencies had all "grown up together" and had shared aspects of their individual problems over a long period of time. We should, therefore, expect to find interagency communication and collaboration facilitated in the Granger network.

Services.—The situation in Granger did not, in itself, suggest that there would be much to bring the agencies together. Rather, we should expect that highly *specialized* agencies which both serve and are responsible to the same *general* public would be likely to come together most frequently in providing services to a community. But the Granger network included two multiple-service agencies, each of which could, apparently, operate a relatively self-contained program, with one serving a specialized (Catholic) public and the other open to all others.

But the clue to collaborativeness in the Granger network was Mrs. Jones's activities within the county and her use of the other agencies. In effect, she ran a single-service program within the county—a foster family program—and used the agencies outside the county for relatively specialized services. We have typified her department's program as providing the locus of foster family care from which, and into which, Granger's dependent children flowed. Hers, unlike the Abbotsford Home, was not an "end-of-the-line" operation but more a beginning point. And her use of the services of the agencies in Bearpaw had brought her into frequent contact with these agencies.

In addition, as we have previously noted, three of these agencies started and developed their programs during a period of time in which they were all confronted with the same, or similar, problems. Thus, while not participants in a tight, interdependent network of specialized services, they had had occasion to share general problems through the years of their growth; and this gave them a basis for collaboration and intercommunication around issues, if not often around cases.

Extent of professionalization of agency.—Levels of professional education in the agencies, moreover, presented much less variation in Granger than in Norden, where a wider range seemed to influence the communication pattern. At the time of our study, however, agency differences in professional emphasis were beginning to grow and to affect relationships in Granger. The Lutheran agency in Bearpaw presented the most professionalization. The other two private agencies and the Department of Public Welfare did not have trained staff. Still, the two less professional private agencies, in particular, were emphasizing the need for, and making an effort to procure, professionally trained personnel. All three private agencies had undergone recent reorganization leading to some revision of program and modification of services in line with the latest child welfare thinking. These changes and redefinitions of program were having repercussions in interagency communication. And this was starting to affect, adversely, communication between Mrs. Jones and the agencies in Bearpaw.

Mrs. Jones pointed out that, during her twelve years in the county, relationships with Bearpaw agencies had always been quite close. Whenever she had a child to refer, an agency was willing to take the child. However, she was becoming more and more concerned because these agencies were "narrowing" their services—or, as she saw the new situation, retrenching their programs, requiring more formal referrals, and taking longer to decide whether or not they would accept a child for care. As she said, now these agencies were not only wanting to know all about a child's family background and his behavior but also "the color of his eyes and the size of his shoes." These changes seemed to Mrs. Jones to be limiting the resources available to her in Granger County. While referrals were still frequently made to all three agencies in Bearpaw, the loss of resources was placing pressure upon the Granger County welfare department to develop further its own resources. The more general and personal orientations of rural ways of life were to some extent coming into conflict with urban specialization. In part, a growing lack of understanding was beginning to result in barriers to communication between the local department and urban agencies. For the most part, however, Mrs. Jones expressed her irritation openly, and relationships continued to be cooperative. Certainly, no rupture in relationships regarding services for Granger children was yet apparent at the time of our study.

Spatial factors.—The factor of physical distance appeared in Granger to add a deterrent to interagency communication. But in Granger three agencies were grouped together in the same urban center, and only one was "off in the country." Furthermore, despite distance there was an unobstructed flow of case traffic between country and city. In a sense, Mrs. Jones served as a common social referrent, having contacts in the urban agencies over cases as well as close ties to the rural community in which she lived.

NETWORK COMPARISONS AND SOME FACTS OF PLACEMENT

How did these two interagency networks affect what happened to children once they left their own families? What were some of the

specific differences in placement pattern which appeared to be associated with the differences in the interagency networks in these two
communities?

Generally, the Granger network moved proportionately more
children into adoption while the Norden network returned more
children home and, furthermore, permitted more children to grow
up in foster care. In addition to the adoption and return home
percentages presented earlier, figures on all those leaving care in a
six-month period, from January 1 through June 30, showed that
none went into adoption in Norden while one child (out of a much
smaller total of children) did in Granger, and three out of five leaving care in Norden [2] returned home—while one child returned
home in Granger. Granted that we are dealing with very small
totals and that more Norden children in care were in an "end-of-
the-line" placement, the noncollaborative configuration in Norden,
compared to the more collaborative one in Granger, did present a
concomitant picture of a total lack of adoption and more return
home.

Our hypothesis about the general tendencies in agency networks
includes the implication that if a child is once in the care of an
agency offering one particular service, removed from his parents
and his community, and this agency is relatively insulated from
those offering different services, he is more likely to remain in the
long-term care of this one agency. Norden foster care children, as
previously recorded, were in care an average of twice as long as were
Granger children, and time in current placement showed an even
greater discrepancy—a median of twenty-six months for Norden,
compared to nine months for Granger. The mid-length period of
placement—from two years to five and one-half years—was most
common in both communities; but Norden showed only 16 percent
of its children in care for less than two years, compared to 38 percent for Granger, while 41 percent were in care six years and over
in Norden, compared to 15 percent in Granger. Obviously, some
of the data on the length of time Norden children spent in care re-

---

[2] The other alternative was leaving care for "other" reasons—reaching majority
age for example—and this accounts for the remaining two children leaving care
in Norden during this period.

flected the fact that many of them were in a treatment setting. The noncollaborativeness of the agency network remains, however, a concomitant situation.

In a similar way the treatment situation in Norden obscured the effects of a noncollaborative network on the numbers of placements children in care may have. The Norden children tended to have had more placements, and to have had more than one type of placement, more frequently than in Granger. Only 13 percent of Norden cases had had only one placement, compared to 28 percent in Granger, while 70 percent of Norden cases had had more than one type of placement, compared to 46 percent of cases in Granger. The noncollaborativeness of Norden agencies involved children who had come to Norden after previous foster care experiences. This situation was not an appropriate test of whether a noncollaborative network of single-service agencies, involving the beginning and only experience in care of foster care children, permitted only one placement and one type of placement to predominate. Clearly, collaboration, as seen in Granger, tended to reflect a more even distribution of placement experiences just as it also clustered "time in care" at the mid-intervals.

The Norden network did demonstrate a tendency, when compared to Granger, toward children's having more movement within care from one type of placement to another. Thus, 55 percent of Norden children had moved out of a foster family to a different type of placement, compared to 32 percent in Granger who had so moved. Movement out of institutions to another type of care had occurred for 53 percent in Norden and 45 percent in Granger. While this did not reflect experiences only within the Norden network itself, these findings led us to revise our hypothesis to say that extremes of *least* or *most* replacement would be found in noncollaborative networks, while the more moderate replacement statistics would be found in the more collaborative networks like Granger's.

Our major differentiations, then, between the interagency networks in Norden and Granger have been presented in several dimensions, and the facts of placement have further clarified the pictures. The Norden situation was typified by greater insularity and noncollaboration among specialized agencies, physically and professionally quite separate, and by the problem which a local agency had in interpreting its program within the community. The Granger situation was representative of more interagency referral in a more collaborative and professionally and physically closer network, with more understanding by the local community of the agencies' programs. But in rural Granger, too, a balance built around rural norms of informality and nonspecialization was being upset, and readjustments in expectations of services seemed necessary. Certainly, the children who were our major interest in these settings still presented a challenge to those who wished to quicken the concern of a community for their problems, whether seen from Mrs. Jones's vantage point in the Granger County courthouse or from behind the doors of the neat brick buildings on the gentle slope at the edge of Abbotsford.

5. *The Children and Their Parents*

We have presented, thus far, some aspects of the ways in which two rural communities met their problems of dependency and provided for the care of their dependent children. Generally, we saw that the child in foster care in Norden was more visible in that homogeneous community than was the Granger child in foster care. Our representative children in each setting demonstrated this, and our subsequent explorations of community cultures, legal systems, and interagency networks filled out pictures of the forces obtaining in association with dependency in these two communities. In neither community did the foster care child seem readily "adoptable." The problems of most children in need of parents in each community were not being resolved through adoption. In fact, foster care and adoption tended to represent quite different social-psychological configurations. Let us consider the predominant situations and the possibilities of return home, as well as of adoption, in Norden and Granger. First, we shall look at the placement histories of children in foster care.

Looking at just the Norden children in foster care, we found that over half of the parents of these children were divorced or separated from one another and only about one third were still married to each other. Most of the children had been separated voluntarily from their parents, although neglect and abandonment, death, illness, and economic hardship, were the major precipitating causes of separation. However, psychological problems loomed large as parental conditions at separation in Norden and were many times more prevalent there than among Granger's cases.

Three out of four of the children in foster care in Norden were in the institution in Abbotsford, and over 90 percent of them came to the institution from another county. The average age of these children when they were first separated from their parents was eight years, and only one in seven had been first separated as a preschooler. The Norden children had had at least two or three placements, often four, and fewer of them had had only one placement than was true of the children in foster care in any of our eight other communities. Furthermore, the children who had reached the institution in Abbotsford had been in care, all told, an average of four and a half years, while those in foster families were even more the long-term cases in Norden, having been in care an average of eight years. Fully 40 percent of Norden's children in foster care had been in care over five and a half years. Only a small minority had been in care less than a year and a half. This tended to make the Norden placement picture one of longer-term care than was found

[1] Because of the questions considered in this chapter, many of the percentages concerning the placement of the children are based only on the numbers of a community's children in foster care—that is, the sum of the children in foster families and in institutional care—and not, as in the preceding chapters, on all the children under study in one community. In previous chapters all the children were seen as a single pool of dependent children, some of whom moved on into adoptive placements and others of whom left care to return home or for other purposes, but all of whom together were the focus of our study. In this chapter, it is the placement histories and the family and personal characteristics of the children in foster care with which we are primarily concerned. The conditions of adoptive children or of those children who returned home are examined separately and only to compare them with the conditions of children in foster care—our questions being why did not more of the children move into adoption or return home.

in any other community we studied. Few children in Norden were either returning home or moving into adoption. Three children— 6 percent of all those in foster families or institutional care on April 1—returned home in the six months up to October 1. Briefly, Norden's placement pattern was one of long-term institutionalization for troubled children who came to the Abbotsford institution from all over the state after prior placement experiences and, sometimes, prior separations and trial returns home. These were children whose homes, even if unbroken or reconstituted, still were the scene of tensions that made return home seem improbable.

In Granger, too, well over half of the parents of children in foster care were divorced or separated. Of the remainder, however, twice as many were widowed in Granger as in Norden, and only half as many were still married to each other in Granger as in Norden. Neglect and abandonment were the major precipitating conditions at separation of parent and child, as in Norden, and death, illness, and economic hardship were prevalent in Granger's cases as in Norden's. But there had been less voluntary separation of children from parents and more involuntary removal of the Granger children who were in foster care, and many more cases had involved enforced separation through the death or institutionalization of a parent in Granger than in Norden.

Granger was caring for twenty of its twenty-five dependent children in foster families. The five in institutions were all cared for outside the county boundaries. At the same time, most of the twenty children in foster families were in homes within Granger County. Interestingly, a Granger child in foster care was as likely to have had just one placement as to have had four or more placements, while more than a third of the children had had two or three placements. In Granger, also, more children were leaving care. A fifth of those in foster care on April 1 had left care by October 1, and all of these children returned home.

The average age at first separation from parents was ten and a half years for the children in foster families in Granger. More than half of all Granger children in foster care had been first separated when eleven years old or older. Only about a fourth were first separated as preschoolers. Still, twice as great a proportion were separated prior to age two in Granger (20 percent) as in Norden (10 percent). However, Granger's children stayed in care a much shorter time. Three years was the average stay for the child in a Granger foster family, and the period was only a little over one year for the child in an institution. Just one in five of Granger children in care had been in care over five and a half years—half the Norden proportion—while one in three of Granger's children in care had been in care up to a year and a half—twice the Norden proportion. Thus, the somewhat dispersed foster family program that Mrs. Jones operated in Granger brought some local children into care at a later age, but it kept them in care a shorter time. Still, neither adoption nor return home for Granger's children, apparently less disturbed than Norden's, seemed major avenues for permanent planning at the time we visited in this community.

THE CHILDREN'S OWN FAMILIES

The three Norden children who returned home between January 1 and June 30 were school-age only children with about four years of care, their parents separated, and mothers living alone. On the whole, except for being only children, their characteristics were very similar to those of the children who stayed in care. Why did not more of the Norden children in foster care return home?

The parents of the Norden children who stayed in care, more than those in any of our other communities, had either no other plans than long-term care for their children or conflicting plans which seemed unlikely to be resolved. Two thirds of Norden's children in foster care were in this situation, and the lowest proportion (12 percent) in Norden, when compared to all our communities, had been relinquished for adoption. More parents visited their children in Norden than in Granger, but still in half the cases neither parent visited or did so only infrequently. About half of the fathers and mothers had no relationship with the agency in Norden, although, again, there was evidence of more continuing parent-agency relationships in Norden than in Granger or in many of our other communities. Also, more parents of Norden's children than of Granger's were contributing toward the child's care—about one in three were doing so in Norden—but as we have seen, they were paying for continuance of a situation which showed little promise of a permanent home for the child.

Norden and Granger families of the children in foster care seemed to be somewhat similar. There was one Spanish-American father among those in Norden; otherwise, there was no parent of minority ethnicity in that group. Practically no Catholic families appeared in Norden either, almost all being Protestant with some 40 percent designated Lutheran. But a much larger proportion of the Norden children in foster care were designated Lutheran after they came into care in that Lutheran community. The parents were not especially youthful—the fathers averaged about forty-seven years of age, the mothers about forty—and they were considered by the agencies as generally average or below in intelligence. Both parents averaged about one or two years of high school. Physical health and handicaps did not appear as problems in most cases in Norden. Although fewer than a third of the parents were still married to each other, the great majority of both fathers and mothers had remarried and currently were living with a spouse.

In several respects the Norden parents were in somewhat better economic situations than the Granger parents of children in care. While most of the fathers were laborers, more of them were skilled workers than in Granger; most of the mothers were housewives, but more of them were gainfully employed than in Granger; and the general economic status, while barely adequate, on the average, included more "comfortable" families and fewer "very poor" ones in Norden than in Granger. However, in working out from this rural community, Norden agencies were looking mainly toward families located in urban centers physically remote from the setting in which the children were in care. Distance complicated return home planning at the same time that it tended to add a rural-urban gulf over which perception of the social characteristics we have just described had to pass. These, then, were the familial situations to which so few Norden children returned home.

While five Granger children who were in care on April 1 returned home during our six-month follow-up period, none of them did so until after June 30. Only one child among the total of thirty-two under study in Granger could be classified as returning home within our study dates of January 1 to June 30. She was an infant born out of wedlock, and returned to her mother, under some agency pressure, when it became apparent that the mother felt able to care for her and could not relinquish her for adoption. Once this was clear, plans were made and acted upon. This case departed radically from most foster care cases in Granger both in the infancy of the child and in the short time she remained in care.

What of the Granger parents to whom so few of the children returned home? First, it should be noted that Granger's children in care—over whom Mrs. Jones had usually worked extensively to keep them out of care—were older, on the average, than the children in care in any other of our nine communities. By then, in half the cases parents either had no other plans except for long-term care or had conflicting plans which seemed to us unlikely to be resolved. Parental visits to children in foster care were less consistent or more infrequent in Granger than in any other community—eight out of ten children had parents neither of whom visited at all or visited infrequently. Fewer than one in ten of the fathers, and one in four of the mothers, of Granger's children in care had what could be called an "adequate" relationship with the agency serving their children. No parents in Granger were paying anything toward the support of their children in foster care. Although many of the children had affectionate bonds with their brothers and sisters (also, mostly in care), none had apparently affectionate ties to their own parents. The Granger children in foster care seemed destined for a relatively long-term experience in a situation which would never eventuate in a legal bond to a family in which they could clearly and unambiguously become full-fledged members.

What characteristics of the parents of children in foster care in Granger tended to deter the movement of children back to their families in that rural community? Why did so few parents continue to have relationships with their children or with the agency caring for the children? Were the parents a highly deviant group in this community? First of all, they were all white, over half were Lutheran, and about one fourth were Catholic. These proportions are a close approximation of the characteristics of the total population in Granger. These parents were not perceived as predominantly of low intelligence, although a little more than a normal proportion were said to be below average in intelligence. In education, too, the parents of Granger's children in foster care were generally average for the community. About half of the fathers were laborers, usually on a farm; only 20 percent were listed as farm managers and 14 percent as professional or white-collar workers in this community where 32 percent of the total population were farm managers and 28 percent were professional and white-collar workers. Still, these are not great disparities and do not suggest that the parents of children in foster care were set apart from the normal population to any great degree. Also, most mothers were housewives, a normal expectation in a rural community, although one in five mothers was on relief. Current physical and economic conditions of the parents, however, regardless of their occupation and social background, were the most deviating characteristics associated with them. None was in comfortable circumstances, and most were noted to be in barely adequate or very poor economic situations. These were the parents, most of whom were separated from each other but were now living with a spouse, whose children were finally taken into care by Mrs. Jones and who retained few if any contacts with their children or with the agency. Only about one in ten of these parents—about half the proportion noted in Norden— expressed a definite desire for their children to return home. As we have seen, few of the childen did return home.

THE CHILDREN AND ADOPTION

We went into our rural communities with many unanswered questions about formal agency adoption in such settings. We found little adoption taking place in either setting and we found little evidence of rural readiness to adopt the dependent children brought into care.

Norden was a site in which children having trouble living in a foster family came into institutional care from many counties. Adoption through agencies of even "perfect" babies was not prevalent in Norden, while the large supply of dependent children seemed somewhat of a burden to the citizenry, few of whom were actively sympathetic to the local institution. However, adoption in Norden did reflect some noticeable departures from the normal placement of "perfect" infants. For example, four of the six Norden adoptions were of children with at least one brother or sister. Moreover, two of Norden's adoptive placements were of children who had some slight physical disability, a similar number presented some psychological symptoms, and below average intelligence was apparent in three cases. In regard to these factors, Norden placed proportionately more children who were different than did any of our other communities.

In a few other respects, however, children placed in adoption through agencies were, in Norden, not children whose characteristics might strain the tolerances of adoptive parents. Of the six cases, four were under two years of age, and the median age was less than six months. All were white in ethnicity. Three were boys and three were girls. Two of the six were Catholic, although Norden's foster care and total populations were almost completely Protestant and Lutheran. Four of the adoptive children were placed in the county by two private, out-of-county agencies. Two of the children were placed outside the county by the Abbotsford Children's Home. Most of these six children had been separated from their parents when less than one year of age; most of their parents were never married to each other. Exceptions to these averages—the more unusual adoptive cases—will be presented at the close of this chapter.

The six Granger adoptive children represented less variation than was found among the Norden adoptions. Three were boys; three, girls. All but one were from homes in the local county and all but one were placed outside the county. All but one were separated, voluntarily, from an unwed mother and all but one entered care in the first two years of life, their average age at time of study being a year and a half. However, only two were infants under one year of age, another two were between one and two years of age, and one was over five years old. Four of the six Granger adoptions were of Lutheran children; one involved a Catholic child. One child had a slight, self-correcting physical disability. Only one had any brothers or sisters. All were healthy, had no psychological symptoms, and were apparently of average intelligence or better. Interestingly, the only nonwhite child in the Granger population under study was an adoptive child of mixed ethnicity. The composite profile of these children contrasted sharply with the older children whom Granger tended to keep in local foster homes.

We have mentioned some of the characteristics, as well as the parental situations, of the children who remained in care in Norden and Granger in comparing them with children who returned home but we have not considered why more of them did not move into adoption.

In Norden over twice as many boys were in foster care as girls (70 percent, representing a greater proportion of boys than in any of our other communities), while adoptions were divided evenly between the sexes. Children in foster care averaged fourteen years of age and none of them was a preschooler, while four of the six adopted children were preschoolers. An amazing 90 percent of Norden's children in foster care were ten years old or over, and this rate far overshadowed proportions in this age group in any other community. Thus, the age factor alone, coupled with the obvious concomitant of time in care, was the major discrepancy between the popular image of the adopted child and that of the child in foster care in Norden. Ethnicity, intelligence, physical health, even physical disability did not differentiate significantly between these two groups of children in Norden to favor the adopted child. However, over 80 percent of Norden's children in foster care, but only two of the six adopted children, had psychological symptoms. We did remark that two of Norden's adoptions were of Catholic children, indicating that in this Lutheran community a Catholic agency in a distant city was finding adoptive homes in Norden County. The Norden child in foster care had almost no ties to his parents, and although almost all these children had brothers or sisters they tended also to retain no affectionate bonds with these siblings. They seemed to be an extremely confused group of teen-agers, most of whom (70 percent) were not completely free for adoption but remained in a situation in which no plan other than long-term care was the apparent wish of most of their parents.

In Granger, also, more boys than girls were in foster care, and both rural communities showed a greater imbalance on this sex distribution factor than did any other communities. Granger, too, was second to Norden in the average age of its children in care—eleven and a half years—and in the proportion who were ten years of age or older—72 percent. These figures emphasize the great age gulf which in our two rural communities more than in any others separated children in foster care from adopted children. In most other respects—ethnicity, religion, intelligence, physical health, and disability—the Granger children in foster care were not too different from the adopted children. However, far more of the children remaining in care (46 percent) than of those adopted had psychological symptoms. All of them had brothers or sisters, most of whom were also in foster care, and among almost half of them affectionate relationships were apparent. Predominantly, too, these children in foster care in Granger had, at the time of our study, an affectionate tie to their foster parents and to their child welfare worker, a relationship which these ten to twelve-year-olds had developed in the two to three years, on the average, that they had been in foster care. On the other hand, they no longer had affectionate bonds with their own parents, even though only about a third of the children had been released for adoption, and approximately three fourths had parents who no longer had any relationship with the agency. Their situation by April 1, while not involving many open signs of conflict and tension, had left over half of them with a confused sense of self-identity. These were the children who, unlike at least five of Granger's six in adoptive placements, still lacked the permanency of a home they could really call their own.

We did find, however, in the midst of the preceding modalities, some exceptions to the apparent rule that the rural child in foster care differs by age and psychologically from the child who is adopted through an agency. In a final look at our two rural communities let us examine briefly a few adoptive cases [2] that required added effort toward cultural redefinition and some departures from normal channels.

We had designed our investigation to include two rural counties, in part with the expectation that rural couples, living by standards somewhat different from those of urbanites, might more readily open their doors to some adoptive children of a type whom the values of metropolitan living today tend to keep in long-term foster care. Under what conditions, in these two rural counties, were such children placed in adoption?

There were two cases of minor physical disability. In Norden the infant with a "crooked" foot had so mild a condition that it was overlooked at birth, not noted until after the child's placement, and expected by the family's doctor to "straighten itself out in time." Similarly, the joint difficulty of the Granger child promised to be self-healing. But what of the three adoptive children with psychological defects in the Norden population? Under what conditions were they moved into adoptive homes? And the part-Indian child (the mixed ethnicity case) in Granger?

The Abbotsford Home arranged for the Breits to adopt seven-and-a-half-year-old Roger Wild after he had lived with them—his second set of foster parents—from the time he was about two years of age. Roger, the youngest of five sisters and brothers, had been removed from a seriously neglectful and personally disorganized divorcee when he was not yet two, but he was not relinquished for adoption until almost six years in foster care had elapsed.

Roger's I.Q. was twice measured on a Stanford-Binet, and both times he scored in the slightly below average range. Moreover, Roger had a physical condition entailing heavy medical expenses, and when he first came to the Breits he was much more negative than most two-year-olds should be, presenting many eating problems in addition. But the Breits wanted to keep Roger Wild and did so.

Who were the Breits? [3] They were in their late twenties and lived in their own home on a rural route on the outskirts of Pearl City. They

[2] All adoptive cases are the stories of real children, but the facts about them have been so disguised that they are unidentifiable.

[3] The Breits may be compared with Jane and Harry Smith, a composite of the typical adoptive parents in most of our nine communities. The Smiths' case is presented with other data on over 180 adoptive couples in Chapter 23.

were married only a few years when Roger was placed with them. Since his placement, the Breits had become the parents of two children of their own. Both parents were high school graduates, and Mr. Breit worked as a skilled mechanic, steadily employed by the same company in Pearl City since Roger first came to stay with them. Mr. Breit earned just over $5,000 in 1957.

When the Breits first approached the Abbotsford Home, they requested a small child to visit with them during a Christmas holiday. Roger, despite his psychological limitations, lived on with the Breits for five Christmases before adoption made their relationship permanent.

Minna Eberhard—with an I.Q. between 70 and 80—was just past six when she and an older brother were first placed in the Callum home in Lawrenceville, a town of under five thousand in a rural county to the south of Norden. More than two years went by in the Callum home before the court petition was filed and granted, making Minna's adoption final at age eight and a half. During this time, after a year or more of strife, Minna's brother had to be returned to the Abbotsford Home. Minna's open jealousy of him subsided, and her behavior generally seemed to the Callums and the staff at the Home to be somewhat improved.

Minna's behavior problems were generated during the first five years of her life after her parents were divorced. Her mother sent her off for a while to live with relatives, who then put her in foster care when both her own father and her new stepfather refused to contribute to her support. At about age five Minna was relinquished by her mother for adoption, committed to the Abbotsford Home with two older siblings, and boarded there for exactly a year before she was thought ready to be placed with the Callums.

And who were the Callums? Both in their late thirties, married about ten years, and childless (with a notable health problem), the Callums were a rural family who worked Mr. Callum's father's farm, as Mr. Callum Junior had done since he completed the eighth grade in Lawrenceville, better than twenty years ago. Their in-town home, valued in 1954 at over $10,000, gave some indication of their economic status. The Callums had come to the Abbotsford Home on the recommendation of friends who had been pleased with the adoption the Home had arranged for them. From the time of their initial application the Callums were clear about their willingness to take a child between the ages of five and ten and with some emotional difficulties. Both of them referred to current conflicts with their own families, related to difficulties in their childhood days. Mr. Callum seemed much more reserved than did Mrs. Callum, but both were meticulous about how they thought things should be done. As a matter of fact, both of them were quite exasperated with the Abbotsford Home before Minna's adoption was consummated, although everyone realized that adoption for a girl like Minna was not an easy matter. The Callums were not so unhappy with the Home, however, as to turn down the proposal that a caseworker continue to see Minna through the years ahead, as needed.

Roger Wild and Minna Eberhard were the only children under study whose adoption the Lutheran Abbotsford Home arranged. These cases suggest that planning the adoption of children with problems is itself a difficult process. The agency's image of an adoptive couple for a completely normal child seemed to be modified when a child like Roger or Minna was to be placed. Even church affiliation became less of an issue, for neither the Breits nor the Callums were Lutherans. Clearly, too, parent-agency relations are an important factor. When the Valley Dell Infants' Home placed an infant in adoption—the third of Norden's children with psychological deficits—with an Abbotsford family occupationally and economically well above the average, and the child subsequently showed developmental difficulties, the family retained the child nevertheless. This was the second adoptive child Valley Dell had placed with this family.

In Granger County, too, both Sue Thatcher and her adoptive parents, the Nolans, seen against Daleville norms, were somewhat unusual.

Seven years old and half Indian, Sue Thatcher was placed by the Bearpaw Catholic Children's Services with a Daleville professional man and his wife, both of whom had completed graduate studies during more than twelve years of childless married life together. Settled in Daleville for the past eight years in an apartment close to the Teachers College, the Nolans promised to give Sue a more permanent home than she had ever had before. At age four, together with a half sister, she was involuntarily removed from alcoholic parents, who subsequently failed, though living in the same city, to keep in touch with Sue or with the agency supervising her foster care placement.

The Nolans, in their thirties, had a modest income and a kind of stability which would be new for Sue. When they first applied for an adoptive child at the Bearpaw agency, they said they wanted an infant only and expressed no preferences regarding physical appearance or ethnic background. The adoption worker selected this child of mixed-Indian background for this couple—a man and wife for whom education had extended horizons but had not provided an acceptable substitute for childlessness.

If, then, we were expecting rural tolerances to be broader than urban ones in regard to adoption, we found little evidence in Norden or, especially, in Granger to support our hopes. Only one of the four families with whom a "different" child was placed was truly a rural family. In Granger the only "different" child was placed with an essentially urban family.

We must therefore leave unanswered, for the present, on the basis of information on the few adoptive placements actually made in Norden and Granger, the extent to which such rural counties might offer permanent homes to so-called "hard-to-place" children. The expectations of rural adoptive parents, discussed in Chapter 23, suggest that there were farm families in Norden and other communities where children who were of school age or in some ways different from the average child might be given a permanent home. These two counties were not, however, providing extensive resources of this type for children in need of parents, or at least adoption agencies in the Norden and Granger networks gave no evidence of intensive efforts or explorations in this direction.

III. TWO SMALL URBAN COMMUNITIES: SUMMIT AND LA PAZ

6. Child Placement and Other Social Processes

In approaching Pine County from the east, we saw flat sagebrush country with a shelflike bluff at the foot of hills to the north and a river, with its belt of cottonwoods, to the south. Irrigation had reclaimed much of the sagebrush land. Shrubs, flowers, and abundant trees crowded the streets and yards of the fair-sized city of Summit beyond the river. We were there to learn about 222 dependent children in what was once known as Fort Summit, now a government center and the commercial hub of a sizable agricultural area.

About a thousand miles south and east, still in the shadow of the Rocky Mountains, we looked in also upon 113 dependent children in Santa Ana County. Here in their southern extremities the Rockies begin to tail off, and the jagged edges of snow-capped peaks are replaced by sandstone buttes. To the north and east of the city of La Paz, 7,000 feet in altitude, rise the even greater heights that beckoned the conquistadors as they struggled up the seemingly endless and gently rising *bajada* toward an imagined City of Gold. And to the south lie colorful vistas that enchanted the Anglo-Protestant traders on their journeys southwestward from the settlements of Missouri. The transition from old to new, from Spanish to Anglo, from *ayer* to *hoy*—yesterday to today—has never been completed in La Paz if, indeed, it was ever begun. The consequences of a community arrested in limbo were still apparent in the phenomena of dependency which we had come to observe.

Who were the children in foster care and how were they taken care of, where placed and why, in these two small urban counties, both trade centers and centers of government in their states?   And who, by comparison, were the adoptive children in Pine and Santa Ana counties?

In Summit, where 90 percent of the children in foster care were in institutional placements, the case of Wanda Smith was representative.[1]

Wanda Smith seemed to be a very grown-up young lady for her eight years.   For the past twelve months she had lived in Summit at Children's Home, the institution operated by the Child's Care Society.   One might have believed that all was well with Wanda if it were not for the fact that, despite her superior intelligence, she was completely unable to learn to read.

Wanda's parents, of whom she spoke with apparent fondness, had not been able to care for her or for her three younger brothers, aged seven, five, and three.   All four children lived at the Children's Home, some two hundred miles from Morrow where Wanda's mother resided and where her father used to live.   With surprisingly little show of feeling, Wanda explained, "You see, they couldn't get along, Mamma and Daddy, so they got divorced.   Daddy lives alone far away and Mamma is married to Alfred now."   Here she looked down at the floor, unable to say why there was no word from Daddy and why she was not now living with Mamma and Alfred.   Nor did she refer to the circumstances which led up to the court proceedings, over a year ago, when the judge temporarily removed Wanda and her brothers from Mrs. Smith.   But the records describe how the children had been locked up alone in the apartment for three consecutive nights and days, with only cold food left on a low shelf in the cupboard for their meals.   This was but the last of many similar episodes of "willful neglect" noted by neighbors over more than a year's time, as Mrs. Smith tried desperately to rediscover who she was and why a marital relationship of more than ten years' duration had disintegrated.

Wanda's mother had left high school at the age of seventeen, to marry Wanda's father.   Just discharged from the Service, at twenty-five Ben Smith had found a good job as a machinist in his home town of Morrow. During their first four married years there were no children, and the Smiths maintained a happy social life amidst their childhood friends. Wanda's birth, and then in rather quick succession the births of the three boys, forced changes on the Smiths' social and budgeting patterns, changes which neither of them seemed happy to accept.   "I hadn't planned on any of the children," Mrs. Smith once remarked, half-smiling.   Mr. Smith seemed openly irritated with the mounting demands of a growing family. Mrs. Smith felt that her limit had been reached during his affair with a

[1] See our definition of a "representative" child in footnote 1 of Chapter 2.

girl friend of hers when Mrs. Smith was pregnant with her fourth child. Mr. Smith did not contest the divorce. He claimed his wife had been seeing someone whom she would probably marry. The only barrier to a new life seemed to be the children. Then the court removed them.

In the year Wanda and her brothers had been at Children's Home, their mother, 200 miles away, in Morrow, had had infrequent contacts with them. Nevertheless, it was clear that she was emotionally very much attached to her children. Since neither the Home nor any other agency had regular interviews with Wanda's mother, if any changes occurred in her situation, they would come about without agency help. Wanda's father seemed completely out of the picture.

Five and a half months after we studied Wanda's case—just eighteen months from the day of Wanda's removal from the apartment in Morrow—Wanda's mother and her new husband came to Summit to get the four Smith children. With no guarantees that her status was permanently changed, and with no sound bases for predictions, Wanda's record was filed among the closed cases: "child returned home."

Dolores Lopez typified the children in foster family care in La Paz, where 85 percent of those in care were found in foster families.

Dolores Lopez, like Wanda, was eight years old. Here, likeness between these two children ceased.

Dolores lived with her older sister, Juanita, to whom she was enormously attached, and Maria, another foster child in the home of Mr. and Mrs. Manuel Cordoba on El Camino del Burro in La Paz. Dolores had lived with the Cordobas for two and a half years. Before that she lived for a few months at St. Mary's Children's Home, up on the hill. But Sister Frances found Dolores, because of her frequent bed-wetting and her withdrawal reactions, too difficult to handle. For these reasons, essentially—though the foster mother's "poor health" was the recorded cause —Dolores had had to leave the foster family with whom she and two of her younger sisters were placed when she was five years old.

That was when Dolores first left the little adobe hut where her mother, grandmother, and seven sisters and brothers were living. Dolores's father had deserted many years ago. Dolores's father had stood in the way of the family's getting public assistance because, though out of work, he was "physically able." Gone from the county and probably the state, ostensibly to find work, Mr. Lopez had never returned. Another "father" lived for a year with Mrs. Lopez and the children. Then the family became eligible for relief.

Many people were parents for Dolores. Actually, no legal bond ever tied Dolores's father and mother to each other. Moreover, although sickly, Dolores's grandmother was as much a mother to the children as was Mrs. Lopez. And when Dolores was very young, her oldest sister (aged thirteen when Dolores was born) had looked after her.

When the four youngest children were first removed to foster homes three years ago, no court action was involved. The Department of Public Welfare arranged for the three oldest school-aged children (who were still at home) to live with Mrs. Lopez's oldest daughter, who had married and settled in the city. This daughter had known for years of her mother's prostitution and drinking. "I can't even talk to her anymore," said the daughter. "But maybe I can do something for the older kids, at least."

Dolores's most important relationships were with her sister Juanita and with Maria, the other foster child in the Cordoba home. Just now, after over two years, Dolores seemed less fearful with Mr. Cordoba. She was able to talk to him directly and not only by making rare comments through her sister Juanita. Moreover, Dolores could now speak above a whisper to her teacher at school.

With all the changes in adults who have been parents to her—people who often as not either paid little attention to her or wished she were somewhere else—it was no wonder Dolores seemed to be somewhat confused about who she was. The future for Dolores was only partially predictable. For some years the agency had had no contact with the mother, but the oldest sister reported no improvement in Mrs. Lopez's ways. Now thirty-nine, and reportedly of dull-normal intelligence, Mrs. Lopez was not likely to approach life differently through her own volition. She never visited Dolores and Juanita, although the Cordobas would be willing to have her come. The foster parents were an older couple—Mr. Cordoba a skilled auto mechanic who worked at a service station in town. Their own children had married and lived in a larger city two hours' drive away. The Cordobas would gladly keep the girls as long as they were physically able to do so.

Although Wanda and Dolores were in many ways different from one another, the characteristics of children in adoptive placements in Summit and La Paz were in many ways alike. Some of the resemblances, as well as some of the differences, between Summit's and La Paz's adoptive children are highlighted in the comparison of the cases of Billy and Tita, who represent the children in adoptive homes in these two small urban communities—Billy in Summit, Tita in La Paz:

Little Billy Hatfield was one of the many preschool-aged residents of Children's Home for whom Mr. Chris Spanos made adoptive placements soon after he became director of Child's Care Society. Billy was of white,

Protestant parents. He had no physical disabilities and was judged to have at least average intelligence. Except perhaps in regard to age—Billy was almost three—he was, in short, one of those "perfect" babies for whom there are so many prospective adoptive parents.

By contrast, Tita, placed by the Department of Public Welfare in La Paz, was not yet a year old. Tita was estimated to have at least average intelligence, and she evidenced no physical disabilities. But Tita was of Spanish Catholic parentage, and this made her one of the nation's "hard-to-place" children. For allegedly, there are fewer adoptive parent applicants in the U.S.A. who want or will take an olive-skinned infant like Tita than there are children like Tita available for adoption. In La Paz, only ten children were in adoptive homes when we made our study, but four of these ten were, like Tita, born of Spanish-American parents, and another two were of Spanish mothers and Anglo fathers, while one was of an American Indian mother and an Anglo father. Thus, only three of the adoptive children in La Paz had ethnic backgrounds like Billy Hatfield's, in Summit.

Neither Billy's parents nor Tita's were married when the children were born. Billy's parents were about three years younger than Tita's: Tita's mother was twenty-five, her father, thirty; Billy's mother twenty-one-and-a-half, his father twenty-seven. Both fathers were of similar social status in their own groups. Both had gone to school a year or so beyond high school graduation and were employed in white-collar occupations—Billy's father as an auditor, Tita's as a night club musician and entertainer. Billy's mother, who had left high school in the eleventh grade, worked regularly as a domestic in the city of Tulare.

Billy and Tita had similar placement histories. Both, early in life, were relinquished for adoption by their parents. Tita was free at three months; Billy, at four months. Tita, of course, was separated from her own mother practically at birth, just as each of the other La Paz children in adoptions was separated during his or her first year of life. Billy, too, was separated from his own mother at birth. It should be noted that among the eighty-nine adoptive children in Summit more than two in every ten were separated from their own parents after the first birthday. As a matter of fact, most of these children—about fifteen of them—had lived in their own homes until after their fifth birthday.

Finally, the two adoptive couples were amazingly alike, aside from their ethnic backgrounds. Billy's new parents, the Burnhams, came to Children's Home from the city of Jordan, and the Castillos drove down from the state's largest city to take Tita home. All four parents were in their early thirties and childless. The Burnhams have been married for eleven years, the Castillos for eight. The extent to which Tita's adoptive father had assimilated the same values as Mr. Burnham is suggested in the following facts. Both fathers had a year or two of education beyond high school. For seven years Mr. Burnham had been working in the Jordan funeral parlor, originally as an embalmer and now as manager of the establishment. Mr. Castillo had been a surveyor for the city government and was now the supervisor of his office. The average level of family income is considerably less in Tita's part of the country than in Billy's, but Mr. Castillo's income in 1957 was $5,750 and Mr. Burnham's $5,667. Both families seemed, thus, to be in a relatively secure economic position and well settled in their communities. Information on the two adoptive mothers reinforced our picture of similarities in the two families. Regarding personal characteristics, our evidence suggested that Mr. Burnham may have been slightly less comfortable about expressing his personal feelings and slightly stiffer in his personal relationships than Mr. Castillo; Mrs. Burnham may have fit exactly our norms of a psychologically healthy woman, while Mrs. Castillo was likely to be slightly more "open" than the average in her expression of feelings. Both women were enjoying their first months with their new adoptive children and both were caring for them in a new, single-family tract home.

These digests of the cases of four representative children suggest specific similarities and differences in aspects of child placement in Pine and Santa Ana counties.

Generally speaking, Pine County placed over 90 percent of its dependent children in institutions and adoptive homes, making minimum use of foster family placements, while Santa Ana County used primarily foster families for its children in care. While most of the children known to agencies in both counties came from urban homes, many more of the Santa Ana children were rural—a fourth of them. In these ways the "where" of placement in Pine and Santa Ana differed. But in a few ways they were similar. Both counties served mostly their own (in-county) children. And both found most of their foster family and all of their institutional placements within their own boundaries. A predominant placement fact remains, however: in Pine, foster family placements, and in Santa Ana institutional placements, were the smallest proportions of each such type of placement in all the nine counties we studied. This situation made our small urban county of the Northwest and our small urban county of the Southwest exactly opposite from one another. In addition, Santa Ana County children stayed in care longer than the Pine County children—although, interestingly enough, not many more of the Santa Ana children came into care earlier than did the children in Pine County. Some of the details of these statements are presented in Table 4.

The children like Dolores Lopez in La Paz, who stayed on in care longer than the children like Wanda Smith in Summit, lived in

Table 4

PLACEMENT, LENGTH OF CARE, AND SEPARATION AGES OF
CHILDREN IN PINE AND SANTA ANA COUNTIES

	Pine County (Summit)		Santa Ana County (La Paz)	
Type of placement, by percentage of children in care on April 1, 1957				
In foster family care	6		77	
In institutional care	55		16	
In adoptive homes	39		7	
Average (median) number of years since first separation from parents, for all children under study	1		2½	
Age at which children first entered care, by percentage of all children under study [a]				
As preschoolers (0–5 years)	54		66	
In 1st to 2d year of life		40		42
In 3d to 5th year of life		14		24
As school-aged children (6–10 years)	32		26	

[a] See note *a*, Table 1.

quite different worlds. How did the cultures of Summit and La Paz impinge upon these dependent children? [2] And while more than half of the children in care on April 1 in Pine County and in rural Norden were placed in local institutions, by comparison most of the children in care in Santa Ana County—and in rural Granger— were placed with local foster families. Were there social processes in either of our two small urban counties similar to the processes we have seen in the two rural communities? Do such similarities make more comprehensible the similarities in child placement pattern?

[2] All of our basic facts gathered in these two communities were based upon the respective counties as the geographical units for our analysis. However, as we discuss the respective cultures it seems more relevant to refer to "Summit" and "La Paz" as the two centers which dominate these small urban communities; thus these terms are used when the communities are referred to throughout the text.

THE TWO SMALL URBAN CULTURES

Summit, Pine County

Summit's populace in the early days was heavily weighted with roustabouts and adventurers, many of them discontented refugees from Civil War aftermaths. There was a boom in the metal mines in this Western territory, but by 1870 the population had declined. The fortune seekers headed for the mines of a now adjacent state, and the more docile people settled down to making a living in the valley where previously, as early accounts tell it, only the flag on the Army fort had prevented anarchy in those first few years after the war.

The inhabitants maintained that their community has known no "boom" or "bust" since those days. The town had grown steadily until it could be called not a "small town" but a "small city" with the many differentiated services that the latter term usually implies.[3] Summit inhabitants were mostly the descendants of transplanted Midwesterners, and most of them had grown up in Summit or in the state in which it is located. An influx from surrounding areas, together with an increased birth rate, seemed to account for most of the population growth. It had been a steady growth, accelerated in recent years.

This was a community serving a rural economy but still quite urban in its life.[4] It was a community of individual homes where again sameness rather than gross difference was more apparent.[5] It was a community in which noticeably different ethnic groups were now practically indistinguishable, although Chinese and In-

[3] In 1950 the city of Summit had a population of about 35,000 and the Pine County population totaled about 70,000. What was designated as "Metropolitan Summit" numbered about 55,000 inhabitants. We saw postwar tracts developing in the bench area, on the shelf above the valley floor. The county population had grown by 40 percent in the decade prior to 1950; the city grew from about 26,000 to 35,000 in the same period.

[4] The rural farm population of the county in 1950 was 13 percent of the total and the rural nonfarm population 18.5 percent of the total. The remaining 68.5 percent were recorded as urban dwellers.

[5] The median income of families and unrelated individuals in Pine County for 1950 was $2,877. Only 2 percent had incomes of over $10,000, and 10 percent had incomes under $500.

dians had been conspicuous in the valley in its mining days. It was a well-educated community.[6] And it was a community in which commercial and white-collar employment predominated.[7]

One sensed here, too (as in Norden), a kind of perceived homogeneity among the people, compounded of local pride, displayed in a refusal to emphasize group and individual differences. An early traveler recounted that the pioneers judged an individual by what he did, not by what beliefs he held or who his ancestors were. And this emphasis seemed to have carried over through the years.

At the time of our study, local informants generally agreed that the Summit population was about equally divided among Mormons, Catholics, and Protestants. These seemed to be the major groups around which Summit people organized their differing sentiments; but the sentiments which all shared seem more significant than any bases for difference in Summit. The occupation base had provided a broad cross section of "respectable," white-collar activities. These tended to permeate this preponderantly native-born white population, lessening class differences. Even the religious differences were not dramatized here: for each of Summit's major religious groups had honored antecedents and each reached out to all segments of the population and into all occupations.

There were, allegedly, conflicts with the Mormons in the past, but these conflicts were now forgotten and local attitudes bespoke the constant effort to avoid such antagonism. Summit residents often mentioned the fortunate circumstances that provided a numerical balance among the major denominations. But historical reports also described the local Mormons as having been law-abiding, frugal, and good citizens. Similarly, the Catholics in Summit were time-honored. The record of one early traveler emphasized that there was absolutely no discrimination against Catholics in

[6] The figure for median school years completed was 12 in 1950.

[7] The occupation breakdown of the 1950 census showed the largest proportions in the county to be working in clerical and kindred work (15.2 percent). Professional and white-collar categories accounted for fully 50 percent of the employed working force. Seven percent were farmers or farm managers, 15 percent were employed in skilled trades, and 27 percent in semiskilled, service, and labor categories. Only 7 percent of all these were employed in manufacturing.

Summit in the early days. It seemed to him that a free life and pure mountain air were antidotes for bigotry. The first church established in the region was Catholic, although the first and oldest church in Summit itself was Episcopal.

All these elements combined to make Summit a community that was important enough to an environing region (and large enough) to be a city, yet isolated enough from communication outside that region [8] (and small enough) to be a town. It was a place where domestic business and local social life were of prime concern to the people and where "respectability" and "avoidance of conflict" were watchwords. Wanda Smith's total situation must be seen with the larger Summit setting in mind to be even partly understood. A community's working definition of child dependency and how citizens extend themselves to act upon it may reflect a local capacity to face up to the unpleasant or a cultural process not unlike the personal mechanism of denial.

La Paz, Santa Ana County

The descriptions of La Paz which a Missouri trader recorded in his diary could, with allowances for some crude impressions of the Spanish and Indian people by a nineteenth-century Anglo-American, be applicable today. Many, if not most, local citizens would be pleased that this congruence between the older era and the present one is still apparent. In the 1820s the visitor remarked about the mud houses, the irregularity with which the city was built, and the friendliness of the inhabitants. Shocked as he was by the lack of "correct moral principles" among the inhabitants, he found the people hospitable in the extreme. Some were very wealthy, but by far the majority were, he recorded, the most wretched and poverty-stricken people he had ever laid eyes on, yet apparently happy in the Church-dominated Spanish Southwest.

To the adventurer, as to the present-day tourist, the city of La Paz presented an interesting contrast to the usual American rural or urban (or, now, suburban) settings. While La Paz was a

[8] The Union Pacific completed its overland line in 1869, but a branch line to serve this region was not completed until the 1880's. Even then, Summit was left twenty miles off this short line and was content with a connecting branch to it.

crossroads and trading center in the 1800s, it was, in a sense, abandoned by the twentieth century until its reclamation by artists, tourists, and the retired. Many professional people, also, preferred to come here to get out of the rushing torrents and into the quiet eddies of American culture where unique strains—the old Spanish and the Indian—still persisted.[9] Many aspects of a local folk culture still endure side by side with modern social manners and innovations.

At the time of our study, farm life in this part of the Southwest had declined steadily, and the most recent drought had accounted for much of the migration out of the county.[10] The poorly educated Spanish workers from the rural villages became migrant workers. Seasonal unemployment had always been a problem in Santa Ana County. And always the gross contrasts between aspects of two worlds intruded into one's impressions of this community. For those growing up in La Paz, its mixed culture made it a divided city, an "either–or" community of two well-demarcated groups.[11]

[9] The 1950 census showed about 38,000 as the population of Santa Ana County, with 28,000 in the city of La Paz. The growth from 1940 to 1950 was about 24 percent in the county and from about 20,000 to 28,000 in the city. This was a period in which a new community, a Federal project, grew in a valley near by and brought business to La Paz. However, a local study indicated that the county population decreased by 0.7 percent in 1950–55. Although there was a natural increase (excess of births over deaths) of 4,693 in this five-year period, there was a loss through migration away from the county of 4,946 in the same period.

[10] In the 1950 U.S. Census, Santa Ana County listed only 9.6 percent of its population as rural farm and 16.9 percent as rural nonfarm. In its proportions of urban dwellers it was, thus, slightly more urban than was Pine County. A local economic survey conducted in 1955 indicated that 9.2 percent of the working force in the county was unemployed. Our only comparable figure for Pine County, taken from the 1950 census, indicated 1.4 percent unemployed in that county.

[11] The census showed 93.5 percent of the population as native-born white. The largest group of foreign born was from Mexico. The special Spanish-surname count for 1950 gave the proportion of Spanish as 60 percent. The current consensus was that the numbers of Anglos had been increasing. Census figures which have been broken down by an examination of this Spanish surname group indicate that the aforementioned division in the community tended to leave one group quite "superior" socially. For example, the median of school years completed for the total population was 9.5; for those with Spanish surname it was 7.5. A part of this picture of a divided community was the school situation, with nine public and five parochial elementary schools and one public and one parochial high school listed for the county.

Here in the world of public affairs one was either Anglo-Protestant
or Spanish-Catholic. This major division was perpetuated along
numerous lines although, as we shall see later, many local participants in professional circles tended to transcend, in their values and
attitudes, the traditional demarcation. But the very conditions
which made La Paz attractive to newcomers served also to prevent
them from doing anything to alter the social system. Even those
who did not primarily identify with either the Anglo-Protestant or
the Spanish-Catholic segment of the community, but were most
proud of being a part of the "unique city," might not wish to see
the conditions bearing on this major ethnic division changed, since
such change would alter the very atmosphere which drew them
there.

La Paz was not a prosperous community, and the basis of its
economy was conducive neither to growth nor to great occupational
stability.[12] Not only was manufacturing even more minor than
in Summit,[13] but La Paz did not service a thriving rural area as
did Summit. Its major occupation groups were employed either
in semiskilled or unskilled work, in the professions or in clerical
work, mostly in government enterprises. Government employment fluctuated also, for it was influenced by political shifts; in politics, too, La Paz was a community of "either–or." Much of the
white-collar government work was carried on by the women in the
local populace, and it was the men—those in the unskilled categories particularly, and mostly Spanish-speaking—who suffered from
a high seasonal unemployment rate. Their problems as bread-
winners of large families appeared central in our picture of dependent children.

[12] The median income of all families and unrelated individuals in Santa Ana
County for 1950 was $2,329. But 3 percent earned over $10,000 (a greater proportion than in Pine County), and 15 percent earned less than $500 (*vs.* 10 per-
cent in Pine County). Median income for all urban Spanish surname families
and unrelated individuals for the entire state was $1,400.
[13] The occupation breakdown for 1950 showed the major occupation groups
(45 percent) to be included in professional and white-collar categories; only
4 percent were farmers and farm managers and 15 percent were in skilled occupations. Thirty-three percent were included in semiskilled, service, and labor
categories. Manufacturing employed only 3.5 percent (one-half the Pine County
proportion), while construction work employed 17.2 percent—a larger proportion
in this seasonal work than was found in any other community.

It was in La Paz that Dolores Lopez's story was revealed to us. Hers was the story of a Spanish-American dependent child cared for through a welfare program maintained and serviced preponderantly by Anglo-Americans.

Social Form and Process in the Cultures

We noted that Summit, like Norden, was a relatively homogeneous community, while La Paz was definitely divided into two major ethnic segments. And there were elements of an awareness of class differences in La Paz, too, with economic disparities widening the major sociocultural gulf in the population; while in Summit "respectable middle-classness" was more the pervading norm. Then, too, both Summit and La Paz were small communities. However, an important difference was noted in communities this size in the perceived beginnings of a greater separation between the worlds of private and of public affairs. Still, "sameness" was the keynote in Summit, and the public and private worlds blended so that events and values in one could not be divorced from events and values in the other. In La Paz the maintenance of homogeneity was not an issue, and the public arena was a site for conflicting views while activities in heterogeneous and guarded private worlds involved values that tended to be kept more separate from public values than in Summit.

Secondly, social processes were manifestly different in these two cultures. Seen as total community configurations, neither Summit nor La Paz was a bustling center of shifting achieved status symbols. Summit was a community which did not recognize many social strata through which participants might move, and the people who chose Summit for a home seemed not much concerned with a struggle for preeminence over their fellows. In La Paz there was even less indication of an achieved status atmosphere. The older residents tended to accept and rely upon traditional place and position, and family name, heredity, and ethnicity remained important in locating people in the social system. The newer residents seemed to choose this community particularly because it was a quiet byway, relatively detached from contests for achieved status.

In Summit we saw stress on independence and separateness, on the avoidance of public conflict in maintaining the public balance between slightly different groups. This situation was compounded by the importance of local, private, social life in this relatively isolated community. In La Paz, on the other hand, it was the public separation of the community into Spanish-Catholic and Anglo-Protestant segments, combined with the guarding of diverse private worlds, which was of greatest significance in the social equilibrium.

The "contractual" or impersonal had also appeared in both Summit and La Paz along with occupational specialization and the recognition of more definite public and private worlds. But in both communities the personal was still more paramount than the impersonal and contractual. In Summit personal friendships still provided the tone, the constraints, and the norms for formal dealings in public. And in La Paz, although there were many professional people who were accustomed to the impersonal and contractual relationships of urban settings, it seemed that particularly the Spanish, still not far removed from their rural antecedents, found such dealings unsatisfying and confusing.

Finally, in these contrasting atmospheres, each community was oriented somewhat differently toward the dependent child. Homogeneous Summit, in the past, may well have resembled Norden in many respects. Like Norden, Summit was somewhat rejecting of dependency; it tended to refuse to recognize dependency problems. But there were latent human feelings for children in the culture which were tempered by a tendency to allow parents to bring up their own children in their own way. Thus, slowness to recognize dependency situations and to act upon them through a public program had intensified the problems of the local private agency, which was responsible for providing services to dependent children from the whole southern half of the state. The director of this agency sought to remedy the circumstances which brought children to the doorstep of his institution, at all hours, often without his having prior knowledge of the referral or contact with the family. And in the operation of its program, the Child's Care Society attempted to bring these dependent children, who came from a wide area, as in Norden, within the circle of the "we" where they could receive the emotional support which Summit was prepared to give those it could see as "ours."

By contrast, divided La Paz had always presented a picture of a "we" group caring for a "they" group in its health and welfare programs. It was Anglo money, Anglo medicine, and Anglo welfare programs that took care of the "Spanish needy," and the gulf between the givers and the recipients seemed quite wide. But in child welfare matters, in particular, those who carried on the work were professional people who largely transcended in their own values the local cultural definitions. While mostly Anglos themselves, these professionals operating the public, tax-supported programs leaned far over to identify with the Spanish families and accept their dependent children as "ours." Still, other civic personages largely reflected a "they" attitude, particularly in their misconceptions about these same children. And the social workers within this cultural framework could bring the dependent children —83 percent of them Spanish in our population for study—no closer into the "we" in the community than the professional health and welfare world, which encompassed them with care, could penetrate.

CHILD PLACEMENT

Foster Care in the Two Cultures

The extremely small proportion of children in foster family care in Summit and the large proportion in foster families in La Paz were reminiscent of a similar but smaller discrepancy in Norden and in Granger. The extensive use of institutional placement was not so great in Summit as in Norden, but La Paz's low percentage in institutional care was very close to Granger's. However, the "they" approach to the dependent children in Norden's treatment center and the "we" approach that seemed more typical of Granger are not so simply reidentified in the two small but more complex urban centers of Summit and La Paz.

Earlier, we related a community's awareness of its ethnic homogeneity to its tendency to stereotype visibly different people. At least such persons are more likely in a personalized community to be excluded from the "we" group and defined as a "they." We found support for this idea in Norden and, to some extent, in Summit. Summit was large enough for there to be some social differentiation and growth of contractual, impersonal relations within it. But we saw a surprising tendency, considering the size of Summit, toward perceived homogeneity, toward uniform respectability, and toward a blending, on a basis of personalized relationships, of the private and public worlds which tend to develop in larger communities. And Summit repeated, to a degree, the Norden situation, in which most of its dependent children came initially from outside the community. Thus perhaps an added effort was required in Summit, too, to draw these children within a circle of concern. But the Child's Care Society tried to meet this problem. The previous director, who had been the Society's executive for many years, had resigned after preparing the way for a successor who could introduce new vigor into the program. As the new director, Mr. Spanos, constantly emphasized, the dependent child belonged to the whole community, he was the concern of the larger "we."

In La Paz, the great proportion of children in foster family care indicated that a secular program operated by an Anglo public agency had had great influence in placement in a culture where sacred social definitions still dominated. This was a setting in which a professional culture transcended one that had persisted through many generations. But the split between private and public worlds which tended to be maintained in La Paz meant that community-wide public programs—through which child care practices might bring the child into the larger "we" of the whole community—were largely abdicated by groups and individuals in their primary concern with their own private associations. And the "we" of the dependent child remained that Spanish half of La Paz in which over 80 percent of the dependent children had their origins.

The attitude expressed by the people we interviewed in the two communities reflected these different atmospheres. First let us look at Summit.

At least one community self-perception in Summit was much like

Norden's. Said Summit, again and again, "We don't have problems of dependency here." If communities, like people, can be said to tend to cope with unpleasantness by the denial of it, Summit gave evidence of using this mechanism. Only a crisis, apparently, could be treated as a problem.[14]

A certain latent discontent with the existing program of the Child's Care Society at Children's Home was capitalized upon by the new director, who moved into Summit with his family, bought a home, joined the local Methodist church, and settled down to take care of "his" children. He attempted to interpret to his board, and through them to the community, that these were "our" children.

"When I first came here," Mr. Spanos said, "the youngsters impressed me as being fearful and fretful. The two major things that I felt most important to do were to relax the climate of the institution and to begin effecting foster placements of our young citizens. It took a while to put across our problem. Now I'm sure the board feels as I do about our mission—we are here to serve the child better." And Aubrey Wells, the young, enthusiastic, newly hired caseworker at the Home, said, "My office door is always open when the kids come back from school. That's my primary job here—to give the kids my time when they need me."

But the acceptance of the dependent child was not always quite

[14] Summit had had a few crises that brought about community action on a broad scale. One such crisis was a polio epidemic several years ago in which outside medical help was welcomed. Some of the medical people who penetrated the local community at that time remained and have adapted their professional practices to the Summit way of life. A more recent crisis which brought on the hiring of a psychiatrist to head a mental health program has since resulted in this highly trained professional leaving the local scene. It seems significant that this man—a former Mormon who became a Unitarian, a native of the state who had received his professional training in the East and looked upon the Summit challenge as a chance for administrative experience—was spoken of as "aloof socially" and never could legitimize his public role. Said the Summit *Frontiersman* in an editorial: "Dr. Robert Ford seems to have the unfortunate habit of saying the wrong thing at the right time." On this occasion Dr. Ford is reported to have said that "the schools are being asked to serve as extensions, or substitutions, of parental authority." The editorial warned that such a statement would "invite the ire of thousands of mothers and fathers in the State," nodded approval to "the idea that father is head of the house, and should act accordingly," and observed that "many areas in the State, not to mention thousands of its citizens, are far from sold on the mental health idea."

so open. Mrs. Black, an active woman in politics and a local resident for several years, remarked that the children at the Home had
not been completely accepted by the community in the past.
"Every group in town took things to the Home at Thanksgiving
and Christmas. But a lot of attitudes persisted about children having the 'badness' born in them, though I think there has always
been an honest concern for kids in Summit."

It seemed that any social action in Summit placed great emphasis on personalized relationships in this community where public
conflict could not be tolerated. Judge Allen, a native son, affirmed
this. He said that his efforts to win election over an incumbent
judge of thirty years caught on because a person-to-person telephone
campaign was undertaken on his behalf. And Dr. Prescott, another native son, now head of the state health department and former head of the county health department, remarked that even he
had had to sell himself first as a person to the county supervisors
before he dared to propose changes and hope to get them acted
upon. For Summit was a quiet, small town in transition to being
a small city. Private associations and social life were tremendously
important, since the people there must provide their own enter-
tainment. One Junior Leaguer, who came to Summit from Louisi-
ana some ten years ago after marrying a native of the state, said:
"There are more parties per capita here than New Orleans ever
heard of. And people will tolerate someone on a professional basis
simply to keep from breaking up social affairs." The director of
the Community Council, also a native son, expressed it a little differently: "Everyone in Summit is pretty close. Personally, over
coffee or a drink, one might criticize someone to his face, but we
don't publicly condemn people. We like this atmosphere in which
people aren't taking pot shots at one another."

What did all this mean for those entrusted with care of the dependent child? For a newcomer, it meant that he proceeded cau-
tiously in the world of public affairs while still confirming his sin-
cerity through friendships in the world of private affairs. Malcolm
Yates, a board member at the Home, a resident for many decades,
and a prominent banker in Summit, said: "Our new director is

good for the community, but we do have to put a few restraints on him. People here are really very concerned about children. But they are not concerned or alarmed about specific problems. We don't believe in overdoing this casework business." He continued, "I have faith in Mr. Spanos. He stands up and says what he believes to your face, and none of us doubts his sincere concern for the children."

The La Paz situation appeared different. Whereas in Summit the tie-in by the professional agency to the community was through a large adoption program of long standing in a relatively homogeneous setting, in La Paz the professional welfare community was immersed, almost overwhelmed, in a long-term foster family program which linked it at the grass roots largely to the Spanish segment of the community. The tie of agency people to the Spanish foster family tended to be a "personalized" link and not based upon impersonal or contractual relationships.[15] This was a program which represented an accepting, understanding attitude toward the dependents by the professional health and welfare people. But it was a program that required the support of other community figures who represented less understanding attitudes. There was probably no community that we studied where the difference between board members' attitudes and staff members' attitudes was more marked. At the same time, it was a place where there was little to indicate that a system that was balanced in division would soon have that balance upset.

The accepting attitude of the health and welfare professional workers toward the Spanish dependents was exemplified by the district health officer. Dr. Elizabeth Weston, who, like many La Paz

[15] Lyle Saunders has some relevant comments regarding the Spanish culture of the Southwest in his *Cultural Difference and Medical Care: La Gente de la Raza*, pp. 94–95: "The Spanish Americans and Mexicans come from rural areas and a long tradition of rural living . . . . Urban living . . . brings . . . many changes in patterns of association . . . . A greater proportion of . . . relationships are thus contractual; a lesser proportion are personal." Saunders sees conflict and frustration in this for the Spanish-American with growing urbanization. But the "old Spanish" in La Paz were still very much anchored to their rural patterns and their familism, and agency people worked within this context. We noted few Spanish who had entered into the contractual relationship of formal adoption, while many cared for children in foster families.

professional people, came originally from the East, said: "The Spanish really love their children very much. I see a lot of poverty in this state, but I would think long and hard before I would try to sell these people on an industrial city life. There are a lot of grades of being poor, but this one is not really the worst, in my estimation."

Another physician in La Paz, who was well informed in child welfare matters, not only expressed an accepting attitude toward the Spanish dependents but acknowledged a desire to see welfare agencies push even further in transcending local cultural definitions. "Maybe there should be more insistence," he said, "on exploring the religious preferences of a mother when she releases her child for adoption. It seems it is often assumed that the mother wishes to have the child follow her own [the mother's] religion, but these things aren't tested enough and consequently La Paz ends up with many Catholic babies that can't be placed for adoption. My own belief," he continued, "about Indian Catholics is that they are not so 'Catholic' as the Spanish Catholics. The Indians are still more at home with their tribal customs."

But the attitudes of other important Anglo people in La Paz often varied from those just cited. They illustrate a different orientation among the board member stratum of health and welfare organizations.

The director of the local girls' club, originally from the East Coast, said that her board criticized because not enough of the "nicer" girls were attracted to the club. "I don't have a single Girl Scout in my club. But since a couple of Anglo girls, who live near by, come to the club, my board thinks I should be able to attract more such girls. But if I ask my board if they would send their daughters to the club, they become a little embarrassed."

And Dr. Hyde, a prominent physician whose wife was a lifetime resident of La Paz, said: "This is not really one community but two. This year the Catholic Church came in on the United Fund drive, so many Protestants have stayed out. I know people who made their contributions and then indicated where every dollar should go."

A local banker on the board of the welfare department declared: "This state is spending too much on welfare. Nobody starves here, for a neighbor will always bring over something to keep a family going. I think the world of the Spanish people, but spending more money for welfare isn't the answer."

People in La Paz, then, seemed to live in a world which not only was divided into public segments but which also separated the public from the private, for most participants wished to keep their private associations out of the public arena where controversy was often dramatic. Of private associations, Dr. Hyde remarked: "There are really four main groups in town—merchants, artists, retired, and the government people. The government group changes after every new Administration comes in. And all groups want to be left to themselves." The local Episcopal minister said: "People here are so independent that they don't want to organize. They have an interest in their own private group programs, but they are not oriented to community-wide, public, cooperative efforts." For it seemed that when issues did enter the public arena they became crystallized around the two major, conflicting foci. The former school superintendent in La Paz, who later, coincidentally, served in the same capacity in Summit, summed up the situation: "In La Paz you're constantly dealing with the problem of divided loyalties. Many Catholic people who have their children in the public school will still be out rooting for the parochial school at athletic contests." Thus we saw a community openly divided into two camps in its public affairs and fractionalized in its private affairs.

At this point we can see that La Paz provided a setting in which responsibility for the dependent child continued to be accepted by those who cared for him directly. But it was a setting in which the dependent child remained outside the experience of others who did not participate directly in his care and did not feel this same responsibility for him. Long-term care for children in one segment of the population seemed inevitable so long as the professional community, in neither public nor private arena, could appreciably modify traditional cultural definitions of dependency, or the basic

economic conditions and social cleavages to which in La Paz they
were attached. The requisites for more children's moving out of
care were, however, found within the dynamics of the social system
in Summit.

Adoption in Summit and La Paz

How did the children like Billy Hatfield in Summit and Tita in
La Paz come to be adopted? What social processes were involved
in this phenomenon? We would expect, following our hypothesis
that formalized agency adoption goes with an achieved status at-

Table 5

ADOPTIVE PLACEMENTS AND RETURNS HOME IN
PINE AND SANTA ANA COUNTIES

	Pine County (Summit)	Santa Ana County (La Paz)
Percentages of all children in care April 1, 1957, who were in adoptive placements	39	7
Percentages of all adoptive placements that were in-county	18	29
Percentages of all children in care April 1, 1957, who left care during next six months	53	17
For adoptive placements	8	1
For return home and "other" reasons	45	16

mosphere, social interdependence, and contractual relationships,
that in these two small urban "in-between" communities adoptions
would present a mixed picture. An achievement orientation should
be manifest to different degrees among different groups or social
strata in communities the size of Summit and La Paz. However,
in adoption, too, Summit showed a surprisingly uniform picture
for a community of its size; while, again, in La Paz the major factor in adoption was the split in the community which, in this case,
provided for a surplus of dependent Spanish children and few
Spanish adoptive homes, but a surplus of potential Anglo adoptive
homes and few (almost no) Anglo dependent children. Table 5
gives a general view of the facts on the cases we studied.

The adoptive placement figures for Summit indicate a favorable
atmosphere for the adoption agency's state-wide program. A note

should be added: the best evidence we have suggests that non-agency adoptions outnumbered agency adoptions by well over two to one in Summit and elsewhere in the state. This situation supports the idea that nonagency adoptions thrive in a personalized atmosphere. And since there was little perception of different social strata through which one might move in Summit, all adopted children were not so much symbols of the achieved status of parenthood as welcome new participants in relatively homogeneous families throughout the whole extended community. Our figures show that most of the adoptive placements of Summit's children took place outside the county, where the agency found ready acceptance of children in families and where the visit of the adoption worker was considered more a personal call by a friend than a formal contact by an agency.

In La Paz, a very low proportion of children in care were in adoptive placement. Moreover, La Paz was one of three communities in our entire study in which the proportion of all the children under study who were placed in adoption was smaller than the proportion who were returned by agencies to their own parents. This might be related to the predominance of an ascribed status orientation over an achieved status orientation in the total community configuration in La Paz. In an ascribed status atmosphere, children are returned to "their own kind"—and in a setting like La Paz's, that can only mean "back home." The lack of available resources for moving a child permanently into a new and perhaps "better" home of his own added to the frustration of child welfare personnel, all too conscious of the two worlds in La Paz. For it was the dependent Spanish children who were or could be available for adoption, but few, if any, achievement-oriented (perhaps "middle-class") Spanish couples were on hand to adopt them. And it was Anglo couples who desired to adopt children and who often were willing to overlook a child's ascribed characteristics. But given the local religious, social, economic, and cultural conditions, the gap between supply and demand in dependency and adoption could not be bridged in La Paz.

How did the attitudes of the people we interviewed corroborate

these impressions? Let us look again at Summit. Mr. Spanos recalled the story of an adoption that went awry in days past, when
the personalized atmosphere was less tempered by professional evaluation. This was the case of two part-Indian girls placed in one
of the "better" homes along Coldwater Avenue. One girl was
never really accepted in the home. The adoptive mother began
to account for the child's "unruly" behavior by referring to her "Indian blood," and eventually the girl was returned to the Home, evidently much damaged by her experience. Currently, the Child's
Care Society was reaching out to tap homes in the community and
across the state where children were desired and would be accepted.
Adjustment to the personalized atmosphere of Summit was being
made in the adoption program. Mr. Wells, the young caseworker
at the Society, said: "You know, I have to work fast when I visit
folks around here to make a home study. Everything is so informal
and friendly that it's difficult to maintain a professional role.
People like to get things on a personal basis right away, and I know
that by the second time I visit I'll be considered just a friend. But
I am learning how to use here too, as I did in Chicago, what I
know about what children need to grow up healthy."

Equally relevant, the local Booth Memorial Hospital provided a
ready supply of adoptable children. Major Treat, hospital superintendent, said: "There seems to be a real open-ness to accepting
children in this community. Actually, very few children are hard
to place; even the physically handicapped are placeable. I suppose
the part-Negro child is the hardest to place, but we have few of
those." Then she made a remark which suggested a somewhat different tone toward adoption in Summit than usually we have associated with the middle-class, core-cultural practice. "Do you know
that a much higher proportion of our unwed mothers keep their
children than in any other Booth Memorial Hospital in the country? I'm sure that the Mormon and Catholic doctors and lawyers
counsel private placement within their own groups and that a lot
of this occurs. I would say only a fraction of the adoptions in this
state go through an agency." The local Catholic priest sustained
this impression when he told us he kept a file of Catholic couples

who wanted children and was ready to refer to this list whenever an unwed Catholic mother came to his attention.

So it seemed that the nonagency-adopted children in Summit were placed through informal contacts within private subgroups. The children whom we saw at the nonsectarian Home perhaps had already filtered through this private screen. Those who remained for agency placement were perceived as a relatively homogeneous group, no longer designated as "Catholic" or "Mormon" or whatever, by the time they reached the Home which had the public responsibility for their care. Then the staff at the Child's Care Society accepted this group as a homogeneous "we" and opened waiting adoptive family doors to them.

Adoption in La Paz was a different story. The old Spanish culture still involved an ascribed status atmosphere in which blood ties were highly important. The county superintendent of schools described this situation: "The Spanish have a real feeling for blood relationship. They feel it is a sacred duty that one's own blood should not be left to the care of strangers. I recall an old folk tale told among the Spanish, that if one grows up with a parent who is not really a blood relative, one is subject to epilepsy. Of course it's just a superstition but it illustrates how they feel."

The local Catholic authorities tended to reinforce this emphasis, although Monsignor Daily was anxiously seeking Spanish Catholic couples to adopt Spanish dependent children. But, he said, "I always try to get an unwed mother to keep her baby if possible. We feel that caring for one's own flesh and blood is best, if at all possible." He went on to explain how the adoption process was strange for the Spanish who were unaccustomed to such formal relationships: "In the past there was no formal adoption among the Spanish. The eldest child was placed with grandparents. Adoption became a legal thing when these matters began to come up on allotment and tax forms." This was in line with Dr. Weston's impressions too: "I knew a Spanish father who gave a newborn child to a relative, an aunt, because this woman had set up a fuss and, after all, they had promised her a child. All he said was, 'After all, it is her own blood.'"

What of Anglo couples who wanted to adopt children? The Episcopal minister related both the ethnic imbalance and the age of the adult population in La Paz to the low proportion of local agency adoptions: "Anglo-Protestant couples just can't obtain children in this state. My families who adopt go to Chicago or St. Louis or to physicians either in or out of the state. There are over twenty adopted children in my congregation now. And many couples are still seeking children."

On the other hand, La Paz is not a bustling, middle-class community for Anglos either. It lacks a good, solid group of the young and of the middle-aged. Many people are retired, and the area offers little to younger people who are eager to get ahead. Here too, then, in its relative lack of young and middle-aged couples, is an explanation for the low rate of adoption in La Paz. For those are the age groups from which adoptive applicants come.

Still, La Paz had felt the impact of a vigorous Anglo middle-class community from its nearness to the Federal project community at Sandy Valley. Local social workers had begun to find homes there for hard-to-place children, for the demand for children was great in this new-born Anglo community. The state supervisor of child welfare commented: "We find Anglo couples in Sandy Valley ready to consider almost any child for adoption. We have even had Protestants offer to take a Catholic child and raise it as a Catholic." A record of a part-Spanish child placed in the home of a Sandy Valley research laboratory director and his wife was quite revealing in exemplifying an extreme of the achieved-parenthood approach to adoption by a couple who were eager to accept the "different" child. The whole community of Sandy Valley seemed to reach out to embrace the child after the placement, three pediatricians were vying to care for him, and many showers were given for the adoptive mother by friends.

There was some evidence that Spanish couples in the area were increasingly adopting children, but their numbers were still small and were largely confined to the growing city of Eldorado, where those who sought to move up socially tended to relocate. Mr. Cuevas, a counselor at the local public high school, remarked: "I estimate that many more of our Spanish students go on to college now. In the over-all student population we find a few more students now coming from families whose parents attended college." However, even if these youngsters acquired a skill there would still be little opportunity for them to use it in La Paz, and they too would leave town in order to get ahead. Of this slowly growing minority of upward mobile Spanish couples, Miss Goetz, at the state welfare office, said: "These younger Spanish couples who are now considering adoption are quite sensitive to such things as ethnicity and coloring. Many are in the process of becoming 'Anglicized,' and a child of darker skin than their own is usually not acceptable to them."

Thus La Paz remained in limbo—arrested in social transition. Its gross disparities, existing side by side, were seen to influence the situation of its dependent children. The latter tended to remain in a status which ascribed to them a continuing role as a segmental "we" which the professionals of the health and welfare community continued to care for through such stop-gap measures as long-term foster care.

7. The Legal Systems

The legal gateway to care in Pine and Santa Ana counties involved different codes and interpretations just as it involved different characters in the foster care drama on these two stages. How different or how similar were these legal systems?

LEGAL ROLES IN PINE COUNTY

The Judge

We had chosen to visit Judge Roy Allen in his office in the county building on a morning when he expected to have a clear calendar. Mrs. Spanos, wife of the director of the Child's Care Society, served as a probation officer for the judge, and she had arranged the meeting. Judge Allen joined us in the outer office occupied by Mrs. Spanos and entered into the discussion of children in this community, which he seemed to know so well, with some enthusiasm. A young man in his thirties and a native son, he was new to the juvenile court and freely admitted that, with a newly acquired mandate from the electorate, he was seeking the best advice available in reorganizing the local program and approach to juvenile problems.

"My predecessor," said Judge Allen, "held this judgeship for thirty years. I have only taken over since January of 1957. We have four probation officers now. But we have a long way to go here to overcome the punitive approach to juvenile problems. I guess it's the carry-over from the old Western tradition of hanging the horse thief. There are many archaic statutes on the books in this state."

Our impression had been that Summit was slow to recognize dependency among its families, and we asked the judge about this. "Actually," he replied, "my probation staff does very little work in the dependency field. I would not remove a child from his parents for psychological reasons. It is only cases of physical need that eventuate in removal of the child. Maybe we're not getting enough dependency cases but we are not out looking for them. You see, the public attitude in this state is to let families raise their own children even if they don't use the same methods or have the same standards as their neighbors. And I go along with this."

Still, we had been told that there were frustrations in child care operations in Summit resulting from a reluctance to take action. The judge affirmed that this was true in his experience: "Yes, there are frustrations, all right. I don't want to go into the foster home business myself, but there seems to be a log jam between some of the public health and welfare agencies. We had a case recently on which we had to improvise," he continued. "A sales representative visiting Summit found a foster home on his own for his orphaned brother and sent for him from Kansas City. Now my probation department is supervising the boy in this informal foster home, but we had to define him as a delinquent in order to do this."

Judge Allen was anxious to keep his own staff out of the petition and prosecuting situations. He felt that only in this way could probation workers remain unprejudiced. The Child's Care Society, he said, was the only agency to which he referred a child.

What were the possibilities of permanent termination of parental rights? Did this ever occur? We asked Judge Allen, and he said:

"Permanent termination comes as a formality after a period of time. These are mostly cases of abandonment and desertion and things like that. You see," he continued, "this is an 'easy' divorce state—only six weeks of residence are required. At the time of a divorce the court often makes some disposition of the custody of the child." But would the judge ever terminate parental rights permanently if the parents protested such action? "No," replied Judge Allen, "in no situation that I know of would I terminate parental rights to a child if the parent expressed the desire to keep the child."

In this judicial climate we saw in operation a variation on the parents' rights philosophy. It was more an emphasis that children should not be overly protected, that parents had a right to follow their own child-rearing practices, and that the local situation did not really present flagrant problems calling for drastic answers.

Other Legal Figures

How did children reach Judge Allen's court in Summit? The process might start with someone's concern about a child, perhaps one left alone or poorly treated by adults. Day or night, these cases might come to the attention of the director of the city welfare department, who was on call for emergency financial and medical assistance and also functioned as matron in the police department. The Child's Care Society was the emergency receiving home for dependent children in Summit. The difference in philosophy between that of the police, who wanted children to be taken from an unsuitable home immediately, and that of the Child's Care Society, whose staff wanted to study the situation before taking a child from his home, represented a difficult gap to bridge. The dilemma was acute since the latter agency—in a sense, a quasi-public one, receiving an annual state subsidy unrelated to the number of children in care—might find children brought to its doorstep at any time.

None of the other social agencies took any direct part in the legal process of removing children from their homes. The health department wanted to remain in the position of family friend and consultant rather than be stigmatized as public critic, and did not make reports which might involve it in court hearings. As the public health nurses were quick to point out, "We have access to practically any home in the community. We stay out of court situations because, for one thing, they might undermine the friendly picture people have of us." This was a familiar theme in this community where "respectability" was so important and public antagonisms were avoided.

The county public welfare department, which in some communities offers protective services to children, stayed almost completely out of this field in Summit. The arrangement between state and county offices was such that even if the county office saw a need for court action in behalf of a child, state office approval was needed before such a step could be taken. Furthermore, the belief in the state office was that the parent must ask for service from the agency if it was to be effective service. Charlie Reed, the state director of welfare, said: "We do not believe in putting children on ice. The court," he continued, "wants to refer cases to us and then just have us do the supervision, but this is not acceptable to me or to my department. We decided long ago that we would either do a complete job or do nothing at all. Shelter care is not foster care, and we will only accept cases in which we find the home for the child and then supervise the home ourselves."

The issue here was a technical one; what was more relevant at this point, however, was the upshot of this welfare department stand. It was this recalcitrance which had led Judge Allen's probation staff to define the salesman's brother, mentioned previously, as "delinquent" in order to supervise him in a foster home. But Mr. Reed could foresee a possible change in this situation. He said: "We would be willing to go along with new legislation which would reverse the present situation which tends to reverse the roles of the public and private agencies here. But in any change we would want to have some control over the total situation, including the policies at intake as well as in the follow-up on a case." In its operations the welfare department did occasionally take over planning and financial responsibility for a long-term case, but this was a most infrequent occurrence. And in these cases the legal responsibility was still with the private agency.

We saw in Summit, then, some overlapping between the legal and welfare worlds and some attempt among representatives of the two worlds to understand the other's point of view. But the formal structure, set up by law and emphasized by interpretation, set one part of the welfare world (the public welfare operation) apart from the legal system while it placed the primary responsibilities upon private welfare agency operations. And this format, too, tended to intensify the pressures upon the private agency in this setting in which avoidance of conflict and of action (except in crisis) seemed built into the social system.

LEGAL ROLES IN SANTA ANA COUNTY

The Judge

We met Judge James Corcoran in his private office in the county courthouse in La Paz one afternoon. He talked to us alone, sitting behind a tidy and rather large desk. We seemed relatively shut off, in this quiet office, from the colorful scene afforded by the little shops and cafes of Muleskinner's Lane—the tourist mecca a block away. Judge Corcoran was very cordial. He was somewhat older than Judge Allen in Summit, yet still not past early middle age. We had heard him described as an important lay member of the Episcopal Church congregation. Judge Corcoran, who had held his judgeship for many years, said: "We have a lot of cases in this community where you just have to remove a child from his home. There are many situations involving drunkenness and prostitution. Under the set-up in this state I am both the district judge and the juvenile judge. Neglect cases are filed by statute in the

District Court, not the Juvenile Court. The state is the plaintiff in such cases and brings charges against the parents."

Our impression of La Paz was that agency case loads were extremely heavy, and children seemed suspended in long-term foster care for indefinite periods. We wondered how the court situation was involved in this picture. "When you serve in a full-time capacity as the district judge," commented Judge Corcoran, "and also have the responsibilities of being the juvenile judge, it leaves you with a pretty busy calendar. In this set-up," he continued, "the only time I see or hear of these cases of foster care children is when they come before the bench for custody hearings, or perhaps much later when some change in status is being contemplated for the child by the agency." He elaborated on his impressions of the Spanish families: "I would say that most of the juveniles handled by our department go back to their own families or to relatives away from La Paz. This seems to work out too. The relatives are eager to care for them."

We had noted during our stay in La Paz a certain amount of insulation between the court and the local welfare department. Judge Corcoran was looked upon as a "good man," who followed a strict interpretation of the law, but agency people had few contacts with him. "It seems to me that a lot of neglect cases are not brought to court," said Judge Corcoran on this point. "I read about these cases in the newspaper. Sometimes it appears that the welfare department has simply said to the mother, 'Let us care for your child,' without asking the court anything about it. In custody cases I would rather get the information from the agency than from my own staff; because in custody hearings there must be testimony, and I would prefer that it come from other people rather than from my own staff. My staff," he continued, "have no power or prerogative to return a child to its own home without action by me. I almost always approve their recommendations, but I am the one who must sanction the action. But the welfare department does not notify me before returning a child to its own home, and I feel that it should."

The agency people in La Paz all agreed that Judge Corcoran did not terminate parental rights permanently. When they had children whom they wished to have legally freed for adoption, agency workers often tried to have the hearing in another county, since other judges often interpreted that giving custody to the agency also gave the agency the right to place for adoption without further legal action. Judge Corcoran acceded, in part: "I have never removed a child permanently from his own home. I always tell the parents in court hearings over custody that the children are theirs to claim when they can return to court and show the court that they have straightened themselves out. But," he continued, "I could envision a situation in which I might remove a child permanently if a proper demonstration were made in court. The responsibility for such a showing lies with the welfare department." He went on, in answer to a question: "All adoptions initiate with the welfare department. I assume that where a child is available it is made known. I have great faith in the welfare department's adoption program."

Judge Corcoran thus operated another variation of what we should call a parents' rights program. In La Paz this emphasis seemed to take the form of an affirmation of the traditional blood-tie right of parents to the child. The flaw in the system appeared to lie in the fact that no Spanish parents ever reappeared to lay claim to their children in court, as the judge stated it was their right to do. For Spanish parents were somewhat awed and ill at ease in the contractual relationships that Anglo legal processes involved. Their children thus tended to remain in long-term care.

Other Legal Figures

When we talked to the workers and executives of the health and welfare agencies who might start children on the legal route to placement we found them reluctant to use legal authority to deal with possible neglect. It was difficult to find a definite division between court cases and other cases, and it seemed almost chance that determined which children went to court and which were handled outside the formal legal process. Agencies in La Paz were operated mostly by the Anglo section of the community, and they seemed to be searching for an approach which would bring people of an Old World culture into reasonable conformity with standards of the contemporary world.   This reluctance by agency people in La Paz to use legal authority seemed to have a different basis than the indisposition to action which we saw in Summit.   In La Paz it took the form of a sympathetic toleration of a people whose cultural antecedents were "different" and should be understood rather than condemned by Anglo standards.   At the same time, there was an element of avoidance, too, for the welfare rolls were full in La Paz, the case loads were heavy, and the current possibilities of movement of Spanish children into adoptive homes were discouragingly few.

The health department, in particular, operated on the basis of education, not law enforcement.   Dr. Weston, the district health officer, conscious of the love of children she saw exemplified in her Spanish patients, said: "I don't think you can legislate some things." But her contacts were not like those of the health department representatives in Summit who had access to "every home in the community."   Her department devoted most of its time and ingenuity to meeting the problems of a people who were economically depressed and who had to be convinced of the value of Anglo medicine in the interests of better health.   A primary concern was to adapt Anglo practices to the Spanish culture without upsetting the basic balance of life attitudes and practices which gave the Spanish people their identity.   Still, once in a while there might be cases severe enough to be taken to court.   There was, for instance, the mother with a low I.Q. (on Anglo tests) who might go off and then forget to come back to feed the baby, having little sense of the passage of time; and there was the chronic alcoholic who would promise not to lose control of herself, but then "got upset" and went off on another spree; and there was the tubercular father who came home from the hospital to find his wife gone and the children all locked in the house.   All these situations could still be seen as linked to conflicts that seemed inherent when a people who tended to live for the present moment, and looked to the past, were caught by some of the forces of a culture that was so completely scheduled by the moving hands of a clock geared to the future.   But such severe problems of family breakdown could not avoid the legal involvement for neglect.   And by the time the circumstances became apparent, conditions had become so bad that it was most unlikely that children removed from their parents at that late date would ever again be able to return home.

In considering the welfare of children the welfare department gave much weight to physical neglect. It had more responsibility in the legal system than the health department for protecting the community's children. The first thought of welfare department people was to work with the family, and court action was resorted to only after other avenues seemed to be dead ends. Then too, welfare was not anxious to add to its already overburdened case loads. It seemed to be enmeshed in a long-term care situation and to have little contact with the court over adoptive plans; for this avenue of movement was relatively unfamiliar to staff experiences in planning for children in this community where the "hard to place" were in the majority.

Personal contacts between legal and welfare representatives were quite cordial. Professionally, however, contacts seemed somewhat confused and irregular. The distinctions of state and county welfare responsibility were not clear when they affected legal action, and distinctions between purely legal problems and administrative problems were not always clear to the welfare people. All parties in La Paz, in both the welfare and the legal world, seemed to feel that there was a real need for "a better child relinquishment law," but on neither side was there a clear understanding of what the present statute permitted. In addition, cultural considerations impeded joint welfare and legal efforts regarding adoption, and the lack of shared experiences in planning for children precluded a break-through in the circular process of long-term foster care.

What were the statutory bases for these resolutions of child dependency problems?

THE CODES AND STATUTES

There are differences between the legal codes [1] in Summit and La Paz, especially in the sections which establish procedure, but in

[1] The laws on which legal action relating to placement in these two small urban counties were based are summarized in Appendix D-2.

general there is more similarity than difference.   The laws effective
in Summit went into greater detail in regard to the removal of the
child as a dependent, but a child in any one of these situations in
La Paz could probably be considered dependent or neglected under
one of the less specific provisions of its law.

Summit laws emphasized adoption and permanent removal.
There was provision for relinquishment to an adoption agency, and
removal of a dependent child was considered permanent unless the
court specified that it was temporary.   The law in Summit gave
parents one last chance to reclaim their children before adoption
could be granted under this kind of commitment.   Both sets of
laws permitted adoption without parental consent under roughly
similar circumstances, but La Paz laws provided for a hearing to
determine whether consent would be needed, although there was no
provision for relinquishment to an adoption agency.

It was in the sections regulating placement of children removed
by the court that we saw the greatest differences between the legal
systems in the two communities—and resulting differences in placement pattern.   In Summit the law which authorized placement
with a "benevolent society, individual, or institution" was interpreted by the attorney general and the public welfare department to
exclude public welfare departments, so that the only commitment
made by the court was to a private agency.   In La Paz, the law was
not notably different, but there was no interpretation which restricted the welfare department from involvement.   Consequently,
two entirely different placement patterns developed in these two
communities, one based on a private agency system which traditionally emphasized institutional care and adoption, and the other
based on a public welfare department which was of more recent
origin and emphasized foster family care.   One might expect that
the one local Catholic institution in La Paz, established in 1865,
would still be strong and vigorous in this Catholic community, but
we found that it had dwindled in importance and in the past few
years lacked the support even of its own Church authorities.   Thus,
secular welfare and the Church had joined to emphasize foster family care in the community's welfare programs.   The law gave its
sanctions to this emphasis.

We saw some differences in the way the systems operated in these two communities. Some of these differences can be discussed with the parents' rights and child's rights emphases in mind. We did not see the contrast we saw in Norden and Granger. Both La Paz and Summit had children who reached foster care through the legal system, and both judges might be considered equally concerned with parents' rights. But, as mentioned before, certain qualifications in these parents' rights pictures should be made. For example, in Summit the legal system was in a state of change. Judge Roy Allen had had only a few months to influence, by his authority and philosophy, the children falling in our period of study. When we talked with him he was anxious to alter the direction of the court which had followed a more punitive approach in the past. Judge Allen as the final step in Summit legal channels really represents a direction rather than a well-formulated judicial attitude. Judge Allen seemed to reflect a general feeling of people in Summit that children were not to be too protected, that they would survive even if not treated just as someone else might think they should be, and that parents had a right to different ideas about child-rearing. In the past, children were usually considered to be problems after they had made their mark as delinquents rather than as neglected children. When they *were* seen as problems, a common solution was to place them outside the community. And Judge Allen, too, said: "Summit is a small enough community that rumors and stigmas will build up on a child who is filed on in this community." Thus there was a legal response to Summit's perceived homogeneity which also tried to lessen the visibility of difference of the deviant.

In La Paz, the whole legal system, largely operated by the Anglo community, emphasized the need for tolerance of the different—the Spanish community and its culture which laid great importance on blood ties and care of children by the extended family. Thus, parents' rights would be given consideration as part of a philosophy of family rights. There may have been, too, less need for court authority, since an Anglo government agency such as the welfare department was authority enough in the Spanish culture.

A more visible difference between the two communities was the degree and character of the contact between the legal and welfare worlds. In Summit, the judge, developing a philosophy to guide him in his new responsibility, was listening to welfare people in addition to consulting his legal heritage. His desire to bring a social welfare-oriented program into the court would seem to influence him toward adopting more of a child's rights philosophy himself. In Summit there was more pressure toward change in the legal system, and much of this pressure came from elements in the social work community. Contacts in Summit were more personal and less exclusively professional than one might expect in a community its size. This general character of contacts also applied to the legal-welfare contacts, with representation common to both professions among Summit's probation officers.

In La Paz there was less of a personalized relationship between professional people, representing the court and social work, and one gained the impression that the two worlds, legal and welfare, went their separate ways, personally cordial but with misconceptions of each other's philosophy and problems. Judge James Corcoran was not looking for guidance in formulating a philosophy for himself, but he was seldom asked to make the decisions which welfare workers wished him to make because they avoided bringing issues before him. Consequently, he was not aware of the problems his decisions made for the agencies in their long-term care of children. He, in turn, was not sure what he could expect of the agencies when he wanted their help. There was not the pressure for change, therefore, in La Paz that we saw in Summit.

LEGAL ISSUES AND PLACEMENT PATTERN

What were the comparative facts on aspects of placement which the Summit and La Paz legal systems might affect?

Since both communities have been described as tending to be parents' rights communities, both should, therefore, have relatively low rates of involuntary separation. In fact, however, there were relatively high amounts of involuntary and enforced separation of children from parents both in La Paz and in Summit, and at an equally high level, despite the differences in economic and other conditions in the two communities. The figures showed 34 percent involuntary separations from parents and 8 percent enforced separations in La Paz, compared to 32 percent involuntary and 5 percent enforced separations in Summit.

Parental conditions at time of separation reflected greater differences. Neglect and abandonment were first-ranking causes, involved in 30 percent of cases, in economically less stable La Paz, while they appeared in 23 percent of Summit's cases. Out-of-wedlock birth—a circumstance for voluntary separation—loomed largest in Summit and was involved in 31 percent of cases there, while it appeared in only 17 percent of cases in La Paz. Marital problems and psychological difficulties were more apparent in Summit and were listed as precipitating conditions at parent-child separation in 16 percent of cases there but were noted in only 4 percent of La Paz cases. Physical illness and related parental problems were far more prevalent in La Paz, accounting for 24 percent of cases there and only 11 percent of cases in Summit. Thus, each community with a tendency toward a parents' rights orientation had similar degrees of involuntary separation involving legal action, but the social and economic situations precipitating legal involvement were quite different.

La Paz, in spite of an emphasis on parents' rights for Spanish families, was reaching more of its children for placement at the preschool years. Actually, both of these small urban communities were separating children as preschoolers more frequently than were our two rural communities. The figures on timing of first separation showed 66 percent separated as preschoolers in La Paz, compared to 54 percent in Summit, and 26 percent separated between ages six and ten in La Paz, compared to 32 percent in Summit. Despite the larger proportion of preschoolers separated in La Paz, many, many more of the children in Summit went into adoptive placements—for the most part, children released by a mother at birth.

In spite of our designation of both communities as manifesting the parents' rights emphasis, the La Paz children spent much greater lengths of time in care. The median figures for all care categories were one year in Summit and 2.5 years in La Paz. It seemed that once children were removed from their parents in La Paz there were fewer routes out of foster care for them.   In Summit, children were often returned to parents after a shorter placement when court entanglements, in a divorce proceeding, for example, had been resolved; and there were also more resources for planning toward adoption in Summit.

Summit showed a relatively high proportion of children returning home during the six-month period between January 1 and June 30th, 18 percent of the children under study.   La Paz's 12 percent was closer to the midpoint for our nine communities.   In La Paz, the return home percentage was higher than the adoption rate, as expected by our hypothesis for parents' rights communities.   But Summit did not fit the hypothesized pattern; it coupled a high return home rate with a very high adoption rate.   In Summit, legal deterrents were seldom involved in most adoptions since children went, after voluntary release at the maternity home, through the agency placement process and into available homes.   However, a high return home rate in Summit was consistent with a legal emphasis which tended not to interfere with the right of a parent to raise his child in his own way.

Obviously, many other circumstances, apart from different legal interpretations but somewhat similar legal emphases, contributed to the differences in placement which we observed in these two small urban settings.   Our previous analysis of the two cultures gave us a basis for accounting for greater differences than similarities.   As we turn to interagency patterns in these community configurations our picture of difference is further reinforced.

8. The Agency Networks Serving the Two Communities

How did the services provided for children in need of parents interrelate in Pine and Santa Ana counties?   And how did these networks of services appear to affect the placement of our Pine and

Santa Ana study population of 335 children—about half of whose cases (170) we studied intensively—in the total of five child-placing agencies serving these two small urban counties?

Coldwater Avenue in Summit was the street of oldest and most distinguished residences in the community. Here the lawns were broad, and the houses mostly large, two-story, frame structures, sturdy and unpretentious. Now and then along the tree-lined avenue, side by side with the older dwellings, one noted a newer home that added a bit of color to the view. But the buildings and grounds of the Child's Care Society, occupying a small block fronting on Coldwater Avenue about half way to the city limits west from Capitol Square, were part of the older appearance of the neighborhood. The Children's Home, with its stone facing, looked almost forbidding. But there was an air of movement around the old building. Painters and carpenters and telephone men had been at work, and a small stucco building on the grounds was being converted to accommodate the offices of the director and his casework and clerical staff. It seemed inevitable that in this bustle and "to-do" doors would be opening more frequently at the Home, both for the children who lived there and for people in the community who were interested in these children. Clearly, the greatest amount of activity in the Summit network of services—diagrammed in Figure 3 as it appeared at the time of our study—was going on at the Child's Care Society and its Children's Home.

Pine County's network consisted of three agencies all located within the county boundaries. The one major private agency cared for all but a fifth of our child population; one small sectarian institution cared for the remaining children under study; while the public welfare department, also a child-placement facility, had responsibility for no children (in care for at least a thirty-day period) at the time of our study.

Our analysis of interagency relationships showed that, in effect,

each agency was functioning unto itself with little or no contact
with other child-placing agencies in the community, either about
children or over issues. What happened to children involved in a
noncollaborative network of agency services such as this? We have
suggested that collaboration among agencies leads to the movement
of children, according to their diagnosed needs and the availability
of services, and especially facilitates children's movement out of
foster care into a permanent home. But such movement should
occur also within a multiple-service agency, as, for example, the
Child's Care Society in Summit, which itself offered three kinds of
placement—institutional care, foster family, and adoption. When

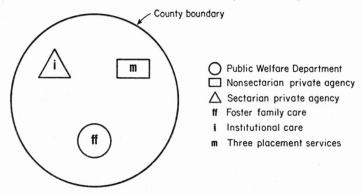

Figure 3. PINE COUNTY AGENCY NETWORK

an agency offers such a variety of services, it would seem not to
need to relate to other agencies in order to complete a plan for a
child, particularly when single-function agencies elsewhere in the
community duplicate the services of the multiple-function agency.
In Chapter 20, the degree to which our data in all of our nine communities supported such thinking is discussed.

Agency noncollaborativeness in Summit had many possible roots.
In Summit emphasis was placed on institutional care. The sectarian agency, the Church Home for Children, offered only institutional care. The nonsectarian Child's Care Society on Coldwater
Avenue offered, during its half-century history, primarily institutional care and some adoptions, with the addition of foster family

care. The communities to which the agencies were responsible were diverse. The two private agencies received children from much larger areas than just Pine County. The nonsectarian agency could receive children from, or place them in, any of the thirty-four counties in the southern half of the state. The sectarian agency received children from an even larger area, covering all the Western states and even reaching into the Midwest. But this sectarian agency had no foster family or adoption program and, therefore, did not place children outside its institution. This agency regarded the "community" which it served as a religious community cutting across political boundaries. It was apparent, then, that the agencies in Summit were not part of a tight network either within the local community or stretching across the state. They were located in a county which acted as a center for services to children, many of whom came from far outside the local community.

Other agencies, not represented in Figure 3 (because they offered no child placement services), must also be considered in the community. In Pine County there was a city welfare department at Summit operated by one staff member who acted both as director and as a worker. She was responsible to the mayor and county commissioners and handled temporary financial aid to families—an expedient which could allow children to remain in their own homes. She was also responsible for the administration of medical care to the indigent. This person had another function which related closely to the care of children—she was the local police matron. She went with the police at all hours of the day or night to pick up children, usually on the complaint of neighbors or interested people in the community. She did not place these children herself but referred them, usually to the Child's Care Society, for further planning.

The Pine County welfare department made available services to children in their own homes also, but only upon direct application by parents themselves. This department would accept complaints from citizens but, as a matter of policy, acted on them only if the complainant was willing to take the matter to court. In each instance, the decision had to be approved by the staff in the state office. As a result, the welfare department had not actually provided such services in the community for several years past.

Pine County also had a private facility for unmarried mothers, a maternity home with a program of prenatal confinement, and postnatal care. If a mother wished to release her child, the caseworker at the maternity home would call in Mr. Spanos at the Child's Care Society. An unmarried mother could receive casework services from the Society, but there was no provision there for her financial help or housing. The State Department of Public Welfare paid for foster care of any kind for the child of an unmarried mother regardless of her residence, whether it was within the state or county or not. This department would provide casework if the mother had her own living quarters; if not, she would be referred to the maternity home, which had its own casework service. At this point the city welfare department entered the picture again because it paid for medical care for residents. Since the Child's Care Society was the major adoption agency within the state—there was one other, much smaller—and this community also had a resource for care of unmarried mothers, one could expect that adoption in the community would be facilitated since services for unmarried mothers and the agency equipped to plan for their children were close together. And we have seen that the number of children placed for adoption by the Child's Care Society represented a high percentage of the children under study.

Agency Antecedents and Present Bases in Summit

History.—As indicated in Table 6, in 1908, long before there was a child welfare program in the public agency and before the Church Home for Children was organized, the Child's Care Society was established by a group of interested citizens headed by the Governor. The original purpose of the Society was to care for orphaned children and to facilitate adoption where this was indicated. In order to help this agency, the legislature agreed to appropriate a fixed amount of money each year for its support, and this subsidy had continued. Originally, the agency offered only institutional care and adoption services, but since 1956, under new leadership, it had embarked on a foster home program.   When the early law dealing with dependent and neglected children was passed this agency was designated as the agency "to whom the probate court might send children," and so it became the primary repository for dependent and neglected children in one half of the state.   The more usual legal pattern, as we have seen in other states, is for such primary

Table 6

CHARACTERISTICS OF AGENCIES IN THE
PINE COUNTY NETWORK

Agency (According to percentage of children under study served)	History	Services	Extent of Professional Education [a] of Staff	Spatial Factors
Child's Care Society (78%)	Organized 1908; auspices private (with public subsidy and responsibility)	Institutional and foster family care, adoption, for children 0–18 years of age	100% of staff (1 member)	Located at Summit; serves 34 counties
Church Home for Children (22%)	Organized 1946; auspices private	Institutional care, for children 2–18 years of age	0% of staff (2 members)	Located at Summit; serves Western and Midwestern states of U.S.A.
Pine County Department of Public Welfare (0%)	Organized 1937; auspices public	Foster family care, for children 0–21 years of age	100% of staff (1 member)	Located at Summit; serves 3 counties

[a] One year or more of graduate study in social work.

responsibility to be lodged with a public agency.   But in 1937, when the present public child welfare program was born in this state, the old law was not changed, and, therefore, the Child's Care Society continued to accept commitments from the court while the county welfare department was not allowed to accept such commitments or to accept releases from parents who wished to have their children placed for adoption.   In the history of placement services, then, we found emphasis on institutional care, given by a so-called "private" but actually quasi-public agency, with the more recently established county welfare department placing only children who needed temporary foster home placement and whose placement was requested by their parents. Each plan had to be approved by the staff in the State Department of Welfare before placement was made. In these circumstances the county department played a very minor role in placement, as seen in the child population which we studied. It had no children in this group.

In 1946 the Christian Church established an institution for the care of dependent children in order, primarily, to give them a Christian education. Pine County was chosen as the site because there seemed to be as little interference there with the establishment of such a facility as could be found anywhere in the area. At the time of our study the Church Home for Children had grown to the point where it was caring for forty-eight children. The Home served a group of children who came to it from a wide area through referrals from congregations of the Christian Church. In effect, the Church Home was considered a mission station by its church.

Thus, in the Summit community, historical development had laid emphasis on institutional care (and sanctioned adoption), while foster family services came late into operation.

Services.—In looking at the services provided by the individual child-placing agencies actually studied in the network we saw little basis for communication and collaboration among them. One private agency served a very specific public—that of its own particular denomination—while the other private agency served the more general, though extended, local public. A staff member at the Church home remarked: "Our institution is affiliated only with the church, and this is on a nation-wide basis. We are not too well acquainted with other people or other church leaders in the community but primarily serve the community of the Christian Church." Similarly, the new director at the Child's Care Society knew very little of the operations at the Church Home, except to recall that there had been a time when the community tried to designate the Home as the community's detention facility for delinquent children. While willing to attempt this responsibility, the Church Home had been unable to cope with the tremendous problems which a receiving home for such children entailed. The public agency, too, had few dealings with the Church Home "except for an occasional conference, together with the Child's Care Society and the court, about a case." These conferences, usually held with the staff in the state department, sometimes included local department staff members. And the public agency, with its apparent reluctance to take on cases of any kind, had few reasons for continuing contacts with the Child's Care Society either. The predominant agency pattern in Summit, then, was generally one of either avoidance of cases or of operation of a relatively self-contained program where cases were acceptable to, or forced by circumstances upon, a more hard-pressed agency. This situation did not smooth the avenues, or enhance the possibilities, of interagency communication.

Extent of professionalization of agency.—Differences in professional education and variations in background and philosophy also seemed to be major deterrents to communication and collaboration in Summit. Until recently, the Child's Care Society was administered by a local woman who had run the institutional and adoption program for many years. But about a year prior to our study an energetic new executive, Chris Spanos, was hired upon the retirement of the previous director, who had prepared the way for a professionally educated successor. Changes in program and outlook of the Child's Care Society were effected. For example, every effort was made to move preschool children from the institution, and adoptive study homes came into use. In short, the new executive put professional standards to work in the agency.

In contrast, the Church Home had no professionally trained staff. It was functioning on a minimal budget, supported entirely by church contributions. Its emphasis was to help children become good Christians and to give them an education based on the Bible. These two agencies neither spoke the same tongue nor served the same children.

The third agency, the county welfare department, with its limited program and "avoidance" policy precluding many contacts with other agencies, similarly shared little common orientation with the other two agencies. But this department did have a trained worker; and some sharing of professional goals, plus a growing appreciation by the new staff at the Child's Care Society of necessary adaptations to the Summit way of life, could provide a basis for collaboration if the local community became the focus of a concern for more services.

Spatial factors.—The factor of physical distance seemed at first glance only a small barrier to communication among the agencies in Summit. All three agencies were located within the local county. Surprisingly, however, the physical location of the Church Home within the community was markedly appropriate to the agency's remoteness from local happenings. The Church Home was "out there" on the fringe of town, where someone's old homestead used to be located, and the staff had few occasions to "go into town" except to attend the Christian Church on Sundays. Also, the great physical distances which were involved both for the Church Home and for the Child's Care Society in serving their extended publics did make their contacts quite diffuse rather than concentrated in a small local area. The foci of their major interest and concern did not direct their attention toward one another in their day-to-day operations.

In summary, we saw in Summit a noncollaborative network of agencies in which each unit endeavored to work out its own problems. The focus or direction of each individual agency program was quite different. A multitude of factors seemed to lead to insularity, lack of communication, and unevenness of service. But the situation also reflected the impact of forces toward change, although problems of innovation and interpretation loomed large in a social system which tended to resist action unless it had been prepared by crisis.

THE NETWORK OF AGENCIES AND CHILD WELFARE SERVICES IN
SANTA ANA COUNTY

The streets of La Paz are narrow, and most of the local inhabitants wish to keep them that way. One does not find here the straight lines of thoroughfares conducive to rapid movement; instead one finds the interruptions of plazas, the encirclements of patios, which lie behind unobtrusive exteriors, and the aimlessness of winding roads that trail off and end quietly against the sunny slopes of the higher ground behind town. It is not easy for the newcomer in La Paz to find the offices of the county welfare department. They are in a newer single-story building, just two blocks from the central plaza on Cortez street—one of those "avenues to nowhere" in La Plaz. There were no signs pointing the way and no external symbols of the department's presence in the building. But within the hall and waiting room and offices occupied by

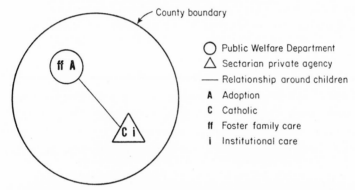

Figure 4. SANTA ANA COUNTY AGENCY NETWORK

welfare were signs of as much efficient and concentrated activity as was to be found anywhere in the community. For welfare was a fair-sized operation in this small urban community, and running a large foster family program called for the employment of a number of persons. The everyday activities of the worker in this agency were the foundation of most services to dependent children in La Paz. Figure 4 pictures this network.

The diagram for Santa Ana County suggests some of the same elements which appeared in Pine County: one large agency cared for almost all our children, and one small sectarian institution cared for the others. The relationship between these two agencies was a tenuous one, based on the few shared cases. Both agencies were located within the county, but the private agency served the whole state, while the public agency served only Santa Ana County. Other characteristics are seen in Table 7.

If we had diagrammed agency relations as they stood at the end of our follow-up period (six months after April 1), there would be no line relating the Department of Public Welfare to the small Catholic institution, St. Mary's Children's Home. At the time of our study there were five children at St. Mary's who were being supported and given casework service by the public agency. But by October 1, these children had been removed, and the public agency

Table 7

CHARACTERISTICS OF AGENCIES IN THE
SANTA ANA COUNTY NETWORK

Agency (According to percentage of children under study served)	History	Services	Extent of Professional Education [a] of Staff	Spatial Factors
Santa Ana County Department of Public Welfare (88%)	Organized 1919 (reorganized 1937); auspices public	Foster family care and adoption, for children 0–21 years of age	75% of staff (4 members)	Located at La Paz; serves the county
St. Mary's Children's Home (12%)	Organized 1865; auspices private	Institutional care, for children 3 years of age through 8th grade	0% of staff (4 members)	Located at La Paz; serves the state

[a] One year or more of graduate study in social work.

no longer had any direct connection with this institution. However, it was still a resource for local children, and referral back and forth with the welfare department was not formally precluded.

How had this pattern affected what happened to children? The large public agency offered foster family and adoption services in the local community, while the private sectarian agency offered institutional care for girls only. The Department of Public Welfare was responsible for service to all children within the county who were in need of placement, while St. Mary's, its program shrinking rapidly in recent years, served only a small number of children who came to it from all over the state. If availability of services were the only determinant of the disposition of children in care, we should expect the small institutional population and the large foster family placement pattern which we found, in fact, in La Paz.

Other services affected placement in La Paz. The county welfare department could be said to offer services to children in their own homes, but this was on a limited basis only and usually occurred as a prelude to placement. The county department investigated situations and made recommendations to the court prior to court action but did not offer a service which could actually be called "service to children in their own homes." There were no psychiatric or treatment services available in La Paz or in Santa Ana County except through one small commercial institution located on a small ranch near town. Nor were there specific services for unmarried mothers within the county. The only maternity homes available to the community were either 350 or 400 miles away, in other states. The public agency was authorized to pay for a woman's care if she were a resident of the state even though the care had to be secured outside the state. It could help her plan for herself and her child and could give her financial aid if she had her own housing. However, even though adoption services were available within Santa Ana County it appeared that few children from these remote maternity homes filtered back to the county for adoptive placement. Thus adoption was a minor part of the La Paz picture.

Agency Antecedents and Present Bases in La Paz

History.—At first glance, the history of services in Pine and Santa Ana counties appeared to be similar, since the earliest service offered in both instances was institutional care. However, the types of placement most used were quite different in the two communities. In view of the fact that foster family care was predominant in La Paz it may seem surprising that the St. Mary's Children's Home was organized as early as 1865. For many years St. Mary's gave practically the only foster care available in the state, and in the recent past the institution housed as many as 125 children simultaneously. Public child welfare services were first organized in La

Paz in 1919 but took on their present form in 1937 with the passage of the Social Security Act. The present emphasis on foster family care reflected the fact that, as we saw in Granger also, this form of care was thought to be much better for children than institutionalization at the time that the public programs of the 1930s were organized. With the advent of the county department, the need for St. Mary's Home gradually decreased. In 1955 the old building was condemned, and the Sisters of the Order were compelled to move to their present, and much smaller, quarters. At the time of our study the capacity of St. Mary's was sixteen children. Thus we found in La Paz a very small institutional population of children even though the local institution was of long standing historically. Almost all the dependent children in our population were in foster family care and under the supervision of the public welfare department in this community where sacred values still had such an important place.

Services.—The broad, general services provided by the county welfare department, with its accessibility to state-wide resources in planning for children, gave this department a measure of autonomy which lessened contacts outside the public welfare family. Until recently, however, the local department in La Paz did attempt to use St. Mary's Home as a resource for institutional placement; group care facilities for school-aged children were the greatest perceived lack in local welfare. But contacts with St. Mary's over services had practically ceased, and the institution continued to operate its shrinking single-service program essentially cut off from other formal welfare agencies. On the other hand, communication among all public agencies dealing with children in Santa Ana County tended to be growing. The health and education agencies were not, of course, a part of the child placement picture, but when the state director of child welfare was asked with whom she worked, she immediately mentioned the health and education departments. And the county director of child welfare services said, "We work well with the Probation Department in this county and confer a good deal over cases with other agencies such as schools, health agencies, and the court." In a sense, the multiple foci of Anglo public welfare services had many points of contact, but contact with private agencies, historically Catholic in this state, seemed to be diminishing as the services of at least one private agency declined.

Extent of professionalization of agency.—The values of professional education pervaded public welfare in La Paz and also facilitated communication between the offices of what we have termed the public health, education, and welfare family. Language difference was no barrier to communication among the professional workers who carried on the public programs. Thus even with the great concern that most professionals in La Paz expressed for understanding the Spanish culture, they often seemed to be talking only to themselves, much as the agency network failed to communicate with its general public. Seen in child welfare terms, the state-administered public program emphasized professional education and uniform standards throughout the state. With financing coming from state and Federal but not from county funds, the tie of the county department to the state office (which was located in La Paz) was very strong. Of four child welfare workers on the staff at the Santa Ana County welfare office, three had completed some or all of their professional schooling. In contrast, St. Mary's had no trained staff. The Sisters concentrated on serving girls from the age of three years until they entered the eighth grade. The focus at St. Mary's was on religious education. And it seemed obvious that the gulf between the public and private agencies in the outlook and emphasis of their staffs was becoming even wider.

Spatial factors.—Geography had little direct bearing on problems of interagency communication in La Paz except to extend the boundaries within which the state-wide public agency units shared their professional values.

The interagency problem in La Paz, as we have presented it thus far, was clearly perceived by the child welfare workers involved. The staff of the public welfare system, both on the county and on the state level, expressed dissatisfaction that their organization offered essentially the only child welfare services in the community. If pressure for change was inaugurated by them it tended to be interpreted as a desire by "the Department" to perpetuate or aggrandize its own position. The paucity of private child-placing services tended to isolate "the Department" in this community where public controversy and partisanship in politics were expected. So, at this time, the administrators in the little offices on Cortez Street, and their superiors in the state building, found themselves in the position of trying, in effect, to create their own opposition at the grass roots in order to legitimize their programs and get backing for their reforms in La Paz and throughout the state.

NETWORK COMPARISONS AND THE FACTS OF PLACEMENT

Earlier in our discussion of interagency patterns we qualified the statement that "noncollaboration implies long-term care" by pointing out that children might move when in the care of isolated agencies if such agencies had within their own programs a variety of services designed to meet a variety of needs. Apparently, collaboration among child-placing agencies was of tertiary importance in both Summit and La Paz in determining movement of children out of care. We would expect that as the number of agency units in a given network is reduced and the importance of a particular agency unit is increased, the importance of relationships between units in the network would decrease. But let us look at some differences in placement pattern between Summit and La Paz to see what network variations may reflect.

The hypothesis that collaboration eventuates in more adoption and a lower return home rate was given no support by the Summit-La Paz comparison which we have typified as relatively a noncollaboration-collaboration comparison. Combined with the adoption and return home rates presented previously, we also saw that of all those leaving care in the six-month period from January 1 to June 30, 64 percent returned home in Summit and 70 percent returned home in La Paz, while 36 percent went into adoption in Summit and 15 percent went into adoption in La Paz. We have suggested that the influence of collaboration on placement pattern diminishes as a single agency gains preeminence in a network so that its program and philosophy, and the resources available to its workers, dominate the total picture. The Summit placement pattern tended to represent the program of one, relatively self-contained, multiple-service agency. In La Paz, cultural factors more than the nature of the agency network seemed key determinants of movement out of care situations.

La Paz had children in care over twice as long, on the average, as Summit. Thus, again, it was the programs offered by particular agencies and the cultures in which they operated that seemed paramount in the one-year median time in care in Summit, compared to the two-and-a-half-year median in La Paz. However, mid-length placements as opposed to disproportions of short or long-term placements did appear as a consistent concomitant of collaboration, compared to noncollaboration, in La Paz and Summit. Summit had 79 percent of its cases in care less than two years, compared to 34 percent of La Paz cases. La Paz had 39 percent in care for the mid-length interval (two to five and a half years), compared to 16 percent in Summit, but had 27 percent in care six years or more, compared to a mere 5 percent in Summit. Adoption played a much greater part in Summit. The program emphasis in La Paz was on foster family care, and permanent planning was frustrated by cultural and economic forces. Our data pointed up the fact that the longer a child stays in care, the fewer are his chances—given any network tendency—for moving out.

Ostensibly, as children's needs change, the type of placement they can most profitably use also changes. In Summit, the single-type care—institution care—was the predominant mode. Thus, 74 percent of the children had had only one placement and only 17 percent had had more than one type of placement. However, a community-wide pattern was beginning there which would tend to differentiate placements more on professional perceptions of a child's special needs. In La Paz, with foster family service the major service by far and with adoption a "difficult problem," even the intraprofessional collaboration which attempted to differentiate placements somewhat on a diagnostic basis was still, given a lack of different facilities, assigning dependent children to a relatively long-term care status. Fifty percent of La Paz cases had had one placement only, and 36 percent had had two to three placements. Thirty-one percent had had more than one type of placement.

Some consistency was found, in the Summit-La Paz comparison, with the hypothesis that noncollaboration goes with extremes of little or much movement between types of care facilities while collaboration goes with moderate movement. In Summit only 7 percent of cases had ever moved out of a foster family to any different type of placement, compared to 22 percent in La Paz. Only fifteen percent in Summit had ever moved out of an institution into any different type of placement, compared to 25 percent in La Paz.

Actually, the over-all sequence of placements in the two communities was very different, children starting in institutional placements in Summit and in foster families in La Paz. In both communities children seemed more likely to return home from an institution than from foster families, and, in any event, they seemed more likely to leave care from an institution than from a foster family. In both Summit and La Paz some children in institutions had been placed by their parents, and when the parents wished to take them back they could do so with little trouble. But multiple-type placement experiences in care were, generally, more typical of the La Paz network than of the separated units of the Summit network.

Our discussion of these two interagency networks has demonstrated major differences in the conditions for operating welfare programs in the two communities. In Summit we saw a noncollaborative system of relatively insulated units with one dominant agency offering multiple services. Insularity was fostered, not by physical distance, but by the social distance between the two private agencies and by differences in social work philosophies among the one public and two private agencies. And compounding the whole problem was the Summit reluctance to take public action and its abhorrence of public conflict. In La Paz, the network was more collaborative by reason of the centralization of its organization and by the blotting out of private programs by the combined forces of secular Anglo welfare. The agents of the Anglo programs now found themselves faced with a situation much akin to "talking to themselves." Not only could this ultimately tend to isolate a professional elite from the grass roots, but it could accentuate problems of bringing pressure to bear for action in a public arena where controversy was an expected part of modes of operation. Professionals in La Paz were attempting to meet this challenging problem.

9. The Children and Their Parents

As agency networks, legal systems, and total ways of life differed in Pine and Santa Ana counties, so did the placement experiences of the children we studied there. If we had hoped that with equally high frequency the children in both of these small urban counties could return to their own families—the parents cured of the ills which had propelled their children into foster care, or the family situations otherwise modified to make a child's return home possible—we soon saw that conditions in the families in these two communities were of a quite different nature. And finally, when we looked at the children themselves, wondering whether adoptive homes could be found for many of them, we got composite portraits of children in foster care which begged questions of the social systems we have described in Summit and La Paz—but did not always answer them. Consolation lay primarily in the cases of at least some children with problems who found their way into adoptive homes in both areas. Our stories of a few of these children and their new parents end this chapter.

PLACEMENT HISTORIES OF THE CHILDREN IN FOSTER CARE [1]

What precipitated the initial placement of the Summit children in foster care? Most of their parents were separated from one another or divorced, and some of the children were removed by court order, not so often as in La Paz because of parental neglect,

[1] See footnote 1, Chapter 5, regarding the base for percentages in this chapter.

but rather sometimes in connection with divorce proceedings until the judge could decide who the better parent for the child might be. In addition, marital conflict and the psychological problems of parents were recognized relatively frequently as precipitators of the Summit children's separation from their own homes.

Once in care, all but a few of the Summit children were put immediately into an institution. This procedure included most of the children placed in foster care before they were five years old, too—and almost a third of the children in foster care were separated from home as preschoolers. No matter who the child, Summit made minimum use of foster families—only 6 percent of the placements on April 1. Once in care, moreover, the Summit children stayed where they were first placed. At the time of our study 77 percent of the children had had no move beyond their first placement. And if, in this respect too, Summit was unique—showing the least movement of children in placement—its children also stayed in care for the shortest time, a little over a year on the average. For more often than in any other community the Summit children moved back to their relatives or into adoption. Of those in care on April 1, about half left care during the following six months; most of them returned to their own families, though some of them moved into adoptive homes. In brief, the Summit placement pattern was one of short-term institutionalization for the children of maritally incompatible, but often remarrying, parents.

In La Paz, by comparison, parents of half the children in foster care had never married, though out-of-wedlock birth itself rarely seemed the major reason for child placement. In only one out of every ten cases of the children in foster care was this a prime cause. Rather, child neglect and such hard realities as parental death, illness, and economic hardship explained why the majority of the La Paz children in foster care had left their own homes. Thus, the children in Summit and in La Paz were ushered into the agency foster care programs under somewhat different conditions.

The situation regarding children's leaving care was different too. In La Paz only a few children left care during our follow-up period —a total of 17 percent of those in foster care on April 1. Only one moved into adoption. And while slightly more than half of the La Paz children stayed on in foster care in the same families with which they had first come to live, about a third of the children had two or three placements by the time of our study, and another 14 percent had four or more placements.

The children's placement histories in La Paz and Summit differed also in the length of time children stayed on in care—an average of three years in La Paz compared to a little over one year in Summit, at the time we visited. And a third of the La Paz children were in care for more than five and one half years, almost two thirds of these children having entered care as preschoolers. In this world of Spanish background the children had little opportunity either to return to their own disorganized families or to move on into adoptive homes, so long-term stay in a single foster family became the major pattern of care in La Paz.

THE CHILDREN'S OWN FAMILIES

Under what conditions did the Summit children return to their own families? What were the families like?

Much more often than for the children who stayed in foster care, the Summit children who returned home had been precipitated into care by marital conflict, but they were in care for merely a fraction of a year when the troublesome situation at home cleared up and return home became possible. In short, those who went home tended to do so quickly. (A typical case would involve a young school-aged child with three or more brothers or sisters in foster care too.) The mothers were housewives. They had had at least some high school education. Economically, they were much better off than their few counterparts in La Paz.

For the Summit children who stayed in foster care, half the parents either had no plans for their children other than long-term care, or had conflicting plans, the resolution of which seemed to us to be most unlikely. More than half of the mothers and about two thirds of the fathers of the Summit children never, or very infrequently, visited their children, and in about a third of the cases, neither of the parents ever visited or had more than a superficial contact with the child. It is true, however, that in Summit—about a third of the cases—more than in the other communities, the fathers or the mothers had at least an adequate relationship with a child welfare agency, a link suggesting some strength in, or concern about, the parent-child relationship. There was also some payment for the children's care in about a third of the Summit cases.

The parents of the Summit children in foster care were also of a somewhat different social group from those in La Paz. About 90 percent of the fathers and mothers were Protestant and Anglo; a very few were of American Indian or of mixed racial stock. Considering the alleged equal proportions of Catholics and Mormons in the Summit population at large, their relative absence from the parent group in our population was of interest. Perhaps, this was because, unlike the situation in La Paz, there were more newcomers to the community among Summit parents, and they failed to reflect the larger population in Summit. A more likely explanation is that the Catholic and Mormon children were afforded help through channels not included in the network of welfare services we studied. Summit's parents who did use the child welfare agencies were relatively young and fairly well-educated. More than half the mothers were high school graduates. At the time of our study they were women averaging about thirty years of age, and the fathers were about thirty-seven years old. In a majority of the cases they were known to be in good physical health. In 14 percent of the foster care cases one parent was dead, but in no case were both parents dead. And if more than half of the parents were divorced or separated from one another, more than a fourth of them were still married to each other, and about another fourth of the mothers were remarried. Economically, they tended to be in adequate circumstances, better off by far than the parents in La Paz. These were some of the conditions which the Summit agencies had to consider in planning for Summit's dependent children.

In La Paz, the very few children who returned home had been catapulted into foster care not by marital conflict, as in Summit, or by parental neglect, as in the cases of most of the La Paz children staying in foster care, but rather by parental illness or death or economic hardship. And as in Summit, the few La Paz children who returned home did so before the end of their first year in care. The family situations were seen to change for the better promptly, or not at all. But in these instances the family situations were far more reparable than in the cases of those children who remained in foster care. For example, the parents of half of the fourteen La Paz children who returned to their own families were married to each other at the time of our study, while only 10 percent of the parents of the La Paz children remaining in foster care were. And intactness or other resources of the families of these children were further evidenced by the fact that only in one case of the returned home children, where there were brothers or sisters, had all the brothers and sisters been placed in foster care; instead, one or more of them had gone on living with some member of the child's family. There was no such evidence of family potential for caring for siblings in four out of ten of the cases of children staying in foster care.

What other reasons prevented more of the La Paz children from returning to their own families? The parents of almost half the children in foster care were clear in their plans: they were ready to relinquish the children for adoption. And for another half of the parents, their desires for long-term care or their lack of a plan or their conflicting plans promised to keep a sizable number of these children in foster care. In almost two thirds of the foster care cases, neither mother nor father visited the children more than very infrequently. And adequate relationships with a child welfare agency were maintained by fewer than 10 percent of the fathers and by 15 percent of the mothers of the La Paz children—about the lowest rates of parent-agency relationships in any community in our study. Ninety percent contributed nothing toward the child's support. This picture of the parents of the La Paz children in foster care fitted together with the other things we learned about them.

If La Paz seemed to have more than its share of parents whose relationships with agencies and Anglo norms presented problems, it was an understandable situation. These parents were a much less well-educated, superficially less intelligent, older, less healthy, and economically less adequate group of people than the Summit parents. About a third of the La Paz mothers had not gone beyond the third grade. About a third of the fathers and more than half of the mothers were estimated, perhaps often because of language barriers, to be of below average intelligence. Mothers averaged about thirty-nine years of age, fathers about forty, by comparison with the mothers of thirty and fathers of thirty-seven in Summit. And if at least 60 percent of parents were known to be in good physical health in our Summit cases, in only 43 percent was this clearly a fact in La Paz. Where genetic disease or defect appeared in 18 percent of the foster care cases in Summit, comparable problems existed in 31 percent of the cases in La Paz. The fact that about half of the fathers of the Summit children in foster care were semiskilled or above in their occupational status, while 70 percent of those in La Paz were semiskilled or below, reflected on our judgment that more than half the families of all the Summit children under study were in economically adequate circumstances but at best only about a third of the La Paz families were this well off. Finally, the ethnic differences in the larger populations of Summit and La Paz were magnified among the parents of the children in foster care. More than 90 percent of the parents of Summit children in foster care were Anglo; in La Paz, only 14 percent of the fathers and 8 percent of the mothers were Anglo, another 7 or 8 percent were Indian, and 78 and 85 percent of the fathers and mothers respectively were Spanish-American—all of these and still others designated as Catholic. These were the parents, about half of whom were not married to each other at the birth of the child in foster care and only 10 percent of whom were married to each other at the time of our study. Another half of these mothers were, at the time of our study, living alone or in an institution. In La Paz the proportion of parents planning on the return home of their child in foster care was by far the lowest in any community we studied—a total of only 2 percent. That only a small proportion of children returned home makes sense.

THE CHILDREN AND ADOPTION

Where return home is not possible, adoption provides another way out of foster care. But for adoption to occur, not only must there be children available; those available must resemble the image that adoptive parent applicants maintain on at least the outer boundaries of their own tolerances for a child they would make their own. What did the child whom the Summit agencies placed in adoption look like?

Boys and girls were placed with equal frequency in Summit, as essentially, elsewhere, and most of the adoptive children, as elsewhere, were under two years of age. However, by comparison with La Paz, Summit placed in adoption many older children, about 40 percent being aged two and over. Of all our nine communities, Summit was the only one to place so many children who were aged ten or over in adoptive homes—17 percent of Summit's sizable number of adoptive placements.

Ethnicity presented no problem in Summit. About 90 percent of its children in care were Protestant and of Northern European origins. In addition, Summit placed a few Indian children or children of mixed Indian background with Mormon parents, a placement that is not unusual in view of Mormon beliefs about American Indians. In all cases of adoptive placements in Summit the children were estimated to have at least average intelligence. In 15 percent of the cases the children showed some physical disability. Almost all of these were of a minor and self-correcting nature; where they were irremediable, the anomaly was one which affected only the child's appearance and not his functioning. Finally, on the whole, the Summit children placed in adoption were psychologically a healthy group of youngsters, although in one out of every six Summit adoptive placements—and here we are involved with proportionately more cases than in any other community—there was some evidence of psychological disturbance. All of these children, it should be noted, were five years of age or older, and their symptoms involved aggression or other behavioral deviations. This is not to deny that for 80 to 90 percent of Summit children placed in adoption, there was absolutely no evidence of any kind of psychosocial problem. In terms of averages, the adopted Summit children tended to be about a year and a half in age, Caucasian and Protestant, of average or above intelligence, physically healthy, and psychologically well adjusted.

The profile of the ten La Paz children placed in adoption was essentially identical with that of the eighty-nine Summit children, except for the children's ethnicity. Four of the La Paz children were of Spanish background, three were of mixed ethnic origins, and the remaining three were Anglo—one Protestant, one Lutheran, and one allegedly of no religious faith. In somewhat more detail, the adoptive situation in La Paz again indicated that sex of the child was not a factor in adoptive placements, but much more in La Paz than in Summit the child's age was a factor, for six of the ten children were under the age of one year, another two had not yet reached their second birthday, and the remaining two children were well under five years of age at the time of their adoptive placement. Thus, in La Paz, no child who had reached his fifth birthday was given an adoptive placement. Every one of the ten children placed in adoptive homes in La Paz had average or above intelligence; in only one case was there any physical disability, and this was minor and self-correcting. Moreover, in no case of an adoptive placement in La Paz was there any evidence of psychological symptoms. If La Paz did succeed in placing, among its small number of adoptive placements, a goodly proportion of children whose ethnicity might elsewhere in the U. S. A. have seemed a barrier to such placement, the other characteristics of the La Paz children in adoptive placements suggested that they fitted a rather narrow definition of the adoptable child—very young, physically healthy, and in almost every way "normal."

With these images of the adoptive children in Summit and La Paz, what now might be said of the children who stayed on in foster care?

In Summit, the children were as likely to be boys as girls. But clearly, these were older children than those in adoption, for they averaged more than seven years of age. In almost equal thirds, the

Summit children in foster care were preschoolers, school-aged children (up to ten years of age), and aged ten and older. Since only 12 percent of the Summit children placed in adoption were in the school-aged group (from age five up to age ten) and another 17 percent were in the age group from ten years on, it is apparent that the age factor alone, even in Summit, was a deterrent to the placement of many children remaining in foster care—at least in the kinds of adoptive homes Summit was using at the time of our study. Clearly, in Summit the ethnic factor was not an issue; the 5 percent of children with non-Caucasian background in the foster care group was paralleled by the 8 percent of Summit children in adoptive placements who were also of American Indian or mixed racial background. The intellectual factor did, however, seem to be a significant one, for a quarter of the children in foster care in Summit were estimated to be of below average intelligence, and it should be remembered that none of the Summit children placed in adoptive homes was judged to have less than average intelligence. Nor was the children's physical health, in any sense, an issue since the great majority of the children in foster care were free of physical disability and were clearly in average or better health.

In addition to the Summit children's age, and the level of their intelligence, the other major deterrent to adoption was psychological problems. More than half the children in foster care in Summit were judged to be psychologically handicapped—55 percent with some symptoms of disturbance with which, it should be noted, they had entered foster care. In about half the cases the children seemed somewhat confused about who they were. In only about half the cases did the children maintain loving relations with their own parents. In 80 or 90 percent of the cases where there were siblings (in only 5 percent of the cases were there no siblings), the ties of the children in foster care to them seemed to be quite affectionate, but in only half the cases where there were siblings were they all also living in foster care—some brothers and sisters lived either with relatives or elsewhere out of foster family or institutional supervision.

Finally, the legal status of the children in foster care is germane:

a fifth of the Summit children in foster care were fully free for adoptive placements; in another half of the cases, parental rights had been modified but, on the other hand, the children's new guardians were not free to relinquish the children for adoption; in the remaining cases parents maintained full parental control. In brief, the Summit child in foster care was a white, Protestant, seven-year-old, of average intelligence and physically healthy, but as likely as not to show some psychological disturbance, to be affectionately tied to his parents, and to be living in a limbo of legal status in which his relationships to his own parents were somewhat curtailed.

And what of the child in foster care in La Paz? Here more than in any other community, the child was likely to be a girl. Was this a reflection of ethnic preferences or disfavor? Moreover, La Paz had somewhat fewer preschool children in care than did Summit— for a fifth of the La Paz children were under five, by comparison with a third of Summit's—and the average age of the La Paz children in foster care was eight and one half years. Thus, the gap in age between the La Paz children in foster care and in adoptive placement was even greater than that found in Summit. The salient factor in La Paz, however, was the children's ethnic composition: over 80 percent of the children in foster care were of Spanish backgrounds, another 10 percent were full or part Indian, and fewer than 10 percent were Anglo. Our estimate was that of all the children in the larger population in La Paz under the age of nineteen, 68 percent (according to the 1950 U.S. Census) were of Spanish origins. Of all the children in La Paz foster families, 86 percent were of Spanish origins, while of the ten children in adoptive homes, only 4. or 40 percent were Spanish. The warping influence of ethnicity in the placement picture in La Paz is thus most clearly presented. Undoubtedly related to the ethnic pattern is the fact that about a third of the La Paz children in foster care were estimated to have below average intelligence. This fact must be noted against the prior observation that none of the children placed in an adoptive home in La Paz had below average intelligence. Also tied into the ethnic pattern is the fact that 90 percent of the children in foster care were Catholic, while seven out of the ten adoptive placements were Catholic.

And if physical health seemed to be no more a problem in La Paz than in Summit, at least 40 percent of the children in foster care, both at intake and at the time of our study, showed symptoms of psychological disturbance, while none of the children placed in adoptive homes were so diagnosed. The issue of personal identity remained a dominant question; for these were children who, in most cases, had no enduring relationship with their own parents or else manifested a marked ambivalence toward them.

Again, as in Summit, relationships with siblings seemed to be a major source of support in about 70 percent of the cases of the children in foster care, and notably these children also showed affectionate relationships with other children. But siblings were a barrier to adoptive placement. Between 80 and 90 percent of the children in foster care had one or more siblings; eight of the few La Paz children placed in adoptive homes had no siblings.

A final barrier to adoptive placement seemed to be the legal system. The severance of familial ties with the child chosen to stay in foster care was made more apparent by the fact that full parental rights were maintained with only 15 percent of the La Paz children in foster care—about half of them living with parental rights somewhat modified and 16 percent relinquished for adoptive placement. But about a fifth of the children were caught in the ambiguities of a legal system which seemed to need clarification. Thus, in brief, the La Paz child in foster care could be profiled as eight and one half years old, of Spanish-Catholic background, physically healthy, but showing evidence from the time he entered foster care of the psychologically disabling experiences he had had prior to placement, maintaining while in care evidence of his psychological disturbance, often attached to siblings who were not living in foster care, and in most cases separated from his own parents by legal as well as psychological barriers. To this extent the children in foster care in both La Paz and Summit looked quite different from the young, healthy, legally free children who received adoptive placements in these two communities.

Not all the children so placed, however, fitted this mold. These were children whose minority ethnicity, physical handicaps, limited intellectual capacity, or psychological ill health made them somewhat different from the majority of children anywhere in America today. In Summit roughly one third of the children placed in adoptive homes were ethnically, somatically, or psychologically different from most children. Note that at least half of the children who were different in the Summit adoptive group were also aged five years or older, as though adoption had been delayed for them. Disguised presentation of a few of these cases illustrates the special conditions under which children whose chances for adoption seemed fewer than those of the physically and psychologically normal Caucasian infant were nevertheless, in the communities we studied and at the time of our study, placed in adoptive homes.

Nellie Clayton, a full-blooded American Indian girl, going on six years of age, was involuntarily separated from her widowed mother a year previous to her adoptive placement with the Clarks. Since her husband's accidental death, Nellie's mother had become increasingly unable to take care of the children, and her history of arrests had increased. Nor was Nellie placed alone; her two older brothers accompanied her to the Clarks.

What combination of forces made such an adoptive placement possible? There were, as we know, a community milieu and an interagency network which were not obstructive to a board's appointment of a new director at the Child's Care Society—one who had redoubled the agency's efforts, especially in rural reaches of the state, to make such adoptive placements. There was a legal system which sanctioned the removal of the Clayton children from their alcoholic mother. And there were the Clarks and their convictions—as well as their big, comfortable farmhouse where three previously adopted school-aged children were already living.

Mr. and Mrs. Clark were strict Mormons. The theological teachings of the Mormons propose a kinship between American Indians and Mormons which made Nellie and her brothers, in the Clarks' eyes, most readily a part of their family. In addition, the Clarks had a feeling of mission in providing a new life for children in need of a home. Mr. Clark, now forty-three, with a bachelor's degree in agriculture, had been born and raised on the large family farm he now owned and managed. Mrs. Clark, ten years his junior, had worked as a church librarian before their marriage. The Clarks had known about the Child's Care Society long before its present executive arrived, but his dedicated activities combined with their moral convictions and religious faith to make possible, in this rural area, the adoptive placement of Nellie Clayton and her two Indian brothers.

Ethnic difference (barring the Negroid) seemed less an adoptive problem in Summit than physical disability. Still another couple —the father, a skilled mechanic, was reared a Mormon—who adopted a second half-Oriental child left town shortly thereafter for a metropolis on the West Coast where Orientals were a much, much larger segment of the public than they were in isolated Summit. The few cases of physical disability were essentially minor problems: a case of anemia in a seven-month-old girl, correctable through diet; a newborn boy with a birthmark on his face; another infant with a slightly turned foot, placed with a couple in their early thirties whose initial expectations for an adoptive child called quite specifically for only a physically and emotionally healthy infant of unquestionable genetic background who was, like themselves, blond. But the child with psychological problems in Summit tended, as elsewhere, to be an older child and to call for just the "right" combination of circumstances in an adoptive placement.

The Tim Johnstons, Steve's adoptive parents, were married over twenty years and were both over fifty years of age, he in his late fifties. They had two previously adopted children, ages twenty-two and fifteen. Mr. Johnston, a college graduate, had an annual income of about $9,000 from his small business, in which his wife worked as secretary. The family lived in a small suburban home.

Since his relinquishment for adoption three years earlier, Steve, aged thirteen years, had experienced five short-term placements—two in institutions and three with families where the agency hoped he might find a permanent home. The Johnstons were the fourth family, and here, at last, things seemed to be working out well and all involved were clear that this was truly an adoptive placement.

Steve's earlier experiences had varied. For years he had been shunted back and forth between divorced and remarried parents, until his father had finally decided to release the boy for adoption. At the institution

Steve had seemed sullen and withdrawn. The first couple with whom he was placed wished to make the boy a permanent member of their family, but Steve resisted such action by running away. He was then ten.

In Steve's second family placement, he began doing well at school but also got involved repeatedly in aggressive skirmishes with age-mates, exceeding the tolerances of his new temporary parents. Illness unexpectedly hit the parents in his third and shortest placement.

At the Johnstons', Steve shared a room with an adopted son, just two years his senior. And during holidays the Johnston's oldest adopted child came down from college. For the first time in years Steve was beginning to hold his head up and to look into the future.

In another Summit case of an emotionally troubled child, somewhat younger than Steve, placement was made in a family quite similar to the Johnstons' where an older adopted child was already in the home. One wonders just what kind of child were these older ones, who could welcome and not be threatened by a newcomer? Systematic psychosocial study of such total family situations might have determined the circumstances under which these psychologically upset children were able to form trusting relationships in a new home. But we had to move on to our next community— and left this problem for others to study.

In La Paz, the child who would elsewhere in the U.S.A. be considered a "different" child was almost the only child available for adoptive placement. Seven out of the ten adoptive placements involved infants of minority ethnicity. Two additional children out of the ten, also in their preschool years, had emerged with psychological damage from experiences with deserting or alcoholic parents. The special conditions for the adoptive placement of such children in La Paz, where the exceptional child was the norm, were apparently not to be found often within the city's limits. Instead, the agency reached out in two directions. It looked to the professional, technical, and other interested couples in the near-by community of Sandy Valley which was fabricated for a special government project, to people who were mostly strangers to the area and quite remote from the center of life in La Paz. In addition, the agency dealt with the more upward mobile, Spanish, lower middle-class, white-collar or skilled worker's families who had moved to the state's biggest and fastest growing city of Eldorado. For such an adoptive case, the reader might turn back to the early part of Chapter 6, where the story of Tita and the Castillos who came to La Paz to fetch her tells as much as we know now about conditions surrounding unusual adoptions in this small urban county where much that elsewhere was unusual seemed typical.

IV. TWO METROPOLITAN AREAS: JAMESTOWN AND CENTRALIA

10. Child Placement and Other Social Processes

Along the Southeastern coast of the United States there are numerous inlets and harbors behind sandy islands that offer protection from the stormy Atlantic. Here some of the earliest colonists in the New World established settlements on land which an English king saw fit to grant in title to a few lord proprietors. Our visit in 1957 to Jamestown—or, more exactly, to James County—on the peninsula separating the Cornwall and Williams rivers as they converge to form the Harbor of James, was occasioned by our concern for 372 children in the supervision of agencies serving Jamestown and its county environs. This old Southern community, about 40 percent of its population Negro, had provided means for the care of these children—means which reflected other aspects of American culture than those we had yet observed.

In another section of the U.S.A., far removed from ports of entry, we had chosen a community similar in size to Jamestown. This was Centralia—specifically Lake County—a prosperous industrial center with surrounding county farm lands in what historians have called the Middle Region of our country. Here the westward migrants of the decades just prior to the Civil War came from the East Coast and, later, from Northern and Central Europe. They were held to the region by the fertile grassy openings of the backlands and were within reach of the factories which enterprising men, needing skilled craftsmen for their labor force, built in Centralia. In effect, Centralia's pattern of progressive growth in this Middle Region earned for it a claim to the description "typically American." In Centralia we studied another 288 children. And through our experiences in the metropolitan centers of Centralia and Jamestown we were able to fill out further our picture of social forces operating in the care which communities were providing for dependent children in the United States.

Let us examine a few cases that represent the predominant situations of children in need of parents in these two communities.

Jody Stanley had just passed his eleventh birthday. He was also nearing the third anniversary of his placement at the Pine Glen institution for white dependent children of the city of Jamestown. Jody came there when he was eight years old, after his father had lost his job. (Mr. Stanley had worked as a clean-up man in the asbestos plant, located on the Williams River just a mile north of where Jody spent his early years in a cramped little house on the north end of the peninsula.) With the loss of his job, Mr. Stanley became discouraged and left Jody's mother, alone with three children. Jody was brought to Pine Glen by his mother, while a younger sister went to relatives who lived in the Victory Homes section of north Jamestown and a baby brother was kept by Mrs. Stanley at home. Since that day Jody had lived in the institution and had learned, somewhat painfully at first, to adjust to the routine.

Jody, a Protestant, was an attractive child of average intelligence, healthy, and with no physical disability. He showed no marked signs of emotional disturbance. He seemed almost overly affectionate with his cottage parents at Pine Glen. Usually he got along well with the other children and was average in his schoolwork. He had only this one foster care placement in his life experience. In the crowded institution he associated with children whose backgrounds were much like his own. He was not overly ambitious about his future plans, but talked, as eleven-year-olds do, about seeing the world someday by shipping out on one of those ships that thronged the harbor of Jamestown.

Jody's mother still lived alone with her youngest child in the small house in which she first began to raise her family. Recently, she heard that Mr. Stanley was killed in a highway accident in the northern part of the state while hitchhiking between jobs. She had no immediate plans for remarriage. In fact, as her youngest grew older, she had begun to consider seriously the possibility of getting a steady job in one of the light manufacturing plants along the river, as so many Jamestown women were doing. Then she would be less of a burden on her sister and brother-in-law, who still cared for her daughter, could afford day nursery care for the baby, and still meet her $30 monthly rent and other financial obligations. She contributed nothing toward Jody's care and really had no plans for him, although she still retained her full legal parental rights.

Preoccupied with her own problems, she had had little contact with Pine
Glen for the past year.

Jody still retained a close feeling for the family he once knew. He had
not been told of his father's death but often saw his sister and aunt and
uncle on weekends when they visited Pine Glen. His mother had not
come around in some time. If he was not sure of his future direction, he
was still not terribly confused about his worth and his place. At age
eleven he was an institution child, and as such he had many companions
in James County. But at age fifteen, according to Pine Glen's policy, he
must leave this institution and assume a new place and a new role in a
culture that was showing pulsations of change and movement. That transition, and his eventual growth to mature manhood, are problems which
the adults in his life must consider for Jody.

Arthur Voegel was of German and Danish descent. He had been in the
care of the Lake County Department of Public Welfare for almost two
and a half years. He was just eight years old and first came into agency
care as a preschooler when the Department stepped in to remove him
from his parents for neglect. At that time, Arthur's home life had been
in constant turmoil. Neighbors complained of his father's drinking and
that both parents, in their marital squabbles, were neglecting Arthur and
his three brothers and sisters. Since Arthur's placement his parents had
divorced and his mother had remarried, moving to near-by Indianola. An
unskilled worker in a community that prides itself on its skilled craftsmen, his father continued to live alone in small $40 per month quarters
in Centralia and retained his job of putting labels on cans in the local
baby food plant. Arthur was in his third foster home and had been in
it for just one year, continuing in the care of the local county welfare department, which had assigned a worker to see to his needs and plan for his
future.

Arthur too was a Protestant child, intelligent, healthy, and without
physical handicap. He had had some school problems—"failure to concentrate," the teacher reported—and his caseworker sometimes noted in
her reports that he had "problems in social adjustment." But Arthur
usually got along fairly well, if somewhat shyly, with other children, and
he seemed to like his foster parents and his caseworker. Arthur had not
seen his own parents in some time, although he had never been released
for adoption. His mother, still young enough at thirty-five to start a new
life with a new husband, had not driven over from Indianola in the past
year to see him. His father had not visited in some eighteen months and
seemed to have forgotten about his son. Neither parent paid anything
toward his care nor did either one have any contact with the agency.

Arthur's brothers and sisters were also in foster family homes in

Centralia—two of them together in one family—and once in a while the caseworkers brought all the children together, so that Arthur had not completely lost touch with his former family. Still, his current situation left him somewhat confused about himself. The Grants, his foster parents for the past year, were good to him and tried to be important in Arthur's life, but Arthur knew, of course, that they were not his real parents. He almost hesitated to let himself like them too much, for he feared that he might be moved soon to another foster family, as had happened twice before. And as he began to seek answers to the questions that eight-year-olds ask, Arthur felt that he was missing something that other boys and girls at school seemed to have. For the months that he had been in foster family care had now stretched into years, and before long even bigger questions and a bigger world would be facing Arthur. How would he be able to meet that world and its challenges?

In contrast to Jody and Arthur, most adopted children of James and Lake counties had quite different experiences. They were released by their mothers, unmarried girls, and moved into adoptive homes usually before they were one year old. Such was the case for both Rex Charles, in Jamestown, and Patrick Mossman, in Centralia. Rex was just nine months old when we reviewed his case, and Patrick was one year old.

Rex was a healthy Protestant infant, placed by Children's Services in Calhoun in the home of a young couple in that community. Rex would never know any other parents than those the agency had found for him. His real mother was just twenty-one years old—a girl who worked in the home of one of Jamestown's finest families—when she became pregnant by a young married man she had met at a dance in the north end of town. She had gone to Calhoun to have her baby, and Rex had found a home in that community. He would doubtless grow up in one of those newer homes, with a picture window, in the suburbs of Calhoun, surrounded by the love of parents who had themselves known many successes and few setbacks to their life ambitions.

Patrick Mossman's real mother was a Catholic convert, an unmarried clerk in a small department store in Centralia, who was twenty-four years old when her baby was born. His father was a young man of Finnish descent, twenty-five years old, who worked in a brewery in Indianola and lived with his parents in that city. Patrick's mother had released him at birth from the maternity home and had gone back to live with her own parents in the country. The Catholic Children's Agency in Centralia had found a home for Patrick with a Centralia couple who wanted children but could have none of their own. Whatever challenges lay ahead for him, his starting point seemed a stable one, surrounded by warmth and love.

How differently were the children in need of parents cared for in these two metropolitan areas? James County used mostly institutional placements, such as Jody Stanley's, and its children in need of parents rarely entered adoptive homes; while Lake County used mostly foster family placements, and adoptive homes were more often found. Moreover, though the children served in both com-

Table 8

PLACEMENT, LENGTH OF CARE, AND SEPARATION AGES OF
CHILDREN IN JAMES AND LAKE COUNTIES

	James County (Jamestown)	Lake County (Centralia)
Type of placement by percentage of children in care on April 1, 1957		
In foster family care	30	58
In institutional care	64	20
In adoptive homes	6	22
Average (median) number of years since first separation from parents, for all children under study	2	$2\frac{1}{6}$
Age at which children first entered care, by percentage of all children under study [a]		
As preschoolers (0–5 years)	46	70
As school-aged children (6–10 years)	28	21
As adolescent children (11 and over)	26	9

[a] See note *a*, Table 1.

munities were alike in coming primarily from urban homes within the county under study, Centralia more frequently than Jamestown went outside county boundaries to place children in foster care. Jamestown, however, seemed more a source for adoptive children than for adoptive parents. Some of the details on the "where" and "when" of child placement in James and Lake counties are shown in Table 8.

The children in these two metropolitan areas were alike only in the fact that they spent, on the average, a two-year period in care. Coming into care considerably older, the children of James County were much more likely to be placed in an institution. And coming into care, on the average, younger, the Lake County children were much more likely to be placed in foster families, and in adoptive homes, too.

Why these differences? A matter merely of history and geography, of tradition in the South and tradition in the North? What constellation of forces helps explain the pattern of child placement in these two metropolitan areas?

THE TWO METROPOLITAN CULTURES

Jamestown, James County

Jamestown was considered in the 1770's to be the most eminent city in the Southern District of North America. In recent years Jamestown underwent a new population growth which saw the outlying areas of James County burgeoning forth with suburban residences.[1] To the south and west, across the Cornwall River, the more respectable homes of a middle class were being built. There the houses were set back from the street, with a wide expanse of lawn, and mothers or their household help watched their children from picture windows. To the east, across the Williams River bridge toward the islands offshore, one found new residential developments with names like Greenbrook Acres and Brookview Meadows. North, following the Williams River between the peninsula and the sea and inland from industrial installations and the Navy Yard, were other new sections, bearing names like Victory Homes, Victory Hill, and Midway Center. For blue-collar and servicemen's families as well as professional people and white-collar workers had sought room for raising their children away from the central districts of the crowded peninsula.

Still, not everyone could, nor did everyone feel the need to, seek room or status by moving outward. Jamestown was a very old city.

[1] James County had a population of between 100,000 and 200,000 in 1950, showing a 36 percent increase over its 1940 population. Nonwhites numbered about 41 percent of the total. Only 1.1 percent of the population was listed as foreign born. The city proper lost population by 1.5 percent in the decade 1940–50. And while only 5.5 percent moved into the county from outside, 15.5 percent of the populace moved to another residence within James County between 1949 and 1950, and 79 percent remained in their same residence.

It still retained its beautiful, colonial homes, protected by high walls, where the oldest families, near Grand Park at the end of the peninsula, remained as visible evidence that "place" and "family name" continued to mean something in the social structure of an old Southern community. This was the part of Jamestown which was the city's showpiece, where one found the iron grille work, the Negro flower vendors, the churchyard cemetery, the Negro mammy caring for the white child. Most of the Negro population remained, too, in cramped quarters in the central district, so that one saw on the peninsula a curious blend of neat but poor homes where both white and Negro lived, hanging out their laundry on a common line. These were visible evidence that an old social order still persisted in Jamestown, a community which was in the process of formation in the eighteenth century but which probably had its character more deeply set by events of the nineteenth century.[2]

In a sense, Jamestown's development had been traumatized by the force of happenings now nearly a hundred years past in its social history. The War of Secession and, more particularly, the Reconstruction, left scars—many of them now implicit and subconscious—that still found expression in the social definitions of the culture. Outside forces once intruded and attempted to upset the basis of an older social order. When the intruders, the Federal troops, had gone, the basis of the earlier social order was reaffirmed as a whole group of people, who could now no longer be simply accounted for and defined by law as occupying the position of slaves, were relocated psychologically in the culture.

Though present-day Jamestown was undergoing change of a different sort, as our statements on physical expansion and economic growth would indicate, the change had not yet affected the

[2] Population figures for James County point up some resemblances to Dollard's description of "caste and class" in the South (John Dollard, *Caste and Class in a Southern Town*), The over-all median income for James County was $1,701, a figure depressed by the inclusion of figures for the Negro population which alone had a median income of $839. Over-all, 19 percent of the James populace earned under $500, while 1.2 percent earned over $10,000. For non-whites alone, 32.4 percent earned less than $500, and 0.13 percent earned $10,000 or more. In schooling, the median of school years completed for the whole population was 8.7. For non-whites alone it was 4.9.

Negro population to any extent. The military installations and the growing industries north of town had brought newcomers to the community and had increased the occupational opportunities of local residents as well.[3] But Jamestown still emerged as more a business, trade, and professional community than an industrial town. And through its current growth the shadows of the past were still discernible in the positions which it maintained for its most privileged and respected as well as for its least privileged and most depressed citizens.

Centralia, Lake County

One American historian presents the thesis that in America it was the frontier, as an outer edge of the advancing wave of movement westward, that furnished the forces dominating the American character. What began on the East Coast as most European, he said, became progressively more American as the wave moved westward, and this was particularly true in the Middle Region where the relatively stable, middle-sized, industrial community which we have called Centralia was located.[4] And our impressions of Centralia lend credence to its description as "typically American."

Even in 1875 Centralia was one of the major manufacturing cities of a rapidly expanding country. In times of economic de-

[3] Professional and white-collar work accounted for 35 percent of James County's employed labor force. Fifteen percent fell in the category of skilled occupations; while 46 percent were in semiskilled, service, and labor categories combined. Only 19.2 percent were in manufacturing industries.

For non-whites alone, occupation figures provide further evidence of the social class line which approached a caste line. Fully 81 percent of employed Negroes worked in semiskilled, service, and labor categories combined (over 33 percent being laborers).

[4] Lake County had a recorded population of slightly over 100,000 in 1950, showing a 16.5 percent county increase over 1940. Non-whites numbered less than 1 percent of the 1950 total (although recent estimates showed their numbers to have increased by four or five times). Foreign-born whites accounted for 10.5 percent of the county population; most of this group were listed as Danish or German, with Swedes, Norwegians, Italians, Czechs, Poles, and Russians also contributing. The earliest base of the population was made up of Northern and Western Europeans. About 85 percent of local residents remained in the same dwelling between 1949 and 1950, 11 percent were noted to have moved within the county, and only 4 percent moved in from outside the county.

pression, which were clearly felt, the populace tended to remain in Centralia, commuting to jobs in the near-by big city of Indianola. Work in Centralia was predominantly skilled or semiskilled labor in light industry–work which was a source of better-than-average income and also of considerable community pride.[5] Centralia did not resemble a factory town. Local industry was proud of its excellent labor force, and labor was proud of the home-grown industry. Centralia prided itself on a reputation for craftsmanship based on a cooperation achieved by managers and employees, both with a stake in the community, who worked together amicably. The employment balance had been relatively unchanged since 1880.[6] The history of the community had been one of steady natural growth with no real boom (except for a more rapid population expansion in the decade from 1910 to 1920). During the depression of the thirties, the population dipped slightly, but the old balance had been regained and was being maintained.

In this relatively stable center of middle-income Americans, life was still community-centered. Larger metropolitan cities to the north and south tended to drain off the professionals with big city aspirations and also made local small businesses relatively unprofitable. For diversion, Centralia housewives enjoyed a shopping spree in the big city, but they would not prefer to live there. Thus, Centralia had a paucity of specialty shops and branch offices, and this contributed to an impression of a small town with a

---

[5] The median income for families and unrelated individuals in Lake County was $3,598 in 1950. Only 7 percent of the populace earned under $500. Slightly more than 3 percent earned $10,000 or more. The median school years completed for the population was 9.2. About one fourth of the population was Catholic, according to a recent survey, and the largest Protestant denomination was Lutheran. Yet neither Catholic nor Lutheran nor non-Lutheran Protestant denominations seemed, in character, very distinct from one another. Perhaps in response to the shared problems of immigrants the churches had shaped the people in much the same moral mold.

[6] Centralia was a blue-collar town which would probably define the color of its collar as at most "very light blue." For 42 percent of the county labor force were employed as semiskilled, service, and labor workers, while 19 percent were listed as "skilled." Proportions in professional and white-collar occupations were the same in Centralia and Jamestown (35 percent). As to industry groups, 49.9 percent of the labor force were employed in manufacturing work, compared with 19.2 percent in Jamestown.

single main street. In a sense, Centralia, with its proximity to the big city of Indianola just twenty-five miles north, had become part of a mammoth metropolitan complex. But it was in no sense a suburb from which people commuted to work, for those who lived in Centralia also worked here. And it was not growing toward new community loyalties, for Centralia's local loyalty was already deep-set.

This was Middle America; a community in which the distinctive elements of Americana—the Boy Scouts, the Y.M. and Y.W.C.A., and, more recently, the Little League—thrived. It was a place where a parade brought out the throngs to watch the home-town prize-winning Boy Scout Drum and Bugle Corps. It was a community of people with roots deeply embedded in their homes, their families, and their jobs.

Social Form and Process in the Cultures

An obvious social differentiation we saw in Summit and La Paz was noted in the emergence of separate private and public worlds in communities of that size, worlds which might complement one another or remain relatively separated from one another. In both Jamestown and Centralia greater size and increasing specialization further enhanced differentiation and the possibilities of segmental human relationships and narrowed the circle within which community participants might easily interact on a personalized basis. But in Jamestown a particular form of categorization persisted in surroundings which provided constant reminders of the past. There, the atmosphere was one in which a high value was placed on tradition. Preserving what was old placed great emphasis on aggregate qualities, on characteristics which gained durability in being identified with specific groups of people. And the tendency to identify these segments with higher and lower class strata also persisted.

In the old city of Jamestown visible evidence remained of the continuing existence of two well-anchored social strata—the descendants of the oldest citizens and the descendants of their slaves. Together with the racial separation in this social system there was also a situation, perhaps best described as a narrowing circle of intimacy, from which outsiders tended to be excluded if Yankee, if Southern but not from the state, if from the state but not from Jamestown, if from Jamestown but not from "near Grand Park."

Centralia presented aspects of a small town with an achieved homogeneity lessening the differences of an initially heterogeneous population. Centralia was still not far removed from the day when the paternalistic factory owner could walk through the shop and call his employees by their first names. So bigness and growing specialization were modified by a situation providing for many values—such as skilled work, clean living, and good neighborliness—being shared by all, just as the common problems which immigrant forefathers faced in a new country were shared in the past. Symbols of class distinction were relatively inconspicuous in Centralia.

Looking at underlying social processes we saw other differences between Jamestown and Centralia. Jamestown represented a cultural setting in which ascribed status forces probably operated more convincingly than in any other of the nine American communities which we visited. If we say that American culture is predominantly a middle-class culture which emphasizes the symbols of achieved status, then communities such as Jamestown seem to have the greatest residues of ascribed status symbols, for they have more visible upper and lower social strata. One approach to "middle-classness" as a process in American life is to define it in terms of those who perceive themselves as upwardly mobile; and to carry out the American dream to its ultimate consequences, such a definition would, with certain variations in modes of reaching toward the goal, tend to encompass everyone. But certain groups in American life either perceive themselves as already at the top or see the climb from the bottom as too difficult, or impossible, to attempt. Jamestown had large segments of these upper and lower strata in its population; it was these strata who tended to rely upon, or were forced to accept, the symbols of ascribed status (place or position) in the social system. Where a caste line also is discernible relative to a particular population segment, a process which is almost the obverse of the normal American culture process operates. In the usual process, ascribed qualities tend to give way to achieved ones for lower classes in American society where groups and their individual representatives are always entering social systems at lower levels and acquiring the means for the upward climb. But the walls of ascription were relatively thick in Jamestown, although Jamestown too had a growing middle social ground in its suburbs. Thus, the residues of ascription, the separateness of segments, and the persistence of personalized human relationships within one's own segment still pervaded the culture.

In Centralia we saw a more typically achieved status atmosphere prevailing. The most interesting impression of Centralia, however, was that the process had reached a stage in which the intracommunity struggle for status was not—and perhaps had never been historically—of prime concern. Like Summit, Centralia tended to lack perceived social strata through which to move. In a word, Centralia's achievement atmosphere involved more a shared pride in what had been achieved by the whole community both economically and socially. A form of ethnic and social homogeneity was being achieved in Centralia, in contrast to rural Norden where homogeneity was ascribed by the historical fact that all who came to the community actually tended, initially, to be the same. Centralia also stressed interdependence, responsibility to the larger whole, while perhaps contractual relationships were more a part of human experience in this urban complex than in isolated, and "separating," Jamestown.

In responses to dependency, again our efforts to classify the tendencies in Jamestown and Centralia must be qualified. In Jamestown we could note a very old and long-time concern for children. Indeed, one of the orphanages, Pine Glen, was the oldest of its kind in the United States. We have used the terms of "we" and "they" to indicate, for the dependent child, a trend toward inclusion in, or exclusion from, the community. It appeared that Jamestown cared for its dependents as many "we" groups, drawing them into partial segments of the whole community—Baptist or Methodist or Episcopal—on the basis of gross social characteristics. But caring for the dependent child and regulating his behavior on a group basis— placement in relatively static child care settings in which the Episcopal or Methodist or Baptist child was defined and placed in accordance with such social characteristics—did not imply social definitions much different in tone from those which operated normally throughout the whole culture. The child in need of parents in Jamestown was usually reacted to in a personalized way as one of the "we" to the extent that all those within the many "we's" in this community normally occupied positions to which they were assigned by gross social characteristics.[7]

The inclination in Centralia was also toward a "we" orientation to the dependent child, but here the qualifying conditions were somewhat different. In Centralia it was the achieved homogeneity and interdependence typifying this community which appeared also in the dependency picture. Informants pointed to the red-brick community centers which this town provided for its youth years ago "when most towns were doing nothing." They were evidence that Centralia too had had a long-time concern for children; but Centralia's children were seen in a homogeneous aggregate, and the answer to their problems was defined as a need for more "recreational facilities." In this uniformly prosperous community those who were different by reason of being dependent had a low visibility. Centralia did not exhibit the more austere exclusion of Norden, nor did it define away problems as did Summit. Centralia was not isolated, it had had dynamic experiences with assimilating different peoples, and it had known the effects of depression days. There was readiness to recognize problems and to attempt to act upon them. Nevertheless, the tendency in Centralia was to perceive homogeneous answer—usually in recreation facilities. And in this setting there was also the inclination to perceive dependent children's problems as uniformly the same if no answer to a special problem was readily available.

Foster Care in the Two Cultures

Our brief description of the two cultural contexts which Jamestown and Centralia represent would lead us to expect to find dif-

[7] Robert Merton's discussions of "relative deprivation" seem applicable to this situation. See Robert K. Merton, *Social Theory and Social Structure*, pp. 227–36.

ferent patterns of placement of dependent children in these two communities. What did the over-all patterns of placement indicate? First let us look at James County.

In this community institutional placements predominated. We have seen this situation in other settings, but of added significance in James County was the large number of institutions involved. Nine institutions represented many religious groups and, of course, also were segregated between Negro and white children within these groups. The James County agencies both reflected and contributed to the social definition of the dependent child in this culture. There was a difference between the impact of an institution in defining the dependent child as deviant in the more segmented setting of James County and its impact as we saw it in a homogeneous setting like Norden. In Norden the child in the local institution was probably the most visibly different child in the whole community, and being in a deviant minority by the simple reason of his dependency he was, and felt himself to be, excluded from the larger community. In serving James County the multiple institutions seemed to exemplify the categorical social definitions which existed throughout the culture. Dynamic change in the physical and economic order had not yet been reflected to any degree in the social system in the placement of dependents. Moreover, the institutional placement did not separate out the dependent child as a dependent *per se* in this culture where divisive social definitions were normal. Such placement was based, in addition, in a strong and persistent belief that institutions were good for children. In part, they expressed a mode of socialization in a culture that had a great stake in maintaining a way of life different from that of the rest of the country. Institutions were the preservers of a cultural heritage at crucial times when other educational facilities were destroyed or invaded.

Miss Cook, director of the Baptist Annie Laurie Orphanage, said: "I take exception to the statement that all children should either be returned to their own homes or moved into adoptive homes. I have a strong feeling that there is a great merit in group care. In this state families are usually so close that even distant relatives are active in most situations. At present all our children have some relationship with relatives, if not with their own parents." And the pastor of a Baptist Church commented: "People feel safer about their children being in an institution than in a foster home. I don't know what foster parents could do for children, but I think institutions like Annie Laurie, with a cottage family plan and definite age groups in each cottage, are good for children. The institution does not isolate the child from his parents as much as a foster home does."

Each representative of a group or segment of the population tended to think in terms of the institution which his own group operated, when a referral for child placement came to his attention. Of course, the public and private issue also came to the fore in this setting where a narrowing circle of trust seemed to operate. The Episcopal minister remarked: "Institutions are privately owned, while the state does foster family placement. People prefer the private to the state but would defend the state to the Federal Government. If the Federal Government is out of the picture, however, they will turn against the state. And they would throw out county government to get local government."

Perhaps a most significant fact among our findings in this community was that in all our interviews it was difficult to find statements from informants that stood out as representing attitudes toward the dependent child *per se.* Such statements as we did obtain were always permeated with attitudes toward a group or classification of people, identified by gross social or ethnic characteristics, and only incidentally reflected attitudes toward dependency within a group. This categorization was the vital clue to Jamestown's handling of dependency. It seemed possible to retain a reciprocal bond between individuals in different groups in this culture when a comfortable classification of each group in the social structure was recognized. A Negro minister said: "The Negroes are divided here. We haven't been able to produce leadership that can get a cross-section of support. People get to a certain point, they are on the verge of achieving something, then there is a withdrawal."

This "withdrawal" seemed to indicate a falling back on an ascribed category that provided certain emotional supports in this cultural setting. In the old-line white families, too, one found problems of identity among the aged and infirm. Yet these old people could live on the peninsula side by side with Negro families, perhaps because they carried the mental image of the past when Negroes lived on their property and worked in the kitchen—and this context still placed things in a proper psychological ordering for them.

A Catholic priest made some statements that were revealing of what was happening to those who were in social flux, the middle classes of the suburbs: "It is the salaried people who are hardest hit when problems come. They can't get on welfare and they wouldn't accept our help. They don't dare ask it for themselves, but sometimes we can get medical care and private hospital rooms for them in a way that 'saves face' just as we do for the old people."

How did these people take to the associations, the friendship patterns, the activities which the public school—the great democratizer of middle-class America—provided and promoted? Mrs. Monroe, speaking from her well-arranged parlor in one of the pillared homes near Grand Park, said: "A lot of the parents in the suburbs are sending their children into the city to the private schools. And of course most of the white children in the city, at least those who can afford it, go to private schools." In this recurrent return to the old strongholds of ascribed status we saw a desire for more complete and personalized relationships with "one's own kind." This was a desire which seemed unsatisfied by the more superficial contacts that the growing middle class setting of the suburbs provided.[8] And the private children's institutions were a part of this milieu in which persons and, in this situation, children in need of parents were defined and located in the social order by their gross social characteristics.

---

[8] C. Wright Mills says: "The prestige market of the big city is often a market of strangers, a milieu where contacts having relevance to prestige are often transitory and fleeting . . . . The metropolitan man is a temporary focus of heterogeneous circles of casual acquaintances, rather than a fixed center of a few well-known groups . . . one has contacts, rather than relations, and these contacts are shorter lived and more superficial . . . . Rather than cohesion there is uniformity, rather than descent or tradition, interest . . . ." See the discussion of white-collar status in the metropolitan setting in C. Wright Mills, *White Collar— the American Middle Classes,* pp. 251–54.

In Centralia, as we have suggested, there was also a genuine interest in children, but the propensity to perceive more extended recreational services as the answer to all children's problems tended to conceal the importance of the particular problem of the child without a permanent home. Those who had not achieved that homogeneity which typified this community, or who had not yet achieved an expected level of responsible commitment to the interdependent whole, were those least legitimized in the social system. But the social forces in this community inclined toward permitting this achievement rather than toward shutting out or excluding new elements.

Apparently, Centralia's problems of dependency were not too great, and its dependent children did not stand out significantly from all children. A Catholic priest said: "This is a good community for children. We keep building schools. The Chest drive stresses youth, people give generous support, and industry matches the amount the employees give. I see a need for more social centers and for a couple more public swimming pools." The supervisor of the county nurses remarked: "We seldom have neglect cases. When we do I refer them to the welfare department. Actually, our back-country areas, where we have more transients and some truck farming, are the source of most of our problems." A county probation officer commented: "There are no slum areas in Centralia. No *one* school contributes a disproportion of problems. Most cases we have are school problems, and the kids complain they don't have enough to do." So the community's recreation programs were being designed to meet this need.

The mayor, formerly a small businessman, stressed the unity in Centralia's heterogeneity: "This is a diversified community. It's a real melting pot—almost another Singapore. I am amazed that we get along so well. But I love this atmosphere because I love to meet different nationalities."

The community's approach to the problems of people new to the system was to school them in the ways of those who had been a part of Centralia's troubled but steady growth. The chairman of the county board of supervisors said: "Centralia has pioneered in one phase of social work. If a man can't manage his money we assign his pay check for a year. Then we set up a budget for him. We take power of attorney and manage a family through the year. Some people haven't had the experience with money that those of us who were tried in a harder school have had."

The patterned response of industry to welfare in Centralia was to give large sums of money for recreational facilities and camping scholarships. Mr. Jensen, the executive of one of Centralia's most renowned manufacturing plants, which his grandfather had founded, said: "I am on the executive board of the Boy Scouts. I don't see any big gaps in services to children. And I know, for I know our people. I went to public school here with the sons of laborers, professional people, and businessmen. The Y.M.C.A. and Y.W.C.A. and the Boys and Girls Scouts have good programs. We have stable people here in Centralia, and newcomers seem to become that way too." Mr. Jensen's grandfather pioneered the Community Chest idea in Centralia and once gave a park to the community. And Mr. Jensen's father had served on both the Community Chest board and the park board for many years.

There was no union in Mr. Jensen's plant, but unions had grown elsewhere in Centralia. Their importance dated from the depression years when, again, the whole community faced a common problem—a problem that touched many workers' families and many local industries. The unions also gave most of their support to the Community Chest drive from which funds flowed into recreational facilities.

A Boy Scout executive said: "It isn't necessary to put on a campaign for funds for the Scouts. Private industry stepped in to see that our Drum and Bugle Corps got to the Valley Forge jamboree a few years ago. The support we receive is a real credit to the big men here in Centralia who back us." But others were not sure that community philanthropic funds were expended in the most propitious way. One man active in welfare said: "There is no basis whatsoever for the distribution of Chest funds. The Scouts and the Y.'s get all the money they want. The child welfare agencies need to develop their public relations so that they can interpret their programs to the community. What we actually need is a 'traffic engineer' to steer our welfare programs."

Thus we found that people who were close to the child-placing agencies and their problems felt that some obvious blinders obscured local perceptions. Mrs. Stancich, of the Welfare Council, commented that recreational services did not serve the "borderline kids." And a local psychiatrist added: "This town as a whole is vitally interested in the welfare of its children. We set up clubs of all kinds. But we are so close to big cities that people tend to go there for specialized services. We get general—and superficial—answers here."

Like homogeneous Summit, Centralia had many service organizations for local people to join, but the shortcoming of such associations was not that they did nothing of a civic nature but, as one physician expressed it, that they did "nothing coordinated," although their concern was clearly centered on public responsibilities. Thus Centralia, a community which was vitally interested in children, moved slowly toward more specialized and diagnostically oriented definitions of those in need of care. For the forces which tended to move this somewhat heterogeneous community toward a form of achieved homogeneity had similarly shaped for it relatively homogeneous answers to its problems.

Adoption in Jamestown and Centralia

The adoption figures, together with the return home rates, for the two communities were consistent with our impressions of the cultures and the other facts on placement in Jamestown and Centralia as may be seen in Table 9.

James County had one of the lowest agency adoption rates of any of our nine communities. At the same time, it was one of three communities in our study—Santa Ana County was also included in this group—which had more children under study returned home than in adoptive placements. As in Santa Ana County, welfare operated within a cultural milieu which seemed oriented more toward moving a dependent child to a situation like the one from which he came, than into a new situation, perhaps perceived as "better." In

Centralia, on the other hand, we found one of the three highest adoption percentages among our nine communities, and this was coupled with one of the lowest return home rates. Percentages on the local county within which adoptive placements were made indicated that some of Centralia's adoption orientation was influenced by forces outside the community, and these influences were part of the larger urban complex of which Centralia partook. But let us begin with the adoption situation in Jamestown.

In a cultural setting in which tradition still clung like the old Spanish moss, we would expect that a practice like adoption—at least the formal, agency kind—could not have taken hold too firmly.

Table 9

ADOPTIVE PLACEMENTS AND RETURNS HOME IN
JAMES AND LAKE COUNTIES

	James County (Jamestown)	Lake County (Centralia)
Percentages of all children in care April 1, 1957, who were in adoptive placements	6	22
Percentages of all adoptive placements that were in-county	36	53
Percentages of all children in care April 1, 1957, who left care by January, 1958 (nine months later)		
For adoptive placements	6	12
For return home and other purposes	15	7

We should expect, moreover, that those adoptions which did occur would tend to be placements strictly within a category—that is, for example, from a Baptist institution into a Baptist home, or from a Methodist institution into a Methodist home. Furthermore, we should expect to find certain hindrances to this form of achieved parenthood in a culture where family name and place were still most important and where a suburban middle class, being a fluid and relatively unanchored stratum of the society, had particular problems of psychological identity and of emotional security. Let us look at some attitudes which express significant outlooks of groups in this culture.

The older families near Grand Park in Jamestown still retained a position as style-setters. As the director of the Chamber of Commerce said, "Jamestown proper is small and static, but it is the generator for the whole metropolitan area." And it was still the generator of cultural values or, perhaps, the preserver of the heritage. It was "down by Grand Park" that one found ladies like Mrs. Yancey, whose son asked her one day why he was named Beauregard since that was the name of a street. She replied that the day would come when he would appreciate the value of a family name. Still, a lady like Mrs. Monroe, a relative newcomer to this neighborhood who had successfully achieved a position there, said that adoption was now the accepted thing in her set, particularly among childless couples. "I have seven adopted children," she said. "Most of them I obtained from private sources, but two were adopted through local agencies." Mrs. Monroe saw changes coming to the society ladies. She went on to say: "You know, ladies are doing more things now since the Second World War. But much is made of 'belonging' here, though some outsiders have slowly been accepted. And adoption is like that too; it has finally been accepted."

Among the Negro families, where dependency problems were serious, a far different set of circumstances existed. A Negro Methodist minister said: "I know of a few adoptions in substantial families, but very few Negroes are applying to adopt. Perhaps they don't know of the opportunity or how to make application. Families are large, and many young couples live with parents. An illegitimate child usually becomes the responsibility of the mother. Illegitimacy is mostly among the poor and illiterate. The higher a girl's social status, the more she loses through illegitimacy. The more economically able ones put the child into a home, and friends would not know of it. A girl rarely gives her child up for adoption."

The director of guidance at a Negro high school felt that adoption was increasing: "But they go outside the community to adopt, and some won't even tell you about it. Actually, very few children live with other than blood relatives, however." Other informants indicated that for many Negro families, perhaps particularly among those who strove the hardest to rise out of their ascribed position, family solidarity of any degree did not come until the grandparent stage. The current generation of ambitious parents were in a tenuous situation for raising children. A Negro high school principal said that almost 50 percent of his students lived with their grandparents. Their parents were in New York, or elsewhere, carving a new life. And apparently those aspiring parents who stayed in Jamestown—where teaching was the major occupational outlet for the Negro high school graduate—turned to sources outside the area when they adopted children, perhaps to escape the social stigma which they might feel was associated with dealing with local agencies.

It appeared that a large number of applicants for adoptive children had not developed among the more mobile James County whites, either, although suburban living might make adoption more attractive to some of them in time. A Baptist minister said: "People don't think about adoption when they put a child in an institution. They want that institution to take care of him." And Miss Cook, of Annie Laurie Orphanage, remarked that most children came into care as families rather than singly, adding: "There is much common-law marriage, and people don't get divorces. Any Aid to Dependent Children grants cannot be more than $99 per month, so we have a lot of group care for family groups of children."

Some people, however, reflected a changing attitude toward the separating and static child care processes typical of Jamestown. An industrialist in the North Area was disturbed that juvenile delinquents were returned to the same home and family from which they came. And a Catholic priest, in Jamestown for twelve years, said: "A high percentage, I would say, of my parishioners adopt children. A lot of it is done independently. Certainly the orphanage is no substitute for a home, to my way of thinking."

By contrast, in Lake County, adoption was a major part of child welfare practice. But many adoptions were effected by agencies located in the near-by metropolis of Indianola, and many of the adoptive placements were also in the larger urban centers.

Centralia was a community in which home and the raising of children were important parts of the total way of life. Still, Centralia itself was not the source of a growing professional or white-collar class. Mr. Kelly, a local newspaperman, said: "Less than 15 percent of the news staff in our office come from Centralia, but all the clerical and printing staff are natives. This is a poor community for retail business, and we have a small white-collar group here."

Family relationships seemed to be aligned, for the most part, with a pattern of family life that was still close to that of the Old World, even though assimilation had been going on for decades.

A Lutheran minister said: "I can recall but one adoption [from a Lutheran agency] and there are not many applicants. In my six and a half years with this congregation I have known of only two unwed mothers. We have had 201 baptisms in that time."

The Catholic priest who was director of the local St. Vincent de Paul Society told us: "We have lots of just ordinary wage earners in our parish. There is much less illegitimacy here than one might expect in an industrial city this size. This parish was once a German parish, but now it has mixed nationalities. In my twenty-two years I have seen all together no more than fifteen or twenty adoptions in the parish."

Another Lutheran minister said: "People are as strict as possible in raising their children. Families tend to be large, and most young couples live separately from their parents. My parishioners are mostly working people. Half of them were on relief in the depression, but there is little illegitimacy and families tend to take over in broken home situations."

The culture pattern which these people lived by was like the industry in Centralia—largely of the home-made variety. "Achievement" had not caught them up in the status struggles that typify the mobile American middle classes. These people were "midway" in American life, located quite stably in the American cultural process. We should expect that adoption would not express for them such a vital aspect of the achievement of parenthood. Mrs. Dee O'Hanlon, the assistant probation officer who investigated all independent, agency, and "relative" adoptions for the county court, said: "I have about sixty adoptions a year to look into. Most of them involve remarriages where a second spouse is being declared the legal parent. We get only about four or five independent placements a year."

Our impression of Centralia was that families did adopt, there were no cultural deterrents to adoption, but also there was no large segment actively seeking adoption as a means for fulfilling their life ambitions, just as there was no visible upper-class stratum from which a "fashion" of adoption might filter down. Many who did seek to adopt children did so through agencies in the urban centers near by where more specialized professional services were provided. But apparently there was no great problem of social divisiveness connected with accepting local children into family homes in this community. A board member at Graham Home said: "There is no real 'society' here. All families have been here many years. Wage rates are high, and this raises the status quo of the whole community." This comment was a significant one, for it seemed to typify the frame of reference within which social definitions took on meaning in Centralia. It tended to highlight a form of achievement that was shared by all in this community.

There were some suggestions of change that might influence the creation of a different adoption public in Centralia. The director of the Community Chest said: "We are moving here from a small-town life to a city way of life. The greatest in-migration is of executive and managerial people. Some family-run businesses are taking on outside managers from big industries. There is a new leadership emerging, a new management group more remote from personal knowledge of employees and local citizens." Such developments could contribute to a modification of the local culture, emphasize a different form of achievement, and make contractual human relationships more common within this community which already stressed interdependence within the larger whole. This could also change the milieu within which local agency adoption took place, and more children like Patrick Mossman might find adoptive parents through the child welfare agencies serving Centralia.

11. The Legal Systems

The law relating to dependent children was quite old in Jamestown; it had been newly codified in Centralia. How did this situation, coupled with the respective approaches of persons involved in the legal process, influence the placement of children who were temporarily or permanently deprived of parents in these two distinctive settings?

The Judge

In the very heart of the crowded peninsula where Jamestown is situated stands the old-fortress-like building which once was the site of the state military college. Across a back courtyard and an alley from this structure, which now housed most of the municipal departments in Jamestown, was a newer annex in which Judge Ward and the employees of the county probation department had their offices. The judge's office was quite large, though modestly furnished. Judge Cornelius Ward seemed pleased to talk about the dependent children of James County.

"It seems to me," he began, "that most of the dependent children in this county come from what I would call 'catch-job' families. You know, that kind of people is peculiar to this part of the country." He continued: "I would say that about 60 percent of the cases come from Jamestown and the other 40 percent from the county." Did there seem to be many obvious situations that contributed toward dependency? "There is a lot of illegitimacy, of course, among the colored. The moral standards of a large segment of the group are particularly low. But there is no stigma attached to illegitimacy in that group. The cases that come before the court are usually the ones that are so serious that neighbors were up in arms and contacted the police."

Judge Ward had been a judge in James County for eleven years. He was a small man, perhaps in his sixties, but with a big booming voice. The law within which he operated provided for adoption only with parents' consent. There was no abandonment provision, or any other way of declaring a child free for adoption except with parental consent.

"We look on foster homes as short-term placements," the judge continued. "We feel that the institutions are for longer term care. We also use foster family homes for younger children. Generally, placements are made in accordance with the religious faith of the child." What reasons did he consider cause for removal of a child from his parents? "Both physical neglect and disturbed relationships are reasons for removal—cases where getting out of the environment would help." In what ways did he attempt to facilitate adoption under the present legal set-up? "I permit a mother to give up custody of a child for adoption without actually making a court appearance." (Many courts in the state required the parent to be present.)

Because of the administrative arrangement and the responsibility for the foster family home situation carried by the welfare department, Judge Ward was somewhat dependent on the social work staff at that department. He was irritated that the welfare department had the money for placement yet was not able, often, to place children he wanted placed. The children that the department could not take, went, of necessity, to relatives, to free foster homes, and (perhaps most frequently) to institutions. "You know, I am required by law," he said, "to visit the institutions to which I commit children, and each year I go to each institution in the state where we have children. I try to make the child see that we care about him and that we haven't forgotten him." This sincere feeling about children obviously came from within a person whose concern extended beyond the constraints of his professional role.

Other Legal Figures

The county welfare department was *the* protective agency in James County. But to some extent both welfare and probation departments were involved in protective service cases. It was the welfare department which had access to foster family homes to which the police could take children for emergency shelter. The probation office had no funds for foster family placements, so it turned such cases over to the welfare department. The relations between the two departments were personally quite friendly. Still, there were "fuzzy" areas in their formal operations which seemed to call for clarification.

There were conferences between the judge and welfare department social workers about legal questions. But there was no regular reporting about children—neither by legal provision nor by the court's regulation. However, when problems arose which required legal action, a conference would be scheduled. There were differences between the two departments which seemed to result from a lack of understanding, or even knowledge, of the other's point of view. Apparently, the welfare department wanted to stay out of court whenever possible. However, the department was pressing the court on termination cases to the fullest extent. The public welfare department had one special worker assigned to handle long-term placement cases. These were children legally in temporary care whose cases actually were not reviewed by the court and who had little prospect of returning home or of being adopted (because of legal limitations). The pressure to do something about these children came from the welfare department rather than from the court. The philosophy of the welfare department was that foster family care was temporary and institutional care permanent, or at least long-term. The department used foster family homes whenever it seemed that a child might be able to return to his own home before too long. This was in spite of the fact that often the easiest thing for the department to do would be to ship children off to institutions; institutions, however, would not always take the children. No public funds were allocated for children in institutions, so that type of care would have cost the department nothing and would have removed the children from the community.

It should also be noted that there was an obvious distinction between the kinds of neglect cases coming from the Negro and those from the white population in James County. Workers at the welfare department commented that they had comparatively few Negro cases in Child Welfare Services but a large number in the Aid to Dependent Children (ADC) case load. The Negro cases they did get were always very serious, since the less serious ones would never reach the court or the welfare department. Relatives seemed more likely to take care of those children. Doubtless a different standard was used in evaluating Negro families and, as the workers would phrase it, "only the flagrant cases arouse interest" (although the judge laid this to the department's reluctance to antagonize anyone).[1] In a sense, it seemed that in Jamestown both the court and the social agencies tended to function "outside the law." No one seemed to move toward changing the law; they merely tried to bend the interpretations in order to operate as effectively as possible under the circumstances. And in some instances the judge appeared less bound by precedent than the Department of Public Welfare in child welfare operations in James County.

LEGAL ROLES IN LAKE COUNTY

The Judge

Judge Joe Lejeune's office was located in the county courthouse in Centralia. The judge appeared to be a man in his early forties, but his serious demeanor somewhat belied his youthfulness. He was thoughtful, almost cautious, in his answers to questions. We settled back in rather luxurious leather chairs in his wood-paneled office and waited for him to finish signing papers before beginning the interview.

"The typical dependency situations that involve removal of a child," said Judge Lejeune, "are cases of children who, in effect, have no parents. This often is because parents are in prison, or are out of the picture for some such reason, and children have no one else to care for them. Before intervening the court must, by law, find a child dependent or neglected. Then the court can place a child outside the home either with a private or public agency,

---

[1] It is significant that informants in Jamestown invariably seemed to evaluate such things as "status" or "neglect" in "relative" terms—looking at the person within his given category in such evaluations. This came out in statements such as, "A Negro doctor makes less than I do, but he has more status than I have"—obviously rating the man's status in accordance with his standing within his own ethnic group. It would seem that this process in social evaluation operates most readily in a setting in which what we have termed "categorization" of people predominates. See the reference in footnote 7, Chapter 10, to Merton's discussion of "relative deprivation."

or with a relative." What were his own feelings about the necessity
of removing a child? "I would consider," he said, "that if there
were any type of adequate home life the child should stay at home;
but if he is removed, then I am in favor of a placement where the
child can have home treatment rather than an institution placement." He continued: "In my two and a half years on the bench
I have had a number of cases where one or both parents have been
committed to an institution and the children were in the custody
of the Department of Public Welfare. When the parents have re-
established a home we may return the children but leave custody
with the DPW for a while."

Judge Lejeune was the juvenile judge in Centralia by reason of
being the municipal court judge assigned to that position by vote
of the judges of the Courts of Record of the county. He had been
a municipal judge since late in 1955. He was responsible for the
termination of parental rights, but he was not called upon to give
approval of adoptions. In dependency and neglect cases he relied
on the social work reports of the private agencies, the county welfare department, and the Probation Department. "There seem to
be more cases designated 'dependent' than 'neglected,'" he said,
"but I can't say that I consciously use one designation more than
the other and I see no reason for sparing a parent by calling the
child 'dependent' if the parent was neglecting the child. I have
never had to terminate rights in the face of a bona fide contest in
court. There have been cases where parents were reluctant to
relinquish their rights, but there have been no contests involving
attorneys."

We asked the judge with what agencies he placed children. "I
have no general rule," he replied. "Usually children are committed
to the state when they don't seem adoptable or when satisfactory
placement in the community seems improbable. But I fear that
children may become lost in such public commitments." What
needs did he see? "There is a need for more institutions for delinquent children. There is also a shortage of foster homes, especially for the 'unusual' child who demands understanding and a
chance to achieve emotional stability but does not require in-

stitutional care. You know, it's easy to get committees together in this community," he concluded, "but what we need is less talking and more acting."

Judge Lejeune operated under a Juvenile Code which had been enacted in 1956. This law was written cooperatively by both social workers and lawyers, and the highly professionalized welfare system in Centralia was familiar to the judge. There was professional respect between welfare people and the judge, but not complete agreement. Judge Lejeune seemed concerned with protecting individual human rights from a system that might become bureaucratic. "But change," he said, "is a legislative, not a judicial, function and should not come through 'strained interpretations' by a judge."

Other Legal Figures

It was the county welfare department which started cases moving toward Judge Lejeune's court in Centralia. There had been a recent reorganization of agencies but not of the staff who provided this service. Over the years the responsibility had been delegated to Miss Miller and Mrs. Bicek, who now operated through the county department. These women were personally known in the community as the people to call about children who needed help. It was not unusual for them to be called at home about a case. "We try to be professional," they said, "but we'd rather take the calls at home than pick up the pieces later." They had high case loads, and the urgent situations were the ones which got their attention. Neither had professional training, although both were interested in improving their work and were trying to keep up with current ideas. "We used to think foster family homes were the answer to many problems," they said; "now we try to explore other alternatives first. But people criticize us for working too slowly toward permanent removal of children from their parents." These women also had a preference for voluntary termination of parental rights. Their efforts to keep children in their own houses were supported in the agency by a new casework supervisor with social work education and by the director who had hired him. On the whole, there was a continuing trend in the county department toward working with families. However, the new casework supervisor expected to become more aggressive in requesting termination of parental rights.

The local probation office was also involved in the legal process, although less directly so. This office was no longer responsible for the cases of neglect and dependency. But in such cases it served as a coordinator for the court, to help arrange the court calendar, and was a liaison between the court and private agencies. The probation office was fairly well separated from public and private child welfare agencies and was principally involved in delinquency cases, but it still investigated all adoptions. There was no conflict in Centralia between the probation office and the welfare department over which one should have charge of protective cases, since this question had been settled by the law.

The private agencies in Centralia, and the state Department of Public Welfare, had little direct part in the process of legal action in behalf of children until after a court decision had been made. Since many of their cases came as commitments from the court, they were often involved with the court in connection with children placed in their care. Annual reports to the judge were required by the new law. But even with the contacts between the agencies and court and with the good feeling the agencies had for the court, there was some lack of knowledge of legal limitations on the part of agencies. Still, there was cooperation on all sides. But, as we suggested earlier, uniformity and a tendency toward homogeneous perceptions can have a stultifying effect in a community if different problems call for different answers.

THE CODES [2] AND STATUTES AND THEIR USE

The laws relating to child welfare in Jamestown and Centralia presented many contrasts. However, a generally liberal use of Jamestown's much older laws did tend to lessen the differences in end results in the care of dependent children.

[2] Appendix D-3 summarizes a comparison of pertinent sections of the codes in the two communities.

The actual organization of the law was very different in the states in which Jamestown and Centralia were located. The Southern state had provisions relating to children and their placement scattered in various sections of state code. Some sections seemed to duplicate; others overlapped. In both states there was some special legislation for particular cities. In Centralia's state, however, there seemed to be special legislation only for the northern metropolis Indianola, while in Jamestowns' state there was a series of special provisions for individual counties. The entire law relating to courts in this Southern state had different bases for the various counties in the state. It appeared that as each county wanted to set up a children's court a new section was added to the law to authorize this. The section in effect for Jamestown dated back to 1936, and no section dealing with neglected children was found to go back farther than 1911. In the northern state the move toward codification of statutes seemed to have started about 1929 and had gradually made the Children's Code quite comprehensive. Almost all the legal issues which we have considered in our nine communities—the temporary and permanent removal of children, placement restrictions, and adoption—were treated in some way in this code.

The allocation of funds influenced children's placement in somewhat different ways in the two communities. In James County, laws limited the amount of ADC funds which could be paid and also restricted their use to children in the homes of relatives. Other funds from state and county were available for foster home care. However, institutional placement, public or private, was of no cost to the counties since there was no provision for "purchase of care." The laws, therefore, tended to make institutional placement cheaper in James County.

In Lake County there was less influence of fund allocation on the placement pattern; but even there, with much codification of statutes, allocation of funds favored certain placements. ADC funds could be used for foster family care only if the child were placed by a county agency, so a private agency either had to make some collaborative arrangement with a county agency or care for a child from its own funds. The other alternative was to persuade the county to use purely county funds. Most expensive of all for the county was placement in a private institution. The fact that Lake County set a maximum figure for such payments tended to limit its children to custodial-type institutions since treatment institutions had rates considerably above the top amount set by the county.

The customary religious restriction was more strongly stated in the James County laws although such restrictions seemed more strictly adhered to in interdependent Lake County. In "separating" Jamestown there were many more sectarian agencies which simply limited their intake to children of their own denomination. With facilities initially set up on a sectarian basis the possibility of placement in a home operated by another religion than that of any particular child was not much of an issue.

Adoption laws, also, were very different. James County had practically none, and did not permit adoption without parental consent. Although there was no provision for termination of parental rights, some judges were willing to take such action if it seemed clear that a child had been abandoned. There was a provision in the law in James County that an adoption could be set aside at any time "for cause." Another old provision in the Jamestown laws was the one which authorized the "deeding" of child. Also, there was no provision that adoptions must go through agencies (except that one agency was given authority to place children for adoption), and no period of time was set for a probationary or investigation period. Thus, adoptions could be completed almost immediately if the judge approved. The report on adoptions in the state said that the mean average time required to process an adoption was twenty days. Some were completed in one day. The result was that nonagency adoptions were given, by the absence of public controls, substantial support.

The Lake County law, in contrast, encouraged—practically required—agency adoptions. Thus, its state had the highest rate of agency adoptions of all adoptions in the country. Court approval was required before independent placement for adoption, and this approval required agency investigation. Procedure was carefully

detailed, and there were specified reasons for termination of parental rights and for guardianship of the child until adoption was completed. This made for uniform procedure among agencies and
courts.

In discussing the relative positions of these two communities
along the parents' rights—child's rights continuum some qualifications must be made. Roughly, Jamestown based legal operations
more on an older parents' rights doctrine, while Centralia had enacted the Children's Code, which stressed the child's rights point of
view.

In Jamestown, parents' rights were emphasized throughout the
law—parental consent was needed for adoption, parents could still
deed children, and adoption could be revoked at any time, presumably with the child going back to the parents. Omissions in the law
relating to adoption and the absence of legislative efforts to refine
and reconcile the various statutes relating to children were apparent. The fact that changes had not been made certainly reflected
an attitude in the state which considered the laws as fairly adequate.
And the separate independence of institutions likewise reflected a
parents' rights philosophy; that is, it left institutions free to take
children whenever parents so requested.

In Centralia, the laws written in recent years were more along the
line of a child's rights philosophy. This statement must be qualified by noting the balance maintained between protecting parents'
rights and promoting the welfare of the child. The legal provision
probably most clearly at the child's rights end of the continuum
was the requirement of court approval of a nonagency adoptive
placement, with agency investigation required as a preliminary to
such approval. This section really took away what some would call
a fundamental parental right—the right to place one's own child for
protection. But there were restrictions on agencies in Centralia to
prevent them from misusing the authority they had been given.
One such restriction was a recent change in the law which made the
refusal of a guardian to consent to an adoption a subject of the
court's review. The law prevailing in Centralia was one written
with agencies and their philosophy and procedures clearly in mind,

but certain precautions were written in. It represented a legal review of welfare authority and reflected a belief in welfare "within limits."

In both communities the contact and communication between legal and welfare worlds were close and cordial. There might be misunderstandings between legal and welfare people, but some of these were caused by frustrations for both groups, going back to such elements as inadequate staff, funds, training, and facilities. When one moved to the state level in both communities, the situation was different. In Jamestown there seemed to be little understanding at the state level between the legal and welfare worlds. The state legislators were described, usually, as attorneys who wanted to continue with independent adoptions and who did not want to change the deeding laws. In Centralia, on the other hand, understanding at the state level was at least as apparent as at the local level. This was illustrated by the collaboration of social workers, attorneys, and judges in writing the Children's Code.

The two communities contrasted, then, in many ways. Both judges took part in, and had considerable knowledge of, welfare activities and welfare philosophy in their communities. But Judge Lejeune in Lake County was more important to more agency people, his court was involved in more cases. In James few of the agencies had many dealings with Judge Ward. By contrast, Judge Lejeune was more of a community figure and agency people often consulted with him. For, as we have seen, the law itself placed Judge Lejeune right in the middle of the welfare picture where he operated under a philosophy expressed in a code which had been threshed out in recent years by both legal and welfare people. But in James County, Judge Ward was less drawn into the welfare world in a cultural setting in which autonomy—of public departments, of private institutions, and, finally, of parents and their rights—was stressed.

LEGAL ISSUES AND PLACEMENT PATTERN

In the two previous community comparisons—in our rural and small urban counties—we found similarity rather than difference in

laws to be the norm. In Jamestown and Centralia greater differences were found. Did these differences in legal systems show up
also in the facts on child placement in the two communities? Varying degrees of difference were noted among the placement variables.

In Jamestown, with a predominance of private institutions offering custodial child care at the behest of parents, 67 percent of the
placements were cases of voluntary separation of children from parents. In Centralia, 61 percent were voluntary placements. Twenty-
four percent of Jamestown placements were involuntary separations, compared to 31 percent in Centralia, and enforced separations accounted for 7 percent of Jamestown cases and 8 percent of
Centralia's cases. A breakdown by categories was more revealing,
however. The institutions in Jamestown received mostly (68 percent) children under voluntary commitments by parents. In Centralia, institutions received mostly (74 percent) the child involuntarily removed and placed by agency and court action. We saw
previously that there was more returning home in Jamestown than
in Centralia. But in Jamestown an involuntarily removed child
accounted for one in five of the return home cases, while none of
the children who returned home in Centralia was initially involuntarily placed.

Generally, the court was more active in dependency cases in
child's rights Centralia than in Jamestown. It was particularly
more active in institutional placements (85 percent of them) and in
40 percent of cases where children returned home. In Jamestown
the parental-agency relationship, apart from court entanglements,
was a far more predominant situation in a setting which emphasized
parents' rights. There, the court was involved in only 23 percent
of institutional cases and in 22 percent of return home cases.

Physical and economic conditions were of greater importance at
time of child-parent separation in Jamestown—conditions which
tended to eventuate in voluntary placements by parents. Thus,
parental death, illness, or economic difficulty was the primary cause
of child separation in 36 percent of Jamestown cases but in only 15
percent of Centralia cases. Unwed motherhood ranked first among
the cases in Centralia, accounting for 30 percent of our cases; while
in Jamestown it accounted for only 18 percent. We have seen how

legal provisions for the protection of the child born out of wedlock
were in the forefront of the legal system in child's rights Centralia. Marital conflict and psychological crises were slightly more
prevalent as parental conditions at time of separation of child and
parents in Jamestown than in Centralia, accounting for 15 percent
of cases in Jamestown and only 9 percent in Centralia. In both
communities from one fourth to one fifth of removals were due to
parental neglect and abandonment.

Children were separated from their parents earlier in Centralia—
70 percent as preschoolers, compared to 46 percent in Jamestown.
Over half (54 percent) of Jamestown's cases involved separation
after age six, while only 30 percent of Centralia's cases involved
separation at these ages. Problems were recognized at an earlier
age and tackled earlier in Centralia; Jamestown was not so ready to
remove children. Parents in Jamestown might decide to place their
older children in institutions, where an educative as well as foster
care function was performed, yet manage to keep the younger ones
at home or with relatives. Then, too, the greater emphasis on adoption in Centralia accounted for more preschool placements there.

Children in care in Centralia were in care only a slightly longer
time than were children in care in Jamestown—a median of twenty-
six months, compared to twenty-four months for Jamestown. This
was true for the total population studied, despite the greater occurrence of adoption cases in Centralia, and also for each placement
category. The difference was greater when comparing children remaining in care than when comparing those leaving care. Added
to the fact that fewer children returned home in Centralia, these
data suggested that under some circumstances in a child's rights
community—for example, where professional perceptions are
brought to bear on the needs of a child and planning resources in
the community are perceived not to meet these needs—there may be
a resulting tendency toward a longer term care experience for the
child. Evaluation of the positive and negative aspects of such different situations calls for a closer, and a more controlled, examination of the consequences of total care experiences, in which time in
care itself is certainly one factor.

The patterns of movement out of care were reversed in these two communities. In Centralia, 22 percent of our April 1 cases were in adoption, and only 4 percent of all the children studied returned home during the six months from January 1 to June 30. In Jamestown, the adoption figure was only 6 percent, while the return home figure was 14 percent. These facts could be said to strengthen our impression of two legal systems, surrounded by other forces, in which different emphases on the child's rights or his parents' rights were manifest.

Thus, the state of the laws and the practices of those operating under them could be logically associated with some aspects of placement pattern. There were major variations in conditions at initial intake, obvious differences in the sanctioned settings and conditions of care, and variations in movement out of care. All these elements reflected trends in two quite different communities that had fashioned distinctive modes for caring for their dependent children.

12. The Agency Networks Serving the Two Areas

The 372 children of James County in our study were served by thirteen different child-placing agencies—more agencies than served any of the eight other communities which we visited. How did these thirteen agencies relate to one another? And what kind of network did the eight child welfare agencies serving Lake County form? How did two different networks operate in serving children in two different cultural settings?

THE NETWORK OF AGENCIES AND CHILD WELFARE SERVICES IN JAMES COUNTY

When an explanation of the apparent preference for institutional care in Jamestown was sought among agency directors and board members one element that was mentioned was the "demonstrability" of institutions. As one man phrased it, "institutions are the bricks and mortar of fund raising." For the visibility of the structures, together with the relative invisibility of the dependent children, seemed to typify the interagency situation with its segmented and far-flung agencies caring for the children in our James County population. A diagram of the agency picture is presented in Figure 5.

Five of the thirteen agencies in the diagram were within the confines of the county boundaries, and eight were outside. Four of these eight were in one community approximately a hundred

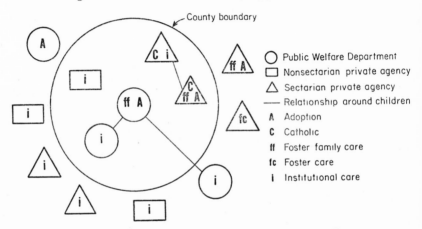

Figure 5. *JAMES COUNTY AGENCY NETWORK*

miles from Jamestown and the other four were scattered throughout the state. In spite of this multiplicity of agencies, 76 percent of the children studied were cared for by five agencies located within James County; the other 24 percent were distributed among the eight agencies outside the county. Characteristics of the individual agencies are outlined in Table 10.

No agencies within this network offered the three placement services of foster family, institutional, and adoptive placement. Nine agencies provided only one service, while the other four had two placement services. There was little adoption service among the thirteen agencies. Two of the agencies offering adoption were in James County, and two were outside. In line with the prepon-

Table 10

CHARACTERISTICS OF AGENCIES IN THE
JAMES COUNTY NETWORK

Agency (According to percentage of children under study served)	History	Services	Extent of Professional Education [a] of Staff	Spatial Factors
James County Department of Public Welfare (27%)	Organized 1923 (reorganized 1937); auspices public	Foster family care and adoption, for children 0–21 years of age	22% of staff (9 members)	Located at Jamestown; serves the county
Pine Glen Home (22%)	Organized 1790; auspices public	Institutional care, for white children 6–14 years of age	100% of staff (3 members)	Located in James County; serves Jamestown
Smith Children's Home (12%)	Organized 1891; auspices private (with city and county funds)	Institutional care, for Negro children 6–12 years of age	0% of staff (1 member)	Located in James County; no limits to area served
Jamestown Orphanage (11%)	Organized 1829; auspices private (with city funds)	Institutional care, for white, primarily Catholic, school-aged children	0% of staff (1 member)	Located at Jamestown; serves the city
Children's Services (7%)	Organized 1919 (reorganized 1930); auspices public	Adoption, for children 0–10 years of age (mostly infants)	50% of staff (6 members)	Located at Calhoun; serves the state
Annie Laurie Orphanage (4%)	Organized 1891; auspices private	Institutional and foster family care, for white children, Baptist preferred, 0–16 years of age	71% of staff (7 members)	Located at Gaines; serves the state
Catholic Child Welfare Services (4%)	Organized 1945; auspices private	Foster family care and adoption, for Catholic children 0–18 years of age	50% of staff (2 members)	Located at Jamestown; serves the state
Mark La Plante School (4%)	Organized 1797; auspices public	Institutional care, for white children 7–18 years of age	0% of staff (2 members)	Located at Meredith; serves the state

Table 10 (Continued)

Agency (According to percentage of children under study served)	History	Services	Extent of Professional Education [a] of Staff	Spatial Factors
Children's Home (3%)	Organized 1850; auspices private	Institutional care for white children, Episcopal preferred, 6 years of age through high school	0% of staff (1 member)	Located at Sumner; serves the state
Christian Home for Children (2%)	Organized 1894; auspices private	Institutional (limited foster family) care, for white children, Methodist preferred 6 years of age–adulthood (accepts 4-year-olds)	0% of staff (5 members)	Located at Calhoun; serves the state
Southern Home for Children (2%)	Organized 1909; auspices private (state grants)	Institutional care, for white children 4 years of age–adulthood	0% of staff (1 member)	Located at Calhoun; serves the state
Bailey Home for Orphans (1%)	Organized 1909; auspices private	Institutional care, for Negro girls 4 years of age through high school	0% of staff (volunteer workers)	Located at Calhoun; serves the state
Interstate Children's Aid (1%)	Organized 1876; auspices private	Foster family care and adoption, for Jewish children; no age limit	100% of staff (2 members)	Located at Georgetown, in neighboring state; serves 5 states

[a] One year or more of graduate study in social work.

derance of institutional care and the fact that there were many single-function agencies, a great deal of agency isolation could be noted in the total configuration. Religious segmentation existed as we had not seen it in other communities. Of the thirteen agencies, six were sectarian agencies, and four of these offered institutional care as their predominant service.

Additional services, not recorded, also presented a somewhat different aspect from that in other communities. Four agencies offered some service to children in their own homes. Two of these four agencies were within James County and two were outside. Five agencies offered protective services to the extent that they received complaints about neglected children from various community people or from ministers of their sponsoring churches and investigated to determine whether placement was necessary. A maternity home located in James County made its service available on a state-wide basis. The county Department of Public Welfare offered casework service and help in planning for mothers who were referred from welfare departments outside the area. In addition, four of the agencies offered casework services to unmarried mothers, and one agency was equipped to give financial aid to provide maternity and hospital care for an unmarried mother. Moreover, the county Department of Public Welfare also could pay for the care of an unmarried mother. The Catholic agency could help an unwed mother by securing free medical care from Catholic hospitals, but it provided no boarding or maternity home facilities. Also located in Jamestown was a mental health clinic which gave some service to children and families in the community.

Agency Antecedents and Present Bases in Jamestown

It must be pointed out that many agencies duplicated efforts as they served specific religious groups in Jamestown, and this situation meant that services were not, therefore, oriented toward a large general public. For James County was a setting in which the whole tended to be broken down into specific categories. Let us look at some of the elements which contributed to this situation.

History.—The oldest agency in the James County network, the first municipal institution for children in the country, was organized by Jamestown in 1790. Of the four earliest agencies, two were sectarian in sponsorship and two were under public auspices— one operated by the state and one operated by Jamestown. In the years after the Civil War four other agencies were established, only one of which was located in Jamestown but all of which served the city and county children of James. These services, too, were limited to institutional care, and, at one time, all these institutions provided education as well as custodial care. This was the period when private institutions, during and following Reconstruction days, became increasingly important as "preservers of a cultural heritage."

In 1909 two nonsectarian agencies were organized. One received a small subsidy from the State Legislature but was actually under private auspices. The other was for Negro girls and was quite small. Around 1920 two new public agencies appeared. One agency was located in the capital city and was authorized by the Governor and the Legislature to provide services, including adoptive services, for children. Shortly after the establishment of this state-wide agency Jamestown set up its own Department of Public Welfare which included limited child welfare operations. With the later passage of the Social Security Act and the establishment of the State Department of Public Welfare, the Jamestown department were reorganized and became a part of the state department, although it was still a county agency. Concurrent with this growth in public child welfare services under Federal, state, and county auspices, the original public agency began to limit its program until it became chiefly an adoption agency. These two agencies existed side by side, both publicly supported, with completely different patterns of organization and responsibility, although within the last two years the State Department of Public Welfare, through the county departments, had begun an adoptive service of its own.

The most recent addition to the interagency network in James County was Catholic Child Welfare Services. There was a perceived need for foster home and adoption service among the Catholic population, and the Church was concerned that such service should meet certain minimum standards. Thus Catholic Child Welfare Services came into being in 1945 for the Catholic population of the entire state, largely centered in Jamestown.

As our previous statements have intimated, the tradition in

James County as well as throughout the state had been toward provision of institutional care, usually under sectarian auspices. But the history of services in James was significant from another standpoint. The provision of public services for the care of neglected and dependent children as early as 1790 indicated a long-standing feeling of responsibility on the part of the community to provide for children in need of care. Not only had the tax-paying public supported certain programs over this long period of time, but the Catholic institution located in Jamestown also received a lump-sum subsidy from the city in order to care for dependent Catholic children. This responsibility had, for the most part, been taken on by the community without benefit of state or Federal funds. In addition to this emphasis on local responsibility there was a strong belief in this region, among sectarian agencies and groups, in the principle of separation of Church and State. Thus, there had been no development of a purchase-of-care plan by either the State Department of Public Welfare or by the James County welfare department.

Services.—Our description of Jamestown suggested that there was little interdependence of services that might lead to communication and collaboration among agencies either over issues or cases. Agency services tended to be crystallized around, and oriented toward, many segmented publics. It seems important to reiterate that experiencing citizenship in Jamestown was quite different from experiencing citizenship in a community like Centralia. In Jamestown the individual was perhaps most significantly a part of a definitive segment of the whole community. And the agencies which had grown through the years still tended toward providing general services to their own specific clienteles.

Discussion with executives and staffs of agencies revealed some of the deterrents to communication which this pattern of services entailed. One executive of an agency in Jamestown said: "Agencies don't get together on an organized basis but generally as they come across joint cases." A staff member at the Department of Public Welfare said: "Few children are referred to institutions from the department. When this is done the case is closed after the child is placed." Even the communication that we did note in James County was usually on the basis of a referral which did not involve a continuing responsibility by the referring agency, so that no joint work was entailed. In addition, with no public agency purchase-of-care plan each agency assumed total responsibility for the children in its care. Agencies spoke of this situation with pride. Said one executive: "You won't find much transferring back and forth here. One agency 'sticks with the child.' " Also to be noted was the fact that most children came to institutions directly upon application of parents—they were not referred from other agencies. In many ways, then, the lack of interagency transactions tended to deter communication and collaboration.

Extent of professionalization of agency.—There were two agencies in the network whose entire staff had completed some or all of their social work education. The Jewish agency, which was located in an adjoining state but served James County too, had a fully professionally trained staff. It served primarily severely disturbed children. The Pine Glen institution also operated with a staff all members of which had some graduate social work training. However, although the Department of Public Welfare had the largest child welfare staff (nine members), less than one fourth of them had any training. Children's Services, in Jamestown, operated with the second-largest child welfare staff, and half had had training. The small Negro institution had almost no paid staff, most of the work being done by volunteers. The total picture showed seven agencies out of thirteen having no trained staff whatsoever. These disparities certainly did not contribute to the emergence of a "professional culture" which might serve as a basis for freer communication through shared professional ideas and values.

Spatial factors.—At first glance, physical distance would also appear to be a major barrier to collaboration. Agencies were widely scattered. And Jamestown itself has been described as a relatively isolated community. There was evidence that geographical separation did strengthen the tendency toward the "narrowing circle" common in this region, but physical distance did not seem to be the major deterrent to collaboration. For even agencies located within Jamestown did not all relate to one another. The Department of Public Welfare seemed to be the chief source of communication. The only other collaborative relationship was that which we have shown between the two Catholic agencies.

Perhaps, in summary, the concept of "separateness" can be used to organize our thinking about patterns of agency care in James County. Racial segregation was just one part of this process. The separateness of the Negroes tended to regulate their behavior as a group with certain aggregate, ascribed characteristics; it did not lead to an approach to their problems on the basis of individual (perhaps achieved) characteristics. And it must be noted that the placement of a dependent child in Jamestown was always influenced by the child's gross (perhaps ascribed) social characteristics—a reflection of the same separating categories which affected so large a share of other aspects of life in Jamestown. Such factors as place of residence, religious affiliation, age, and race were prime considerations in placement. The presence of segmentation such as this emphasizes the atmosphere of separateness and insulation in which agency care in James County was carried on.

THE NETWORK OF AGENCIES AND CHILD WELFARE SERVICES IN
LAKE COUNTY

Some twenty-five miles from Centralia, farther north along main railroad lines over which sixty-five passenger trains passed daily, was the large metropolitan center of Indianola which was the hub of professional services for this East North-central state. There specialized legal and medical, as well as social welfare, consultation was available within an hour's journey from Centralia's unimposing business district. One did not need to explore too far to sense that the major ties of this "typically American" community were with the larger metropolis. The rural backlands west of Centralia, where the county boundaries were the most distant from the city limits, remained relatively unserviced and remote from the city of Centralia. The flow of traffic and of sociocultural values

was along a north-south axis. But this flow did not wash over
Centralia unimpeded and unchanged. Centralia had ways of doing
things that were its own. It had social welfare services of its own.
This picture of a community both proud of local values and
methods yet influenced by, and accepting of, external ones is represented in our diagram in Figure 6 of the network of agency services in Lake County.

The eight agencies of the Lake County network were equally
divided between those within the county and those outside. There

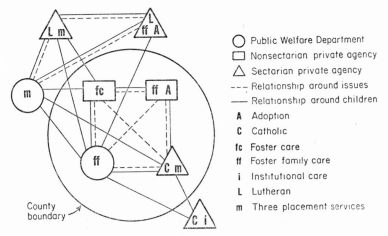

Figure 6. LAKE COUNTY AGENCY NETWORK

were four agencies, among the eight, serving almost equal proportions of our children—each caring for between 17 percent and 25
percent of the total. The other four agencies served small numbers
of our children, dividing approximately 15 percent of all cases
among them. Sixty-seven percent of the children under study were
cared for by agencies within the county, and the remaining 33 percent were cared for by agencies situated outside the county. All
the outside agencies were located in the near-by metropolitan
center to the north. Table 11 indicates some characteristics of the
eight agencies involved in this network.

In the interagency network in Lake County there were only two
single-function agencies: one, the local public welfare department

which offered only foster family care; and the other, the Catholic institution for boys caring for an extremely small proportion of our children. Three agencies offered multiple or three-placement services, while the other three offered not only foster family care but one other placement service, either adoption or institutional care.

Our diagram also shows that of the eight agencies four were sectarian and, therefore, served specific segments of the public.

Table 11

CHARACTERISTICS OF AGENCIES IN THE
LAKE COUNTY NETWORK

Agency (According to percentage of children under study served)	History	Services	Extent of Professional Education [a] of Staff	Spatial Factors
State Department of Public Welfare (23%)	Organized 1921 (reorganized 1947); auspices public	Foster family and institutional care, adoption for children 0–21 years of age	75% of staff (8 members)	Located at Indianola; serves 4 counties
Catholic Children's Agency (22%)	Organized 1924; auspices private	Institutional and foster family care, adoption, for Catholic children 0–14 years of age	100% of staff (1 member)	Located at Centralia; serves 2 counties (part of diocesan agency)
Lake County Department of Public Welfare (21%)	Organized 1932 (reorganized 1956); auspices public	Foster family care, for children 0–21 years of age	33% of staff (3 members)	Located at Centralia; serves the county
Graham Home (17%)	Organized 1868; auspices private	Institutional and foster family care, for children 0–18 years of age	67% of staff (3 members)	Located at Centralia; serves the county primarily
Lutheran Service Society (9%)	Organized 1936; auspices private	Foster family care and adoption, for children, National Conference–Lutheran preferred, 0–21 years of age	94% of staff (18 members)	Located at Indianola; serves the state

Table 11 (Continued)

Agency (According to percentage of children under study served)	History	Services	Extent of Professional Education [a] of Staff	Spatial Factors
Children's Aid Society (5%)	Organized 1889; auspices private	Foster family care and adoption, for children 0–18 years of age	100% of staff (1 member)	Located at Centralia; serves 3 counties (part of state-wide agency)
Lutheran Homefinding Society (2%)	Organized 1896; auspices private	Foster family and institutional care, adoption, for Synodical Conference–Lutheran children 0–18 years of age	61% of staff (13 members)	Located at Indianola; serves the state
St. Vincent's Home for Boys (0.3%)	Organized 1920; auspices private	Institutional care, for boys, primarily Catholic, 6th through 9th grade	100% of staff (3½ members)	Located at Indianola; serves 10 counties (diocese)

[a] One year or more of graduate study in social work.

These four agencies care for one third of our population, and indications were that in spite of serving specific religious groups these agencies used the services of other agencies when necessary. All the agencies outside Lake County served the whole state. The two branch offices of outside agencies in Centralia served two or three counties.

Services to children other than placement services may also be seen in the total community picture. Six of the eight agencies offered casework services to unmarried mothers. There was no maternity home within Lake County, but mothers could be helped to plan and could receive service within the county. None of the agencies actually operated a maternity home, but agencies were able to refer easily for maternity home care. The county Department of Public Welfare could provide financial aid to unmarried mothers in their own homes and could also purchase care for county residents in maternity homes. Two agencies could also provide wage home or foster family home care for unmarried mothers. If the unmarried mother were a nonresident of the state, the public agency, operated by the State Department of Public Welfare, could use Federal funds for maternity care, subject to certain regulations such as commitment to the agency and the qualification that the unwed mother must be a minor. All illegitimate births had, by law, to be reported to the State Department of Public Welfare, and this agency in turn reported to the appropriate county. The law made communication between the state and county offices necessary and also made financial as well as casework help for all unmarried mothers mandatory.

Protective services to neglected and abandoned children were offered by the county Department of Public Welfare. Upon complaint of someone in the community, this department would work with a family, hoping to help them meet community standards without necessitating placement. There was also a child guidance clinic, financed by the county public welfare department. The clinic was available to the community as a whole primarily for diagnostic and consultative services but it could also accept a small number of children and parents for treatment.

Agency Antecedents and Present Bases in Centralia

What lay behind the relatively collaborative network in Lake County which Figure 6 has pictured?

History.—In 1868, more than twenty years prior to the establishment of any other services in Lake County, Graham Home was organized as an institutional facility to care for orphans. But as early as 1896 one of the Lutheran agencies in our study was founded specifically to offer foster family home care. There were, thus, precedents in Lake County to the emphasis on a variety of services. And this emphasis on more than one kind of service was expressed in the total network of services available to children and also in services provided within the individual agencies, since all but two offered more than one kind of placement.

While private agencies' services had a long history in the state it was also true that within a short period—from 1920 to 1936—the bulk of its social services, both public and private, were organized, so that in many respects the agencies in Lake County had developed simultaneously. There was an arrangement whereby a public agency could purchase service from a private agency even though there were certain limitations to the ways in which public funds could be used. Both state and county funds were available to support not only children directly under the care of the public agencies but children serviced by private agencies as well.

The history of child welfare services in Lake County seemed to indicate a pattern of encouragement of the growth of many services. No one religious group had been dominant, and neither public nor private factions had been dominant. One might conclude that the climate was conducive for the growth of agencies to serve professionally perceived needs.

Services.—Since several agencies provided the same kinds of services, even though their clientele might be limited to a particular religion or to a particular county, a basis for collaboration was established when their very existence encouraged shared information and ideas. For example, issues which arose over practices or the charging of fees were matters for discussion among all adoption agencies. One agency representative in Centralia said: "There is a variety of child-placing agencies, and if one agency is stumped for placement resources it may call other agencies for help." There were also committees in Centralia, under the auspices of the Welfare Council, which brought about participation by both child welfare and other agencies. Then, too, as one executive pointed out, there was a natural alignment of private agencies located within the community and the Lutheran agencies which served the community but were not located there. These agencies shared problems and exchanged referrals. On the other hand, as the same executive mentioned, "the public agencies have not been that close, although we work frequently with them since they are a source of many of our cases."

Extent of professionalization of agency.—We may note in Table 11 that regardless of size or auspices, no agency within the network had no professionally trained workers. The percentages of workers

with training varied considerably, but those agencies which were
not fully staffed with professional workers were making efforts to
recruit trained staff and to gear their programs toward more professional services.   In fact, one agency which, because of lack of
finances and lack of staff, felt that it could give intensive service to
only six children had limited its institutional program to just six
children.   The Graham Home had modified and changed its program to focus more completely on care of children with emotional
disturbances.   The Catholic Children's Agency formerly provided
institutional care to preschool children.   However, in line with
professional thinking that institutional care is damaging to preschool children, the institution had been closed.

Spatial factors.—Four of the agencies in the Lake County configuration were located outside the county.   Even so, physical distance did not seem to promote remoteness from other agencies in
the network.   The director of the Lake County welfare department
did point out that the factor of distance between Centralia and
Indianola sometimes made referrals difficult because it was hard to
"get hold of the worker, particularly in the Lutheran agencies."
This had seemed to lead to "getting together over issues" being
limited to the agencies with offices within Centralia.   But agencies
outside the county were used, and collaboration was primarily on
the basis of cases.

Common language, common goals, and common philosophy,
then, tended to promote collaboration and mutual acquaintance
among agencies which shared problems, cases, and values.   With
agencies working toward the same goals, and offering many of the
same types of services to similar groups (even though not organized
to provide specialized services to a general public), we would expect that agencies would be brought together to work out problems
of policy and to plan for specific children.

NETWORK COMPARISONS AND THE FACTS OF PLACEMENT—
JAMESTOWN AND CENTRALIA

In spite of the fact that there was wide variation between Jamestown and Centralia in patterns of communication and interagency

network, these great differences did not show up in many of the factors of placement. Let us begin our presentation of placement experiences and the interagency networks where we left off in our discussion of the legal systems—with a look at movement out of care.

Movement out of care in noncollaborative Jamestown was consistently more oriented toward return home to parents with whom "separated" agencies tended to maintain ties. In addition to the trend shown in figures cited previously we note this tendency in the figures for the nine-month period following April 1 which show that of all those leaving care only 29 percent went into adoption while 63 percent returned home. Conversely, in Centralia during the same period 58 percent of those leaving care went into adoption, and 28 percent returned home. In more collaborative Centralia, referrals between agencies often occurred in this planning which consistently tended to move more children toward adoption.

The time-in-care situation was one of more similarity than difference when explored beyond the total median time in care which indicated an average of a few months longer for Centralia. Median time in current placement was eleven months for both communities. Jamestown had a larger proportion (41 percent) in care less than two years than did Centralia (34 percent), but each community had a similar proportion in care six years and over—22 percent in Jamestown, 25 percent in Centralia. The mid-length period was more predominant (41 percent) in Centralia, but Jamestown had fully 37 percent of its cases grouped at this interval of years also. We must conclude that collaboration among relatively more professional agencies did not, just as a child's rights orientation did not, shorten the time in care for Centralia children as compared to Jamestown children.

A far greater proportion of children in Centralia than in Jamestown had had more than one placement and more than one type of placement. In Centralia, only 20 percent had had one placement only, compared to 51 percent in Jamestown, while 40 percent had had more than one type of placement, compared to 29 percent in Jamestown. At the same time, 21 percent of the Centralia children had had four or more placements while only 9 percent of the Jamestown children had had four or more placements. Again, more professional agencies providing more diversified services in a collaborative network contributed to more placement experiences within care for Centralia's dependent children.

Sequences of movement also revealed differences in the two networks. While children were as likely to have moved out of foster families to a different type of placement in their care experiences in Jamestown as in Centralia—25 percent compared to 23 percent who had had this experience in Centralia—they were much less likely ever to have moved out of an institution into some other type of placement, 11 percent against 28 percent in Centralia. In non-collaborative Jamestown, institutional care was considered for long-term planning, while foster family care was for temporary planning. In collaborative Centralia, institutions were used more for specific problems of specific children, while foster family care was used for long-term placement. But the different set of values did not increase the relative movement out of foster families in Jamestown as compared to Centralia in the way that it appeared to increase the relative movement out of institutions in Centralia as compared to Jamestown.

Generally, our two total configurations and their placement patterns reflect different milieus. There was a continued faith in Jamestown in the value of institutions and a tradition that groups should take care of their own. The circle of the "we" was drawn around many subgroups in this community and its environs. At the same time, there was a pride in autonomy in Jamestown and a set of forces operating there that seemed to narrow the circle of trust, as it narrowed circles of acquaintance, for participants in the community while it kept agencies and families closer together. In Centralia, a professional set of values tended to permeate the whole welfare world just as common goals and values tended to permeate the larger social world of the community. People in Centralia had shared many experiences, involving change and growth, in the history of the community. And in the ongoing process, by which things which were different became part of an interdependent whole

in Centralia, a faith had developed in relatively uniform answers to
meet problems which were also seen as relatively uniform. Certainly, professional services to children in Centralia, while not highly
specialized, were based on far different perceptions of children's
needs than those which obtained in Jamestown. At the same time,
those who participated in the drama of dependency in these two
communities doubtless had somewhat different bases of determining their self-identities in the two distinctive cultures.

13. *The Children and Their Parents*

The varying cultures, legal systems, and agency networks of Jamestown and Centralia provided quite different configurations of foster
care and adoptive placements in these two communities. And in
the Old South and in Middle America social forms and processes
in foster care tended to be distinct from those in adoption. In
Jamestown foster care usually meant custodial care in an institution. In Centralia, professional agencies were quite actively en-
gaged in caring for dependent children, mostly in foster families
where local people had opened their doors to the city's children.
Adoption through an agency was not usual in Jamestown; it occurred much more frequently in Centralia. How did foster care
in these two communities compare in light of the possibilities for
permanent planning for children—either for return home or for
adoption—in each setting?

PLACEMENT HISTORIES OF THE CHILDREN IN FOSTER CARE [1]

More than in any other community, death, illness, and economic
hardship were the precipitators of foster care placement in Jamestown. Neglect and abandonment were next in importance. All in
all, however, voluntary separation of children and parents, in which
the parents themselves often selected the institution of placement,
was the predominant situation in Jamestown.

[1] See footnote 1, Chapter 5, regarding the base for percentages in this chapter.

As we have mentioned, institutional care was the usual type of placement in Jamestown—just as in Norden and Summit—and many institutions were involved. Almost 60 percent of the foster care children in Jamestown were first separated from their parents as school-aged children—one in four at age eleven or older—and this high rate of late separations was surpassed only by our two rural communities and by "institutional" Summit. The average age at separation of the child in institutional care in Jamestown was seven years. Institutions usually could not take preschool children, and parents often had to wait for a placement until children reached school age. Moreover, Jamestown children moved infrequently after their initial placement. Slightly over one half of them had only one placement, and only one in ten had had four or more placements—a picture of little movement in care surpassed, again, only by Summit. In Jamestown the average length of time in institutional care was 2.6 years—much longer than Summit but much shorter than in Norden. There was little adoption but considerable return home to parents taking place in Jamestown. And where adoption did occur, 64 percent of it represented placements outside the county. The ratio of adoption to return home movement for Jamestown was 1 to 3 in a nine-month period following April 1. We saw, then, that the Jamestown placement pattern was an institutional one somewhere between the short term of Summit and the long term of Norden. It was set against a background of economically deprived and conflictful home situations to which, nevertheless, children often returned after a stay at the institution to which their parents had entrusted them.

Centralia presented a contrast in which neglect and abandonment and separations, both involuntary and enforced, were predominant. Centralia had a lower proportion (45 percent) of voluntary separations than did any of our other communities. It seemed that an active professional welfare group which applied fairly uniform standards to families in this relatively prosperous and homogeneous community and a newly codified juvenile law with few gaps or omissions were largely responsible for this highlight in the Centralia placement picture.

The Centralia children were usually cared for in foster families, and only two of every ten in care on April 1 were in an institution. The children studied in Centralia also became dependent at an earlier age. Fifty-nine percent in Centralia were first separated from their parents prior to their sixth birthdays, and this was a higher proportion of preschool separations than was found in any community except economically poor and ethnically divided La Paz. Once in care, moreover, children moved much more frequently in placement in Centralia than in Jamestown. Half of them had moved two or three times, and the rest had experienced, in equal proportions, either one placement only or four or more moves. Centralia's children in foster family care were in care, on the average, much longer than Jamestown's and those in institutional placement were in care twice as long. The predominant category—foster family care—showed a placement average of 2.3 years in such families at the time of our study in Centralia. Institutions were used somewhat selectively in Centralia, and the 20 percent of dependent children who were in institutions on April 1 had been in care an average of 5.3 years.

Few children were returning home in Centralia—a lower proportion than in any community except our two rural ones—but a sizable proportion were being placed in adoptive homes by agencies. Actually, there was the same amount of movement out of care noted for Centralia as for Jamestown in the nine months following April 1; but in Centralia, five children moved into adoption for every three who returned home in that period. Meanwhile, large numbers remained in the foster families where they had been placed after removal from homes which the community and its welfare and legal agents considered inadequate.

THE CHILDREN'S OWN FAMILIES

What conditions in the children's own families seemed related to the rates of return home, higher in Jamestown than in Centralia? When children returned home, did they go back to families that resembled normal families in the community more than they resembled families of children who remained in care? What were the children and families like?

Comparison of the situations of the Jamestown children who returned home with the situations of the Jamestown children who were still in care yielded fewer differences than similar comparison in most of the other communities produced. In this respect Jamestown was most like Summit but quite different from Centralia. Compared to children still in care, Jamestown children who returned home were somewhat more likely to have been separated from their parents on the latters' volition (74 percent compared to 61 percent) and less likely to have been separated involuntarily (18 percent compared to 28 percent). Conditions of parents at separation from their children were much the same in the two groups—death, illness, and economic hardship were just as frequent—but neglect and abandonment were slightly less prevalent in the return home cases in Jamestown. The children who went home, however, were much older when first separated—an average of eleven years, compared to seven years for the child still in an institution—and they had stayed in care almost a year less than the average child who remained in an institution. Parents were likely to be divorced and to be living with a spouse, presumably a new one, but not living alone or with relatives. Mothers were more likely to be housewives and fathers to be fairly well educated among return home cases in Jamestown. On the other hand, almost all these children, like those remaining in care, had minor brothers or sisters. A discriminating factor was the physical proximity of fathers (but not of mothers), for in 77 percent of return home cases the father lived in the same county as the child and had no problem visiting, while this was true in only 47 percent of cases of children remaining in care. Thus, the child returning home entered care an older child in Jamestown although he had been in care a shorter time; he was a child, evidently, for whom institutional care was no longer needed.

The Jamestown children in foster care included a greater proportion for whom long-term care (or no other plan) was desired by parents than was found in any community except Norden. Almost twice the proportion were in such a situation in Jamestown as in Centralia; however, when the groups for whom parents' plans were conflicted and resolutions seemed unlikely were added to the long-term care groups, Jamestown and Centralia seemed to have equal proportions (54 percent) of their dependent children in limbo. Despite the extent of voluntary placements noted in Jamestown, almost 60 percent of the children were in a situation in which neither parent visited, or visited, at most, infrequently; while only one out of seven fathers and one out of four mothers were described as having an adequate relationship with the agency. Since the parents of all children who returned home had paid nothing toward their support, such payment in Jamestown could not be cited as evidence of interest adumbrating parents' removing their children from care—quite the reverse! Even with these situations, however, a greater proportion (43 percent) of Jamestown's dependent children still had affectionate ties to their parents than was noted in any other community except Summit (Centralia had only 24 percent recorded in this manner). But almost twice as many of those who returned home as of those who remained in care in Jamestown retained affectionate relations with their parents.

Social characteristics of the Jamestown parents whose children were in foster care compare interestingly with what we know about the total population in that community. Approximately 75 percent of the parents were white and Protestant. Catholics were represented about as frequently as Negroes but, of course, much more in line with their over-all representation in the total population. Negro parents, in spite of their being members of a segment that was extremely depressed socioeconomically, were underrepresented on the child dependency rolls, compared to their ratio in the total population. Interestingly, when Negro families did have their children placed in foster care, such children were about as likely to be adopted as were white children in Jamestown; but the Negro children were much less likely to return home than to be adopted and were even less likely to return home than were the white children in this community.

Jamestown fathers of children in foster care averaged about forty years of age, and mothers averaged close to thirty-five. Health and physical condition of parents were considered good in 80 percent of the cases. In four out of ten cases parents were divorced or separated, and in another one fourth of cases one parent was dead. However, 43 percent of the fathers and 33 percent of the mothers were either living with the other parent or with a new spouse. Thus agencies could look toward two-parent homes for over one third of their children in planning a return home for the child in foster care. An interesting contrast appeared in evaluations of parents' intelligence and education: agencies perceived three fourths of the fathers, but only about one third of the mothers, as having average intelligence or better; but fathers averaged only a seventh-grade education, while mothers, on the average, had achieved the tenth grade in schooling. The largest proportion of fathers (39 percent) were skilled workers, and the next largest proportion (29 percent) were laborers. It was noted, however, that in no instance when a child returned home was the father a laborer. Similarly, most mothers of children in foster care were working women—only 32 percent were recorded as housewives —but 56 percent of the mothers of the children who returned home in Jamestown were housewives. Generally, parents of Jamestown children in foster care seemed to be in barely adequate circumstances, but a smaller proportion of them seemed very poor than in Centralia. At the same time, in only one in ten cases in Jamestown was there said to be no sleeping space available at home for the child—and many children returned home—while in over half of Centralia's cases there was said to be no sleeping space available, and, as we have seen, very few children returned home to Centralia's families.

The Centralia children who returned home contrasted greatly with those in foster care. All of them were voluntarily placed in this community where, more than in any other, voluntary placement was least prevalent. Also, none of the Centralia children returning home had been first separated from his parents because of neglect and abandonment, and marital conflict was three times as prevalent as a precipitating condition among these cases as among the cases remaining in care. Children who returned home were in care a shorter time—two years—but not much less time than were the children still in foster family placements; and the children returning home first entered care a year older in life on the average, than did the children still in foster families. All children returning home in Centralia had retained affectionate ties to their parents (compared to only 24 percent of those remaining in care). In 80 percent of return home cases parents were divorced or separated; the remaining 20 percent had never married. Most fathers were living with a spouse, and most mothers were living alone or with other adults. The absence of brothers and sisters for children returning home was five times more prevalent in Centralia than in Jamestown. And in 80 percent of Centralia's return home cases, parents had been paying at least something toward the cost of the child's care—a significant item in a community which valued economic responsibility. Thus, Centralia's few return home children did not return to the large, economically deprived families that greeted their foster care brethren in Jamestown. Centralia's younger dependent children returned to a small family, broken by divorce or separation, or perhaps to a mother who had never married; but none ever returned to a home where neglect or abandonment, as perceived by legal and welfare agents of the community, had brought about the involuntary separation of children and parents.

Why did so few children return home in Centralia? Let us look further at the children in foster care. Twenty-eight percent of Centralia's children in foster care had parental clearance for adoption, and for only 9 percent was return home definitely desired by parents. (Only La Paz had a lower proportion for whom return home was desired.) Thus, over half of Centralia's children in foster care were in the limbo where parents either had no plans or had unresolved conflict in their plans for them. Parents visited even more infrequently in Centralia than in Jamestown. Of all our communities Centralia had the highest proportion of fathers who did not visit or visited very infrequently. And Centralia had few parents of children in care who had continuing relationships with agencies. The lowest proportion (5 percent) of mothers who had an adequate relationship with the agency was found, and this was but one third of the proportion so recorded for the community (La Paz) next lowest on this variable. In 50 percent of the cases the parents of Centralia's dependent children paid nothing toward support. These tendencies did not point toward movement out of care through return home.

How did the social characteristics of these parents appear in this prosperous, achieving, homogeneous community? In ethnicity they were like most everyone in Centralia. In religious affiliation, it appeared that Catholics were slightly overrepresented (39 percent of fathers and 33 percent of mothers) and Lutherans somewhat underrepresented (5 percent of fathers and 16 percent of mothers) in comparison to their estimated numbers in the total population. Parents in Centralia were about the same age as their counterparts in Jamestown—fathers about forty-one and mothers about thirty-six, on the average. No more of these parents than in Jamestown had physical health problems, but more children in foster care in Centralia (17 percent) had one or both parents deceased. Interestingly, agencies in Centralia seemed to perceive many of the fathers and mothers as below average in intelligence, although fathers averaged an eleventh-grade education and mothers averaged only a year or two less. This rather harsh situation was found in families where the greatest proportion (36 percent) of fathers were skilled workers, 28 percent were unskilled, 29 percent of mothers did household work, 18 percent did clerical work, and only 26 percent were housewives. Being a housewife apparently did not increase the chances for a mother to have her child returned in Centralia as it did in Jamestown, for only 20 percent of the mothers whose children returned home were recorded as housewives. About four in ten of Centralia's parents of children in foster care were divorced or separated, but a similar proportion of both mothers and fathers was currently living with a spouse at the time of our study. Far fewer mothers in Centralia than in Jamestown were still living alone—19 percent, compared to 36 percent. As previously reported, more of Centralia's families of children in foster care than of Jamestown's were said to be in very poor economic circumstances, although our information indicated that in any absolute comparison (except, perhaps, in living space and housing), the Centralia parents were socially and economically less deprived than their Jamestown counterparts. But in the Middle Region of the U.S.A., as contrasted to the Old South, parents who were seen to have failed as citizens and as parents had little likelihood of receiving their children back home; for their role as parents was more a community-wide issue just as their role as citizens involved them more on a community-wide stage.

THE CHILDREN AND ADOPTION

What image did adoptive parents have of the adoptable child in the Old South and in Middle America? We can explore this question to some degree by taking note of the characteristics of the average child who was adopted in Jamestown and in Centralia. How different were these children from those who remained in foster care? How much would the popular image of the adoptable child have to be changed in order that more of our children might find permanent adoptive homes in these two settings? Our findings suggest some answers—and pose some further questions.

In Jamestown boys and girls were adopted with about equal frequency, but in every case adoption involved infants or very young children. More than in any other community, the child placed in adoption through an agency in Jamestown tended to be an infant. Over 90 percent of such placements were of children under age two, and no case involved a child as old as five. The conviction that adoption is for the parent who desires a baby to raise from infancy still seemed to prevail among agency adoptive parents in Jamestown.

Ethnicity figures represented some interesting findings in Jamestown. Divided ethnic groups are often presumed to compound the problems of adoption in a community by making it more difficult to match "like" parents with "like" children. However, segmented and separated Jamestown placed proportionately as many Negro children in adoption as it brought into foster care from the total population. In other words, segments supplied dependent children and then absorbed their own in adoption so that, although agency adoption was not prevalent in any group in Jamestown, a Negro child had as good a chance as a white child of being adopted *once he came into care*. But we saw that Negro children were greatly underrepresented in the foster care population over all—about half the children from birth to age nineteen in Jamestown were Negro, but Negro children accounted for only 20 percent of our foster care population. However, Negro children were adopted proportionally as often as white—22 percent of all recorded agency adoptions. Catholics were also proportionately represented in agency adoptions in line with their numbers in the foster care population in Jamestown.

All the agency-placed adopted children in Jamestown were considered of normal intelligence, and none had a serious physical disability or health problem, although over one fourth had slight and remediable disabilities. These were very young and attractive children, showing no evidence of any ties to parents or other family members, completely free, legally, for adoption. Only one case in twenty-five manifested any psychological symptoms, and in only one case out of five were there brothers or sisters. In effect, the Jamestown child placed in adoption through an agency was almost as different from the average child in foster care as an infant is from a teen-ager.

Agency adoption in Centralia, according to our figures, was three times more prevalent in absolute numbers than in Jamestown and, considering that James County actually had a somewhat larger population than Lake County, the disparity in incidence of placements per person or family was even greater. About one half of Centralia's agency adoptive placements were made outside the county (compared to about two thirds of Jamestown's). In Centralia the ratio of boys to girls in agency adoptive placements was almost 3 to 2, but this reflected their exact proportions in the city's foster care population. Centralia was also placing some older children, although the average age of the adopted child was just one year; one in ten of Centralia's agency adoptive placements was of a child five years old or over. Still, 82 percent were of infants under two years of age.

All the adoptive children were considered at least average in in-

telligence. No more of them than in Jamestown had health or
physical disability problems.   One in twelve manifested some
psychological symptoms, which doubtless appeared in the older
children. Two out of five had minor brothers or sisters.

A few children being placed by agencies in adoption in Centralia
were of minority ethnicity.   One out of ten was either Spanish-
American or of mixed ethnicity. However, no Negro child fell into
our sample of agency adoptions, and of course there were not many
Negro families in that city. The religious representation in adoption seemed to reflect the agency set-up rather than group representation in this mid-region community. Protestants and Catholics were equally represented in the foster care populations, with
Lutherans—recorded separately—accounting for the remaining 20
percent in foster care.   But the specifically sectarian label appeared more predominantly in the adoption picture.   Lutherans
accounted for 30 percent of agency adoptions, the number of Catholics rose to 44 percent, and those classified as Protestant accounted
for only 26 percent of agency adoptions. Apparently the sectarian
agencies, even in interdependent Centralia, were aiming toward
their own sectarian publics in their adoption programs and dominated adoptions more than they did the foster care picture in the
community. But in a community in which years of growth and
shared achievement had, as we stated earlier, cast most of the people
in the same moral mold, there were signs in adoption of community-
wide tolerances of the older child and the child who was somewhat
different.   In Centralia these cross-community tolerances might
never be taxed to the degree they could be in a highly segmented
community. But in finding permanent homes for more children
Centralia agencies seemed in a position to capitalize upon a long-
standing recognition of the importance of family life and, perhaps,
upon a growing emphasis on the achievement of parenthood in
that community.

How different were the characteristics and the situations of
children who remained in care from those of children who were
adopted?

We may highlight the foster care configuration in Jamestown

more completely. Boys outnumbered girls three to two in foster care in Jamestown, although this disparity did not hold for adoption. Of course, a most important disparity between children still in foster care and those in adoption was age—the average age of those in foster care being ten and a half years, with only 7 percent under two years of age. We have already noted that minority ethnicity constituted no more of a barrier to adoption than it did to foster care placement in Jamestown. Below average intelligence, however, was recorded for one fourth of Jamestown's foster care cases but was never noted in adoption cases. Minor physical disability actually appeared slightly less prevalent, proportionately, among Jamestown's children in foster care than among those in adoptive homes, and physical health problems were practically nonexistent in both groups.

We might expect psychological symptoms—concomitant with greater age and varied experiences in care—to appear much more frequently in the children remaining in care than in those adopted. This was definitely the situation in Jamestown where such symptoms were ten times more prevalent in the group still in foster care. Along with this we found confusion over a sense of self-identity in more than half the children in foster care but undetected, if existing, in any adoptive child. There were minor brothers or sisters in over 90 percent of the cases (with affectionate bonds to siblings in more than half of these instances), and strong, affectionate relationships with parents more frequently among Jamestown's children in foster care (43 percent of the cases) than in any other community except Summit. Furthermore, the Jamestown children in foster care tended to be tied to their natural parents legally, for the parental rights of more of them (59 percent) were completely unmodified and fewer children (6 percent) had been completely freed for adoption than was true in any of our other communities. Compared to the infants placed in adoption in Jamestown—96 percent of them born to unwed mothers and all legally free for adoption—the older child in foster care, with his many and perhaps confusing ties to parents and siblings as well as to people in his institutional or foster home world, presented a far different configuration of social-psychological forces in that old and slowly changing community. Not only was he very different from the adoptive child in Jamestown, but it seems doubtful whether, in the eyes of his natural parents, agencies, and prospective adoptive parents, he was ever remotely considered a candidate for adoption in that community.

By comparison, the total situation of the Centralia child in foster care seemed more like that of the adopted child than of the return home child in that community, although it was certainly very different from either, on the average—in much the same way that the Jamestown foster care child seemed more like the return home child than like the adopted child in his community. The implications of this statement bear upon differences between the two cultures and upon differences in their welfare practices, which all of our preceding analyses have dramatized. In noting that the average Jamestown child in foster care more nearly resembled the return home child in Jamestown than the average Centralia child in foster care resembled the adopted child in Centralia, we mean to suggest that movement back to a child's own home is easier to facilitate in Jamestown than movement to adoption can be facilitated for most children in foster care in Centralia.

The Centralia child in foster care averaged about the same age as his counterpart in Jamestown—much older, of course, than the average adopted child. But we saw at least a few adoptions of ten-year olds in Centralia, and ten was the average age of the foster care population. Proportions of the two sexes in foster care were exactly the same as in adoption—57 percent boys, 43 percent girls. Ethnicity too was represented about the same in foster care and adoption. Although one Negro child appeared in our foster care sample and none was adopted, actually a slightly larger proportion of other minority or mixed ethnicity children were adopted than was represented in foster care in Centralia. We have already noted that religious affiliation showed a greater Catholic and Lutheran emphasis in adoption than in foster care. Otherwise, the characteristics of average or better intelligence, good physical health, and no physical disability were only slightly less prevalent in the foster care group than in the adoption group in Centralia, and none of these elements, except serious and irremediable physical disability, could be considered a major deterrent to adoption in that community. Of course, psychological symptoms appeared frequently in the older foster care group to the same degree as in Jamestown, but they also appeared in a few more of Centralia's adoption cases (8 percent, compared to 4 percent in Jamestown). Affectionate relationships to parents were apparent with only 24 percent of Centralia's foster care children, while bonds with brothers and sisters appeared strong with only 37 percent (and in 20 percent of adoption cases too), full parental rights were retained by parents of only 20 percent, and only 15 percent had been completely freed for adoption. Centralia's children in foster care were almost as old, on the average, as Jamestown's but they had far fewer emotional and legal ties to their families than did the children in Jamestown.

The Centralia community, through its professional welfare agents, was reaching out quite actively to children who were the victims of inadequate home environments. Still, the children taken into care by these programs which tended to bespeak the conscience of a whole community were not, predominantly, moving toward the permanent, and improved, home situations desired for them. At the time of our study, 67 percent of these children were reported to be confused about their worth, place, and direction—a slightly greater proportion than were so diagnosed in Jamestown (56 percent). From the foregoing analysis the barriers to be surmounted—chiefly age and psychological symptoms—before adoption could appear as a frequent outcome of planning for children in need of parents in Centralia move into focus.

Some departures from the norms we have described were found in our metropolitan communities. Let us examine at least one case where the image of the adoptable child was somewhat remolded and redefined by agency and adoptive applicants.

In Centralia fewer than half of the adoptive placements were in any way unusual, and almost half of these were of children with minor remediable physical difficulties. In Jamestown, about half the adoptive cases involved children who were in some way different. Slightly more than half of these children had physical disabilities, and slightly fewer than half were Negro. Kathy was the one adoptive Jamestown child whose psychological problems were notable. Similarly, in the Jamestown group of adoptive parents, 70 percent of whom were employed in white-collar positions, the world of Mr. and Mrs. Barker, with whom Kathy had been placed, was unique:

Kathy was a three-year-old Negro girl, adopted by Mr. and Mrs. Elmer Barker, a Negro couple in their mid-thirties who had one other child, aged fifteen. Neither parent had been to school beyond the ninth grade, and both worked in the fields for a combined annual income of $3,000 to $4,-000. Mr. Barker's high blood pressure was a problem which he let only moderately restrict his daily living.

The Barker home was in a tenant house without plumbing; there was an outdoor toilet. Although Kathy had her own bedroom, this was made possible only because Mr. and Mrs. Barker now used the living room as their bedroom. In spite of these factors the agency, acknowledging that it was making some exceptions to its standards, decided to use this home since there was no other available Negro couple with dark skin and it was thought Kathy was greatly in need of a permanent home, having been in foster care almost all her life.

Kathy's parents' rights had been temporarily terminated, when Kathy was four months of age, because of neglect. She was then taken into foster care. Eight months later Kathy became legally free for adoption, but she remained in the same foster home until at age twenty-two months, malnourished and moribund, she was placed in a second foster home. This was a very difficult move for Kathy who, in addition, experienced a third temporary foster home placement before she was placed with the Barkers when she was two and a half. During her many months in foster care Kathy had exhibited various psychological symptoms: withdrawal from one of her foster mothers, refusal to talk with her foster parents or to play with other children, and extended periods of inactivity. Currently, at the Barkers, Kathy's symptomatology included difficulties in social adaptation and ready crying, but her almost twelve months of continued living with one set of parents seemed to have made Kathy less frightened and more certain of the grown-ups in her immediate world.

V. TWO BIG CITIES: KING CITY
AND WESTPORT

14. Child Placement and Other Social Processes

In the great Southwestern spaces of the United States the traveler drives for miles over roads that only jack rabbits cross. Traveling from the west one hears mostly the Spanish language and Mexican music on the car radio. But at some point in the journey east and south the landscape vistas, like the tones on the radio, begin to change. The open range is replaced by cultivated fields, and the accents on the air waves also turn. First the twang of the local newscaster intrudes; then, the more urbane tones of young men likely to have been born or schooled in Chicago and points east lay greater stress on news of the larger world; and, finally, the patter of the disk jockeys provides a curious blend of the local and the universal. As we approached King City the buildings that rose out of level lowlands seemed shockingly new. The highway became a hustling freeway that rushed on to the south. But we came to King City to stay for a time, interested in the 1,099 dependent children for whom this metropolis of the New South was providing foster care and adoptive services.

At a distant point in the Far West we located another community, very close in size and rate of population growth to King City. For Westport, too, was a fast-growing metropolis. It was, perhaps, more typical of urban cosmopolitan America than representative of distinctively regional variations, for Westport had grown much as America has grown through the decades. It represented, in size, the end of a progression of communities with a predominantly Northern European base of population whose dependent children we observed from Norden and Granger through Pine and Lake. And

here in the newness of the West foster care and other services for
some 1,811 dependent children were being provided.

Comparing these two big cities, with an eye to their care of dependent children, we immediately noted that King City had many
fewer children in care than did Westport—1,099 to 1,811. Was
there less demand for child placement in the big city of the New
South, or were there fewer facilities for such care? And how else
did life in these two big city settings provide different destinies for
the child in need of parents? Again, let us meet some of the children first.

Bobby Jo Callen had been in the care of Children's Home of Hope in
King City for almost four years. He was just four years old when his
mother first requested help from the Home and placed him there. He
was a healthy child, attractive, apparently intelligent, but somewhat "holding back" in his relationships with most other people. Bobby Jo was a
white, Protestant child. He had no physical handicaps. But an adoptive
home had not been found for him as yet, although his mother had recently expressed a willingness to relinquish him.

Bobby had been in his present foster home for ten months. Prior to
that he stayed at the cottage at Hope Home for a time, and was with another foster family even earlier when he first came into care. He had two
sisters and a brother, and they too were in foster care—the two sisters in
a foster home together and the older brother also staying in the cottage
at the Home. Bobby saw his brother and sisters now and then and still
felt affection for them, but he had not seen his father in three years and
his mother's visits had become infrequent and undependable in the past
year. Consequently, Bobby Jo now seemed to deny any feeling for either
of his parents. His world was a world of foster parents and other children, and of child welfare workers who came in and out of his life—three
different ones in his four years in care. And of course the world of the
public school was now becoming more important, although he had not
yet become much interested in it. For Bobby had other problems that
troubled him, problems that he had not allowed to come too close to
the surface as yet. If he seemed to show affection for his foster mother
and father—they were the anchors in his present world—and to like his
worker from the agency, as the years passed his confusion about who he was
and where he belonged would deepen the doubts that he kept concealed.

Bobby Jo's mother was thirty-two years old; his father, if he was alive,
was now forty-six. His father was a machinist at a company that made
oil drilling tools. A war veteran, he married and then found the respon-

sibilities of home life and the pace in King City too much to bear. One night after his father had been drinking heavily, Bobby Jo's mother just up and "ran him off"—told him not to come back. She had found another man who often visited the house, but she had not divorced or remarried. Bobby's mother placed her children at Hope Home, promising to make plans for them, but increasingly lost touch with the agency and with her children. She was last known to be living in an old apartment in the central section of town, doing household work that enabled her to pay her monthly rent of $45.

Bobby Jo's mother seemed to be groping toward a new start of some kind in the bustling, changing metropolis of the New South. The little boy himself was still looking for the road signs for his first real start.

Hugh Guffey, in Westport, was also one of a family of four children. He had been in foster care slightly over three years, since he was barely five years old. He had just entered the third grade in one of Westport's public schools. He lived in a foster family home under the supervision of the Makah County Department of Public Welfare, who assigned a child welfare worker to his case. He first came to the attention of the welfare department when neighbors complained to the police about the home conditions in which his parents were keeping him and their other children. He, too, was an intelligent, healthy, attractive child with no physical handicaps. He, too, like Bobby Jo in King City, was white and Protestant. He, too, awaited the plans that others would make for his future.

Hugh had been with his present foster parents for eleven months. This was his third placement, and recently his worker, knowing that the foster parents were talking of moving, began to discuss with Hugh another home farther out in the country where there would be more room for him to play. He was not too sure he wanted to move—he liked his foster parents—but then he was not especially open in expressing his feelings with his social worker and sometimes made things a little tough for her when she came to see him. Hugh was rather attached to his school friends, and he was beginning to like his teacher. She had praised him for his good work in arithmetic, and he was beginning to be interested in school. He scarcely heard of his real parents any more and no longer spoke of them openly to his foster parents. His sisters—all three of them—were together in a foster home in Westport. He visited them occasionally and still felt some affection for them. But he was closer now to his friends at school and to the foster brother who lived with him. Actually, Hugh had shown some improvement in his behavior since coming into foster care, although his sense of who he was and where he belonged had not clarified along with his improved behavior. He was not so backward socially and he had learned to trust people who seemed sincerely to care about him. Still, a life situation that had no guarantees of permanency for an eight-year-old posed threats that he could not shut out of consciousness.

Hugh Guffey's mother, like Bobby Jo's mother, was thirty-two years old, but his father was only thirty-six. Both parents had had some high school education, though neither one was graduated. His father worked on the assembly line at the aircraft plant. Mother and father were divorcel now and each was living alone. Mr. Guffey had not been in touch with Hugh or with the agency in two years, and Mrs. Guffey had almost no contact with them. Both parents had gone their separate ways. Mrs. Guffey moved quite frequently, but now rented an apartment in an older house on Founders Hill for $55 per month.

The welfare department had tried to get Mrs. Guffey to relinquish Hugh, but found it difficult to keep in touch with her. They had planned to refer Hugh to an agency in Westport for adoptive planning once they could demonstrate in court that parental rights to him should be terminated. Meantime, a boy whose teacher said he might have a real aptitude for mathematics and science waited for the signs that would tell him, "This is permanent—this you can build upon."

As in all our communities, most adopted children in Stark and Makah counties had had quite different experiences from those of the bulk of the children in foster families and institutions.

Patti was freed for adoption when she was few months old when Hope Home completed the legal action surrounding her release by her mother at the maternity home in King City. She was first kept at the Home nursery for a time and then went to a foster mother while the agency selected her adoptive home from among its many applicants. Her real mother—a pretty, intelligent, twenty-two-year-old Protestant girl who worked as a domestic in the Bayou Pines section of King City—could not keep Patti because she was unmarried to the airman who had fathered her baby and was ashamed for her parents in the country to know of her trouble. Patti's mother continued to live with two girl friends in King City, her baby now a part of the past. But Patti found a home with the Clements when she was ten months old and had been with her new parents, the only ones she will ever remember, for six months. Her daddy and mamma were proud of her because they had waited what seemed a very long time for her. Patti had delicate little features, a shock of soft brown hair, and, her parents said, "a wonderful disposition." Mr. Clement was already anticipating the day when he would be helping his daughter ward off overzealous suitors. In the meantime, he and Mrs. Clement had been busy fixing over another room in their suburban home as a nursery, hoping that soon Hope Home would find a little brother for their Patti.

Craig, in Westport, had an experience much like Patti Clement's. Craig's mother was only nineteen and two years out of high school, which she had quit in the eleventh grade, when he was born.   At the age of four months Craig was completely freed for adoption when Associated Children's Services received the final release from his mother, a salesgirl in a Westport department store who thought at first that she might wish to keep her baby.   But the twenty-six-year-old merchant seaman who fathered Craig had no desire to marry, and Craig's mother returned alone to her parent's home on Bayview Hill from the maternity home.   Since Craig was a white, Protestant, "perfect" baby, Associated Children's Services had no trouble finding a home for him.   He was placed with the Watsons when he was nine months old after a brief stay in the agency's adoptive study home.   Of course, Craig's new dad and mother had big plans for him.   Mr. Watson, who used to play football at the state university and was now a successful lawyer in Westport, already envisioned helping the coach at State get into a Bowl game, about New Year's Day 1978, by supplying a flashy halfback to carry the brunt of the offense.   For the present, he and Mrs. Watson had given up their weekends of sailing on the bay; but they would be back there soon, this time with another hand to help mind the tiller.

Although the "modal" child in both communities was in foster family care, markedly more of the King City (Stark County) children in care than those in Westport (Makah County) were in insti-

Table 12

PLACEMENT, LENGTH OF CARE, AND SEPARATION AGES OF
CHILDREN IN STARK AND MAKAH COUNTIES

	Stark County (King City)	Makah County (Westport)
Type of placement, by percentage of children in care on April 1, 1957		
In foster family care	51	62
In institutional care	31	17
In adoptive homes	18	21
Average (median) number of years since first separation from parents, for all children under study	$2\frac{1}{8}$	$1\frac{3}{4}$
Age at which children first entered care, by percentage of all children under study [a]		
As preschoolers (0–5 years)	59	62
In 1st to 2d year of life	34	45
In 3d to 5th year of life	25	17
As school-aged children (6–10 years)	27	19

[a] See note *a*, Table 1.

tutional placement on April 1. To this extent King City had not yet lost the Southern tradition of institutional care for dependent children, so integral a part of child care in Jamestown.

There were few differences and some similarities in the "where," "how long," and "when" of foster care and adoptive placements in our two big cities, as shown in Table 12. In King City, with its much smaller total number of dependent children, there was more institutional placement. In other respects the big cities tended to be alike, with the children in care, on the average, about two years, and six out of every ten of them becoming dependent as preschoolers. Does big city life, no matter what its heritage or unique patternings, tend toward a particular approach to its care for dependents? Let us explore these settings for their differences as well as for their similarities.

TWO BIG CITY CULTURES

King City, Stark County

The earliest settlers of the Anglo Southwest were largely self-reliant frontiersmen from the back country of the American East. The farms which they established varied from small, one-family operations to large plantations worked by slaves. This was a region of ranchers and farmers, of cattle barons and slaveholding cotton growers. In 1845 there were still no factories throughout the entire area. At about that time the population of King City was less than five thousand. But in 1957 the population of the metropolitan area was nearing the one-million mark. This tremendous expansion had gone on through each decade in which a census was taken. King City was a community in which growth and economic prosperity had stolen the scene from history. Still, this was a Southern community that remembered Reconstruction. And it was a Southwestern community that had never quite forgotten that another war was once fought—by Anglo-Americans, against Spanish-speaking peoples from across our Southern national boundary.[1]

1 Stark County had a population of over three quarters of a million, according to the 1950 census. The county population showed a 52.5 percent increase for the decade 1940–50. The population in 1950 was 18.5 percent Negro. A count

Stark County was the extended base of this young community
that was also a young people's community.[2] Population growth
had been most pronounced in the younger age groups. It required
youthfulness to keep up in this setting of economic and social opportunity, and many of the young couples who made their homes
in King City raised their growing families in the spacious suburbs
that had developed rapidly since the Second World War. King
City had never had a major setback in its expansion. Even the
great depression was flouted there. Consequently, King City was
brash and confident, cocksure of its bigness and of future claims to
greatness. Its people were restless and eager. Most of them had
rural antecedents, and many had had little time to put down deep
roots in the city. The city boundaries, like the local economy,
had also expanded outward constantly.[3] It seemed that people
who had known the open spaces of range lands also needed space
for living when they became urban dwellers; and the structures of
the central metropolis provided showpieces and a work arena in
King City for folk who wanted room for individual homes.

Forty-story skyscrapers in King City marked the home offices of
major oil companies, banks, and insurance concerns. But refin-
eries and factories and assembly plants on the fringe of the city
indicated that there was employment for blue-collar as well as
white-collar workers.[4] Perhaps the most significant aspect of this

---

of Spanish surnames showed there were approximately 5 percent Spanish-Ameri-
cans. Only 2.5 percent of the total population were listed as foreign-born. The
median of school years completed for the total population was 10.4; for non-
whites, 7.6; and for "Spanish surnames," 5.2.

[2] By certain age groups, Stark's population increase from 1940 to 1950 appeared as follows: under 5 years of age, 123.7 percent; 21 years and over, 48.9
percent. The median age of the total population was 28.8 years. Only 4.7 percent of the population was 65 years old and over.

[3] Home construction, like commercial building, had gone on at a rapid rate.
The 1950 census showed that 71.9 percent of the population resided in the same
houses in 1950 as in 1949, while 19.3 percent occupied different houses in the
county and 7.1 percent moved in from a different county. The city grew from
76 to 156 square miles in 1950 and doubled in size again in 1957.

[4] Occupation figures were as follows: 44 percent were employed in professional
and white-collar occupations (9.8 percent listed as professionals and 10.6 percent
as managers, except farm); 16 percent were employed in skilled occupations; and
38 percent were employed in semiskilled, service, or labor occupations combined.

whole picture was the stress on bigness and on large-scale "organization" in King City. The social forces which were implied by this situation, both in transforming local life and in attracting "organization" newcomers, were an important part of this big city culture.[5]

The apparent brightness of the future in King City had increasingly turned its people away from the past. Incomes were relatively high, schools were crowded, and even the Negro population had found channels for upward social mobility more pronounced than, perhaps, in any Southern community in America.[6] The Spanish-American population too, even more depressed socioeconomically than the Negro, had, since the war, begun to make strides of its own. For the contagion of growth, movement, and progress was pervasive in this community. And the problems of dependent families and their children might, too, be perceived as another challenge to progress.

Westport, Makah County

The settling of Westport, in what we have called Makah County, in the mid-1800s has been called a replication in miniature of that of America, but with the added momentum of more than two centuries behind it. The first settlers came by sea. The community started in an isolation that diminished only gradually, and it was

(Only 7.3 percent were laborers.) Industry groups showed 21 percent employed in manufacturing.

The nonwhite population was represented in the labor force as follows: 83 percent employed in semiskilled, service, and labor occupations (over 20 percent laborers); 5 percent in skilled occupations; and 11 percent in professional and white-collar brackets.

[5] Whyte's discussion of the "organization man" has particular relevance to the analysis of the culture of Stark County (see William H. Whyte, *The Organization Man*).

[6] Median income for families and unrelated individuals in the county was $3,078 in 1950 with 8.9 percent making less than $500 and 3.4 percent making $10,000 and over. Median income for nonwhites alone was $1,681 (considerably better than in James County): 15.3 percent made less than $500 and 0.2 percent made $10,000 and over. Median income for urban dwelling families of Spanish surname (figures available only on a state-wide basis) was $1,134 (below the figure for La Paz).

not until the decade prior to the First World War that this area really merged with the rest of America.

The railroad was long in penetrating to this Western outpost, but once it came (in the 1880s), capital began to flow in and population growth became steady, even, at times, spectacular.[7] Westport had been a melting pot of many nationalities for a hundred years. It experienced riots against the Chinese laborers following the early building of the railroads and felt the effects of a rapidly expanding Negro population in the aftermath of the Second World War. But it still was building upon a population base that was predominantly Northern European and heavily Scandinavian. In many respects Westport resembled a larger, faster-paced version of the typically American community we called Centralia. And in the Far West the continued process of Americanization had found new frontiers leading to a further cultural synthesis.

Westport, too, provided a setting to which young people were attracted. In fact, the child population of Makah County increased at an even greater rate in the decade prior to 1950 than was true for Stark County. Still, Westport was not quite so youthful over-all as King City, the median age was several years older, and there were more elderly people in the population.[8] This Western community had not boomed quite so strikingly as had its Southern counterpart and, perhaps, had more second and even third generations of local residents. Westport proper, much like Jamestown, did not have limitless room for expansion, being constricted by natural water boundaries. Thus, expansion had taken place in Westport around a somewhat more stabilized central core,

[7] Makah County had a population of a little less than three quarters of a million, according to the 1950 census. The rate of increase over 1940 was 45.1 percent for the county and 26.5 percent for the city. The nonwhite population in 1950 was 2.3 percent Negro and 1.8 percent "other races." Foreign-born whites accounted for 10.6 percent of the total, and well over half of this group were from Norway, Sweden, Canada, or England and Wales. The median school years completed over all was 12.1.

[8] By certain age groups, Makah's population increase from 1940 to 1950 was as follows: under 5 years of age, 164.7 percent; 21 years and over, 38 percent. Median age of the population was 32.5 years. And 9.1 percent of the total was 65 years old or over.

and the city had not so much reached out to incorporate new areas as it had let the suburbs grow around many small centers. Movement and activity and the signs of restlessness were indicative, here too, of people who sought the good life for themselves and for their children.[9]   Newcomers, however, tended to be city people for whom Westport was the second or third urban stop in the quest for new opportunities.   There might be, for many of them, shallow roots and a newness of community commitments; but perhaps more in Westport than in King City one sensed that newcomers felt they had reached a final stopping point and aspired to put down deeper roots and develop stronger local ties and loyalties.[10]

Blue-collar workers outnumbered white-collar in the community; but again there was a close balance between the groups.[11]   However, Westport's economy had been geared to support its expanding population primarily through the impetus of wartime and defense contracts.   Big industries were closely linked to the exigencies of the cold war.   Periodically, unemployment in Westport had cast longer shadows than in King City, and labor disputes had been a significant part of the community's history.   Westport's labor organization was on a large scale, and work was quite removed from the small-plant atmosphere in which the employer knew the man on the shop floor by name.   Wages were high, although living costs were also among the nation's highest.[12]   And

9 The 1950 census showed that 73.5 percent of the population resided in the same houses in 1950 as in 1949, while 16.9 percent occupied different houses in the county and 7.3 percent moved in from a different county or abroad.

10 On the average, homes were less crowded in Makah (2.92 persons per household, *vs.* 3.27 for Stark); and a greater proportion of children in the 14–17 age bracket were still in school in Makah (91.4 percent *vs.* 83.2 perecnt in Stark). See Whyte, *op. cit.,* pp. 295–344, for a description of the "transiency," the "new roots," and the "classlessness" which typify, in part, social processes operating in the newer suburbs of both Stark and Makah counties.

11 Occupation figures showed 50 percent of the employed labor force in professional and white-collar occupations (10.5 percent were professionals and 10.7 percent managers); 17 percent were in skilled occupations; 31 percent in semiskilled, service and labor occupations combined (only 5.3 percent were laborers); 17.3 percent of the total were employed in manufacturing.

12 Median income of families and unrelated individuals in Makah County was $3,222 in 1950 with 9.2 percent making less than $500 and 2.7 percent making $10.000 and over.   Local figures for 1949 showed Negro males to have had a

dependency among families was met not only by a concentration
of local economic resources but by a mobilization of professional
ideas and methods as well. For Makah prided itself on the quality
of its professional services, and in the field of child welfare had
made an effort to bring highly professionalized skills to bear on
problems of the child in need of parents.

Social Form and Process in the Cultures

Increasing size of communities first brought to our attention the
growing distinction between separate private and public worlds.
In still larger settings, further differentiation promoted segmentation and heterogeneity, as we saw in Jamestown and Centralia,
modified by different historical and contemporary conditions in
those two settings. In King City and Westport the population
was so large that differentiation produced a tendency toward shading back into sameness coupled with anonymity, and individuals
and groups lost their unique identity and became absorbed in the
mass.[13] Thus, "massness" as a social process in these large communities might be said to involve the social form and process of
achieved homogeneity combined with an extreme tendency toward
impersonality in human relationships. Again these statements
must be qualified.

Both King City and Westport had powerful radio and TV stations and large newspapers from which the populace gained many
social images and norms and through which people participated
vicariously in the many daily dramas of community life. At the
same time, King City still retained its categorization of relationships with two major segments of its population—the Negro and

---

median income of $2,199 compared to $3,125 for white males in that year. Thus,
nonwhites in Makah County seemed less economically depressed on the whole
than in Stark County.

[13] Large numbers alone are not the requisites for the formation of "masses."
We have used the term to indicate a situation where aggregates of people relate
to one another in many specialized ways but, through the weakening of traditional bonds, individuals are only loosely bound together. Yet in counties like
Stark and Makah individuals in the mass are bombarded with many stimuli to
which they react more as members of an audience. We suggest ways in which
masses shape into more articulate publics (in these two settings) through which
interests and desires form into issues where viewpoints are defended and discussed.

the Spanish-American. In addition, King City residents seemed to maintain or find their identity in traditional groups in which they shared traditional values. Thus, for example, publics which took form out of the mass in King City still might be primarily organized around a Baptist or Methodist or Catholic affiliation, although the incoming "organization families" from distant points provided a notable exception to this trend.[14] Class distinctions were also operative in King City, as were some overtones of a continuing caste line relative to the two most visible ethnic segments. The symbols of status which the King City middle classes attempted to appropriate for themselves were usually those (like private schooling) retained by a moneyed upper class (though not so much as in Jamestown).

In Westport an inclination toward achieved homogeneity (that we noted also in Centralia) had operated more forcefully in this larger setting. There was a tendency for the publics that were formed out of the mass in Westport to be based on new interest groups of local origin. One example was the force of professionalization in Westport that influenced the Catholic or Lutheran or even, to a degree, the Negro professional person toward sharing more interests and values with his professional colleagues than with members of his ethnic group. And distinctions of a class hierarchy were not so apparent in Westport. In this pervasive middle-class setting the blue and the white collar mixed frequently and their shared values tended to reflect a pride in the Westport way of life —including the boating and water skiing on the bay—rather than an aspiration toward the symbols of status which a well-defined upper class, had it existed, might guard.

[14] Evidence of a desire for a more articulate group identity, counter to the strain toward anonymity, could be seen in the shift in church membership which many rural people underwent when they came to the city. One Baptist minister explained that the Baptist church in the city was probably too "rational" and "intellectual" for rural folk and, also, that such people felt "left out" since offices which they once held in their country church were now filled by others. Thus they might start a new congregation in conjunction with other newcomers, and in so doing, share a certain disenchantment with a way of life that had not yet become as meaningfully integrated for them as the one they left behind.

Both of these big cities provided settings in which an emphasis on achieved status was predominant, or gaining preeminence, over that on ascribed status. Certain groups in King City still felt the impact of historical events in being assigned an inferior position, and many people still sought identity in a traditional group. But, basically, King City was a place where people came to achieve, to leave the past behind, and to acquire a new and, as they saw it, better identity. Even the Negro in King City now aspired to a form of middle-classness and did not feel so strongly the need to escape from this Southern community in order to achieve some social mobility.[15] Still, separateness was more apparent than interdependence in King City, while contractual relationships were relatively new and unsatisfying to many people from rural backgrounds. The result was a continued separation of people into traditional groups where more personalized relationships obtained, despite an atmosphere of change and achievement.

In Westport, too, achieved status and the symbols of achievement were paramount, as reflected in the pace of life and the philosophy that went with it. Westport was a place of opportunity in which the past was remote and the future was what one made it.[16] And in Westport interdependence of individuals and groups was stressed while contractual relationships were an acceptable part of the urban experience of a more sophisticated population.

In general terms, the growth of professional specialization in King City and Westport implied that the dependent child, regardless of his group identifications, was treated by the professional as one of "ours," to be claimed for the community by those charged

---

[15] A Negro professor at a local Negro college in King City reported that he had recently been requested by a group of downtown businessmen to do a market study of the Negro. This revelation caused one person to comment, with some irony, that apparently "a man is a man when he's a consumer."

[16] Perhaps Riesman's analysis of "consumer-oriented" and "other-directed" people is most applicable in the populations of our two largest communities (see David Riesman, *The Lonely Crowd*). Whyte, *op. cit.*, pp. 345–64, presents an interesting discussion of "inconspicuous consumption" which suggests that in suburbia, at least, people seek to achieve only what the Joneses achieve, but guard against becoming conspicuously different.

to care for him. In King City there were obvious differences in attitudes between professionally educated workers who were native to the county and those who came from distant areas. On the whole, however, in King City there was still a strong degree of traditional segmentation so that a dependent child was perceived more as a member of, and claimed more often by, a segment of the whole. Thus, even the professionals in King City seemed primarily committed to particular parts of the community's population and operated within the relatively insulated case load of a given agency. Individual benevolence by private donors with pet projects was common in King City. At the same time, the anonymity of urban life bred callousness toward persons in the mass, and trained welfare workers often found their problems of interpretation to the community, regarding concern for the dependent child, quite difficult to solve. There were strong precedents in King City for defining the "unfit" as "unworthy." But the direction of change in approach and attitude was toward more interdependence of professional groups which attempted to bring the community's dependent children within the accepting circle of the larger "we."

In Westport professional values were of greater consequence in shaping local cultural definitions than in any community we visited. The emphasis was upon perceiving the dependent in terms of diagnostic needs, regardless of his traditional group identification, and upon accepting responsibility to claim him for the community as a whole. The larger community tended to support this treatment approach and prided itself upon a willingness to support professional persons in their ventures. Achieved homogeneity in the population of Westport seemed now to be passing to a stage where a new social differentiation of the dependent child was taking place as diagnostic terms superseded older group identifications. As part of this new differentiation the harshness of the urban setting was somewhat softened as professional workers tried to lead the community toward greater acceptance of dependent children. Still, there were those who saw dangers of "sovietization" of children in this process. In Westport there was much participation and active seeking for answers to social problems, but the complaint of some was that "in Westport there is too much specialization of services," perhaps a step beyond the emphasis on the perception of homogeneous answers we saw in Centralia.

Foster Care in the Two Cultures

The dependent population was considerably larger in Westport than in King City. In Westport, as we have noted, 1,811 dependent children were in some type of foster care placement, under agency auspices, while only 1,099 children were so cared for in King City. Our information on the comparative economic situations in the two communities does not indicate great disparity in the conditions leading to dependency. It would seem that much of this difference could be accounted for only by different social perceptions of dependency and by different social service resources in the two settings. Evidence suggests that those segments of the King City population which by reason of a lower socioeconomic position might be expected to contribute disproportionately to dependency rolls were not reached uniformly by agencies in the community. In Westport a more uniform set of behavioral norms was applied to the total population. In other words, behavior of individuals in King City was evaluated relative to their own segmented group, while the predominant trend in Westport, compounded by a highly developed set of professional values which tended to shape local cultural values, was toward a more uniform standard for evaluating the behavior of all members of the community. This professional standard seemed to eventuate in more specialized placements determined by diagnostic perceptions of the needs of the individual. Let us turn first to child placement in King City.

Three agencies, each of which provided multiple services in the community, seemed to represent the configurations of forces—Catholic, private nonsectarian, and public—around which major issues of dependency became of community concern. Let us look at some attitudes expressed by participants in the community's drama of dependency. We note two major emphases that find expression: the harshness of urban life (particularly for the newcomer) and the difficulty for community participants to perceive responsibility toward dependents in either their own segment of the community or in the larger whole; and the protected traditional group identity which was apparent in efforts to bring children more into segments of the "we."

King City was a fast-paced urban setting to which newcomers did not easily adjust. The director of the public health nurses for the county said: "King City is composed mostly of a rural population that has come to the city to make money. Many people are here just because of employment and are not really 'married' to the community. This is also true of the 'better' classes too. A big insurance company recently moved in hundreds of families from the East Coast when it opened a home office here."

A Baptist minister said: "Rural Baptists often feel left out in the urban church. And most groups in the city have to be led to accept greater responsibility for their own. This is partly my job in speaking at different churches each Sunday. More fortunate people in the city tend to turn their backs on the less fortunate and dissociate from them."

An adoption worker told us: "Sometimes the judge will give parents the alternative of going back to the town from which they came or losing their children here in the city. But it seems to me that people seldom go back."

An adoption worker at the Bureau for Colored Children said: "I think that more of the Negro girls at the maternity home come from outside the county now. And more of them seem to desire anonymity than in the past. Negro foster mothers are still too busy working to care for infants, and of course they lack transportation to and from the clinics."

A welfare agency executive said: "This state still operates under the old Reconstruction Constitution of the 1870s. The ceiling on ADC is partly directed at the rural Negroes who come to the city and who, it is felt, don't need more than ten dollars a month to live on."

The head of visiting teachers in King City noted increasing pressures adding to children's problems in that city. "In our central schools we seem to have more of the 'pressures from parents' problems in families that moved in during and since the war."

Groups in the community were more inclined to protect an ascribed identity than to seek a new one, although such groups did try to improve their situations much more than we noted to be true in Jamestown. There was increasing cooperation but still not complete mutual trust. The Baptist minister remarked that religious groups did cooperate but that they also jealously guarded their denominational ties. The head of the King City Council of Churches, who came to the city from Detroit five years earlier, said that the Council had grown on the basis of a growing concern of individual congregations for cooperation rather than on the desires of whole denominations. But the Baptists, most of them Southern Baptists, were still the largest single denomination in King City and maintained their own association; and cooperation even between separate Baptist congregations was said to be difficult to obtain. Presbyterian churches were all represented in the Council of Churches but were a much smaller group of churches in King City than in most big cities, while the Methodists, who frequently cooperated on the Council, were highly organized for interchurch participation within their own denomination. The minister from Detroit made clear to us the continued emphasis on separateness in the community life of King City. He felt, however, that the newer churches in the suburbs seemed more willing to refer parishioners to the Council for counseling and other services, perhaps, he said, because the suburban pastor was often overwhelmed with a building program.

The Catholic hierarchy noted changes taking place, but it maintained a strong feeling of responsibility to the specifically Catholic segment of the local population. Father Welch, at Catholic Children's Home Society, said: "Most marriages in the newer parishes now are interfaith marriages, and the Catholic population is really cross-sectional socioeconomically. Still, our parochial schools can't keep up with the demand. People seem to prefer a parochial education for their children."

José Ramirez, the leader of the Latin American Citizens League, expressed some of the problems of his group: "A few years ago people were alarmed about our Citizens League. There was some fear that it was subversive or full of troublemakers. Our organization is now stressing an educational program to give the pre-schoolers some training in the English language. We are trying to break the circle of circumstances that has deprived us of economic opportunity."

The movement toward interdependence and some degree of assimilation had begun in King City, but currently it proceeded on the basis of reaffirming strong segmented group identifications. Among the Negroes was a noticeable identification with the problems of their own group and a struggle for status within that group. And the struggle often bred dissociation of the more fortunate from the problems of the less fortunate. There was, too, a persistent tendency in King City to take an interest in welfare matters over which one could exercise some personal control. As one person put it, "so much philanthropic money is still tied up in pet projects where it is least needed in this community."

In Westport observations on placement could also be articulated with reference to two major themes: the anonymity of life in the big city enhanced the problem of bringing dependency to the attention of an informed and concerned public; and the tendency toward a new, achieved social differentiation increased the importance of professional and other interest groups and defined the dependent child in more diagnostic terms.

Westport was also a fast-growing urban center whose populace was caught in the tensions of a rapidly paced life. Still, newcomers seemed to have had urban experiences in the past, though some, initially, had great difficulty in becoming at the same time both assimilated and newly differentiated in this social system. They were the persons who felt the impact of urban anonymity to the greatest degree.

The Juvenile Court judge said: "In the past our dependent families tended to be located on the fringe of town—out in the 'sticks.' Now they tend to be people in our crowded metropolitan area.

There seems to be less neighborhood tolerance of families for one another than previously. Financial problems are paramount. Usually a local loan company has first call on the pay check each pay day."

The counselor at the sheriff's office said: "Vandalism has increased here in the past two years. Children are getting into trouble at younger ages." She continued: "I think the Protestant groups need to take greater responsibility for those in their particular denominations. The Catholics here are certainly above the average in their home life, and we get referrals from this group. But the Protestant kids are too apt to be lost in the crowd."

The counselor at a local high school said: "This district used to be more middle class, but now families are constantly moving in and most of the fathers work at the aircraft plant. Every Monday we have five or six enrollees and there are many drop-outs during a semester."

Negroes in Westport were subjected to perhaps greater tensions than whites in the urban setting. Their population increased by 300 percent in ten years. Warren Volt, director of the Urban League, said: "Although nonwhites constitute only 4 percent of the population, 13 percent of those applying for unemployment are nonwhite, and most of them are Negro. The Negro population remains concentrated in certain census tracts, and population density there goes up and up. Newcomers join together in clubs for companionship. They also tend to take care of one another's dependent children. But over all, Negro families are pretty stable when they get here to Westport. This city may be the third stop for a Negro family."

A professor at the university commented: "The incoming Negroes have difficulty in learning how to be 'middle class.' Their real problem is budgeting. Negro families that have been here for a longer time find it difficult to identify with these newcomers and to see their problems in a common light."

A worker at the Lutheran agency felt that there was really not a very highly developed social conscience in this middle class community—people were too busy being consumers to worry about their fellows. As he put it, people were too involved in fishing and gardening to care much what was happening to others.

A recurrent note sounded by informants in Westport was that, to a large degree, a pride in the community as a whole served to claim people's loyalties. This was particularly the emphasis of civic leaders, and where a given leader found it difficult to draw elements of his particular group into identification with the whole he would tend to draw away from these elements. Among religious groups, denominationalism seemed on the decline. At the Council of Churches it was stated that new churches had been growing at a rapid rate, particularly in the suburbs. One staff member said: "Sometimes a new church will be affiliated with a particular denomination, but it is quite likely to become a community church and be interdenominational. Community churches are growing fast in the outlying areas." A Jewish professional man in Westport said that although he lived in the suburbs he sent his son into the city to attend the Orthodox synagogue, because the Reformed synagogue in his neighborhood was too subject to the "cliquishness" and "conformity" that seemed to him to typify suburbia. Our informant at the Council of Protestant Churches said that highly visible ethnic groups, like the Orientals who accommodated to their elders, still stayed much to their own churches. Even for them, however, the future seemed to indicate greater assimilation, although the break with the past had not been violent.

The director of the Lutheran agency told us: "The Lutherans have grown with the middle class in Westport. Years ago we opened a Skid Row Mission for Scandinavian seamen. But now our two major emphases are first, an effort to reach the larger community because of the traditional Lutheran concern for welfare activities and second, a prior obligation to Lutheran families, specifically."

The Catholics in Westport were also an integral part of the whole. Many members of the Catholic agency staff had worked in other social agencies in the community. A board member said: "When I was a boy a Catholic was pointed out more than now. The old bishop was quite a 'separatist.' But I married a non-

Catholic, and most of my brothers and sisters did too. Not too many years ago marrying a Catholic might have been considered marrying 'down'; but not today."

In the public schools the influence of social uniformity was also apparent. One high school principal said: "There is no easy identification of a particular social class or ethnic group with a particular school. School clubs are based on service and academic standing. The Hi Y died out here some years ago. Our boys say that everyone feels he belongs to the whole school community."

It was interesting to note in Westport that where segregated schools had developed inadvertently, both whites and Negroes had become concerned because this process seemed counter to the normal processes in this social system. Generally, however, Westport's schools were becoming more cross-sectional, with the "lower" schools sending more children on to college and the "higher" ones now getting more children from the lower economic groups.

The labor picture, too, in Westport was one of respectable acceptance, community-wide commitment, and movement toward middle class values. A representative of the local carpenters' union said: "This is more a blue-collar town than a white-collar town. Labor is respectable here. Our union doesn't include the category of race on its membership or employment forms. We have close relationships with employers and get along much as 'one big family.' Labor is even given a special day of recognition in the public schools."

In summary, both of our two large cities reflected the conflicts and the tensions of fast-paced urban life in their dependency pictures. A more uniform set of standards, effected through a larger number of agencies, led to the care of more dependency cases in Westport than in King City. Both communities required professional groups to lead them toward a greater acceptance of the dependent child into the "we" in order to avoid his being lost in the anonymous mass. But in King City a people with rural antecedents were led more toward concern for those who belonged to the same segmented group as their own, and care involved more general facilities with a wider use of institutions. In Westport, an older urban populace was led toward acceptance of newer diag-

nostic terms for differentiating the dependent and claiming him
for the interdependent "we" through the use of more specialized
facilities.

Adoption in King City and Westport

More dependent children in Makah County than in Stark
County moved into adoptive homes.   The over-all figures on adoption through agencies indicated noteworthy disparity between the
two communities in the prevalence of agency adoption, since Westport provided considerably more adoptive services through its more
specialized agencies.   Adoption relative to total placement is presented in Table 13:

Table 13

ADOPTIVE PLACEMENTS AND RETURNS HOME IN
STARK AND MAKAH COUNTIES

	Stark County (King City)	Makah County (Westport)
Percentages of all children in care April 1, 1957, who were in adoptive placements	18	21
Percentages of adoptive placements that were in-county	89	62
Percentages of all children in care April 1, 1957, who had left care by October 1 (six months later)		
For adoptive placements	9	9
For return home and other reasons	22	14

Both King City and Westport were dynamic centers of middle-
class values and had large suburbs where childless couples might
be increasing the demand for adoptable children.   Let us look at
them separately, however, to see what differences we may discern.

In King City an achievement atmosphere was still permeated
with ascribed symbols, and separation of groups was more apparent than interdependence.   There was a more anchored upper
class there—visibly identified by wealth and place of residence—
which functioned as standard-setters.   This segment adopted children largely through a high-status agency located elsewhere in the
state.   The middle-class suburbanites of the community tried to
emulate, in many ways, this upper segment.   In this atmosphere
it seemed that adoption through local agencies was still geared

much to an orientation toward, and placement within, a segment of the community, although this was less true in King City than in Jamestown. One private agency, Children's Home of Hope, seemed to move furthest toward interpreting adoption to a cross-sectional and interdependent public. At the lower end of the social ladder, groups in King City that were most anchored socially by characteristics that inhibited their social mobility were not much in the market for adoption as yet. However, some Latin Americans were becoming more adoption-conscious through their ties to the Catholic community, which was becoming predominantly middle class. And a Negro middle class was taking shape in King City too. Still, Negro families who adopted were inclined to do so outside the community, for local agencies seemed to connote, for them, a stigma of welfare, from which they were desirous of dissociating themselves.

Among our informants in King City was the Junior Leaguer who said that most of her friends who adopted children did so through the Emma Hapworth Home in Midtown. A certain "status" was attached to such adoptions.

An adoption worker at the Probation Department said: "Not many people know about the Probation Department as an adoption agency. There is a stigma attached to probation. But sometimes people read in the newspaper about a dramatic case of dependency, and then they want to adopt the 'unfortunate' children involved. Most of my placements are families of children."

Father Sheridan, at the Catholic agency, expressed his primary commitment in the community: "We look for the emotionally mature, practicing Catholic family in our adoptive placements. I have explicit faith in our agency director's ability to evaluate a good Catholic family. We're not too worried about all the professional formalities but we're out to find good Catholic homes for children who need them."

At the Children's Home of Hope—the large, private, nonsectarian agency in King City—a board member said: "We still think of ourselves as a public agency to a degree, because we are interested in all the children in King City." The director of the Home added: "We are making a concerted effort to get the hard-to-place child adopted—particularly the older child and the emotionally and physically handicapped. We have a long waiting list of couples who want babies; but now we are able to interest more of our applicants in an older child."

Mr. Ramirez, of the Latin American League, spoke of the changing motivations of many younger Latin Americans: "Since a few of our people have made the grade into professions, a lot more are willing to try. Returning veterans with only five years of schooling used their G.I. Bill benefits after the war."

An adoption worker at the Catholic agency remarked: "Latin Americans who adopt children are quite concerned about avoiding 'Indian' features in a child. The adoption process is still pretty new to most Latin Americans."

Dr. Willard Mays, a Negro professor at the local Negro university, said: "This is the most attractive city in the South to Negroes. The number of households is increasing faster than the population is increasing. The proportion in the professions was 2.9 percent in 1940 and is now at about 4.6 percent. Many Negro professionals still hold down more than one job. I see a changing attitude toward children. There is an increased investment by more Negroes in the child as a person of value who should be given dancing and swimming lessons, etc. And Negroes here are losing the 'deep South' tolerant attitude toward illegitimacy."

A Negro adoption worker at the Bureau of Colored Children commented: "In the recent past our adoptive applicants were found for the most part among thirty-five-to-forty-year-old couples. Younger ones were all working too hard to have time for children. Now this is changing, although it still seems to me that Negroes who adopt are apt to get their children from somewhere outside the community. But lots of unwed mothers are still influenced by relatives to go back on a plan for releasing a baby. I hate to see this happen because I know we can do so much better for the child."

In Westport, achievement symbols were more uniformly manifested in the whole community. The atmosphere thus engendered, coupled with a familiarity with contractual relationships and a stress on the interdependence of groups within the whole, seemed particularly conducive to achieved parenthood and agency adoption within the community. The norms of a mobile middle class encompassed blue-collar workers as well as white-collar people and were much in line with the social values of professional welfare people as well. Where the trend toward achieved homogeneity, now approaching a new social differentiation, was so paramount it would appear that professional welfare staffs should have considerable success in gaining acceptance for adoption of many ordinarily hard-to-place children. However, this did not seem to be the case in Westport, although the child of mixed ethnicity was certainly more placeable there than in King City. Nevertheless, agencies stressed highly professional standards in adoptive placements. But social interdependence was also stressed, and adoption agencies in Westport that began as sectarian operations now were largely nonsectarian, and even the Lutheran agency accepted non-Lutherans as adoptive applicants. The Catholic agency, of course, still served only Catholic children and families, but it was not militantly striving to claim dependent children for the Church and utilized professional values in studying a home even as it looked for Catholicity in the home. Negro adoptions, too, were not so common as white, but Negro workers shared, in integrated agencies, the problems of all social workers and treated the unique aspects of Negro placements merely as problems among many problems. There were even those in the community, like one prominent Negro, who spoke of the possibility of adoptive placements of white children in Negro homes as well as Negro children in white homes, although this view was still not prevalent.

Let us explore some of the statements reflecting the situation in Westport:

A professional member of the staff of Associated Children's Services said: "Probably 50 percent of adoptions in this state are through agencies.[17] This agency began under Methodist auspices,

[17] For 1957, 56 percent of the nonrelative adoptive placements in the state were made by agencies.

and prior to 1938 most adoption referrals to us were through churches. But that would be rare now. We are developing guilds tremendously to stimulate lay participation."

A volunteer worker at the Crippled Children's Hospital said: "I think this is probably the most organized city in the world. We have a broadly developed volunteer auxiliary system that reaches across the community. This hospital, from the very beginning back around 1900, never allowed any race, creed, or color discrimination."

A worker at the Lutheran agency remarked: "We used to get a lot of people who asked for a child with Scandinavian background. But this is seldom true any more, and I suspect it was partly the workers who projected these ideas on the clients." The head of the agency said: "We are beginning to have interracial congregations in the Lutheran churches now, and this may open up more adoptive homes for hard-to-place children. But the hybrid child is still not too accepted by the Negro either."

A board member of the Catholic agency said: "Families are getting bigger. This is true of both Catholics and non-Catholics. When I was a boy I was one of six children, and it was fairly certain that a family as large as ours was Catholic. There is a high value placed on adoption now. An adoption has become an event, like a birth. Formerly, a childless couple didn't feel so much left out. Now all their friends have large families, and it increases their desire to adopt." [18]

Negro adoption in Westport was both similar to, and different from, that in King City. A Negro worker at Associated Children's Services said: "Negro adoptive families have tended to be somewhat older than the average. They are also somewhat lower on the socioeconomic scale than the majority of adoptive couples. We let them pay whatever they can as an adoption fee. Last year we placed twenty-five Negro children in adoptive homes throughout the state. I think a lot of Negro families earn enough to adopt children, but they haven't settled back in the struggle for security

[18] See Whyte, *op. cit.*, p. 393, for further documentation of the view that having children, through adoption if necessary, is crucial to adjustment to some forms of suburban living for young couples.

enough to have time for kids. Actually, most of the Negro community still doesn't know about the services of this agency, and most of them think of us as having terribly high standards. Housing problems are also critical for Negroes here in Westport."

A home recruitment committee member at the same agency said: "We are finding that it is best not to use the word 'Negro' when asking colored people to form an interest group relative to adoption. It is better just to ask them to 'get a few friends together who are interested in adoption.' We find that advertising alone isn't enough. You have to 'infiltrate' through clubs and more personal contacts."

Thus the agency adoption process even in interdependent and sophisticated Westport presented a mixed picture. The great task which welfare professionals there had set themselves in attempting to move children into permanent homes was to explore the variations required in their own practices at the same time that they continued to influence and shape the local culture and its definitions of dependency and the "adoptable" child.

15. The Legal Systems

Within the social contexts of King City and Westport, legal systems related to the care of dependent children had developed and, in the course of their operation, were continuing to change. How might we describe those systems at the point in time which was of interest to us? And how did the law and its agents appear, differentially, to be affecting child placement?

LEGAL ROLES IN STARK COUNTY

The Judge

The new courthouse in King City was an impressive structure, although it could not rival the massive commercial buildings that marked this community as the hub of the New South. Across San Carlos Street from the new courthouse the old courthouse building

still stood—newly renovated within—and it was in the older building that the hearings were held at which the fate of many dependent children was decided. Judge Baker had a large courtroom on the second floor as well as a more confidential inner hearing room. Beyond the hearing room were the judge's chambers,
where we met him.

A recent letter to the King City Press, signed by the chairman
of the Christian Life Committee of the local Baptist Association of
Churches, concluded: "Stark County should be congratulated for
having such an outstanding Christian gentleman heading up our
Domestic Relations Court." Judge Baker, a Methodist, came to
the bench from the welfare world. He was chief probation officer
in Stark County as far back as 1919 and held that position for
many years until he became clerk of the district court. He came
to the bench in the new Domestic Relations Court in 1953. How
did he currently see his responsibility in dependency matters?

"My primary concern is to consider whether parental rights
should be terminated," he said. "First, I must look at the parents
and try to decide whether they are capable of carrying through a
plan for continuing to care for their children. Then I consider
what alternatives there might be in getting care for the children.
I want to know whether there are other relatives who might have
an interest in the situation. Many families coming to King City
have a hard time of it, and I believe sometimes the only hope for
these people is to return to their home area where they had previously made a success of their family life." Investigations of dependent families were carried out by the Probation Department.
"I don't ask directly for a recommendation," Judge Baker said,
"but the department is never very far from my own position in the
recommendations which they make."

What did the judge think, specifically, had been accomplished
in his tenure on the bench? "We reorganized the Probation Department," he said, "and I recommended the present director for
his job. I had known this man previously through Boy Scout
work." He continued: "Secondly, we reopened the Warm Springs
School for predelinquent boys, and I feel we have some fine men
operating the program there. Thirdly," he said, "I hired the first

full-time psychologist employed by an agency in this state when I brought Dr. Chase to the staff of the Probation Department. I have also worked hard to convince the County Juvenile Board of the need for new housing for the juvenile section of the Probation Department, together with a facility for detention care for children, and these new facilities will be opened very soon now."

What were some of the continuing problems which he faced? "Stark County cannot, by any means, meet the need of all the children who require substitute care. Therefore, I am trying to encourage agencies to look outside the county for more foster homes. There should be a greater use of ranch-type settings where children can have plenty of room. I am requesting the help of various Protestant churches in soliciting homes that the court can use. Incidentally, I think the Catholic agency here has the best attitude of any agency toward assuming responsibility for their own children. They will try to find foster or adoptive homes for all the Catholic children we refer to them. We also have a real need," he continued, "for a dependency institution for Negro children. All in all," concluded Judge Baker, "we need more aggressive protective services in Stark County, but that is a problem in this state where people like to be self-sufficient."

What were some major controversies at this moment? "My major disagreement has been with the private agencies and particularly with the Children's Home of Hope here in King City. I used to be on the board of that agency but resigned in 1950. I feel that agency should be extending a broader service rather than becoming more exclusive about whom it serves and leaving the long-term care cases to the Probation Department." The judge added: "The local agencies just have not done a very good job of defining their services and deciding who should take what type of case. The larger private agencies should accept responsibility for extending services throughout the community."

Other Legal Figures

In Stark County the Probation Department was a major child-placing agency, performing the functions ordinarily carried out by a public welfare department. This meant that Judge Baker, through his long affiliation with the Probation Department, was acquainted with the social workers, the agency directors, and the Council people in Stark more as a probation officer than as a judge. He had legal differences with the local district attorney, who was spearheading the effort to lower the juvenile age to 14 years, beyond which a child could be tried as an adult, as part of a move to control juvenile crime. But the major crystallization of issues around the legal situation in Stark seemed to involve the judge as at least a partial spokesman for the public agency world in controversy with the spokesmen for the private agency world typified by the widely respected Children's Home of Hope in King City.

The Children's Home of Hope had moved through the years toward a more well-defined intake policy, although it still saw itself as being concerned with "all the community's children." It felt that the judge was not clear enough in distinguishing between Community Chest money (which it received) and tax money, and felt no compulsion to accept into care all children referred to the Home. But Judge Baker was critical of private agencies which would not readily accept referrals from the court; he was tired, he said, of "talk and do nothing" and had decided to spend his time and energy on getting new facilities for the children who came before him.

The pathway by which a child in Stark County might come to the judge's attention was almost exclusively through the Probation Department. For if a child was considered dependent or neglected it was the Probation Department which would look into the situation and bring the case to court if deemed necessary. This agency operated protective services, providing placement for dependent children and even making adoptive placements. The Domestic Relations Court was a separate unit, apart from the Probation Department. Judge Baker, as the juvenile judge, was also a member of a five-man County Juvenile Board. Still, with his background in welfare and his continuing ties to the Probation Department which he had helped to reorganize, Judge Baker expressed in his own philosophy that of this public agency which he championed. Thus the relationship between the judge and the major agency bringing neglect cases before his court did not reflect varying philosophies and different vantage points so much as it involved a shared frame of reference. The emphasis of the judge and the Probation Department was on movement out of long-term care wherever possible, and proceedings for termination of parental rights were frequent.

The Probation Department used the private institutions and agencies of Stark County each on a somewhat different basis. The small Filippo Orphanage received a few boys and girls from the court where group care was indicated and termination proceedings not contemplated, since this institution wanted parents to be available for visiting. The somewhat larger Home on the Range for boys also received some boys from the court where group care seemed advisable, although it was primarily an agency accepting voluntary placements made by legal guardians. The Catholic Children's Home Society was willing to accept responsibility for permanent planning for any Catholic child referred to it. This agency did not itself move toward termination of parental rights, since it held that man is inadequate to judge something which only God can decide.

The Children's Home of Hope had had, in the past, a large share of court wards, but by the time of our study it had cut the proportion of these cases sharply until it had a much larger proportion of children in care on a voluntary basis. Even with voluntary placements, this agency asked parents to sign an agreement which stated that if plans agreed upon with the agency were not carried through, the agency would refer the case to court for whatever action seemed advisable. Thus, in spite of agency differences, the trend toward aggressive efforts to terminate parental rights rather than perpetuate long-term foster care was exemplified by the two major agencies, the Probation Department and the Home of Hope, which between them cared for nearly 70 percent of our child population. In fact, the one point on which welfare people in Stark County seemed most able to reach a consensus was their affirmative evaluation of the careful and persistent way in which Judge Baker moved toward permanent plans in dependency cases.

LEGAL ROLES IN MAKAH COUNTY

The Judge

The Juvenile Court in Westport had been in existence since 1913. In 1952 it moved into the newly dedicated facilities of the Youth Service Center on Sullivan Street, centrally located but in one of the more depressed areas of town. The Youth Center was constructed at a cost to the community of about one and a half million dollars. It was constructed from the ground up for the specific services it would provide, and Judge Dean, who had served as the juvenile judge in Makah County since 1933, was a principal figure in its planning and erection. Our tour of the building revealed an up-to-date detention and court setting for youth that few cities in America could rival.

Judge Dean was a colorful figure in the public dramas of Makah County. He conducted a weekly radio program, called the "Court Corner," through which he had become known to a fairly large section of the county's populace. He belonged to no fraternal organization and described himself as a nonactive member of the Congregational Church. He was first admitted to the bar, in another state, in 1916, without having completed his studies for the law degree. He told, with some relish, the story of how he then returned to the university to make a bonfire of his law books in celebration of his passing the bar examination. As we began our conversation, Judge Dean removed his coat, leaned back in his chair, and waited for us to speak.

What were the major dependency problems in an urban setting like Makah? "Makah County has one of the highest rates of growth in child population in this state, and this has meant increased crowding in our central neighborhoods. Many families have great problems in making ends meet. People are swamped in debt. Also, I notice an increased shading of our delinquency cases over into the dependency ones. More delinquency, now, seems to be the result of some form of dependency."

What was his attitude toward permanent removal of a child from parents? "I start with the basic philosophy that if at all possible a child should be maintained in his own home. I deprive only as a last resort and when I do remove a child permanently I feel that, in effect, I am saying to the Almighty: 'In this case I think you did a poor job in giving this child a home and I'm going to start him all over again with a new one.' But I don't believe any juvenile judge can shrink from this responsibility. In my courtroom," he continued, "a parent faces sworn witnesses. The record which the caseworkers have prepared is open to all parties to the hearing, and the defense counsel has complete access to this record. If something which comes up is challenged I merely swear in the person whose statement is being challenged. The overwhelming majority of dependency cases over which court hearings are held come directly on referral from law enforcement agencies and not from the social agencies in Westport." The judge emphasized that his legal procedure resulted in many cases coming to the court wherein agreement had been reached with parents and their attorneys on a pretrial basis.

How was the court administered, how was the public currently represented? "There is a board of managers for the Juvenile Court now. Under a special law of this state, four laymen constitute this board, and I am the chairman ex officio of the board. I have four of the community's most respected business executives backing me up. The board meets twice a month at 7:30 A.M., and these men are interested enough in this work to meet at that hour, and quite willingly too."

What did he see as major problems currently? "We always have the problem of guarding against allowing children to be 'sovietized' by agencies, particularly public agencies. The law makes no provision for me to place a child in the custody of the Department of Public Welfare unless there is no private agency that can place the child, and this fits my own philosophy on these matters. I don't want to see any arm of the state crowd out other facilities for caring for children. In some states the juvenile judge has become a mere arm of the welfare department. Whenever I do give custody to the welfare department for planning I always give personal custody to the director there, since the law authorizes commitment to an individual, and I never give custody to the department as an abstract entity." He continued: "I encourage community participation and interest in the problems of dependent children. We have a guild at the Youth Center with seventy-five active members. My radio program helps to stimulate community interest." He concluded: "I think that there is a much better atmosphere in this community now for youth services than there was just five or ten years ago when I had to fight the battle for the Youth Center. But of course our problems will continue just as this community continues to grow."

Other Legal Figures

Judge Dean and his staff at the Juvenile Court in Makah County controlled the removal, both temporary and permanent, of children from their homes and to some extent determined the kind of placement made. But there were points in this decision-making at which the process was not completely under the control of the court. For example, if a private agency could not place the child, the judge was forced to call upon the public agency. Then, too, it was the welfare department which controlled the public funds which could be used for placement. If parents were able to pay the full amount for foster care, Judge Dean could order whatever placement he saw fit. If parents were not so able, the judge believed that he should be able to order public welfare to pay part of the cost and set an amount for the parents to pay. But the welfare department was responsible for the public funds for care and thus considered itself the authority for determining how much a parent should pay toward his child's support. This was one point at issue in the controversy between the judge and his staff and the welfare department. Without control of public funds for foster care the court people could not operate a foster home program. But they hunted up foster family homes which were originally listed as free homes, and if these homes worked out satisfactorily they were referred to the welfare department for foster home licensing and payment. Judge Dean continually championed groups in Makah that uncovered prospective foster homes for referral to the welfare department.

The first step in the legal route to placement in Makah usually involved one of the local law enforcement agencies. Judge Dean pointed out that of 1,156 dependency cases referred to court in 1957, only 170 were from social agencies. Most cases came from law enforcement agencies. The police and the sheriff's office, as well as the court and the Probation Department, were all theoretically screening or intake agencies, operating in the protective services field. Final placements, after referrals, were made either by a private agency or by the welfare department. The sheriff or the police would bring to the Youth Center a child they thought should be removed from his home. The court would then make the decision on removal, and where removal seemed appropriate the child was committed to some other agency, with the public agency a last resort. The welfare department, the public agency, seemed to worry the most about overly long detention at the Youth Center, and it tried to get children into foster homes as soon as possible. Thus, in Makah County there was no definite designation of an agency as a protective service, although almost all the agencies operating in child care were willing to sign dependency petitions to bring court action for the removal of a child from his parents.

In spite of disagreements over emphasis and methods, Judge Dean's actions in termination proceedings were largely approved within the social work community in Makah. Thus, although he expressed a certain antipathy toward social workers, Judge Dean carried out court procedures in a manner which permitted permanent planning for children. He was considered decisive but somewhat unpredictable. He utilized the medium of radio to enlist support from a broad public, and such support invariably provided him a degree of freedom in bargaining and discussion with other public figures, including agency directors. But the major controversies which developed did not relate, primarily, to legal practice or procedure in the disposition of children in foster care.

THE CODES AND STATUTES AND THEIR USE

As we found in most of our community pairs, the laws relative to child care practice in Stark and Makah were similar rather than

different. In summaries we have condensed the Makah laws more
than those in Stark. Makah County law gave many more reasons
for bringing children before the Juvenile Court and gave these
reasons in greater detail; but some sections were repetitious and
could probably be included with the general sections of the Stark
County law.[1]

Both Stark and Makah laws were not too specific about placement after removal, and neither seemed to recognize the existence
of public welfare departments. In both laws there appeared to be
conflicts and a lack of specificity which permitted a variety of judicial interpretations. In Stark County only local funds were used
for foster care, and the court controlled the granting of these funds.
This local control expressed the emphasis on local autonomy in
that county, but specific provisions for this did not seem to be explicit in the law. In Makah, state funds were used for foster care,
but their allocation made for the aforementioned conflict between
the court and the county welfare department over their use.

Neither law had a definite provision for terminating parental
rights, but the law in both communities permitted adoption without parental consent. Stark County made this determination only
at the time of the adoption hearing, but Makah allowed both for
a permanent commitment to an agency in advance of the adoption
hearing and for a separate hearing before an adoption was finally
granted to let the court determine in advance whether the adoption would require parental consent.

In their relationships with ther respective probation departments
and with other agencies, both judges were like executives of large,
powerful administrative agencies as well as judicial figures in their
communities. But Judge Baker had moved up from an administrative position, while Judge Dean infused his personality into the
administrative agency. In a sense, Judge Baker was still operating
a placement agency in Stark County, whereas Judge Dean in
Makah kept more specifically to a judicial role.

How did these two legal personages appear on our child's rights

[1] Appendix D-4 presents comparable sections from the two sets of laws which
influence movement into and out of foster care.

–parents' rights continuum? Viewed across the span of all our communities, certainly both appeared as "welfare" judges, oriented toward protecting the child. But it was welfare by his own definition toward which each was oriented. With Judge Baker in Stark it was a probation department's definition of welfare that expressed his philosophy, and the Probation Department operated in Stark in a situation which required that it be both a legal and a social agency. With Judge Dean, the philosophy of child welfare expressed was more a personal one, certainly indicative of a sincere concern for children. For Judge Dean's approach and philosophy could not be defined by a description of the view-point of any particular agency or interest group. His position as crusader and champion of facilities for children had to be seen more in individual terms, and his individualistic approach promoted, at times, a greater measure of unpredictability to his activities.

Perhaps both of these judges could be typified as relatively unassimilable parts, but still parts, of the welfare world in their respective communities. Everyone in the welfare agencies knew them and saw them as powerful forces working in the interests of children but precipitating certain conflicts because of their feelings about segments of the social work profession. Judge Dean in particular preferred to by-pass the professionals and go to the broader public for his support. He favored private agencies over the public welfare department. Judge Baker, on the other hand, found the one big private agency in Stark—also the most professional one—the most irritating. Perhaps if King City had had a powerful welfare department actively placing children, Judge Baker's antagonism might have centered there. But Stark's probation department largely replaced the welfare department, whereas the Makah welfare department was a large, powerful, and impersonal force. Still, both judges were somewhat detached from the legal world: Judge Baker was carrying on an open controversy with the district attorney, while Judge Dean required strong cases from agencies on permanent custody matters because he had once been reversed by a higher court.

Both judges, in their concern for protecting children, were apparently willing to remove children from their parents, either temporarily or permanently. A certain difference in emphasis could be noted, however, between the two communities. In Stark County agencies generally mentioned first Judge Baker's philosophy of permanent planning and his willingness to terminate parental rights, but then would add that the judge was fair about this and did protect parental rights. In Makah County, the emphasis was in the other direction, with agencies mentioning first the strong case they had to make in order to get a termination decision from the court. But in both these large urban settings, with relatively long histories of juvenile court facilities, dependent children tended to move fairly freely through the legal gateway into placement.

LEGAL ISSUES AND PLACEMENT PATTERN

Some of the experiences in placement of children in King City and Westport fill out the discussion of the legal systems in these two big cities. First let us examine the degree to which legal steps seemed involved in dependency cases.

Little difference was noted between the two communities on percentages of children separated from parents voluntarily, by court order, or because of the physical absence of parents. Stark County had only a slightly greater proportion of involuntary separations—32 percent compared to 26 percent in Makah—and the child's rights judge in King City may have seen proportionately more families from which involuntary removal of children for placement appeared necessary.

A major difference between child's rights Stark and child's rights Makah unfolds when we look at parental conditions at time of separation of children from parents. In Stark, as in James County, physical factors—death, illness, economic difficulty—were much more prominent than in Makah. In Stark 22 percent of the cases involved such conditions as primary, compared to only 6 percent in Makah. In Makah, marital conflict and psychological crises were paramount, accounting for 28 percent of cases, compared to 18 percent in Stark. With a low ADC grant in Stark, removal of a child for his protection when one parent died was often necessary. In Makah, there were many specialized facilities to which referrals could be made, and agencies were more likely to take children into care when marital conflicts and psychological crises were the contributing parental condition. Out-of-wedlock birth was also proportionately more often a contributing condition in Makah—it actually accounted for the most (31 percent) cases there compared to 23 percent of cases in Stark. Neglect and abandonment were almost equally represented in the two big cities, 26 percent among Stark cases and 23 percent among Makah cases.

Differences in over-all proportions of children first separated as preschoolers were negligible in these two child's rights communities—59 percent in Stark and 62 percent in Makah—but proportions separated between birth and two years of age showed greater differences—34 percent in Stark and 45 percent in Makah. Makah's greater emphasis on adoption doubtless showed up in these figures. Proportions first separated from parents between ages six to ten were 27 percent and 19 percent for Stark and Makah respectively.

We also found, consistently, that Makah had a lower median time in care. The over-all median figures for total time in care were 26 months for Stark and 21 months for Makah. By separate placement categories the differences also held true: 45 months for children in foster families in Stark, compared to 37 months in Makah; 35 months for children in institutions in Stark, compared to 24 months in Makah. Thus, somewhat earlier separations eventuated in shorter time in care in Makah. The comparative picture of agency services, which we have not yet presented, may be more influential in this situation than legal codes and their interpreters.

We saw, also, slight differences in the movement out of care in Stark and Makah: 18 percent in adoptive care on April 1 in Stark, compared to 21 percent in Makah; 14 percent of all those studied returned home between January 1 and June 30 in Stark, compared to 10 percent in Makah. This may point up the somewhat different contexts within which our two big city child's rights judges operated. A major answer for Judge Baker in Stark to the problems of rural families who became dependent in the city was to return their children to them when the family would return whence it came. In Makah, there were more agencies specializing in adoption to which Judge Dean could refer children for planning. We know, further, that not only were more people reached by social agencies in Makah, but, in absolute numbers, twice as many agency adoptions occurred there as in Stark.

As we recall how the preponderance of cases came before these two juvenile courts, the reasons for which they came, and the cultural fields in the communities, the varying tones of concern for dependent children and of desire and readiness for adoption, the preceding facts again express similarities and variations in two big cities. However, our total pictures do not really become clear until the services provided and the networks of agencies are described and analyzed.

16. The Agency Networks Serving the Two Cities

The services designed to care for children in need of parents are both an expression of, and an influence upon, a community's approach to dependency. What were the agency patterns in King City and Westport?

THE NETWORK OF AGENCIES AND CHILD WELFARE SERVICES IN STARK COUNTY

Close to town on the west the freeway entering King City passes the buildings and grounds of Children's Home of Hope. A section of Hope Home property had been sliced off to make room for highway progress, but the buildings of this distinguished child care facility had been untouched. Not far from this westside location the new structures—still unoccupied—for housing the Probation Department and the youth detention center of Stark County were taking form in late 1957. On the southeast side of town the new, but small, Filippo Orphanage sat alone beside the freeway, occasionally catching the attention of travelers, who might stop and inquire about children seen playing in the yard. Far beyond city limits and at the extremities of the county boundaries, one could find the old colonial-style mansion that housed the Home on the Range for boys. But a quick glance was not sufficient for locating other parts of the interagency puzzle in Stark County. In late 1957 one had to explore the northside area behind the railroad station to look in on the Probation Department in its old quarters in the annex of the Robert E. Lee Hospital. To find the Bureau for

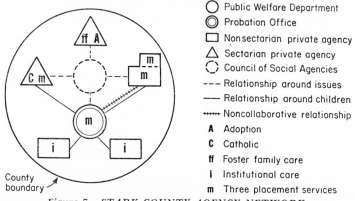

○ Public Welfare Department
◎ Probation Office
☐ Nonsectarian private agency
△ Sectarian private agency
◌ Council of Social Agencies
--- Relationship around issues
— Relationship around children
⇢⇢ Noncollaborative relationship
A Adoption
C Catholic
ff Foster family care
i Institutional care
m Three placement services

Figure 7. STARK COUNTY AGENCY NETWORK

Colored Children, a separate facility of Hope Home, required an even deeper exploration into semi-industrialized neighborhoods on this northside. And Catholic Children's Home Society operated out of tenth-floor offices in a downtown building.

How did these parts of the agency network relate to one another? What services did they provide to the children of the county?

The diagram for Stark County in Figure 7 introduces a new element—the Council of Social Agencies. It acted as an instigator and facilitator of communication among the major agencies in our study. The reader will note that the dotted lines indicating communication over issues all go through the Council.

The three largest agencies were all multiple-service agencies and differed primarily in the fact that one was public, one was sectarian, and the third was nonsectarian. Each tended to duplicate the other's services. It was among these three agencies that 93 percent of the children in our study were distributed. The nonsectarian multiple-service agency (Hope Home with its Negro affiliate) cared for 51 percent of the child population in placement. However, influence was relatively balanced in Stark County.

In addition to the three major agencies there were three very small ones, two of them single-function institutions and all three having little connection with the larger agencies in the network. We have pictured the two small institutions as having a relationship only to the county Probation Department. The small Jewish agency offered foster family and adoption services and related to other agencies over issues and through the Council of Social Agencies.

Another feature of the Stark County network was the concurrent existence of two types of relationship between the Probation Department and the Home of Hope. One was a relationship over cases and the other was a negative relationship. In this particular case the negative relationship not only involved the referral of children and the fact that the Probation Department believed Hope Home should take more children, but reflected the over-all conflict in deciding the proper functions of the two agencies in the community.

In essence, the situation in Stark County offered conflicting impressions in that the three large agencies and one of the small ones communicated with each other (on issues) through the Council, but there was little communication among the agencies over cases. The two small, peripheral institutions were brought into the picture only for referral of cases. We cannot, then, define the network clearly as either collaborative or noncollaborative, for it is some of both and is dominated by three multiple-service agencies that were somewhat insulated within their own case loads and problems.

Did agencies also offer duplicated nonplacement service? Three placement agencies reported they offered protective services and

Table 14

CHARACTERISTICS OF AGENCIES IN THE
STARK COUNTY NETWORK

Agency (According to percentage of children under study served)	History	Services	Extent of Professional Education [a] of Staff	Spatial Factors
Children's Home of Hope (38%)	Organized 1892; auspices private	Foster family and institutional care, adoption, for white children under 13 years of age	48% of staff (23 members)	Located at King City; serves the county
Stark County Probation Department (28%)	Organized 1914; auspices public	Institutional and foster family care, adoption, for children 0–16 years of age	22% of staff (9 members)	Located at King City; serves the county
Catholic Children's Home Society (14%)	Organized 1952; auspices private	Foster family and institutional care, adoption, for Catholic children 0–21 years of age	67% of staff (6 members)	Located at King City; serves the county and accepts unmarried mothers from the diocese
Bureau for Colored Children (13%)	Organized 1939; auspices private (attached to Children's Home of Hope)	Foster family and institutional care, adoption, for Negro children 0–17 years of age	50% of staff (6 members)	Located at King City; serves the county
Home on the Range (4%)	Organized 1946; auspices private	Institutional care, for non-Negro boys 6–17 years of age	0% of staff (2 members)	Located in Stark County; serves the county primarily
Filippo Orphanage (2%)	Organized 1955; auspices private	Institutional care, for non-Negro Christian children 4–10 years of age	0% of staff (1 member)	Located in Stark County; serves the county primarily
Child and Family Service (0.3%)	Organized 1912; auspices private	Foster family care and adoption, for Jewish infants for adoption	100% of staff (4 members)	Located at King City; serves the county

[a] One year or more of graduate study in social work.

services to children in their own homes. The Probation Department was the major protective service agency, but Catholic Service
Home Society and the Child and Family Service, the small Jewish
agency, also considered protective service as part of their programs.
Referrals of cases in Stark stemmed primarily from the Probation
Department, and one would suspect that much of the protective
service eventuated in placement.

There was one maternity home in Stark County which was a
separate agency offering casework services, medical care, and institutional care to unmarried mothers. In addition, of the multiple-
service agencies, the Child and Family Service and the Catholic
Children's Home Society offered casework to unmarried mothers.
The two other agencies with adoptive programs served the unmarried mother only when she wished to release her child. These two
agencies also offered prenatal care and would provide foster home
care for the unmarried mother.

Stark County had two services which have not appeared in our
communities heretofore—homemaking and day care. Homemaker
service was offered not only by Jewish Child and Family Service
and Catholic Children's Home Society, but also by the Family
Service Agency. These same three agencies had, as a part of their
programs, family counseling. They looked upon these two services
as preventing the necessity for placement. Day care homes were
provided by Child and Family Service; in addition, day nurseries
operated in the community as separate agencies with many children in care.

Agency Antecedents and Present Bases in King City

History.—Stark County has been described as a rapidly growing
community having certain strong traditions but with fewer ties to
the past than we noted in Jamestown. A look at the history of
placement agencies suggests how tradition was influencing the
county.

Children's Home of Hope was not only the most respected
agency in the community but was also the oldest. It was organized
in 1892 by a woman who took in a few homeless children. The

name of the agency recalled that when things looked darkest for this woman in her child care efforts she still had hope. Hope Home grew into an agency offering institutional care. Later, as foster home care was considered an essential part of a child welfare program it, plus adoption, was added to the Home's services. Therefore, Hope Home became a large multiple-service agency. In 1939, in response to community demand, the board of this agency agreed to establish under its auspices a multiple-service agency to care for Negro children.

In 1912 the Jewish Child and Family Service was organized to give financial assistance. Since that time this function had been given up completely, and the Jewish agency became primarily a family agency, with foster family and adoption services available but amounting to only a small part of the total agency program.

About this same time (in 1914), the county Probation Department was established, supported entirely through county tax funds. It was established at the time of great development of juvenile courts in this country. Since there were no public services for dependent and neglected children, the Probation Department took on this function in addition to the usual one of caring for delinquent children. This plan for public services to children continued, perhaps reflecting the community's desire to avoid any opportunity for state or Federal "interference" in their programs. Thus, the Probation Department was the source of referral of many of the children cared for by other agencies.

As the population of Stark County grew, demand for services increased, and there was pressure on all agencies to offer more service. There were resultant conflicts in determining each agency's role in the community. The board and staff at Hope Home retained a feeling of responsibility to the larger community, yet it seemed necessary, in order to develop a sound program in the private agency tradition, to limit the children served to the group that Home of Hope believed it could serve best. Recent developments somewhat reduced tensions on these issues with the establishment, in 1952, of the Catholic Children's Home Society and the organization of Filippo Orphanage and Home on the Range. Although these programs were not large, Catholic Children's Home Society in particular had publicly stated its feeling of responsibility for all children and families of the Catholic faith in the community.

The history of the most recent agency to enter the Stark County picture illustrates how services may emerge in this community. Filippo Orphanage, opened in 1955, was the fulfillment of a dream of an Italian immigrant. This man and his wife had no children but had always wanted to provide care for deprived and neglected youngsters. After retirement, Mr. Filippo bought land outside the city and set about building an institution for children. Many people in the social work profession were concerned because they were sure that Mr. Filippo was not acquainted with proper standards for child care. They attempted to discourage him. However, he persisted. When the bishop of the Catholic Church refused to bless his institution, Mr. Filippo found a priest in a neighboring parish who would agree, and early in 1955 Filippo Orphanage was opened. Mr. Filippo died shortly after the opening; his will established a foundation, with a board of trustees composed primarily of his relatives, to provide financial support for the home. At first there was some hesitation on the part of the State Department of Public Welfare in licensing the institution, but finally the license was granted and Filippo Orphanage became a full-fledged agency in the Stark County network.

In summary, the early history in Stark County emphasized institutional care under private auspices with gradual growth toward a variety of services offered by one agency. Thus Filippo Orphanage began somewhat as did Children's Home of Hope, but some fifty to sixty years later.

Services.—One might think that there was much duplication of services in Stark since many agencies offered the same services. But let us examine the kinds of children served by the various groups. Table 14 indicates that all agencies helped children within the county, that the two institutions served non-Negro children, and that the largest (private) agency served both white and Negroes but under two separate organizations. Were there other distinctions separating the clienteles? The two sectarian agencies worked with their own groups but did not delimit their services on the basis of color. Nor did they limit on the basis of age, both serving children from infancy to age twenty-one. The Probation Department also helped children of all races and religions, but legally served children up to the age of sixteen only. Children's Home of Hope cared for white children under thirteen years of age, while their branch agency, the Bureau for Colored Children, served only Negro children under seventeen years of age. In other words, services were limited on the basis of religion or on the basis of race, but no agency used both criteria for delimitation. Collaboration was not completely absent. Communication over issues, which was largely a responsibility of the Community Council, was enhanced by the fact that all agencies, whether they participated actively or not, were members of the Council and, therefore, the Council had access to each of them.

Extent of professionalization of agency.—The two small institutions in Stark County were the least professional, having no trained workers. Among the other agencies, all staff members of the small Jewish Child and Family Service were trained. The three major agencies were about comparable in professional emphasis except that the Probation Department had not been able to secure a large proportion of trained personnel. (It should be said, incidentally, that the Council was staffed with professionally trained people.) An examination of our network shows that most communication was among the more professional agencies, particularly on the basis of issues in the field. While the Probation Department did not have many professionally trained staff members, there was some recognition of a need for this. However, professional education was not a major goal of the judge or of the administrative staff of Probation. Other agencies, approximately half of whose personnel had had some social work training, wished, if at all possible, to have only trained people on their staff. But those agencies that had no trained staff did not indicate that they felt professional education was particularly important, nor was there a professional social work emphasis in their programs.

Spatial factors.—The six agencies serving Stark County children were all located within the county, and four had their offices in King City. The two small institutions were located more peripherally, and this might have a bearing on their lack of communication with other agencies. However, not only were all agencies located within the county boundaries (admittedly, a wide area), but all of them served Stark County only, or at least primarily. The Bureau for Colored Children of Hope Home had penetrated beyond county boundaries in seeking adoptive and foster homes, but its responsibility was for Negro children in Stark County. Catholic Children's Home Society served Stark County except for services to unmarried mothers, offered on a diocesan basis. Home on the Range indicated it would serve the entire state, but in point of fact it served primarily the county and did not receive referrals from a much wider area. The same could be said of Filippo Orphanage. Thus, we saw a rather county-bound situation, with Stark County services offered for Stark County children only, and little apparent flow in and out of county. But the distances involved in this large county reinforced the insulation of the peripheral agencies from the whole.

In light of this description, how could we typify the interagency picture? Perhaps, "professionalism with a difference" expressed the Stark County configuration. There was not the staff interchangeability that one would expect to find in a highly professionalized social work setting. Professionals retained a general framework of values, shared among the major agencies; but the distinctive loyalties which divided agencies—their commitments to segments of the whole and to their individual programs—seemed of greater significance than a shared professional value framework in defining the tone of interagency operations. Stark County seemed to represent a growing and a somewhat undecided community, with the Community Council serving as a central moderator for interaction among agencies. There were few referrals of children among agencies, although there was a rather formalized committee set-up through which issues were handled. Children were served much on the basis of the group to which they were ascribed membership, and services were limited by the resources of the agency through which children were reached. A broader perspective of community need was still unclear in Stark. This situation promoted some tension and resultant discussion through the Council in this rapidly expanding and changing metropolis.

Actually, none of the parts of the interagency network in Makah County was highly visible in that community. The parts distributed themselves much as the populace was distributed—somewhat heterogeneous and specialized yet tending more toward uniform "respectability" than toward difference. Perhaps the most conspicuous element was the welfare department, located in a renovated warehouse by the bay, passed by thousands of motorists every day but doubtless recognized by few as the home of county welfare. The other agencies largely blended in with the diversified features of a complex metropolitan setting. The Catholic and Lutheran agencies each occupied downtown office space, near doctors, lawyers, dentists, and other Westport professional men. One adoption agency was in a "close-in" neighborhood surrounded by residences; another was farther out, in a newer residential neighborhood. One institution was in the old and colorful Bayview Hill area in the northwest section, also surrounded by family dwellings; another, the highly respected Hindley Treatment Center, occupied several acres on the edge of an outlying suburban development. The relationships among these agencies as they serviced Makah County are diagramed in Figure 8.

Ten agencies were in the Makah County network. A wide variety, in size and function, of agencies were represented with the public welfare department serving the largest group of our child population and the Catholic Bureau for Children and Associated Children's Services representing the other two points of a major service triangle. These three agencies alone were responsible for 75 percent of the children in the study, with the remaining 25 percent divided among seven agencies. However, although there was this variation in size, communication was fairly general, and no agency was completely isolated. Only two agencies offered all three placement services, four offered two services, and four operated as single-function agencies. Of the ten agencies, four were sectarian, but among these only one—the Catholic Bureau for Children—was a large agency. In Makah County, then, we found mainly private agency services, but with a public agency as the largest single agency. No one agency seemed to dominate except for the fact that the public welfare department and the Probation Office were focal points for communication over cases.

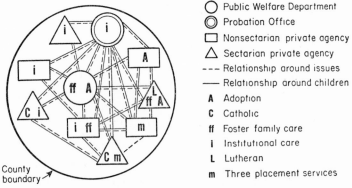

○ Public Welfare Department
◎ Probation Office
☐ Nonsectarian private agency
△ Sectarian private agency
--- Relationship around issues
— Relationship around children
A Adoption
C Catholic
ff Foster family care
i Institutional care
L Lutheran
m Three placement services

Figure 8. MAKAH COUNTY AGENCY NETWORK

Makah County, then, presented a collaborative network with a variety of somewhat specialized services. Few agencies offered institutional, foster family, and adoptive services all under one agency roof. Within this picture, two specialized elements emerged which we had not seen previously: the private, nonsectarian Hindley Treatment Center and the Probation Office, which offered only detention care but served as a source of referral to all other agencies. We have included probation offices in other communities usually because they operated direct placement programs. In Makah, the Probation Office was included because it was a vital factor as the initiator of child placement and exerted an influence among child welfare agencies.

Other services, not specified as placement services, were also complex in Makah. Casework to unmarried mothers and prenatal and

Table 15

CHARACTERISTICS OF AGENCIES IN THE
MAKAH COUNTY NETWORK

Agency (According to percentage of children under study served)	History	Services	Extent of Professional Education [a] of Staff	Spatial Factors
Makah County Public Welfare Department (35%)	Organized 1935; auspices public	Foster family care and adoption, for children 0–21 years of age	78% of staff (40 members)	Located at Westport; serves the county
Catholic Bureau for Children (21%)	Organized 1936; auspices private	Foster family and institutional care, adoption, for Catholic children 0–21 years of age	84% of staff (19 members)	Located at Westport; serves the state
Associated Children's Services (19%)	Organized 1896; auspices private	Institutional and foster family care, adoption, for children 0–18 years of age	95% of staff (26 full-time, 14 part-time members)	Located at Westport; serves the state
St. John's School (7%)	Organized 1909; auspices private	Institutional care, for children 9–14 years of age or through 8th grade	0% of staff (1 member)	Located in Makah County; serves the state
Lutheran Child and Family Service (6%)	Organized 1944; auspices private	Foster family care and adoption, for Protestant (Lutheran given preference) children 0–21 years of age	100% of staff (4 members)	Located at Westport; serves the state
Children's Services League (5%)	Organized 1907; auspices private	Adoption (some foster family care), for children 0–21 years of age	100% of staff (5 members)	Located at Westport; serves the state
Westport Home for Children (4%)	Organized 1884; auspices private	Institutional care, for boys 6–14 and girls 6–18 years of age	75% of staff (4 members)	Located at Westport; serves the county primarily

Table 15 (Continued)

Agency (According to percentage of children under study served)	History	Services	Extent of Professional Education [a] of Staff	Spatial Factors
Makah County Probation Office (2%)	Organized 1913; auspices public	Detention care and referral, for children 0–18 years of age	86% of staff (35 members)	Located at Westport; serves the county
Hindley Treatment Center (1%)	Organized 1935; auspices private	Institutional and foster family care,[b] for children 2–18 years of age	100% of staff (13 members)	Located at Westport; serves the county
Protestant Federated Home (1%)	Organized 1956; auspices private	Institutional care, for Protestant boys 13–16 years of age	100% of staff (1 half-time member)	Located in Makah County; serves the county primarily

[a] One year or more of graduate study in social work.
[b] Adoption service available for those children admitted initially for treatment.

confinement care were offered by four agencies—the Catholic and Lutheran Agencies, the county welfare department, and Associated Children's Services. The latter had a rather extensive foster home program for unmarried mothers and had developed a program of medical care which was quite progressive. The Catholic Bureau for Children also provided a limited foster home service for unmarried mothers. In addition to these two programs, Lutheran Child and Family Service operated a maternity home, and there was another, independent, maternity home in Makah. The maternity homes, too, including the one under Lutheran auspices, communicated with other agencies and particularly with those offering adoptive services.

One agency offered a limited homemaker service. None of the child-placing agencies said that it specifically provided protective services for children. A department of the sheriff's office and a department of the Westport police accepted complaints regarding neglect and acted on them, but protective services, as such, did not exist in Makah County. However, there had been community concern about the lack of protective services, and after some deliberation among community agencies and boards it was decided that the county welfare department should take on this function. At the time of our study that department was about to launch such a program.

No agency in the community listed service to children in their own homes as a part of its program except on an extremely limited basis (usually just prior to placement). However, three active family agencies offered family counseling: one, a growing family service agency; another, the Lutheran Child and Family Service, having counseling as an important part of its program; the third, the Jewish agency, operating a small program in counseling.

In-patient psychiatric care for children was available through the Central Home for Children, and there was a psychiatric clinic for children in connection with the University Medical School. However, because of limited finances and staff these two agencies were not able to offer as much service as the community agencies believed were needed.

Agency Antecedents and Present Bases in Westport

History.—In Makah County one would have a difficult time deciding whether precedent favored institutional or foster home care, for in the history of services we do not find one or the other kind of care predominant. The two oldest agencies, Westport Home for Children and Associated Children's Services—organized in 1884 and 1896 respectively—grew up side by side, one offering only institutional care while the other began as a foster family agency and developed institution services at a later time. About ten years later, other services emerged—the Children's Service League, St. John's School, and, in 1913, the Probation Office. St. John's School began as an educational institution, and education remained the major area of emphasis even though the program was now geared to dependent children. The Children's Service League began as a relief-giving organization and developed through the years into an agency operating an institution for infants plus an adoption program. Later, the agency became a foster family and adoption agency with emphasis on adoption. The Juvenile Court, organized in 1913, originally administered Mothers' Aid, as did many other juvenile courts throughout the country, and established a probation service.

Over twenty years later two of the largest agencies—the Catholic Bureau for Children and the Department of Public Welfare—came into being and the Hindley Treatment Center was established. A need for additional services had been seen, and the Community Chest encouraged development of the Catholic agency and Hindley Treatment Center. Hindley had had a much earlier beginning, as a children's institution operated by a prominent person in the community. When this person died the function of the agency was changed. A new administrator was brought in, and treatment services were introduced. Here was an instance of general community planning toward essential social services. All of this occurred after the Social Security Act was passed, when public services were unfolding so rapidly throughout the nation.

In 1944, when the Lutherans decided to assume a specific responsibility for child welfare services, the Lutheran Child and Family Service was organized. Since institutional care was already available in the community, this agency became a foster family and adoption agency.

The most recent addition to child welfare services in Makah County was the Protestant Federated Home, a small institution for older boys established in 1956. The sponsors of the Home were encouraged by Judge Dean to establish services for Protestant children since there were no institutional services in the Community specifically sponsored by a non-Lutheran Protestant group. The original sponsors were members of various local Protestant churches. Their first effort was to recruit foster homes for the public welfare department. Since there seemed to be a dearth of facilities for older boys, this Protestant group decided to fill a part of this need by establishing a small institutional setting. They conferred with the Council of Social Agencies, with the public welfare department, and with the State Department of Public Welfare about standards of care and how such a facility might be set in operation. The agency was finally admitted to the Council of Social Agencies. The sponsors expected eventually to develop an institution offering a variety of services to Protestant children.

Throughout the history of the growth of services in Makah mutual cooperation and participation in planning formed the pattern. Since institutional care, foster home care, and adoption developed simultaneously and in a parallel fashion, one type of care did not predominate. Almost since the beginning of services there was a variety of service available to dependent children in Makah County.

Services.—A purchase-of-care plan operated in this state through the public welfare department. Since the welfare department purchased care for dependent children who might be physically under the protection of another agency, there was a necessity for communication over these cases with all agencies in the community. The Probation Office, as a referral source of children for several agencies, was also responsible for much interagency communication. Likewise, there was communication among adoption agencies and among other agencies having representatives on state committees and on committees of the Council of Social Agencies.

To note further the basis for interagency collaboration, it is important to look at the groups of children being served. There were four sectarian agencies and several single-function agencies. One might think that the sectarian label would be the basis on which services were defined. It was true that the Catholic Bureau for Children served primarily Catholic children, but St. John's School accepted both Catholic and non-Catholic children. Protestant Federated Home, a small operation, would not refuse a Catholic child, and admissions were not strictly determined on the basis of religion. The Lutheran agency was committed to serving children who needed the kind of care the agency offered. This did not necessarily limit the service to Lutherans, although they were given priority. In light of the sectarian aspects of this picture, it is interesting that although agencies might be affiliated with specific religious groups there was easy and frequent referral to other agencies. In other words, the services given by the agencies in Makah

County were offered more on the basis of perception of the particular problem of a child rather than determined by the religious or racial group from which the child came. Children were referred for care from the public welfare department or from the Probation Office to the agency which could meet the child's need, and agencies expected to receive referrals on this basis which involved a professional, diagnostic differentiation of the dependent child.

Extent of professionalization of agency.—As we looked at Makah County, we found that there was no agency in the community, except St. John's School, that did not have some professionally trained social work staff employed. In four instances, as indicated in Table 15, 100 percent of the staff had some professional training, and in no agency was the proportion less than 75 percent. We have suggested that lack of variation in level of professionalization enhances communication. The fact that many of the professional personnel had formerly worked with other social agencies in the community certainly typified a situation in which a professional value system tended to pervade the social work community, facilitating interagency communication and strengthening collaboration over cases and issues.

Spatial factors.—Although some services were offered on a county basis, the majority were offered on a state-wide basis even though most cases seemed to originate within Makah County. In three instances—at Lutheran Child and Family Service, the Catholic Bureau for Children, and Associated Children's Services—the agencies participating in this study had branches in other communities throughout the state. The public welfare department, too, was a part of a state-administered welfare program. Therefore, there was a concentration of resources for an entire state within Makah County. All ten agencies were located within the boundaries of the county, and most agencies had their offices within the city limits of Westport. Only Protestant Federated Home and St. John's School were located outside the city limits, and these two agencies were thus somewhat isolated from the general community.

Collaboration and communication in Makah were frequent between individual agencies over referrals of cases and through the Community Council over issues. Children received service from the agency which could best meet their professionally perceived social and psychological needs. Segmentation was not so much segmentation along religious, age, or ethnic lines as, primarily, by services. Some services were established in Makah, at the urging of the Community Chest, as an expression of the community's desire for stronger programs. The Council, although not as crucial to collaboration as in Stark County, was still a major force in Makah. But there was increased chafing within agencies at the controls which participation in United Good Neighbor Funds entailed. There was evidence that the movement toward central coordination had reached a stage in Makah where individual agencies, particularly the smaller ones, were now seeking to acquire a greater measure of autonomy over their own operations, suggesting coalitions with other agencies on the basis of common interests and shared problems. As a part of this sentiment was the theme, now sounded from several vantage points in Makah, that agencies had become too specialized and even too interdependent. Still, in 1957, healthy competition in the shared social welfare venture seemed the keynote by which agencies in Makah said they operated.

NETWORK COMPARISONS AND THE FACTS OF PLACEMENT

Were there great differences in placement pattern which could be related logically to differences in interagency networks in Stark and Makah counties?

The emphasis in movement in more specialized and collaborative Makah, where adoption services were such a major part of all services, was toward adoption more than toward return home to a greater degree than was true in Stark. Figures on all those leaving care in a six-month period showed that 36 percent went into adoption in Stark, compared to 52 percent in Makah, while 57 percent returned home in Stark, compared to 39 percent in Makah.

The figures for time in care in Stark and Makah were not too dissimilar when explored beyond the total medians, which

showed twenty-six months for Stark and twenty-one months for
Makah. Time in current placement showed a one month lower
median for Stark than for Makah—eight months, compared to nine
months. But the breakdown by year intervals showed Makah
more skewed toward shorter term care, generally, than Stark: 42
percent of Stark cases had been in care under two years, compared
to 50 percent in Makah; 38 percent of Stark cases had been in care
from two to five and one-half years, compared to 35 percent in
Makah; 20 percent of Stark cases had been in care six years and
over, compared to 15 percent in Makah.

The predominance of the mid-number of placements stood out
only slightly more boldly for professionalized Makah, and in most
respects the two systems showed only negligible variations in numbers and types of placement experience. In Makah 56 percent of
children had had two to three placements and only 23 percent had
had one placement only, while 21 percent had had four or more.
The comparable figures in Stark were: 50 percent with two to three
placements; 27 percent with only one; 23 percent with four or
more. Makah children had had more than one type of placement
in 57 percent of cases; Stark children had had more than one type
of placement in 56 percent af cases. Multiplicity of care experience was the norm for both large communities in which collaborative specialized and less collaborative multiple-service agencies
operated.

Differences which appeared in sequences of movement were a
little more pronounced. In Stark 42 percent of all children in care
had moved out of a foster family to another type of placement at
some time in their care experience, compared to 37 percent in
Makah; but 41 percent in Stark had similarly moved out of an institution into a different type of placement, compared to only 32
percent in Makah. Apparently, the multiple-service agencies in
less collaborative Stark were more likely to move a child to another type of care within the same agency than were the more
specialized agencies in more collaborative Makah.

In Stark, we have said, "professionalism with the accent on difference" typified the tone of collaboration in a community seeking

answers to increasing child welfare problems. One agency executive said: "We usually work through the Council on anything new concerning child welfare in the community. But" he added, "there is a need for a better coordination of services. Clients have to shop around too much to find an agency that will accept them and meet their problems."

In Makah, we noted "professionalism tending toward a shared viewpoint" but with growing fears of overspecialization apparent. An agency worker said: "Shared ventures among agencies are important and always have been, in getting things done here." Still, amidst a healthy rivalry between agencies in Makah, some evidence of discontent could be noted at the restraints which a high degree of agency interdependence entailed.

Thus, in both big cities, striving to meet new and growing problems, tension could be noted in the ongoing equilibrium of the interagency networks. But without some perceived tension, change within a system could not occur and new challenges could never be met. That the challenges of child welfare in Stark and Makah would be met somewhat differently in these two communities could be predicted from the character of the two systems, which we were able, in part, to determine.

17. The Children and Their Parents

Our two largest communities presented many complexities that taxed any efforts to make generalizations. Still, we attempted to account for distinctive tendencies in foster care and adoption in each setting viewed as a whole, building our composite pictures from the several viewpoints presented in the three preceding chapters. Our major question still remained: Given these contexts, how frequently did children without parents find a permanent home, and how could more of them do so? King City and Westport—more specifically, the counties of Stark and Makah—could each, fruitfully, have been studied more intensively to throw light

on ramifications of this question in much of urban America today.
However, even our exploration, which gave these communities no
more than equal billing with smaller communities, uncovered findings about children in foster care and their parents in big cities in
this country that clarified some major deterrents to permanent planning for such children.

PLACEMENT HISTORIES OF THE CHILDREN [1]

Of all our communities, King City had the highest proportion of
voluntary separations of the children in foster care and, together
with Jamestown, one of the lowest proportions of involuntary
separations of children and parents. As in Jamestown, though not
so frequently as in that older, Southern community, death, illness,
and economic hardship were the most common conditions precipitating the placement of children in foster care in King City. Neglect and abandonment were also recognized rather frequently, while
parental psychological problems were relatively of more importance
as precipitators of foster care in this big city than anywhere except
in Norden with its treatment institution. This picture of family
conditions and the predominantly voluntary nature of parent-child
separations could be expected in a community which was much
less prone to perceive dependency and take on the formal care of
children than was Westport or most of our other communities.

In spite of some similarities in placement pattern between our
two Southern communities, King City was using institutions to
only half the extent that Jamestown was. Most of King City's dependent children were being cared for in foster families—although
a smaller proportion than in Westport—and we have already seen
that far more adoptions were taking place, proportionately, in King
City than in Jamestown. Considering all types of placement, King
City tended to confine its foster care and adoption to Stark County
alone and surpassed even Westport in the proportions of its adoptions within the local county. The children in foster care first became dependent at fairly early ages in King City. The average age

[1] See footnote 1, Chapter 5, regarding the base for percentages in this chapter.

was actually younger than in Westport, and similar to the average age in Jamestown. About half were first separated as preschoolers. And once in placement, the King City child in foster care had just about a 50 percent chance of moving two or three times while in placement, and in only one in four cases did he have only one placement. In this respect King City closely resembled Westport (and Centralia too) and was quite different from "one placement" Jamestown (and Summit). However, the child in foster care was staying in care a longer time in King City than in most of our other communities—the average stay was 3.7 years for those in foster families at the time of our study and 2.9 years for those in institutions—and his stay was from about one-half to one full year longer than for the comparable child in Westport. But our evidence suggested that King City was shortening time in care. For example, a greater proportion of these childen in King City left care in the six months following April 1 than in Westport, and King City's total rate of movement out of care was surpassed only by the rate in Summit. We found that about twice as much movement out of care in those six months involved return home as involved adoption in King City.

Westport was a community with many professional and specialized welfare services. Like Centralia, it tended to reach dependency through active agencies and courts to a greater degree than did our other communities. In Westport we found a 12 percent greater prevalence of other-than-voluntary separations than in King City. Quite obviously, conditions of neglect and abandonment dominated the separation picture in Westport more than in any other community. Other parental conditions were of lesser importance, but marital conflict appeared much more often than in King City, and death, illness, and economic hardship were much less often perceived as conditions precipitating placement than in King City.

As they came into care in Westport, children were distributed among the community's many agencies in a manner closely resembling that in Centralia—not quite two thirds in foster families, about one sixth in institutions, and one fifth in care in adoptive homes on April 1. These children were divided into almost even proportions, as in King City, between those first separated as pre-schoolers and those separated at school age; however, more of them, proportionately, than in King City first came into care when less than two years of age. At the same time, the average age at separation for the child in a foster family in Westport at the time of our study was four years, one year above that of the child in a foster family in King City, while the average child in an institution was first separated at age nine in Westport, two years above the average age for King City. But Westport kept children in foster care a shorter time than did King City, as we have seen. Compared to Centralia, however, its children in foster families at the time of our study had remained in care over half a year longer than their counterparts in that smaller community. On the other hand, Westport was using institutions quite differently than was Centralia, and its children in institutions had been in care a much shorter time than had children in institutions in Centralia (2 years compared to 5.3 years).

Over all, children in Westport had been moving into adoption at a greater rate than in King City, although King City seemed to be catching up. Our pictures of movement for the date of our study showed less return home, proportionately, for Westport than for King City (but more than for Centralia). And while Westport was operating an extensive child welfare program that reached across the whole community—kept children in care a shorter time than did the program in King City, created more specialized services for children, and moved more children into adoption—yet, this program ran athwart many problems in attempting to find permanent homes for children in this large, heterogeneous, and somewhat sophisticated urban center.

THE CHILDREN'S OWN FAMILIES

Returning home seemed more common for King City children in foster care than for the children in Westport. What parental conditions could we associate with this tendency?

One fact which stood out quite clearly in comparing the return home situation in King City with what occurred in our other communities was the large proportion of return home children who were originally separated involuntarily from their parents. This was true of about half the cases in King City, where, otherwise, voluntary separation was so predominant. The interesting contrast was that in most communities the tendency was so definitely in another direction—involuntary separation was much less likely to lead to return home. We could couple this finding with the fact that 70 percent of those who returned home in King City were originally separated because of parental death, illness, and economic hardship or neglect and abandonment. We could recall, too, that a major practice of welfare and legal agents in the community was to return children to families that were reconstituted after joining forces with other relatives, often in the outlying regions from which they came to the city. Another explanation was that newcomers might lose their children to foster care for a time in the fast-paced city but would get them back quickly after a short period during which the family became acculturated to big city ways. For these children averaged only one year in care, and 71 percent were in care less than a year and a half. They averaged six years of age at the time of return. And this return home experience occurred disproportionately among dependent Negro children, although it occurred less than proportionately among Latin-American children and among Catholics in care. The Latin-American child, of all groups represented in foster care in King City, had the greatest chance of growing up in foster care, according to our findings. Return home occurred largely where the father was a semi-skilled or unskilled worker and where the mother was a household worker or a housewife. It occurred only where there were other brothers or sisters in the family—and King City was the only community where this was always the case. It seemed to occur more with the socioeconomically less-than-average dependent families in King City (except that the Catholic agency was moving deprived Latin-American children more toward adoption than toward return home), and may have indicated that return home planning in the harsh big city often meant parental surrender to overwhelming urban forces.

In about one third of the foster care cases in King City parents wished to give up their children for adoption, and fewer children— although a sizable proportion (43 percent)—than in any other community were in a conflicted limbo. Apparently, a large number waited for adoption planning, while for one in five return home was still desired by his parents. Still, more of these children were seldom if ever visited by parents than was true for children in Westport though more retained affectionate ties to parents. Often, however, neither parent had an adequate relationship with the agency, and in this regard King City and Westport were quite similar although both manifested less complete severance from parents than was found in Centralia. Parents were paying nothing toward the child's support in two thirds of the cases of children in foster care in King City.

We have seen that King City had a much larger Negro population than did Westport; but King City was reaching this population segment only about as frequently, in proportion to all children in care, as Westport was reaching its much smaller Negro population. Thus similar proportions (19 to 20 percent) of parents of all children in foster care were recorded as Negro in King City and Westport, and Negro families were represented on child dependency rolls in King City only to the same degree they appeared in the total population. The Latin-American group, on the other hand, was contributing about twice its normal population proportion to child dependency rolls. Catholic families contributed no more than their proportionate numbers.

As a total group, mothers of children in foster care averaged about thirty-four years of age, most of them were of average intelligence, and their average education amounted to completion of the ninth grade in school. Half of them were household workers, and only one fourth were housewives (a departure from the more domestic pattern in Southern Jamestown). Fathers averaged close to forty-five years of age, were of average intelligence, and their educational attainment averaged a little less than that of the mothers. The greatest proportion of the fathers was made up of skilled workers (31 percent), although one in four was unskilled. (Recall that children returned home to the semiskilled and the unskilled worker's family but not to the skilled, who, perhaps would not leave a city job to reconstitute a family elsewhere.) This total group of parents of the children remaining in care were about on a par socioeconomically, except in education, with the corresponding group of parents in Westport. Only about one fifth were still married to each other, and one tenth were widowed. Still, almost half of the fathers and over one third of the mothers were living with a spouse or mate at the time of our study. Whether their future plans included their children then in foster care could only be surmised by those who worked with them amidst the distractions of the big city.

In Westport the child who returned home was seldom one who had been initially separated from his parents involuntarily. Nor had he often been the victim of neglect or hardship. More often than in any other community, the child who returned home in Westport had been separated from his parents because of marital conflict which was, apparently, resolved with some professional assistance. Thus he was likely to stay in care longer than the corresponding child in King City (1.8 years, on the average, compared to one year). He was an older child (eleven years of age, compared to six years of age in King City) and was usually older than the average child who remained in care. Divorce, usually accompanied by remarriage, seemed to pave the way for return home in Westport; three fourths of the mothers of the children returning home were living with a spouse, while only a little over one third of the mothers of all children in foster care were living with a spouse.

The presence or absence of brothers and sisters appeared to make no difference whatsoever in the return home picture in Westport— contrary to our findings in King City—for the child who returned home was neither more nor less likely to have siblings than was the child who remained in care. Westport did not seem to be planning so much around the family unit when return home was contem-

plated; workers and agencies seemed to be planning more around
an individual child who was their responsibility, and if his parents'
home, perhaps newly constituted by one parent, was perceived by
them to meet his psychological needs they then returned him to this
home.

We have noted that fewer children, proportionately, returned to
their parents or relatives in Westport than in King City. What
other parental conditions and motivations contributed to this fact?

Actually, only a slightly greater proportion of the parents of
children in foster care in Westport than in King City could be considered to have left their children in an unreconciled limbo situation, but still this included almost half of the cases. About the
same proportions in the two communities had either released the
children for adoption, or definitely desired to have their children
return home. Parents were somewhat more likely to visit their children in foster care in Westport than in King City, although in half
the Westport cases neither parent visited more than very infrequently. Continuing, adequate relationships of the parents with
the agencies appeared with about equal infrequency in both communities (one in four or five cases). But in King City adequate relationships were almost twice as prevalent where children returned
home; in Westport, adequate relationships by mothers were three
times as prevalent where children returned home, while the father's
relationship with the agency seemed to make little difference in
distinguishing between the child who returned home and the one
who remained in care. Also, parents were paying something toward
a child's support in Westport in three out of five cases where children returned home but in only two out of five cases where the
child remained in care. (Payment for care seemed of negligible
importance in increasing chances for return home in King City.)
Finally, of all comparisons to be noted between Westport and King
City, there was a most apparent difference in the ties of children to
their parents, both for children who returned home and for those
who remained in care. In a comparison of the over-all foster care
picture in the nine communities, Westport children manifested least
often any apparent affectionate bonds with parents, except for the

children in our two rural counties. King City did not show a large proportion of foster care cases with affectionate ties either, but in King City fully 59 percent of those children who returned home were recorded as having affectionate relationships with their parents. In Westport, only 23 percent of those who returned home were recorded as having retained affectionate bonds to parents; so whatever the bases for determining the psychological needs of the individual child were in Westport, ties to parents did not loom large among these evaluations.

Other characteristics of the families we studied in Westport illustrate further contrasts between planning in an interdependent community in which quite uniform standards are applied to all and in a more "separated" community where diverse standards still apply to different groups. Negro families were disproportionately represented in foster care cases in Westport. Although only 4 percent of the child population from birth to age nineteen in that community was Negro, 18 percent of our foster care population was Negro.[2] Most significantly, perhaps, no case of a Negro child who returned home was recorded by us in Westport. The contrast to King City was great, for return home was more likely for a Negro child there than for a white child, and it must be presumed that such return was seldom to a greatly improved situation. On the other hand, Negro children were coming into care in great numbers in Westport—in total numbers, far more were in care there than in King City—but few were being adopted, and none was returning home. This may suggest aspects of a dilemma appearing in child welfare operations in Westport, but it certainly offers food for thought to professional workers who have the conviction that every child has a right to his own home. An added facet of this situation was the finding that 40 percent of the children in our sample who left care for other reasons (e.g., grew to majority age) were Negro children.

As a total group, the parents of the children in foster care in

[2] Granted, this 4 percent was a 1950 figure, as were all our census figures for all our communities. The Negro population had grown by 1957 but not to anything near 18 percent.

Westport were slightly younger than their counterparts in King City (fathers averaged about thirty-seven and mothers about thirty-three), they were an even healthier group than in King City, more were recorded as at least average in intelligence, and they were a better educated group by some two to three years of schooling on the average. There were a few Oriental, Indian, Latin-American, and "mixed" families represented in Westport, but, aside from the situation of the Negro population, minority ethnicity did not seem to be a deterrent to return home although it presented some barriers to adoption. On the whole, occupation groups were represented similarly in Westport and in King City—mostly skilled workers among the fathers, followed by the unskilled and the semiskilled—but a greater proportion of the mothers were housewives in Westport and more of them were clerical workers. And being a housewife or a household worker definitely increased a woman's chances of having her child returned to her in Westport. Available housing space and other economic characteristics were much the same for the parents in Westport and King City. It seemed obvious, however, that different expectations of them as citizens and as parents obtained in Westport, much as in Centralia, as opposed to King City. And quite obvious too was the fact that affectionate relationships between these older children and their parents were less apparent in Westport than in King City even when the children were eventually returned to their parents.

THE CHILDREN AND ADOPTION

How can we distinguish the adoption image and the probabilities of adoption for the children in foster care in King City and Westport?

King City departed slightly from the norms of adoption found elsewhere. Some older children were being placed there, and King City had the lowest proportion among our five largest communities —but still fully 74 percent—of children under two in adoptive placements. Boys and girls were equally represented. Negro children were not being placed in proportion to their numbers in care (we saw that they tended more to return home), while Latin-American children, usually given attention by the Catholic agency, were being placed in adoption in proportion to their numbers in care (but we saw that they were less likely to return home than were other children). Catholic children, generally, were being placed in adoption more frequently than Protestant children in proportion to their numbers in foster care and in the total population, although the over-all ratio of Catholic to Protestant adoptions was about two to three. Adopted children as a total group were recorded as intelligent and healthy, and in no case did a child with an irremediable physical disability appear in an adoptive placement in King City. Even with a few older children represented in the group, 97 percent of adoptive cases were noted to be free from psychological symptoms at placement, although only 86 percent were so recorded at the time they first came into care.

Our findings did not reveal many revised tolerances or changed images of the adoptable child in King City. And it must be recalled again that in a "separated" community like King City ethnic minorities could be placed within their own sizable segments. The Catholic agency seemed particularly able to revise standards in evaluating Latin-American families for Latin-American children so that these children as a group kept pace with whites in movement into adoption. But an adopting public among the Negroes was still ill-defined and relatively inconspicuous in this Southern community.

The profile of Westport's many adopted children revealed that the city's highly professional agencies seemed to be guarding the traditional image of the adoptable child as the "perfect" infant perhaps more than did agencies in any other community. A few Negro children were being placed but not in any degree in proportion to their numbers being taken into care. Westport was placing children of mixed ethnicity to the same extent, compared to all agency adoptions, as Centralia and King City were, but Westport's record of "mixed" placements was much less impressive than that of either of these other two communities when the proportion of dependent children with mixed ethnicity in this heterogeneous community was considered. The median age of the adopted child was eight months, although a few older children were being placed, as in Centralia, but not so frequently as in King City. The adopted child in Westport was almost invariably intelligent, healthy, without any physical disability and, except in rare cases, without psychological symptoms. The bare facts that of those adopted 91 percent were white children, while only 65 percent of those in foster care were white children; that 97 percent had no physical disability, while 80 percent of those in foster care had no disability; and that 97 percent were of average or better intelligence, while 78 percent of those in foster care were of average intelligence, revealed the selective nature of the characteristics of the adopted child in this heterogeneous Western metropolis.

Let us make a final survey of the children who remained in care in King City and Westport to crystallize some of the apparent deterrents to their movement in the light of the family configuration and the adoption image in each community.

In both King City and Westport the average age of the child in foster care was ten years. In King City this meant that he was four years older than the average child who returned home and nine years older than the average adopted child. Three fourths of the children remaining in care in King City were school-age children. Almost half were ten years old or over. Movement out of care for these older children, given the situations we have described, seemed unlikely without changed practices and changed images. However, ethnicity was less of a barrier in King City, since adoption could be made within each given ethnic segment, but return home was a more likely route for the Negro child. Less than average intelligence was a slight deterrent to adoption in King City. On the other hand, a physical disability, recorded for one fourth of King City's children in foster care, was not a deterrent to adoption if it was self-correcting or remediable. The presence of psychological symptoms was, however, a major factor discriminating between children in foster care and those in adoption; but such symptoms apparently were not a factor deterring return home.

The child in foster care in King City usually had affectionate ties to his brothers and sisters and showed affection for other children.

He was no longer very close, however, to his own parents. And in 60 percent of the cases the child in foster care manifested a confused sense of self-identity. In only one fourth of the cases was he legally free for adoption, and in almost four out of ten cases his parents retained full legal rights to him. To all intents he was a child for whom special efforts would have to be made if his personal confusion and his status of impermanency were to be remedied.

In Westport, the age disparity between the child still in care and the adopted child was even greater than in King City, though on the whole, the age distribution of children in foster care was much the same in both cities. In Westport, however, the impact of a professional value system and of a uniform set of behavioral norms seemed to apply across the whole community. Ethnic minorities were quite disproportionately represented on Westport's dependency rolls, but adoption seldom occurred for these groups and return home never occurred for Negroes. Boys were slightly more prevalent than girls in foster care—on a par with King City and Centralia—while boys were more likely to return home, but either sex had about the same chance of being adopted. We have already noted the disparities between the popular adoption image and most characteristics of the average child still in care; but it is noteworthy that Westport's diagnostic approach did not perceive many children in care as below average intelligence or with physical disabilities; nor did it detect a greater prevalence of psychological symptoms than was detected in King City (45–46 percent in both communities).

The situations of the children in care in Westport did emphasize some problems of planning and dramatized some differences in comparison with King City. These children actually less often showed affectionate ties to their parents (the least found in any urban community) than their counterparts in King City. Fewer than half of them had affectionate bonds with siblings (about 80 percent in both communities had siblings). Yet they were frequently affectionate with other children just as were the corresponding group of children in King City. However, in the midst of the complexities of life in Westport, these children were more often confused about their sense of self-identity than were the children in foster care in King City. Thus, the dependent child in Westport reflected the indeterminacy of his unstable position in that community.

Only half as large a proportion of these children were still completely tied legally to their parents as in King City, and more of them (36 percent) had been released or were in a legally adoptable situation. But the ambiguities of their total situations could not be clarified by clearing up legal entanglements alone. The gap between the position of these children in the culture—perhaps now becoming legitimized in a status of children in indefinite care—and the position of a child anchored in the permanency of adoption was wide. The social agencies of Westport, and indeed of all our communities, with few exceptions, had shown few tendencies to bridge this gap or actually to approach the problems of children in foster care as, literally, problems of children in need of parents and permanent homes.

It would be unfair to allow the preceding statement to stand without again presenting some examples of exceptions to the adoption norm found among placements in both King City and Westport. A few cases were noteworthy. In King City there were Judy, with a suspected physical disability, and two Latin-American children, Ann and Jimmy, with troublesome parental backgrounds.

Judy Blank was originally placed with the Davidsons on a foster care basis when she was two weeks old. At that time it was feared she was suffering from congenital heart disease. Six months later this home became a free home. After another period of six months had elapsed, and Judy was given a clean bill of health, this same home became her adoptive home. At the time of our study Judy was a year and a half old.

The Davidsons already had four children in their family, ranging in age from eighteen to seven years, the three youngest being adopted children, when Judy was placed with them. The family lived on an annual income of about $6,000 from a small business which they owned. A Catholic couple, the Davidsons were both in their forties, and both had moderate health problems.

Although Ann, aged four, a little Latin-American girl adopted by the Quintanos, was reported to have average intellectual capacities as measured by the Gesell Developmental Test, her mother, a patient in the State Hospital for Mental Defectives, had an I.Q. of 35. Ann's mother's parental rights were terminated when she abandoned Ann in a bus. The little girl was two years of age.

At that time Ann was placed in a foster home which the agency thought might develop into an adoptive home. Since this did not eventuate as hoped for, Ann was removed two years later and placed with her present adoptive parents.

Mr. and Mrs. Jose Quintano, a Catholic couple, were in their middle forties and had two other children, aged six and eight. Mrs. Quintano had completed the third grade, and Mr. Quintano had no formal education at all. Despite this fact, Mr. Quintano was employed as a skilled craftsman with an annual income of over $4,000.

The sparse record of the adoptive study of this family seemed to have been written primarily for the court and told us relatively little about this couple who were giving a permanent home to a four-year-old Latin-American girl whose own mother was mentally defective.

Mr. and Mrs. Francisco Luna were a Mexican-American couple who adopted Jimmy, a three-and-a-half-year-old boy of similar ethnic background. Both of the Lunas were illiterate, and Maria Luna spoke no English. Until Jimmy was placed with this couple, she had referred to a statue of Christ in their home as *"nuestro unico hijo."* The Lunas lived, moreover, on an annual income of $2,880. In addition, Francisco Luna was in his early fifties and Mrs. Luna in her late forties—ages much beyond what is usually thought desirable for adoptive parents of a child as young as Jimmy. The picture in this situation was made more complete by the knowledge that Jimmy had low-average tested intelligence, though he had no noted physical disability and seemed to be making a symptom-free psychosocial adjustment. He was born, however, of an incestuous union, his father was in prison, and his mother also was in an institutional setting.

In Westport, exceptional adoptive placements included the case of psychologically troubled Laura and that of Billy Varnum.

Mrs. Duncan Gordon was epileptic, although her seizures had been under control for about five years. Of different religious faiths, the Gordons were both about forty and childless. Duncan Gordon, employed as a brick mason, had an annual income of about $5,000. At their earliest visits to the agency the Gordons had indicated that they would readily accept a child with questionable genetic background. Laura's was not, but her behavior called for a kind of devotion which is likely to be generated only by a biological relationship, or by a great desire for a child to be one's own, such as the Gordons' feelings for Laura.

Laura, far more than a two year old should be, was hyperactive, aggressive with grownups, and periodically destructive. Described as attractive and appealing, with an average I.Q., she had been relinquished by her parents at the age of three months in response to pressure from the court because of their neglect and abuse of her. Laura was then placed in a foster home where she remained for almost two years, at which time she was placed with Mr. and Mrs. Gordon.

In this case a mother's health condition, the parents' age, and the differences in their religious background seemed less important than is sometimes true in adoptive placements.

Billy Varnum was a five year old whose journey into adoption was greatly influenced by a newspaper advertisement. Included in the symptomatology of this child with deep-seated psychological problems were withdrawal in social relationships, serious sleep disturbances, and other evidences of anxiety. His intellectual capacity was assessed as average in a psychiatric evaluation, and no physical disability was noted. Billy's parents were not married, his father's whereabouts was unknown, and when the boy was about three years of age his mother had demanded the court's assistance in arranging foster care for her son, who was found then to be an extremely deprived child. Temporary arrangements were then made for Billy in a foster family. Because of Mrs. Varnum's unverified complaints about sex play among the children in this home, Billy was removed within three months, at her insistence, and placed in an institution.

A few weeks later, Mr. and Mrs. Baker, a middle-aged couple with an income of under $5,000, answered a newspaper advertisement seeking a couple to care for an emotionally disturbed child on a foster care basis. Billy went to live with the childless Bakers. Some diminution of Billy's fears and symptoms of anxiety were noted by Billy's caseworker.

In over two years of erratic efforts to plan with the agency for Billy's future, Mrs. Varnum gave simultaneous evidence only of her deep-seated dislike of the child and her inconsistencies and rages regarding her own personally disorganized life. The Bakers seemed right for Billy. When, over his mother's protests, Billy became legally free for adoption a year and a half later, the Bakers requested permission to adopt him. The request was granted, and what was originally intended as a temporary placement became for Billy an adoptive home.

These were children who were different but for whom big city agencies found adoptive parents—children who otherwise might have lived on through their childhood and adolescent years in the uncertainties of foster care.

VI. THE SUMMATION AND A TEST IN BRIGHTON

18. Community Life, Foster Care, and Adoption

Let us review briefly some of the relationships which we may now hypothesize between community dynamics and the care of dependent children before looking at the community we called Brighton as a testing ground for some of our hypotheses.

COMMUNITY FORCES AND FOSTER CARE PLACEMENTS

We can now look back across eight communities to note the patterns of, and reactions to, foster care that appeared related to the social forms and processes we hypothesized for community cultures. The separating or interdependent orientations, the ascribed or achieved orientations, and the personalized or impersonalized orientations—each was found to be associated with particular patterns and manifestations of care. Furthermore, homogeneity, segmentation, and heterogeneity each produced particular conditions that were manifested in the community's approach to dependency.

A general hypothesis that guided our explorations into foster care was that *foster care placements reflect the normal social process tendencies in the culture of a community.* More specific hypotheses follow from this one:

1. A *separating* orientation tended to be associated with more institutional than foster family care in a community. This was true in Jamestown, Norden, and Summit.

2. An *interdependent* orientation tended to be associated with more foster family than institutional care in a community. This was found in Granger, Centralia, and Westport most conspicuously,

not only in their current pictures but in their historical patterns of growth.

3. An *ascribed* orientation tended to bring about a static care setting, and the atmosphere of planning emphasized maintenance of the status quo in community life. Jamestown and La Paz exemplified this, and their return home rates were higher than their adoption rates. Children moved on relatively infrequently into families other than their own. Norden demonstrated this propensity in the long periods in which dependents were in care. But in Norden this operated more specifically to set the dependent child apart from others in the community and to imply that his status as a deviant was one which he could not easily outgrow.

4. An *achievement* orientation tended to bring about an atmosphere of planning which emphasized more planning toward a new and "better" situation. Centralia and Westport exemplified this most clearly; King City was also achievement-conscious, but there the tendency operated differently on and within different segments of its population.

5. A *personalized* orientation was more accepting (less rejecting) of the dependent child in a setting where he was not considered greatly deviant, but was more rejecting of him in a setting where he was considered greatly deviant. The former situation obtained most in Granger and perhaps in some of Jamestown's institutions. The latter situation appeared most conspicuously in Norden.

6. An *impersonalized* orientation was more accepting (less rejecting) of the dependent child in a situation where this orientation was not conspicuously new for him, but was more rejecting in a situation where this orientation was most conspicuously a new experience for the dependent child. Rural dependents in the King City or Jamestown public care settings would probably feel most rejected by this experience, while urban dependents in the Centralia and Westport public care settings would probably feel less rejected by this experience.

We may also discuss the predominant social forms obtaining in communities as they relate to foster care placement. First, let us hypothesize some variations on *homogeneity*.

A general hypothesis, developed in our initial explorations, was that *in a highly homogeneous community dependent families and their children will be more visibly different and, thus, more deviant in the community.*

In the smaller, personalized, "separating," and homogeneous rural setting an exclusion of the deviant dependent child existed. This was the case in Norden where, actually, most dependent children came initially from outside the community.

In the somewhat larger and more dynamic, but still personalized, "separating," and homogeneous setting where difference was a threat to the ongoing social equilibrium, a denial of the existence of dependency was found. This was the case in Summit, with the lowest prevalence of dependent children of all our communities.

In the still larger setting, where difference had been assimilated through achieved homogeneity and interdependence was stressed, problems of dependency were not denied, but a process of perceiving homogeneous answers tended to appear. This was the case in Centralia.

Our more *segmented* communities also revealed some consistent patterns which could be formulated into hypotheses. A general hypothesis which developed was that *where there is much segmental differentiation in a community and the participants have had many experiences with difference, dependency* per se *will be less a differentiating phenomenon.*

This general hypothesis could be derived, with variations, from findings in Granger, Jamestown, and La Paz. Granger was too small for us to note segmentation, but sociocultural differences were apparent and had been accommodated to, just as economic fluctuations were met through the years. A major corollary of this hypothesis applied most specifically to Jamestown: *Where norms are ordinarily applied differently to different categories (segments) of people, the norms of dependency will be applied separately within, and relative to, each segment.*

This occurred most forcefully where an implied social stratification accompanied segmentation, as in "separating" Jamestown. Professional welfare workers in La Paz, on the other hand, seemed to form an interdependent bridge of uniform professional standards across the ethnic gulf in the community. A continuance of the tendency toward separate standards for separate segments could be discerned in King City.

Finally, our findings suggested hypotheses particularly relevant to large, complex, *heterogeneous* community settings. A general hypothesis developed was that *in complex urban settings where social heterogeneity is combined with extreme impersonality, the dependent child becomes less visible as a deviant but may tend to be lost in anonymity.*

Some variations on this tendency were noted:

A community welfare leadership (more specialized in such a setting) tended, at times, to quicken the concern of segmented publics, ethnic and religious groups, for their own kind in drawing dependent children into a separated circle of concern. This was true in King City, where an institution for the most depressed ethnic group was said to be needed and foster family programs operated largely within insulated case loads of agencies that were only slowly reaching toward more interdependence.

A community welfare leadership also tended, at times, to quicken the concern of the larger public as an interdependent whole in drawing dependent children into a circle of concern. This was true in Westport where treatment programs were interpreted to the whole community and a foster family program reached across the whole community and involved exchanges of cases and ideas between agencies. But the first tendency was also apparent in Westport too, although it seemed to lead from the quickened concern of separate publics toward a pooled community of concern.

A final statement will close our review of relationships between community forces and foster care placement. The specialized and diagnostic perception of the dependent child we noted in Westport led at least one key person in that community to fear impersonal "sovietization" of dependent children. This was perhaps the last stage we saw in processes of reaction to dependency, which began with the most reluctant differentiation of the dependent in our smallest and most homogeneous rural setting and ended with fears of sovietization of the dependent child in our most complex and heterogeneous urban setting.

Agency adoption can now be examined in association with the forms and processes manifested in the eight communities thus far discussed. One general hypothesis guided our explorations into adoption: *Agency adoption is more legitimized and acceptable in some cultural climates than in others.*

On the basis of this initial statement we derived a major hypothesis which accounted for our three social process tendencies and related them to agency adoption in our communities. This hypothesis was: *Agency adoption tended to go with the achievement orientation, with the impersonal or contractual orientation, and with the interdependent orientation in a community culture.*

Conversely, we would expect to associate nonagency adoption in its "purest" form (placement with relatives) with tendencies opposite to those stated above.

Let us elaborate briefly on this broad hypothesis. We noted that the most professional adoption agencies stressed the achievement of parenthood and de-emphasized blood descent and heredity in interpreting adoption to clients. Also, agencies maintained a professional contractual relationship with clients and stressed the legal factor. Further, professional adoption agencies were inclined to be nonsectarian and to operate across a broad and interdependent cross section of the community rather than within a separated population segment. Westport and Centralia exemplified all these tendencies most clearly and operated the most professionalized adoption programs.

Variations on the three orientations cited in the last hypothesis could lead to a high agency adoption rate, and variations which we saw showed how agencies may adapt to the cultural setting. The adoption agency in Summit, for example, accommodated to a highly personalized setting by playing down the contractual aspect and placed proportionately more children in adoption than did any other agency. Also, sectarian agencies might operate within a separated population segment, as the Catholic agency in King City did, but might stress interdependence within that segment and make many placements.

A corollary hypothesis seemed to develop: *The achievement orientation (interpreting achieved parenthood to adoptive applicants) was less important where an agency operated in a more "separated" setting and/or where it operated in a more personalized setting.* This seemed true of the rural placements through the agency in Summit and of some Latin-American placements made by the Catholic agency in King City.

We also found that our major forms of social differentiation came in for consideration in adoption. Generally, a homogeneous setting (like Summit) seemed to present the most ideal situation for like children to meet like parents. But in Norden, on the other hand, homogeneity was a complicating element in that the most available children were most visibly different, as deviants on the local scene, from prospective adoptive parents.

However, a major cultural element in adoption barriers was found where sociocultural gaps separating dependent children and prospective adoptive parents were widest in a community. For in this situation the problem of bringing available children and adoptive parents together was greatest. An interesting aspect of our findings was the variations in agency practice suggested for bridging such gaps. Some of these practices are discussed briefly at the end of this chapter.

This review of our groundwork has not been at all complete and exhaustive. But it suggests some of the relationships we can look for in foster care and adoption in Brighton once we have learned something about form and process in that community. So, then, let us turn to Brighton.

A NEW ENGLAND COMMUNITY

Brighton, the Greater Brighton Area

Brighton might be one of those American communities around which sociologists have pioneered their studies of social class in this country.[1] It is fairly old (though not so old as Jamestown or La Paz), it is in New England and on the Atlantic Coast, it is industrialized and highly urbanized,[2] and it is intermediate in size, providing relevant comparison to similarly sized Jamestown and Centralia. Brighton was the one community we studied in which the designation "Yankee" indicated a definable segment of the population. At the same time, it was a community in which, in 1950, one fifth of the total population was foreign born.[3] This would seem to indicate that Brighton had experienced successive waves of immigration through the 200 years of its history. And through these years Brighton had known periods of great prosperity and of depression. Another significant fact, which the census did not reveal, was that Brighton was a community in which well over half the population was Catholic. But, unlike the situation in La Paz, Catholicity did not coincide with other social characteristics to divide the community into two parts; for segmentation was more typical than bifurcation here, and even Catholics were divided into ethnic parishes in which Old World languages were used in the services.

This New England community was barely holding its own in numbers. The city proper lost population slightly between 1940 and 1950. Even Greater Brighton, the larger area which we focused upon, gained only slightly over 2 percent in population in that decade although those were years when most metropolitan centers grew extensively. Brighton was old in its urbanness. Its pop-

[1] See Vol. I of Warner's "Yankee City" series in which the commonly used American stratification designations are set down dividing a community into "upper-upper" and "lower-upper," "upper-middle" and "lower-middle," and "upper-lower" and "lower-lower" classes. (W. Lloyd Warner and Paul S. Lunt, *The Social System of a Modern Community.*)

[2] Measured by such criteria as high proportions of multiple-family dwellings, low fertility rates, and high proportions of women in the labor force, Brighton was the most urbanized of all our communities. Also, women outnumbered men significantly (about 54 percent to 46 percent beyond age twenty-five), and the population, over all, was an older one. The median of school years completed was 8.3 for the total population.

[3] England and Wales contributed some 18 percent to this foreign-born group and French Canada about 17 percent. But the largest group of foreign born, over 21 percent, were listed in the census as from "other Europe," and exploration on the scene indicated most of these were Portuguese who were not otherwise designated by the census.

ulace moved about less within the community,[4] and more of them lived in multiple-family structures, than was true of the population in any other community we studied. They worked, predominantly, as operatives and craftsmen in manufacturing trades.[5] And over half of those employed as operatives, and 45 percent of those employed in manufacturing generally, were women. We learned in Brighton that most of these women were employed as stitchers in the needle shops—a job traditionally avoided by men in this community.

Incomes were not high in Brighton. In 1950 the median income was some $1,000 below that in Centralia, although it was well above the figure for Jamestown [6] (where the income figures for Negroes considerably depressed the over-all median). Thus, although new industries were beginning to invigorate the economy, the pace of change was not a fast one in Brighton. There was a sense that this community looked back longingly to a day a century ago when it was the richest city per capita on earth.

Social Form and Process and Predictions on Placement Pattern

The forms of social differentiation which we found in Brighton seemed to show a predominant tendency toward heterogeneity that crystallized in an implied social class system. Ethnicity, occupation, place of residence, all had coalesced into class layers with a Yankee stratum at the top and the most recent immigrants at the bottom. But time and a changing occupation base had modified this picture. The Yankees of the imposing homes were a shrinking minority, and it had been some years since a sizable immigrant group had entered the system. Thus, "upper-uppers" and "lower-

---

[4] Physical mobility figures showed: 90.7 percent of the families occupied the same house in 1949 and 1950; only 6.4 percent moved from a different house in the county; only 2.3 percent moved in from a different county.

[5] Only about 28 percent were in professional and white-collar occupations in Brighton (12 percent were in professional or managerial positions alone); 58 percent were in semiskilled, service, and labor categories combined (38 percent of these operatives and 6 percent laborers). Manufacturing occupied 47 percent of the labor force.

[6] Median income for families and unrelated individuals was $2,580; 11.2 percent earned under $500, while 1.7 percent earned $10,000 and over.

lowers" were now hard to find. Sameness in occupation (approximately 50 percent were blue-collar employees in manufacturing) had widened the middle social ground by broadening the base of experiences which a majority in the community shared. But social mobility had been deterred by continued crowding in multiple-family structures where ethnic groups remained close to their own kind. Thus, the middle social ground in Brighton was more inert, did not have the room or the feeling for change and expansiveness that one identifies with a middle class in America. Its members remained relatively tied to ethnic neighborhoods, parishes, and tenements.

Social processes noted were further expressions of the situation. The atmosphere in Brighton appeared to be one in which emphasis on ascribed status took precedence over emphasis on achieved status. Our preceding statements bear this out—the lack of perceived mobility; the social strata anchored by heredity, place, and position; the constrictions on movement and expansion in the middle social ground. Likewise, Brighton's population was an older one, and perhaps the middle-aged group rather than the young married set with their children best expressed the outlook of the community. Moreover, separateness rather than interdependence seemed to typify groups in Brighton, although in the "social middle" some feelings of interdependence were developing. Still, loyalty to the part was much stronger than to the whole. Contractual relationships were a part of human experience in this highly urbanized setting when people ventured outside their own segment. But the separateness which kept people close to their own kind in crowded ethnic neighborhoods also enhanced the importance of personalized relationships with those in one's ethnic group whom one knew more as whole persons.

In such a setting we should predict that the emphasis in care would be on a given segment of the community looking after its own. Child dependency (as visible difference) should not be highly stigmatized. Dependency had undoubtedly hit a broad span of families and would not be so much identified with a lower or inferior segment except, perhaps, in the eyes of those in the highest social class. Knowing the history of professional welfare developments country-wide, we would expect there to have been a history of private institutional placements in Brighton determined, as in Jamestown, on the basis of ascribed social characteristics. However, if a public program had operated for many years (and New England communities were among the earliest arenas of community-wide public action in America), we would expect a wide use of foster family placements and a movement toward more use of them coupled with a more uniform set of behavioral norms applied in an increasingly interdependent middle social ground.

However, given a low proportion of young married couples and little room for raising children, we should expect that Brighton would have a low adoption rate. But even where formal adoption did occur within the community we should anticipate its being a practice still filtering down slowly from an upper class of standard-setters (as in Jamestown and, to a degree, in Stark). And it would seem that adoption below the upper stratum would still proceed on the basis of a separating placement within a social category, made by persons known and trusted personally by the adoptive family, in which heredity of the child was of much importance. With a declining population we might further expect to see, as in Granger, agency adoptive placements being made outside the community in other, more vigorous, urban centers.

When we consider the relative acceptance or rejection of the dependent child, certain relationships can be inferred between social form and process and the impact of dependency. With multiple difference and a history of community-wide experiences of economic fluctuations, we should expect the dependent not to be too visibly different and excluded but to be accepted into the "we." Also, Brighton was not so large and impersonal that anonymity bred rejection of community deviants. Continued segmented stratification would indicate that institutional placements in Brighton, perhaps mostly in private care facilities, reflected, as in Jamestown, the interested concern of a community segment for its own. At the same time, with no dramatic lower stratum specifically identified with dependency and with dependents probably coming from a broader social "middle," foster family homes should not be near-marginal or substandard homes but should also reflect "we" placements. This would be particularly true if there were an active public program in Brighton recruiting foster homes from a broad and increasingly interdependent, though relatively inert, middle social stratum.

Let us now look at the facts of placement and movement and listen to the statements of those we interviewed in Brighton to fill out our picture of foster care in this New England metropolitan area.

CHILD PLACEMENT

Foster Care in Brighton

Basic facts on the placement of children under study in Brighton are shown in Table 16. As demonstrated there, Brighton pre-

Table 16

PLACEMENT, LENGTH OF CARE, AND SEPARATION AGES OF
CHILDREN IN BRIGHTON

Type of placement, by percentage of children in care on April 1, 1957	
In foster family care	58
In institutional care	37
In adoptive homes	6
Average (median) number of years since first separation from parents, for all children under study	3.4
Age at which children first entered care, by percentage of all children under study [a]	
As preschoolers (0–5 years)	56
As school-aged children (6–10 years)	29

[a] See note *a*, Table 1.

sented more a foster family placement picture than did Jamestown, but less so than Centralia. Conversely, Brighton's institutional care was more extensive than Centralia's though less so than Jamestown's. It had a smaller dependent population for study than either Jamestown or Centralia.

As in Jamestown, we saw in Brighton a segmentation of groups; but Brighton's public welfare program counterbalanced the extent of local private institutional care. Similar to that in Jamestown, there was a primary concern for dependent children within one's own segment of the population. Unlike the situation in Centralia, there was little money available to be diverted into welfare so that Brighton was reaching fewer dependent families through its agencies than was Centralia. In Brighton, wherever the gulf between social classes was the widest the rejection of the dependent child from the lower class was greatest. This tendency paralleled the separation of dependent Spanish and upper-class Anglos in La Paz. At the same time, Brighton was perhaps more like Centralia than Jamestown in increasingly applying uniform behavioral standards to all its people.

As we present the words of those we interviewed in Brighton we shall attempt to identify class layers in the social system. Our use of Warner's terms for social classes will indicate, generally, whether an informant seemed to perceive himself, or the group alluded to, as relatively *more* or *less* anchored to an upper or lower stratum, or whether he perceived himself, or a group, *more* or *less* achieving social mobility in the middle, with a concomitant broadening of perspectives. In a community as socially differentiated as Brighton, class affiliation not only affected how or what one perceived in regard to dependent children; it complicated child placement and the community bases for its support. The "we" and the "they" became more clearly defined by multiple-group boundaries.

Whatever went into social definitions, the insulation of group from group was still typical of Brighton. Mrs. Morgan, an adoptive parent who lived in one of the old whaling houses in Brighton, and who probably could be classified as at least a "lower upper," related an incident that exemplified this situation: "When my husband was an officer in the Marine Corps during the war he was with a friend one time when they both saw a sailor with 'Brighton' written on his tee shirt. He was sure he wouldn't know the man, but his friend insisted he speak with him. My husband found that the man was from Brighton all right but lived on the North End, had never been south of Center Square in his life, and didn't even know where Brighton High School was." She added, "This is pretty typical of people who live here."

Miss Silva, a stitcher in a needle plant, of Portuguese descent and probably somewhere in the relatively "mobile middle" socially, said: "This will be a hard town for you to learn about. Whichever group of people you speak to will know of that group and no other. There are lots of different nationality groups in our shop, but I am different from most of them because I pay attention to civic matters that other workers are afraid of. It has only been in the last year or two that I knew the Community Council existed. Now when I try to get people interested in things they tell me 'That's too high-brow for me,' or 'They wouldn't accept me.' " She continued, "You see we have classes of people here, and one class doesn't step out to find out what the rest of the city is doing."

Father Leonardo, who ministered to a parish composed largely of descendants from colored immigrants from the Cape Verde Islands (probably Brighton's largest "upper lower" group), said: "National groups here founded their own churches with a priest from their own country in charge. Thus we have French, Portuguese, Polish, Italian, and Cape Verdian parishes. The Cape Verdians feel that they are the last ones hired and the first ones fired. But Puerto Ricans are moving in now, and they are many years behind the Cape Verdians. These two groups dislike one another."

A local newspaper editor told us: "Brighton is a place where nationality remains important. It is always recognized in elections. There are over 450 clubs and organizations here with largely 'nationality' memberships. The Franco-American societies sponsor their own Rifle, Drum, and Bugle Corps." This last statement rang in sharp contrast to the common civic feeling we recalled in Centralia's pride in its Boy Scout Drum and Bugle Corps.

On this segmented basis, and allowing for harsher attitudes across the greatest class gulfs, there was still evidence of a concern for dependent children in Brighton.

A Negro Protestant minister, perhaps a "lower middle," said: "We Protestants are in the minority here. Lack of money hampers us, but other churches are no more concerned than we are with kids. Catholics will support the United Fund, but they support Catholic drives first and are probably more devoted to the policy of their church than they are concerned about the entire community."

Mr. J. C. Flynn, owner of a furniture store and active in Catholic welfare activities (probably an "upper middle"), said: "We never come across child neglect. The average mother and father who are poor are more desirous of having their kids behave than are some of our better families. And, you know, this city would be in a constant turmoil about what to do with eighty orphans if it weren't for our Catholic institution. Most kids are entered by relatives, but a few are referred by a parish priest." He added: "People here are conditioned to be less opulent. Because of local conditions they have to trim their sails all the time and are alert to the other fellow's plight."

Miss Silva, our Portuguese-American informant, commented: "It seems that parents, regardless of the situation, want their children and don't feel they should give them up. The Cape Verdians, for example, keep their illegitimate kids. Homes are found within the family, or the priest handles placement in the Church."

Father Manuel, pastor of a large Portuguese congregation on the North End, said: "Most of the kids at the St. James Orphanage are Portuguese. The Father there has done a great job of inculcating in the nuns and workers an attitude of charity and real affection toward the children."

The retired president of one of Brighton's mills, perhaps a "lower upper," said: "The younger industrialists who come here say that Brighton was never educated in welfare. The Jewish groups and the Catholics can always collect money for their own—their drives always go over the top. But our United Fund drives have had a terrible time in getting support."

Mr. Sylvanus Strayer, of the local Society for the Prevention of Cruelty to Children (SPCC), said: "It is hard to find a child here who does not have a relative near by. I think there are many informal child placements."

And informal placements in Brighton's neighborhoods still largely reflected the personalized concern of ethnic groups for their own kind. But Brighton was changing, slowly; and these changes were expressed in a shifting orientation to child neglect as a community problem, particularly in the middle social strata.

Mr. Tom Tascali, a labor representative on the board of the United Fund and probably identifiable in the "mobile middle," said: "I live on a typically American street. There are a bus driver, a newspaper editor, a factory worker, the owner of a laundry, and a street sweeper all living on this street." Mr. Flynn added: "In another generation all this factionalism will be over. The Portuguese are becoming assimilated, and when the economic situation permits they move out of tenements into nicer districts."

Mr. G. Paul Priddy, a personnel manager and past president of the Community Council, probably a very "upper middle," remarked: "Until recently there was a complete lack of community spirit. But I see changes now. I heard that the rector at the Episcopal Church in the South End was criticized because he began to make the church a neighborhood church. A lot of Portuguese families had moved in there and he let their kids play in the yard and encouraged them to come to young people's groups. The church became about 35 percent Portuguese." He continued: "The neighborhood Protestant churches are pretty much the working people's churches. The 'society' churches are the ones in the center section of town. People in the neighborhoods go to center churches when they get society-minded."

This pattern was reminiscent of the process by which suburbanites in Jamestown still returned to the central peninsula to partake of the older symbols of status. But in Jamestown this was an effort to reaffirm status in terms of older symbols, while in Brighton it represented a quest for new status by those few who now were perceiving themselves as socially mobile.

Mr. Alfred Winslow, an old Brighton Yankee, a lawyer, and probably the closest to an "upper upper" that we interviewed, said: "What's left of old Yankee families are very cliquish. All the foreign elements are Catholic. But the town is much less split up than it used to be. My father's generation is out of the picture, and mine is about to fade out. I think the racial groups that went through the public schools were more Americanized, although they still have their own festivals. One thing that we can be proud of here is our highly skilled labor force."

The skilled worker in Brighton, as in Centralia, was achieving a middle position in the social system from which his community perspective might be broadened, although physical and economic constrictions had slowed the pace of his mobility.

In this shift toward more of a community approach to problems of dependency there were variations in people's perceptions and attitudes which, again, seemed identifiable with their class position in Brighton, whether "lower upper," like Dr. Knox, or cognizant of the ways of the "mobile middle," like the union official and Miss Silva.

Said Dr. Calvin Knox, a pediatrician, "I see some children whose parents are on ADC, and most of these people are intellectually and morally inferior. Most of them don't have what it takes to be competitive human beings. But I am sure that all the other doctors in town are sympathetic to child welfare, although not too many are involved in agency programs. Support of welfare is pretty well spread out, and the United Fund is well enough organized to induce people like factory workers to contribute. However, I understand that all the agencies have a hard time finding boarding homes."

Miss Silva said: "Foster children are always referred to as 'state' children. They stay for a certain length of time, and parents are paid for their care. I know only a few foster parents. I guess lack of money keeps people from asking about adoption." While the head of a textile union, also in tune with public attitudes in the middle social ground, said: "It is public knowledge that you can place children in foster homes. I know of many people taking care of state boys and girls. There are good people who do that and some who don't have to do it for money but are just willing to help children."

In public agencies, placement procedures seemed to follow certain priorities. A juvenile probation officer described a case: "We got a report on a fifteen-year-old illegitimate girl living with a man.

Her mother was given a short sentence in the women's reformatory. An aunt—a big, warmhearted woman who felt responsibility for her niece—agreed to take the girl. When this aunt died we found another placement. The first two foster homes we tried didn't work out, but now the girl is in a successful foster home placement where she is happy." We note in this public case that relatives were explored first, but other community doors were also open when relatives were no longer available.

In Brighton children still tended to be cared for by extended families and neighbors or within the facilities of a specific church or ethnic group. The "lowest" classes, particularly, seemed to absorb their own dependents, while the "upper" classes either had none or absorbed them in private care. But when children came to the attention of public agencies—and the court received predominantly voluntary commitments—they tended, as the local SPCC noted, to be referred by individuals who were personally concerned for their well-being. With an economic situation somewhat more depressed than Centralia's, Brighton foster homes were apparently hard for agencies to find. But in the middle social strata there were open doors for "state" children, and community-wide welfare activities had begun to receive a broader base of support in Brighton.

Adoption in Brighton

The adoption figures for Brighton placed it among our lowest communities in the prevalence of such placement. The facts we gathered appear in Table 17. In addition, Brighton was one of our three communities having the fewest agency adoptions. It was also

Table 17

ADOPTIVE PLACEMENTS AND RETURNS HOME IN BRIGHTON

Percentage of all children in care April 1, 1957, who were in adoptive placements	6
Percentage of adoptive placements that were in-county	53
Percentage of children in care April 1, 1957 who left care by January 1, 1958 (nine months later)	
For adoptive placements	7
For return home and other purposes	14

one of our three communities (La Paz and Jamestown were the others) which had a return home percentage higher than the adoption percentage.[7] Adoption, as reflected in the statements of people we interviewed, was much an extension of cultural process in this "shabby, but charming," old town, as one person referred to the community. Old World patterns persisted in Brighton. Young people went to work rather than to college and left home in increasing numbers; ties to ethnic groups, of people who stayed on, remained strong; and there had been little room, or economic spark, for social mobility. Adoption even among the "upper" classes still stressed ascribed characteristics of children, and the process of adoption through an agency had not reached many in the lower strata.

Mrs. Morgan, the adoptive parent in the old whaling home, said: "I know quite a few who are adopting, but it certainly isn't a popular practice. The ones I know are like me—married a long time, talked about it a long time, and finally acted. I am Dutch and my husband is English and I wanted a child who was Dutch and English or all one or the other. It didn't occur to me that I would even consider another nationality. Our adopted daughter is all English —she's blond and has nice little features."

Dr. Knox, the pediatrician, said: "The children available for adoption here are inferior to the families that want children for adoption. Parents of the same social groups as the children available are not interested in adoption. The people who want to adopt are not average people, and the problem is a difficult one."

Miss Silva, in the social "lower middle," said: "I know of one person who adopted a child. I heard of someone else who wanted to adopt and went to Portugal. She felt that if she were going to help she would help someone of her own family."

A clerk of the district court, French-Canadian by descent, said: "The older French-Canadian families used to adopt a lot informally without adjudication. Now they see the need for legal action. Many went to Canada for children. But most adoptions were direct; people wanted a French child, and they didn't go through agencies. I would say, however, that the feeling is shifting so that

[7] See Table 32, columns 4 and 5, in Appendix C.

now they don't much care if a child is Irish, Portuguese, Italian, or whatever so long as the religious strain is kept the same. Priests make many adoptive arrangements, and there is no better go-between than a priest."

The Catholic priest at a North End church said: "People are somewhat afraid of adoption. They say: 'You don't know what you are going to get.' Heredity is involved." But Mr. Priddy, the "upper middle" personnel manager, who chided his wife a bit for "status-seeking" but was now himself attending a church in the center section of town, said: "I have several friends who have adopted children. All of these people are at about my social and economic level. I don't know about people below or above us. But it does seem that adoptions are increasing a bit."

The Negro Protestant minister, who had many contacts with those more anchored to a lower social stratum, said: "I think foster homes are more popular than adoption because you get paid without the responsibility of providing everything for children. I would encourage adoption if I felt the inquiring couple were the type to adopt."

Father Leonardo said of the Cape Verdians: "Their families are quite large. Adultery and illegitimacy are recognized facts, and people care for their own children or relatives take over. Very few Cape Verdian children are adopted, because most people already have large families."

Thus in Brighton adoption was not a popular practice. For the most part, it still remained for the "upper" few, and even with these people the matching of ascribed characteristics took precedence over achieved parenthood. For in Brighton those things which persist were more apparent in the culture than were those things which change.

OUR NINE COMMUNITIES COMPARED

At this point we shall put together our pictures of all nine communities and place some relevant facts side by side. This may help to give us a better total perspective since we are now familiar with each community. Before looking at our composite pictures of foster care and adoption, it is suggested that the reader glance at the comparative facts on all nine communities, compiled in Appendix E, for a final view of social differentiation and social change as it is suggested by relevant census data.

Foster Care and Adoption in Nine Communities

The foster care placement and adoption figures for all our communities, including a figure on prevalence of foster care and prevalence of adoption in the populations, appear in Table 18. Several things stand out in this table. Our statements recall the hypotheses presented at the beginning of this chapter. The prevalence of foster care figures indicates a composite of many things. In a sense, they reflect an interplay between actual physical and socioeconomic conditions contributing to dependency in a given community and the social definitions, expressed through social welfare resources, by which dependency was perceived and acted on. The Norden and King City figures on prevalence of children in foster care (per community population) represented the two extremes encountered. We know that Norden's high figures in large part reflected the fact that an institutional facility located there handled dependent children from all over the state. This accentuated the visibility of the dependent child in highly homogeneous Norden, and associated dependency with the more extreme deviation of out-of-county families in that community. King City stood out for its very low proportions of the population in foster care. This was particularly surprising in view of the fact that King City had a depressed population segment and suggested that multiple standards tended to influence different groups in defining dependency in this somewhat "separating" community. But apparently King City was relatively reluctant to perceive dependency in any population segment.

Separate figures on Jamestown (not in the table) showed that only 20 percent of our foster care population was Negro although 49 percent of the child population up to age nineteen was Negro. This indicated that a double standard for defining dependency prevailed most of all in segmented and "separating" Jamestown. In

La Paz, 83 percent of the foster care population was Spanish while 68 percent of the population group from birth to age nineteen in La Paz was counted as "Spanish-surname" by the census. Thus La Paz seemed to reach dependents, through its professional social workers, with a more uniform set of standards than did other divided or

Table 18

PREVALENCE OF FOSTER CARE AND ADOPTIVE PLACEMENTS [a]

	Children in Foster Care (Per child population ages 0–19)		Children in Adoptive Homes (Per numbers of married women ages 20–44 with husband present) [b]	
	Children in Foster Care on April 1, 1957	Children Whose Own Homes Were in the County	Children in Adoption on April 1, 1957	Children Whose Placements Were in the County
Rural Communities				
Norden County (Abbotsford)	11.5	1.0	2.3	1.6
Granger County (Daleville)	4.0	3.2	2.3	—
Small Urban Counties				
Pine County (Summit)	4.7	0.9	6.7	1.5
Santa Ana County (La Paz)	5.8	1.9	1.4	0.4
Metropolitan Areas				
James County (Jamestown)	4.7	4.1	1.2	0.3
Lake County (Centralia)	6.0	5.2	3.8	2.0
Greater Brighton Area (Brighton)	6.0	3.9	0.8	0.4
Big Cities				
Stark County (King City)	2.9	2.9	1.2	1.1
Makah County (Westport)	5.9	5.2	3.0	1.8

[a] Stated as numbers per 1,000 in population groups indicated.
[b] For smaller communities proportion of married women ages 20–44, with "husband present," were taken on "state-wide urban" or "state-wide rural non-farm" basis, and this percentage applied to female population ages 20–44 in our communities to obtain a base for calculating the index.

segmented communities, since the Spanish were a more depressed group socioeconomically in the total population. However, the low in-county prevalence of agency-supervised dependent children for La Paz indicated that welfare professionals in that community did not apply, on the whole, as rigorous a set of behavioral standards as was applied in more prosperous Centralia and Westport where the prevalence figures of 5.2 for dependent children from in-county homes were highest of all.

The low figures on proportions of the population in foster care in Summit should be evaluated in light of the fact that only 45 percent of all cases there came from homes within that county. Summit served a broad area, and dependency, apparently, was not common within the local community nor was it often perceived there. Summit had a problem similar to Norden's in adjusting to children who initially were usually "outsiders." But the dependents who were cared for in Summit were not so visibly different or excluded as were the dependents in Norden and they moved much more readily into adoption through the local agency. Centralia and Westport, serving their communities more professionally and perceiving dependency through a more uniform set of standards, had the highest proportions of their local child populations in care. The figures for these two communities, compared with all the others, strongly suggest that the availability of services was a major determinant of the in-county prevalence of children in foster care, even as the low figures for Norden and Summit suggest that a relative absence of socioeconomic problems may also have contributed strongly to this index.

Summit stood out for its high prevalence of children in adoptive care on April 1. But we found that a very small proportion of the Summit adoptions were placements in the county. Centralia and Westport ranked highest in proportions of adoptions in the community. The highest proportion of all King City adoptions were in-county placements, but it ranked quite low in prevalence of adoption per county population. The figures for King City were colored by the fact, as we saw before, that very low proportions of the population were in any kind of formal welfare care in that community.

Brighton, Jamestown, and La Paz stood out for their low proportions of agency adoptive care. Brighton and Jamestown were particularly low in adoptions per community population, while a very low proportion of the few adoptions in La Paz were in-county placements. Each of these communities had a low achievement orientation, had broad sociocultural gaps in their populations, and had large segments who were strange to contractual relationships.

The Norden picture suggested strongly that such a small community might be the scene of more adoptions if more children were available or if dependent children cared for locally could be perceived by local residents as adoptable. The King City picture suggested that in the growing suburbs of a large metropolis there might be many prospective young adoptive couples that had not been reached. Even more, in such settings, there might be many couples of a thriving middle class who would increasingly be less concerned with the ascribed characteristics of a child and who would be more amenable to accepting the "different" child. Let us return briefly to some considerations that our earlier hypotheses suggested.

It appeared that for people of rural antecedents, the *contractual* emphasis in agency adoption was most strange and threatening. Many Negro newcomers in our communities demonstrated this, as did the rural Spanish around La Paz, the rural whites newly arriving in King City, and most people in Norden and Granger. For those newly *achieving* upward social mobility, the ascribed characteristics of a child were still of great importance. Young educated Spanish couples in La Paz and King City and the young educated Negro couples in King City and, to a lesser degree, in Westport manifested the fear that certain characteristics of a child might detract from their own achieved status. These were not the couples with whom children who were "different" might be placed in adoption. For those couples less knit into the *interdependent* larger community, separated contacts and emotional reinforcements through shared experiences with other prospective adoptive parents of their own group seemed important. The Negro adoptive applicants in Westport seemed to need these experiences with "friends who were also interested in adoption" more than they needed to be accommodated for either of the other two tendencies.

Further elaboration here of the manifold implications of our findings would serve little purpose. Our picture of foster care and adoption, across a wide spectrum of nine American communities, has been painted in broad strokes. We have merely penciled in the bold outlines of social form and process in widely disparate total community configurations. A major task we faced was to make discrete communities which were not immediately comparable, comparable as arenas in which phenomena of foster care and adoption occurred. This was done by conceptualizing them as sociocultural systems. If the questions which arise from this sketchy, and still indistinct, picture stimulate a closer, and a more controlled, focus on smaller areas of our canvas, then our explorations will have served their major purpose.

19. Legal Systems and the Placement of Children

Our "across-the-board' legal material did not contain as many variations in content as our knowledge of differences in legal practice in the nine communities would lead us to expect. This suggested that it was more the way in which a judge perceived his role, and the way in which he was perceived in his role by others in the community, that determined legal practice in child welfare. Thus our analysis placed the emphasis on the philosophy and practices of a judge, on the philosophy and practices of welfare agencies, and on the interdependence of both within a particular community.

For each community we present a list of relevant laws [1] and a brief picture of the individuals who put them into effect. We were particularly interested in those legal practices which were involved when children entered or left foster care. We were interested in the degree to which the law was explicit and consistent and the degree to which it left much to individual judgment. But primarily we tried to look at a total system of "legal forces" as part of a larger system of "community forces" and did not attempt to separate out particular influences. In our paired communities the laws them-

[1] See Appendix D.

selves were often quite similar but had very different usage. It was the total effect of the legal situation on child placement and movement that we wished to indicate.

We identified a parents' rights emphasis in half of our communities—Norden, Jamestown, Summit, and La Paz. In our explorations we anticipated the following effects of this orientation on the placement pattern of foster care children: (1) fewer agency adoptions and more return home; (2) a shorter time in care; (3) separation from parents at a later age; (4) fewer involuntary separations of child from parent; (5) more physical and social rather than psychological reasons for separation. A child's rights emphasis, we hypothesized, should manifest the obverse of these placement tendencies.

In our interviewing and in defining the roles of the judge and other legal agents we inferred a parents' rights or a child's rights orientation from the expressed attitudes of these key people. Now, in summarizing the legal aspects, we will change our order of reporting as we changed our procedure of presentation of the Brighton community data. This time we will review some placement facts in all our communities, present Brighton against a backdrop of findings that have been consistent with a parents' rights or child's rights emphasis in eight communities, and attempt to place Brighton somewhere on the parents' rights—child's rights continuum on the basis of placement pattern findings. Next we will look at the legal situations in eight communities in a manner designed to indicate degrees of judicial freedom for judges in these communities. This will be represented in terms of trends toward consistency or inconsistency in the laws, remoteness of legal and welfare systems from each other, and existence or absence of explicit restrictions. Brighton laws will be presented, and Brighton will also be placed in its context on these judicial freedom variables, the hypothesis being that these factors are related to the freedom of a judge to act and to define his own role. We will follow these summaries with a brief sketch of the judge in Brighton and others who surround him to see whether his and their attitudes are in line with what we would expect in a community presenting a placement picture and a judicial freedom picture consistent with a particular set of roles.

Let us turn to the placement findings that we hypothesized as related to the parents' rights emphasis found in Norden, Jamestown, Summit, and La Paz. Two things are important in deciding whether placement facts were consistently in line with this hypothesis: how a parents' rights community compared with its similarly sized partner (a comparison in which other variables are more likely to be held constant), and how parents' rights communities appeared in a rank ordering of all communities on a given placement variable. The results of looking at the five placement pattern findings demonstrated that only two of them were consistent enough to be considered predictive of a parents' rights or a child's rights emphasis. They were: fewer adoptions; and separation from parents at a later age. We will look at each of these findings separately and then see how Brighton appeared in them.

Fewer agency adoptions and more return home.—This held generally true for Norden and Jamestown when compared to their partner communities. Each had less than half the proportions of agency adoptions that Granger and Centralia, respectively, had. And Jamestown had many more children returned home than Centralia, although Norden had only slightly more returns home than Granger. Summit and La Paz, paired communities but both placed by us on the parents' rights end of a continuum, should not differ and did not differ greatly in having high return home proportions. But Summit stood far out of proportion to La Paz, or any other community, in adoption proportions, and this was not consistent with our "parents' rights–low adoption" hypothesis. This suggested that a closer look at differences in Summit adoption practices was in order since in most of our communities high adoption rates tended to go with ease of release of children from natural parents through legal action, and thus with a child's rights orientation. Likewise, Norden was inconsistently low on return home, and this fact called for a broader look at the kinds of children in care in that community—mostly children whose parents were not in or of that community. In summary, ranking eight communities on incidence of adoption and return home yielded the data in Table 19.

Table 19

COMMUNITIES RANKED BY PERCENTAGE OF CHILDREN IN
ADOPTIVE PLACEMENTS OR RETURNED HOME

(In percent)

Children in Adoptive Homes on April 1, 1957		*Children Returned Home during the Six-Month Period January 1–June 30, 1957*	
Summit [a]	39	Summit [a]	18 [b]
Centralia	22	Jamestown [a]	14
Westport	21	King City	14
King City	18	La Paz [a]	12
Granger	17	Westport	10
Norden [a]	8	Centralia	4
La Paz [a]	7	Norden [a]	4
Jamestown [a]	6	Granger	3

[a] Parents' rights communities.　　　　[b] From Table 32, Appendix C.

Separation from parents at a later age.—The proposition that an emphasis on parents' rights would permit parents a longer time and more deviant behavior before court action would be taken did prove somewhat consistent in our eight communities except in La Paz, where separation was early but the judge was less involved in the welfare picture. Median age at separation was the same for Norden and Granger, but Norden had only half Granger's proportion of children separated as preschoolers. Median age at separation was two years higher in Jamestown than in its partner, Centralia; and percentage of separations as preschoolers was considerably lower in Jamestown. Summit and La Paz had identical median ages of first separation, but La Paz clustered with the child's rights communities in percentages of children separated as preschoolers, as detailed in Table 20.

Where did Brighton stand on these two placement variables? On the first, Brighton clustered with the parents rights' group, being next to Jamestown in low proportion of adoptions (6 percent) but in the middle on the proportion returning home (11 percent). Brighton was low in adoption, particularly when compared to similarly sized and child's rights-oriented Centralia and it was high in return home, again particularly compared to Centralia. It resembled its partner, parents' rights Jamestown, in other words, much more than it resembled Centralia on this variable.

Table 20

COMMUNITIES RANKED BY CHILDREN'S AGE AT
SEPARATION FROM PARENTS

	Median Age (In years)	Percentage Separated as Preschoolers
Norden [a]	8	19
Granger	8	40
Jamestown [a]	6	46
Summit [a]	4	54
King City	4	59
Westport	4	62
La Paz [a]	4	66
Centralia	3–4	70

[a] Parents' rights communities.

On the second variable Brighton occupied an intermediate position in the rank ordering of communities. It clustered with parents' rights communities, compared to Centralia, on the percent separated as preschoolers (56 percent) but resembled Centralia more than Jamestown in median age at first separation (four years).

Thus, Brighton did not rank high among all our communities as either parents'-rights or child's-rights-oriented, but on the basis of the two placement variables which separated our communities most consistently it tended to fall toward the parents' rights end of the continuum.

THE LEGAL SYSTEMS AND JUDICIAL FREEDOM

A reappraisal of legal content and process in all our communities suggested a hypothesis relative to the role of the judge: Judges have more freedom to act on their personal philosophies where: (*a*) laws and codes are not consistent or well-codified; (*b*) the legal and welfare worlds are quite remote from each other; and (*c*) there are few restrictive measures—religious, economic, and judicial—to restrain the judge.

Ranking [2] our eight communities impressionistically on these three characteristics yielded the data in Table 21. From the table we see that Norden and Jamestown were perhaps most alike in

Table 21

COMMUNITIES RANKED BY CHARACTERISTICS RELATED TO
FREEDOM OF THE JUDGE

(a) Codification and Consistency of Laws			(b) Remoteness of Legal and Welfare Worlds			(c) Restrictive Measures		
Least	Jamestown	1	Remote	Norden	1	Few	Granger	1
	Norden	2		La Paz	2		Centralia	2
	Westport	3		Jamestown	3		Westport	3
	King City	4		Summit	4		King City	4
	Summit	5		Granger	5		Jamestown	5
	La Paz	6		Centralia	6		La Paz	6
	Granger	7		King City	7		Summit	7
Most	Centralia	8	Together	Westport	8	Many	Norden	8

ranking high on (a) and (b) and low (although Jamestown was number 5) on (c). Granger and Centralia were most alike in ranking low on (a) and (b) and high on (c). In summary, inconsistent codes and a broad separation of legal and welfare worlds, together with more restrictive measures, seemed to be associated with communities demonstrating the parents' rights tendency. Generally, rankings were consistent with orientations. Norden and Granger (hypothesized opposites in orientation) were ranked as very dissimilar on these three factors; Jamestown and Centralia (also opposite) were ranked dissimilar; Westport and King City (hypothesized as similar in orientation) were ranked similar; Summit and La Paz (similar in orientation) were ranked similar on these factors.

Thus, the factors in bringing about the greater freedom of a judge to act on his philosophy—his room for defining his own role—were not all found in either child's rights or parents' rights settings. Our rankings showed, however, more factors of freedom apparent in our parents' rights communities. Interpretation might

[2] Ranking was done independently by three persons familiar with the legal material on these communities, and the average rank given by all three was assigned to a community.

suggest that when laws were overlapping and not well codified they gave little direction to the judge and permitted him more influence—but his influence could be a strong "legal" one (as in Jamestown and Norden) or a relatively strong "welfare" one (as in Westport and King City). Furthermore, where the legal and welfare worlds were far apart a judge tended to be more legalistic, as in Norden, La Paz, and Jamestown; while where these worlds were close together a welfare philosophy seemed to influence his operations, as in Westport, King City, and Centralia; or perhaps like-mindedness induced closeness. Also, the more restrictions on placement, the more a judge's legal role was defined and constrained for him. This tended to eventuate in a legal emphasis rather than a welfare emphasis in the communities we studied.

It became obvious that a judge's freedom could be either freedom from welfare constraints and directives, or freedom to express a welfare philosophy in his own actions. At the time we studied our communities, with the court and welfare situations then obtaining, judicial freedom seemed to go more with a parents' rights emphasis. Lack of legal recodification and remoteness of the welfare world from the judge tended to free the judge from influences of professional welfare people; but other restrictions, of an older, more ascribed, set of legal and cultural definitions, bound him more tightly in his choice of alternatives as the chief legal figure in child placement. It was this latter combination—lack of newer welfare opposition and direction plus older legal and cultural restraint—that typified our parents' rights communities. By contrast, a combination of welfare opposition and/or legal recodification plus relative freedom from older legal and cultural restraint typified our more child's rights communities.

Where did Brighton rank on these factors? From a perusal of Brighton laws [3] and our previous look at the forces operating in that community, our rankings for Brighton located it in the following positions:

1. On consistency or codification of laws we gave it rank "8" (moving Centralia to "9").

[3] Presented in condensed form in Appendix D-5.

2. On remoteness of legal and welfare worlds we gave it rank "4" (moving Summit to "5").

3. On incidence of restrictive measures we gave it rank "8" (moving Norden to "9").

Thus, Brighton did not fit either the Norden and Jamestown parents' rights pattern or the Granger and Centralia child's rights pattern. Its laws, like those in Centralia, had been highly codified. But it was closer to Jamestown than to Centralia in having the legal and welfare worlds more remote from one another; and it was closer to Jamestown than to Centralia again in having many restrictive measures to constrain the operations of the judge. On all three variables Brighton did not seem to allow for much freedom of action for the judge. His role was apparently closely defined by the laws and the community situation. And this was not inconsistent with a community in which stability was more apparent than change and in which roles throughout the social system were comparatively well defined and relatively static.

Looking at Brighton in the light of both areas that we have discussed—placement variables and judicial freedom—we should anticipate hearing certain themes expressed in the attitudes of the judge and of those who deal with him in matters of child placement:

1. We would expect that the philosophies expressed would emphasize the rights of parents to their children. There should be a closer resemblance to Jamestown in this respect than to Centralia, although children were apparently being reached for placement at younger ages in Brighton than in Jamestown.

2. We would expect that the judge would express a philosophy that indicated he was more a product of the system in which he operated than an innovator within it. If legal codification and restrictions left little room for interpretation to the judge, we could expect that welfare practices would be carried out by other welfare agents with little more than formal attention to the judge's place in procedures. Apparently, all parties to legal considerations in child placement in Brighton would be suspended in a social field in which interpretation was given little free play. And with com-

parative remoteness of legal and welfare worlds, we might expect a certain tolerance between agencies and the judge in Brighton, a tolerance that indicated in other communities where we saw it the relative absence of contacts and conflict between them.

Judge Manuel Caliveri had a suggestion of reservedness in his manner. He was handsome, dark, and quite tanned, as befitted so many people in this community by the sea. He was only in his mid-forties and just recently had stepped out of his position as district court judge, including the juvenile court in Brighton, to take a judgeship at a higher level. He talked freely about his experiences on the juvenile bench.

We understood from talking to other informants in the community that comparatively few of the cases we were interested in came to court. What was the court's position in dependency cases?

"Most cases came in through the work of our local SPCC," said the judge. "Until three years ago we called them 'neglected' children. Now we say they are 'in need of care and protection.' You see, we used to have to adjudicate that the children were neglected. This carried a kind of stigma even though the records were not to be to the prejudice of children. But the newer designation does not have quite the stigma that the old one still carries." He continued, "In most instances the court takes the recommendation of the SPCC since they make a thorough investigation and interview parents and children. If it seemed required, an adjudication would be entered, but there were many cases where I didn't do this. The district Department of Public Welfare didn't care to take children unless there was adjudication, but I was sometimes able to persuade them to do so, particularly in situations that obviously seemed temporary. The court hears a case, passes on it, decides whether there is merit to the petition; then the court pretty much terminates its interest, although I always continued to have a personal interest."

What kinds of cases are adjudicated?

"There are not too many. One stands out in my memory. It was a case of tremendous physical abuse where the father was committed for assault and battery. The cases that get to court are generally ones where the SPCC has given a family repeated warnings. There must be evidence that can be substantiated. Usually, this comes from police department reports in addition to those of the SPCC. There also might be medical testimony. There may be neighbors who complained or relatives who wanted the help of the authorities."

Under what conditions did he permanently remove children from parents?

"I had nothing to do with permanent removal of children. In the District Court after the child is committed to the Department of Public Welfare the court has no further say whether the child should be placed for adoption or returned home. The court simply adjudicates. It can go no further."

What legal action, then, is forthcoming in adoptions?

"The Probate Court handles all domestic relations, including adoption and custody of children. The Department of Public Welfare may recommend adoption in the investigation which is required prior to adoption, but the probate judge's decision is final and he has a right to take the report and use it as he sees fit. The Probate Court handles any termination of parental rights. When the District Court places a child no legal rights are wiped out; all remain."

What dealings did he have with social agencies?

"I am a board member of Family and Children's Welfare Society [a private, nonsectarian agency]. I have had numerous contacts with them and used to call them for suggestions. With other agencies my contacts were not so sustained. Occasionally the Department of Public Welfare had a problem with a child in placement who was acting up. I did not have any contacts with Catholic Charities during my term. I did have contact with St. James Orphanage; sometimes I would make arrangements for them to keep a child for a short time while I was giving further thought to the case. Most of my dealings were with the SPCC [4] and the Family and Child Welfare Society. My relationships with the welfare department were more official ones."

We had noted a social welfare philosophy in the court actions for the cases we had read and asked how this had come about. "This was true when I came to the picture," said the judge, "and I simply fell into the pattern. I just took it for granted that this was a better policy, and perhaps I enlarged on it myself."

Judge Caliveri's remarks must be interpreted in the light of information about the law in Brighton. The law itself was what might be characterized as more of an "agency" law than most laws we studied. Instead of stipulating the reasons for removing a child, it emphasized the responsibility of the State Department of Public Welfare to provide foster care for children under given circumstances. It provided a general authorization which placed a big responsibility on this public department and comparatively little on the private agencies. The new law, revised in 1954, was spoken of by people at the Department of Public Welfare as representing their thinking and practice and was written from the point of view of the agency rather than the court. Also important was the fact that, historically, there had been an emphasis on foster home care in using public funds, and it was only recently that the welfare department could use institutions except on a medical basis. Even in 1957 explanation had been made in writing when an institution was used in placement. There were also restrictions in the law about placement in other than the same religion, both for adoption and for temporary foster care. Exceptions were allowed, but the agency or judge had to explain why an exception was made.

Apparently, all parties to the legal process were somewhat constrained in their operations by definite specifications, and this tended to push both judge and agencies closer together. The con-

---

[4] The Society for Prevention of Cruelty to Children is not a placing agency and handled none of our children. The Family and Child Welfare Society handled about one sixth of our cases.

tinued relative remoteness of the judge from the welfare world was a product of the lack of centrality of his court to the placement and movement of dependent children. However, he knew agency people (in connection with delinquency cases), and where he *was* involved in placement apparently a welfare philosophy infused his operations.

The principal element in the apparent lack of contact between the judge and welfare agencies over dependency cases seemed to be the State Department of Public Welfare. But this absence of contact was intensified by other agencies that might have counteracted the tendency, by the law itself, and by the general climate of the community. Everyone involved in the process which might bring children into court as "in need of care and protection" was either interested in keeping them out of court (at least as involuntary placements) or willing to have the Department of Public Welfare work with families on a voluntary basis. The policy of the SPCC at the state level had changed over the years to a less aggressive removal approach and toward more work with families on a voluntary basis in order to obviate court action. This change was accepted by the SPCC in Brighton. Private agencies which might have referred to the SPCC preferred to work with families rather than encourage court action. The city Department of Public Welfare in Brighton would have preferred to have children removed more aggressively; but this agency would need the help of other agencies that would be involved in the process. And the philosophy of the head of the district office of the Department of Public Welfare, and much the approach of the state office, too, was to work on a voluntary basis with families so that placement, if and when it came, would be voluntary.

While voluntary placement, on the parent's request only, was predominant in child placement in Brighton, there were cases where guardianship by the Department of Public Welfare was involved, either with or without the parents' consent. Guardianship was used for cases of "death, unavailability or incapacity of the parent or guardian, or with the consent of the parent or parents." This kind of arrangement provided the continuity of care that the Department of Public Welfare thought was necessary since the parent could not take the child out of foster care without going to court. About 10 percent of State Department of Public Welfare cases came into care in this way and through commitment by the court. Most such cases were initiated in Brighton by the SPCC. The Probation Department and the police also seemed to accept this policy as a satisfactory one. The court too had no objection, although it would have preferred to retain some control over children committed by it to the public welfare department.

Thus, the parents' rights emphasis, which we anticipated for this community (which also had a particularly low rate of cases involving court commitment and modification of parental rights), was a matter of a common orientation that permeated a whole social system. Emphasis was upon the maintenance of family ties and upon looking to relatives and neighbors as primary resources for enabling family dislocations to be handled without too drastic measures by formal authorities. The law, too, accentuated the positive responsibilities of public legal and welfare agents to the common whole and seemed to take for granted that such agents were of and for the community and should not be feared and artificial appendages. In such a setting the roles of those involved in the child placement process seemed stable, well-defined, and in a reciprocal balance. As the history and picture of services unfold we may find other clues to the character of the Brighton stage on which our drama of foster care was enacted.

20. Child Welfare Agencies and the Placement of Children

During our study of children in foster care we directly involved sixty placement agencies through reading their records and talking with their staffs and board members. These sixty agencies were distributed in nine communities, some communities having as few as two agencies in the study while one community had thirteen. The involvement of agencies was not always dependent on the proportion of our study population in their care, for the range of children for whom a particular agency was responsible was from 0.3 percent of our population for an agency in one community to 90 percent for an agency in another community.

It is extremely difficult to make categorical statements about agencies at any particular moment in time because they were changing and developing constantly. We concentrated our analysis on the interagency configurations as they could be conceptualized in a community. Our examination of agency networks, out of which two major interagency tendencies were deduced, involved four dimensions. These were: history of the growth of services; types of services offered (whether multiple, dual, or single); extent of professionalization of agency; and spatial or geographical location of the agencies. We treated these elements as interrelated and said that they contributed to our diagrammed pictures of interagency relationships which we defined, after analyzing interview material, as either collaborative or noncollaborative.

Granting that there was circularity involved in the processes we described (and it was just this circularity, or interrelatedness, we wished to emphasize), let us reverse somewhat the presentation in this summary to use our findings in eight communities as a test for what we should have expected to find in Brighton. First, we will look at the four elements which we considered in each community in defining interagency networks as relatively collaborative or noncollaborative. Then we will take our eight communities, divide them into collaborative and noncollaborative groups, and finally look at some aspects of their placement patterns. We can then see which placement pattern variables were most consistently aligned with one tendency or the other. A look at Brighton's placement pattern should indicate what interagency tendency we might expect there. A presentation for Brighton of history of services, types of services offered, degrees of professionalization of staff, and spatial location of agencies, together with a sociogram reflecting statements of participants in the system, should demonstrate whether the Brighton network was in line with the collaborative or noncollaborative tendency which the placement pattern suggested.

Looking at eight communities, having prepared sociograms for each to picture their interagency networks, we could place them along a continuum in terms of collaboration (and/or with multiple-service agencies serving all child publics) and noncollaboration (and/or with multiple-service agencies serving only special groups of children). Location on the continuum was determined basically from information on our agency schedule on interagency relations (Item M). These data fed into our construction of a sociogram of the interagency network of relationships in each community. A community's location on the continuum could be computed by considering the amount of observed collaboration on a network diagram (as a proportion of the number of possible linkages) combined with a consideration of the proportion of all children who were cared for in single-, dual-, and multiple-service agencies. Collaborative agencies and/or many multiple services would place a community at one end of the continuum; noncollaborative agencies and many single services would place a community at the other end of the continuum.

The picture was most clear where there were many agency units which either did or did not collaborate. The picture became more "mixed" in Summit, where there was no collaboration, but a single multiple-service agency served the majority of all children in a three-unit configuration; in La Paz, where there was 50 percent of possible collaboration but most children were served by a dual-service agency in a two-unit configuration; and in King City, where most cases were served through multiple-service agencies which collaborated through the Council of Social Agencies but smaller agencies remained relatively insulated and negative relationships also entered the picture. The continuum appeared to line up our communities in this way: [1]

Collaboration ———————————————— Noncollaboration

←——————————————————————————————→

Most   Most

Westport—Centralia—Granger—La Paz—King City—Summit—Norden—Jamestown

[1] A slightly different ranking was obtained when an effort was made to quantify a combination of the degree of collaboration noted relative to total collaboration

Let us look at the elements upon which this comparison was based. Their interdependence is apparent in the difficulty one finds in attempting to discuss one element without bringing in the others.

History of services.—An examination of the histories of growth of services in Jamestown, Norden, Summit, and King City revealed that institutional care was the only type offered during the early periods of foster care in those communities, other services developing at a much later date. In most noncollaborative Jamestown institutional care not only came many years ago but was provided under both public and private auspices in a very early declaration of responsibility to children in that community. In Norden, a similar historical development of public and private institutional care took place. Summit showed an initial emphasis on institutions also, but in Summit a concurrent emphasis on adoption was added to the picture. In the states in which both Jamestown and King City are located a further tradition was noted in the historical emphasis on the development of services along sectarian lines. Thus, a history of both institutions and services developing on a sectarian basis was found in Jamestown and, in varying degrees with other emphases modifying insulation, in our other noncollaborative communities.

In three of our collaborative communities—Westport, Centralia, and Granger—the history of services demonstrated an emphasis not on one type of care but on a variety of services which had grown up together. Similarly, the histories of these communities indicated a more secular and interdependent than sectarian emphasis.

----

possible, and a weighting of cases which assigned heavier weights for cases in single services, lighter weights for those in dual services, and lightest weights for cases in multiple services (without attempting to discriminate quality of a given service or variations in professional training). On this basis the following scores were obtained (where 1.0 would indicate perfect collaboration and/or all cases in multiple-services facilities): Westport = .56; Centralia = .51; Granger = .50; La Paz = .49; King City = .53; Summit = .35; Norden = .29; Jamestown = .20. A definite split between ends of the continuum was obtained on this basis; but King City received higher ranking for collaboration through the Council and 93 percent of its cases were in three multiple-services agencies, while La Paz received 50 percent of possible collaboration out of a two-unit configuration and had most cases in one dual-service agency. Some details on this index are in Appendix A-4.

La Paz was less clearly defined in this manner, but its more recent history—past history reflected more an absence of any services than a tradition on which current services might be based—presented a picture of secular, dual services developing around the central core of a public program.

Types of services (current).—This element could never be isolated from the one above but can be restated briefly in the light of our continuum.   On the whole, most noncollaborative Jamestown and Norden had agencies with single functions which made few referrals and did not discuss issues with other agencies.   But in Summit the major agency was a multiple-function organization, and in King City three of the major agencies were multiple-function and communicated over issues through the Council.   Furthermore, Jamestown and Norden agencies (particularly the institutions) operated on a sectarian basis which enhanced their insulation.   But in Summit the multiple-function institution served all children on a nonsectarian basis, and in King City, although a separating sectarianism was still very apparent, the two major multiple-function agencies were nonsectarian, though somewhat insulated in their separate case loads, and did not refer cases back and forth within the network.

Services in the communities on the collaboration end of the continuum contrasted to those in the other communities.   Westport had many single-service agencies which referred cases back and forth and one large multiple-service agency from which referrals often came.   In Centralia there were fewer single-function agencies than in Westport, although multiple-service agencies were also not prevalent; but, predominantly, agencies with more than one service were developing programs in Centralia in which movement of cases occurred on the basis of the kinds of problems each agency could best handle.   In Granger, three agencies offered more than one placement service, and only the public agency offered just a single service.   Referrals came from this public agency while issues were discussed among the private agencies.   Services in La Paz were differentiated within the broad program of the one, large, public agency, and the single-function institution—different in being highly sectarian—was increasingly excluded as a resource for services to which referrals could be made in that community. Discussion of issues did not take place between this public agency and the private agency in La Paz.

Extent of professionalization of agency.—Disparities in professional emphasis and the incidence of professional staff seemed related to collaboration and noncollaboration. Disparities in professional program emphasis in a given network made communication between agency units more difficult, while fewer disparities facilitated communication. At the same time, professional education might enhance the desire for communication and collaboration by broadening the perspective of an agency and its representatives. In four of our communities there were marked differences in professional emphasis among agencies. Jamestown, again, represented the greatest degree of difference when the many agencies there were considered. In personnel, the range in Jamestown was from an agency staffed primarily by volunteers with no training to one agency with 100 percent professional staff. In King City, there was wide variation in professional emphasis which was most marked in comparing the smaller agencies to the larger ones. Summit and Norden also represented varieties in levels of professionalism, but there were fewer agency units between which disparities could be expressed. The major agency in Summit had a new, trained executive who adopted a broad perspective of community need, but his presence accentuated the great disparity in professional emphasis between this major agency and the smaller, sectarian agency in Summit.

Our two most collaborative networks, Westport and Centralia, represented relatively high degrees of professional emphasis and education among agency personnel and less variation between agencies. Westport was the most consistent and had been highly professional for a longer time than Centralia. Some agencies in Centralia were reaching toward greater professional emphasis, and this had been a recent change; but, over all, disparities between agencies in that community were not so common as similarities. In La Paz a great emphasis on professional education was apparent in the all-encompassing public agency program. The one element which again enhanced the "mixture" in the La Paz picture was the great disparity in professional emphasis between the major agency and the other, very minor, sectarian agency. Granger was changing. The widening range of professional emphasis in Granger agencies was beginning to make communication, and collaboration, more difficult. Granger was a community in transition, revealing the disparities that doubtless occur in the movement toward increased professional care.

Spatial or geographical location of agencies.—This factor was not of primary importance in defining collaborative or noncollaborative networks. However, spatial separation appeared to strengthen the other factors in noncollaborative Jamestown and helped to place Jamestown at an extreme end of the continuum. In Norden, spatial separation went with a rural-urban division to intensify problems of communication between certain agencies. In Summit, agencies were physically close but served wide geographic areas so that, in a sense, they faced away from one another. In King City, physical distance in an extremely large county contributed to the noncollaboration of smaller agencies on the periphery.

But spatial separation and a rural-urban division were also apparent in relatively collaborative Granger and deterred our ranking of Granger farther toward collaboration on the continuum. In La Paz, the move from the center to the edge of town by the sectarian institution had intensified a growing tendency toward noncollaboration between it and the central public agency. Physical distance between some agencies in the Centralia network was modified by the growth of a shared professionalism in a spreading metropolitan region. Finally, distance between agencies in Westport was no problem and, furthermore, the community was a central attracting locus for services that turned attention of agencies, in serving their publics, from hinter regions toward the urban center.

The over-all picture emphasizes that where all four factors operated consistently in one direction or the other our distinctions of network tendencies were most clear. Where the picture was a mixed one, a system was strengthened which, at the time of our study, had in varying degrees what we have called either a more "collaborative" or a more "noncollaborative" tone. Let us now consider some placement variables which on the surface seemed most related to interagency situations.

With a *collaborative* system of specific service agencies (and/or with a group of multiple-service agencies serving all child publics in a community), we hypothesized a high adoption rate among children in foster care and more movement from both foster family and institution to both adoption and return home. Further ex-

Table 22

AGENCY COLLABORATIVENESS AND CHILDREN LEAVING CARE

(In percent)

	Children in Adoptive Homes on April 1, 1957	Children Returned Home during the Six-Month Period January 1–June 30, 1957
Most collaborative		
Westport	21	10
Centralia	22	4
Granger	17	3
La Paz	7	12
King City	18	14
Summit	39	18
Norden	8	4
Jamestown	6	14
Least collaborative		

plorations suggested that under these conditions placement patterns might present more mid-length (two to five and a half years) placements, more placements of more than one type, more age-differentiated placements, and more "mid-number" of moves—that is, more children experiencing two to three moves rather than experiencing only one move or four or more moves. The obverse hypothesis was that in a *noncollaborative* system of insular, specific-service agencies (and/or with single-service agencies limited to serving special groups of children) there would be a lower adoption rate, and movement out of foster care would be largely one of returning to own homes rather than going into adoption. Further exploration suggested the possible tendency for such a network to produce both more short- and more long-term care, more placements undifferentiated by the child's age, more single placements (in one facility only), and more experiences of either one move or four or more moves.

In eight communities five major placement variables seemed somewhat consistent in separating collaborative and noncollaborative networks of agencies. The first was the variable initially stated in our interagency hypothesis: collaborative networks showed

Table 23

AGENCY COLLABORATIVENESS AND COMPARISON OF
ADOPTIVE PLACEMENTS AND RETURNS HOME

	Of Children Leaving Care in the Six-Month Period January 1–June 30, 1957, Percentage Going into Adoptive Homes	Of Children Leaving Care in the Six-Month Period January 1–June 30, 1957, Percentage Returning Home
Most collaborative		
Westport	52	39
Centralia	58	28
Granger	50	50
La Paz	15	70
King City	36	57
Summit	36	64
Norden	—	60
Jamestown	29	63
Least collaborative		

greater incidence of adoption, while noncollaborative networks showed lower incidence of adoption but higher return home rates. The figures are given in Table 22.

There was a tendency to have more adoption in the most collaborative networks, while in the least collaborative networks there was less adoption and the return home rates were closer to, or greater than, the adoption rates. The middle regions on the continuum did not hold to this tendency; La Paz and Summit were the most noteworthy exceptions where other situational elements in these communities took precedence, as determinants of placement pattern, over networks that included only two and three agencies respectively. In Table 23 a further elaboration may be found in the figures on leaving care in a six-month period where greater consistency was seen except for La Paz.[2]

Table 24 makes clear that the number of placements also showed some consistency in discriminating between collaborative and non-collaborative networks of agencies.

Table 24

AGENCY COLLABORATIVENESS AND NUMBER OF
CHILDREN'S PLACEMENTS

(In percentages of children)

	One Placement	*Two to Three Placements*	*Four or More Placements*	*More Than One Type* [a] *of Placement*
Most collaborative				
Westport	23	56	21	57
Centralia	20	59	21	40
Granger	28	47	25	46
La Paz	50	36	14	31
King City	27	50	23	56
Summit	74	20	6	17
Norden	13	60	27	70
Jamestown	51	40	9	29
Least collaborative				

[a] Foster family care is one type of placement, institutional care another.

Our three most collaborative networks showed most consistency on this variable in clustering in the mid-range again. Our three most noncollaborative networks were also consistent when we consider they included the two networks with the largest number falling under "one placement" and the smallest number under "four or more placements" (Summit and Jamestown), and one network with the smallest figure under "one placement" and the largest under "four or more placements" (Norden, although it was most heavily weighted in the middle also). La Paz and King City exchanged

[2] La Paz consistently appears as an exception in our rankings. Thus, we saw it as a child's rights community legally, yet children were separated from their parents at an early age through a welfare operation that was quite insulated from the legal world. Also, it is collaborative, but few children are adopted in this cultural setting, and collaboration again represents an insularity within a welfare community.

places on the continuum on the basis of this variable. Variations on "more than one type of placement" also showed the extreme ranges to appear in the noncollaborative group.

Table 25 shows the sequence of movement in foster care and its consistency in the light of our postulated tendencies.

Table 25

*AGENCY COLLABORATIVENESS AND CHILDREN'S
MOVEMENT IN CARE*

(In percentages of children)

	Out of Foster Family into Any Different Type of Placement	Out of Institution into Any Different Type of Placement
Most collaborative		
Westport	37	32
Centralia	23	28
Granger	32	45
La Paz	22	25
King City	42	41
Summit	7	15
Norden	55	53
Jamestown	25	11
Least collaborative		

Again, the less extreme picture tended to appear in our collaborative networks, while the extremes of little or much movement appeared in the noncollaborative networks. And this over-all picture of intermediate placement tendencies, generally including more adoptions and lesser proportions returning home, was the major basis that set collaborative networks apart from noncollaborative networks.

One more finding (Table 26) fills out the picture. In our preceding chapters on interagency networks we reported the figures on length of time in care for all cases studied, including adoption and return home cases in the population, and looked for an association between collaboration and mid-length years in care. No consistency was found. However, when the comparison was made only on cases in foster care, thus holding the influence of adoption constant, a fairly consistent discrimination between collaborative and noncollaborative networks appeared. Mid-length care tended to go with collaborative networks, and extremes of long- and short-term care with noncollaborative networks. The range in percentages in short-term care in the noncollaborative group was 14 to 72, while the range in short-term care was much less—22 to 35—in the collaborative group. The range in long-term care was 7 to 40 in the noncollaborative group and again was much less—20 to 34—in the collaborative group. Collaborative networks tended to manifest a normal curve humping in mid-length years. King City resembled the collaborative group on this variable, but the other noncollaborative networks had skewed or flattened distributions. Looking just at the foster care populations, those children in foster families and institutions on April 1, and not at the babies who

Table 26

AGENCY COLLABORATIVENESS AND CHILDREN'S LENGTH OF TIME
IN FOSTER CARE

(In percentages of children)

	0–1½ Years	2–5½ Years	6 Years and Over
Most collaborative			
Westport	35	44	21
Centralia	22	44	34
Granger	32	48	20
La Paz	23	43	33
King City	27	46	27
Summit	72	21	7
Norden	14	46	40
Jamestown	35	36	28
Least collaborative			

moved swiftly into adoption, collaboration was associated with mid-length time in care. Thus, where agency units tended to work together in a community a picture of children neither "rushing out" of care hurriedly nor of "staying on" for lengthy periods of custodial care tended to appear.

How did Brighton appear on these placement variables? Table 27 shows the characteristics of Brighton's placement pattern. Clearly, Brighton approximated the noncollaborative network tendency. It had a low adoption rate but a medium return home rate, although reasons for leaving care were weighted heavily toward return home. The placements in Brighton were not concentrated in the mid-numbers (although they showed evenness rather than extremes), and an extreme low incidence of more than one type of placement further grouped Brighton with the noncollaborative networks. Sequence of movement figures put Brighton with the extreme of few movements along with Summit and Jamestown. Finally, length of time in care for foster care children in

Table 27

BRIGHTON CHILDREN LEAVING CARE, NUMBER AND SEQUENCE OF
PLACEMENTS, AND LENGTH OF TIME IN CARE
(In percentages of children)

Percentage of all children in care in adoptive homes on April 1, 1957	*Percentage of all children under study returned home during the six-month period January 1–June 30, 1957*
6	11

PURPOSES OF LEAVING CARE

Movement to adoptive home	*Return to own home*
28	63

NUMBER OF PLACEMENTS

One	*Two to three*	*Four or more*	*More than one type*
33	34	32	28

SEQUENCE OF MOVEMENT

Out of foster family into any different type of placement	*Out of institution into any different type of placement*
15	23

LENGTH OF TIME IN FOSTER CARE

Up to 1½ years	*1½ to 5½ years*	*6 years and over*
28	26	46

Brighton was skewed away from the mid-length period and bunched more toward long-term care.

The preceding placement patterns suggested either a lack of service units or an insulation of existing units in a noncollaborative interagency network. In Brighton the relatively high number of agency units indicated that, as in Jamestown, we should look for insulation of the parts as typifying the Brighton configuration. Let us turn to a description of the network of services in Brighton for explication of the interagency picture.

THE NETWORK OF AGENCIES AND CHILD WELFARE SERVICE
IN THE GREATER BRIGHTON AREA

The interagency network in Brighton is pictured in Figure 9. The diagram presents essentially a noncollaborative, single-function agency network with only two agencies performing more than one placement service. Table 28 fills in the details for the elements of the diagram.

Three agencies in the diagram were under sectarian (Catholic) auspices. Two of these overlapped in that they had the same exec-

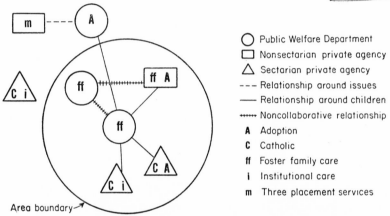

○ Public Welfare Department
□ Nonsectarian private agency
△ Sectarian private agency
--- Relationship around issues
— Relationship around children
⊶ Noncollaborative relationship
A Adoption
C Catholic
ff Foster family care
i Institutional care
m Three placement services

Area boundary

Figure 9. GREATER BRIGHTON AREA AGENCY NETWORK

utive and that families who sought admission of children to the Catholic institution applied at the office of Catholic Charities; but the institution (St. James Orphanage) also received children directly from the district office of public welfare. There were three public agencies which must be differentiated. The center circle on the sociogram represents the district office of the State Department of Public Welfare. We represented the State Department of Public Welfare itself by the circle outside the community through which only adoption, as a direct placement service, involved the department proper in the community. The circle to the left of the center one represents the Brighton City Department of Public

Table 28

CHARACTERISTICS OF AGENCIES IN THE GREATER
BRIGHTON AREA NETWORK

Agency (According to percentage of children under study served)	History	Services	Extent of Professional Education [a] of Staff	Spatial Factors
District Department of Public Welfare (52%)	Organized 1947; auspices public	Foster family care, for children 0–21 years of age	50% of staff (10 members)	Located at Brighton; serves 45 towns
St. James Orphanage (17%)	Organized 1894; auspices private	Institutional care, for children, usually Catholic, 5–12 years of age	0% of staff (2 members)	Located at Brighton; serves the diocese
Family and Children's Welfare Society (16%)	Organized 1843 (merger in 1945); auspices public	Foster family care and adoption, for children 0–adolescence	100% of staff (6 members)	Located at Brighton; serves the Greater Brighton Area
St. Benedict's School (6%)	Organized 1890; auspices private	Institutional care, usually for Catholic boys 3–14 years of age, girls any age	0% of staff (1 member)	Located at Harborview; serves unlimited area
Brighton City Department of Public Welfare (5%)	Organized in 1700s (Brighton became a city 1847); auspices public	Foster family care (limited), for children 5 years of age and up	0% of staff (2 members)	Located at Brighton; serves the city
Catholic Charities (2%)	Organized 1924; auspices private	Adoption, for Catholic infants	0% of staff (1½ members)	Located at Brighton; serves half the diocese
Children's Friend Society (1%)	Organized 1865; auspices private	Foster family care, for children 0–17 years of age; institutional care, for children 4–17 years of age; adoption, usually for infants	78% of staff (28 members)	Located at New Lancaster; serves the region
State Department of Public Welfare (1%)	Organized 1863; auspices public	Adoption, for children 0–21 years of age	73% of staff (11 members)	Located at New Lancaster; serves the state

[a] One year or more of graduate study in social work.

Welfare—an agency administering financial assistance and offering foster family care, and one which at the time of our study was rapidly "going out of the foster care business." The only multiple-service agency in the network was outside Brighton, in the larger community of New Lancaster. This agency, Children's Friend Society, had no relationships with other Brighton agencies and came into our study because it had a few children in foster families in Brighton.

We saw, then, a cluster of three agencies, one of which was declining rapidly in importance and related negatively to the other two. The other two agencies, plus the Catholic agencies, actually carried the major responsibility for child placement within the Brighton community. Institution and foster family care services seemed about equally divided. Adoption services were available, but few children were flowing into adoption. Only one relationship over issues can be noted on the diagram; other relationships were those over cases. Two negative relationships, flowing from a single agency, were also recorded. The total impression was one of insularity and segmented services, though not quite to the degree noted in Jamestown.[3]

Agency Antecedents and Present Bases in Brighton

History.—Brighton was a relatively old community in a state with an even older heritage. The earliest Anglo settlement on this site appeared in the seventeenth century, although the present city charter was not granted until 1847. The most recent service was established in 1924 and the oldest in 1843. The city Department of Public Welfare was established in 1847. The district office of the department was set up only in 1947; this occurred when the State Department of Public Welfare was decentralizing its administration. But the history of welfare in the state as a whole went back much farther than any of these dates.

The principle of public care was established in the state in 1635

---

[3] Brighton received a collaboration index score of .21 by our calculations. This placed it between Norden and Jamestown at the noncollaboration end of our continuum.

when the Governor of the then colony placed a child by indenture. The principle of state responsibility was enunciated just after 1675 when almshouses were created to care for persons displaced "during military action." An outstanding historical point which had current ramifications was that as early as 1863 the state legislature proclaimed the principle that care in a family setting was better for a child than care in an institution. At this early period home investigations of indentured wards by an appointed visitor were undertaken to protect the interests of the children. The principle of using state funds to pay board for children in foster homes was also established at that time. Thus interdependence was affirmed early in the state's history, although Brighton's own history represented more an experience of "separateness" as layers of newcomers gathered through the years of community growth in the later nineteenth century. These principles of care remained in effect until the law was changed in the early 1950s to enable the public department to use institutional care, on a limited basis, for children. Thus, broad acceptance of public responsibility for dependent children was well established in this state. The reorganization of 1947 brought to the fore local program modifications for particular communities. And shortly after this a licensing act, directing the State Department of Public Welfare to regulate the licensing of all agencies, brought about the first real contact between public child care agencies and private institutions.

Private agency services entered the Brighton picture in 1843 when a forerunner of the Family and Children's Welfare Society was established. The Children's Friend Society was organized in 1865. The two Catholic institutions opened in the 1890s, but Catholic Charities did not appear until 1924. The advent of the Social Security Act and the provision of ADC brought about a decrease in the population of institutions, although institutions were perpetuated by some nationality and religious groups. But institutions were always secondary in Brighton, and this was even more true in the rest of the state. The emphasis historically, and currently, was upon placement in foster families with institutions caring for school-aged children in an educative setting.

Services.—Services offered in Brighton were predominantly those undertaken by the non-Catholic agencies, although this was predominantly a Catholic community. The Family and Children's Welfare Society and the district Department of Public Welfare handled a large proportion of the dependent children between them, and most of these children were Catholic. It was difficult, therefore, to distinguish child publics by nationality or ethnicity or age group except to say that Catholic agencies served only, or largely, Catholic children and that institutional care was offered primarily to school-aged children. Services had developed, in this mixed picture of separation and interdependence, so that the two major agencies divided responsibilities, with the district Department of Public Welfare handling long-term foster home care (referring children for adoption to the state office in New Lancaster) and the Family and Children's Welfare Society handling short-term foster family care and adoption service to both Protestants and Catholics. In this set-up there was little breeding ground for shared issues, but communication over cases did occur. Communication between the city department and other agencies was legally prescribed, since if public assistance were to be withdrawn, another agency had to agree to take responsibility for the children and work with the family. The city department's emphasis on meeting financial need precipitated a negative relationship with agencies that had a different emphasis in their programs. However, the recent advent of a purchase-of-care plan could promote communication as agencies such as St. Benedict's School became newly aware that they could receive public funds for Brighton children whose parents could not pay for them. Also, the lifting of the prohibition against use of institutional care by public agencies might promote more, and stronger, relationships between public agencies and private institutions.

Extent of professionalization of agency.—Professionalization in Brighton was revealed in as wide a variation as we noted in Jamestown. This ranged from no professional staff in one agency to 100 percent professional staff in another. The two agencies within the community that cared for 68 percent of the children were the most professional and also communicated the most with each other. The sectarian division was added to disparities in professionalism in deterring communication from this two-agency configuration to other agencies. The other agencies cared for few children in or from the Brighton area and lacked a common professional base upon which consensus in ideas could more easily develop. Likewise, they had fewer day-by-day dealings over cases which could establish channels for communication.

Spatial factors.—Spatial location entered the Brighton network as another deterrent to communication. A rather widespread geographic area was involved, with one institution in Harborview and two agencies located in New Lancaster. However, only 8 percent of our children were served by agencies outside the Brighton community.

Four agencies, and three of them single-service agencies, served over 90 percent of our children. The total picture seemed to reveal a segmented network that was more noncollaborative than collaborative.

The character of the Brighton network of agencies was reflected in statements of participants in that network. Mr. Lafferty, at the district office of public welfare, said: "In theory, we have the responsibility for leadership in child welfare matters, but we lack the staff to stimulate community activities and community organizations. Agencies here don't get together frequently, and when they do it's apt to be about a particular problem like mental health. There is no continuing interaction through committees of the Council either." Nationality and religious divisions seemed partly involved in this. And the district office had no administrative relationship to the local city welfare office. "Our philosophies are quite different, and the Brighton city agency does not request our consultation," added Mr. Lafferty.

Miss Olsen, of the Family and Children's Welfare Society, said: "We work better with some agencies than with others, but this is the kind of community in which we know each other and can call each other fairly easily. We are friendly with the city Department of Public Welfare but we have a different philosophy and are still fighting a battle, so to speak, with them. We have good relationships with some of the outlying public welfare departments. It has always been with the Brighton city public welfare department that we've had our difficulty. I've never met with city or district people socially except perhaps on one or two occasions."

Mr. Wallace, at the city welfare office, told us: "Most of the time, I think the district office does a good job; but the state has granted them terrific powers. Recently we turned a case over to the private Family and Children's Welfare Society. We had investigated and felt they could supervise more closely. They gave glowing reports on a rejuvenated home; but we heard the children were still eating out of ice cube trays. We give them facts, and they give back the phrase 'mother love.'"

Father O'Hara, at the Catholic Charities in Brighton, said: "We deal with other agencies mostly through the Community Council. The Council provides the leadership here in welfare, working through committees. But we are set up primarily to help Catholics. Catholic principles are the basis of our work. Our support is by Catholics for Catholics. Our adoption referrals usually come through parish priests. We are placing into good adoptive homes and we are using St. Benedict's School to try to give children what they can't get at home."

Sister Theresa, at St. James Orphanage, said: "We have very little to do with other welfare agencies since parents themselves bring children here. Our teachers get together with other teachers from parochial schools and institutions since our school does have problems in common with other parochial schools."

At the Children's Friend Society, in New Lancaster (fifty miles from Brighton), Mr. Wheatcroft, the executive director, said: "The feeling among agencies here in New Lancaster seems a good one. We asked around recently for impressions on our fund-raising for a new building, and the consensus in other agencies was 'Whatever helps you, helps us.'" But Miss Ligget, the director of children's services at this agency, added: "We have little contact with Brighton now, although the district welfare office there once used us more for diagnostic study on cases. It doesn't seem to me that agency people in Brighton are particularly active in state groups."

Thus, the Brighton picture unfolded, showing a pattern of services that suggested a very old historical emphasis on community-wide interdependence, a later growth of separateness, as sectarian groups took on more responsibility specifically for their own, and a current tension toward the interdependent emphasis again in this community. Our summary has attempted to emphasize what each of our prior sections was intended to show: that particular phenomena—particular facts of placement and of services, for example—often take on more clarity for child welfare planning when they can be seen in a broad context in which interrelated particulars begin to shape the tendencies of a more coherent total configuration.

21. *The Children and Their Parents in Brighton and in the Nine Communities*

PLACEMENT HISTORIES OF THE CHILDREN IN FOSTER CARE [1]

We have seen that the community we have called Brighton was economically poor but, nevertheless, had a long history of child welfare services that reached fairly large numbers of the population. A first look at Brighton's placement histories further revealed that Brighton had a greater proportion of enforced separations of children and parents—separations caused by the death or institutionalization of a parent—than did any other community. At the same time, Brighton had the lowest proportion of involuntary separations of all our communities. Similarly, neglect and abandonment were least often recorded as precipitating children into care in Brighton of all our communities, while the combination of marital conflict and out-of-wedlock birth accounted for more cases there than anywhere else except Westport. Brighton seemed more toler-

[1] See footnote 1, Chapter 5, regarding the base for percentages in the section on Brighton children.

ant of lower physical and economic standards than were other communities with deprived population segments (like Jamestown and La Paz), since comparatively low standards operated in a broad middle social ground. But more interdependent Brighton apparently applied more rigorous and uniform social and ethical standards of behavior to this broad middle group in its population.

Brighton, like Centralia, used foster family placements predominantly, but institutions continued to be far more important in Brighton than in Centralia and a paucity of agency adoptive placements put Brighton among our communities with the fewest adoptions. This was not because children came into care late. Actually, Brighton appeared to be separating children from their parents at a relatively early age. Among its children in foster families the average age at separation was one year—only Summit recorded a lower average for a comparable group of children—and for children in institutions the average age at separation was seven years. Only La Paz and Centralia had slightly higher proportions than Brighton of children in foster care who were first separated from their parents as preschoolers.

Perhaps in line with a mixed picture of predominant foster family placement, but with institutions continuing to be important, Brighton manifested a U-shaped curve in its pattern of number of placements of dependent children. Thus there were two clusterings at the extremities of "one placement" and "four or more placements" in Brighton, while this was the only community in which "two or three placements" were the least frequent experience of children in foster care. If this New England community tended to separate dependent children from their parents at an early age, it also kept many of them in care a long period of time. In fact, the average time in care (7.6 years) recorded for Brighton's children who were living in foster families was the highest average recorded for any of our seven largest (urban) communities. Brighton had a greater proportion (46 percent) of children in foster care more than five and a half years than even long-term-care Norden. Movement out of care was somewhat similar in Brighton and Jamestown; few children were adopted, and more returned home than were adopted. The proportion of return homes to adoptions in the community was two to one in the nine-month period following April 1. Briefly, the Brighton placement pattern was one of relatively long-term placement in foster families, and less often in institutions, for children whose parents usually were no longer married to each other. In the case of institutional placements the dependency situation often involved a widowed parent in this community where the average age of the population was relatively high.

THE CHILDREN'S OWN FAMILIES

In what ways were the situations of the children who returned home in Brighton different from those of children who remained in care?

The majority of children who returned home in Brighton had been precipitated into care by death, illness, and economic hardship; this was true of almost twice the proportion of cases that were similarly recorded in any other community. Apparently, economic problems could be tolerated in this New England community, without placing a continuing stigma on the family, to a greater degree than could problems of social adjustment. This tendency was opposite to that noted in Centralia, where divorce and unwed motherhood were not highly stigmatized but economic mismanagement was. These children usually returned home during the first year in which they came into care. All but 6 percent of them had been voluntarily placed with an agency. They were older at time of separation (averaging eight years of age) than were the children remaining in care, but they averaged two years younger at the time of our study than the children in foster care on April 1 (nine years of age, compared to eleven years of age). The mothers of these children were usually housewives or household workers; the fathers were as likely to be unskilled workers or laboring men as to be skilled workers, but only infrequently were they the semiskilled in Brighton's labor force. It also seemed that the Portuguese-American and French-Canadian-American child had a much greater probability of returning home than did the child of less well-defined ethnic groups in Brighton's population. The Negro child in our sample did not return home although he represented about one tenth of those in care.

Much as in all our communities, almost half of the children remaining in foster care in Brighton were in a situation in which parents either had no plans other than for long-term care or had unresolved conflict over plans. The most frequent situation involved the apparent desire for continued care, although one child in four could have been given up for adoption and for one in seven return home was desired by his parents. And in populous Brighton at least one parent was likely still to visit the child in care in over half the cases—more than was true anywhere else except in Summit —but in less than 20 percent of the cases did either parent have an adequate relationship with an agency. In half the cases, too, no payment for a child's support was being made by parents, but this fact did not seem to affect chances of return home noticeably since payment was being made in only a slightly greater proportion of cases where children returned home.

The parents of the Brighton children in foster care seemed to come from a fairly representative cross section of the community, if one were to eliminate the upper social strata. Child dependency seemed to cut across the many ethnic groups in Brighton, but the older Protestant Yankees were not represented to any degree; for 75 percent of the mothers and 70 percent of the fathers of our children in foster care called themselves Catholic (as did 87 percent of the children). In addition, about one in ten parents was Negro, two in ten mothers were Portuguese-American, and about one in seven mothers was French-Canadian. The more uniform behavioral norms which applied in Brighton, as compared to Jamestown, tended to discern dependency in Negro families at about three times the normal rate that would be expected from that group's representation in the total population. On the whole, the Brighton parents whose children were in care were fairly young, considering the average age in this community, and healthy. Fathers averaged about forty years of age and mothers about thirty-four to thirty-five. In education, fathers averaged eight and mothers between eight and nine grades of schooling. Fathers were almost all in blue-collar work, while mothers were mostly housewives or household workers. They were in a barely adequate economic situation, and crowded housing was almost invariably a problem. In all, these social characteristics, with some qualifications for ethnic representations, seemed to be those of any normal group in the Brighton population. But it was not economic conditions, primarily, that caused parent and child separation. Rather it was the broken homes, brought about by divorce, separation or death of a parent, or illegitimacy, that seemed to be involved in the continued separation of dependent children from their parents.

THE CHILDREN AND ADOPTION

What was the image of an adoptive child in this community where hereditary characteristics were still considered important? Was the interdependence which tended to apply relatively uniform norms to dependency also providing a uniform image of the adoptable child? Or did agency adoption proceed more within many population segments, while dependency was perceived more cross-sectionally and acted upon by agencies which functioned across group boundaries?

First of all, Brighton was one community in which the sex of the child seemed to have a bearing on his adoptability. The sexes were equally represented in foster care, but boys were placed in adoption in a ratio of two to one over girls. The adopted child averaged about ten months of age, and none was more than ten years old, while 96 percent were under age five. No Negroes were placed in adoption in Brighton, but the Portuguese-American child seemed to have a better than equal chance of being adopted. Although 87 percent of the children in foster care were labeled as Catholic, only half this proportion of children in adoptive placements were Catholic. Thus the adopted child tended to be the white, Protestant infant even in heterogeneous Brighton, though some placements within population segments accounted for variations. Our interviewing revealed that people within ethnic subgroups were interested in adopting only a child of their own kind, and these groups varied in the degree of their interest in adoption of any type. Otherwise, regardless of who adopted him, the adopted child was always healthy, almost invariably of average or better intelligence, had no parental ties, and was never found to manifest psychological symptoms. All groups in Brighton seemed to share this normal image of the adoptable child.

How did the children remaining in care compare with this select adoption group?

The age comparison was as dramatic in Brighton as elsewhere. The child remaining in foster care averaged eleven years of age. He was only slightly more likely to be perceived as average or above in intelligence than were his parents; Brighton ranked highest among all communities in proportions of children in foster care recorded as below average in intelligence (46 percent). We recall that 96 percent of the children adopted were considered average or above in intelligence. Almost nine out of ten of Brighton's children in foster care were school-aged children, and 60 percent were over ten years of age—figures surpassed only by the two rural communities of our study. As was mentioned, Negroes, Portuguese, and French-Canadians were heavily represented, with each group contributing about one in ten of the children in foster care. But Negroes neither returned home nor were adopted, while Portuguese and French-Canadian children had a somewhat better chance than other children of returning home and Portuguese children had, furthermore, a better probability than most of being adopted. About one adoption in seven involved a Portuguese child in Brighton. French-Canadian children, however, had much less probability of being adopted, considering their rate of coming into care, and were three times more likely to return home than to be adopted. In the total group in foster care, a large proportion in Brighton had some physical disability. Although almost all were otherwise healthy, one in four had what was considered an irremediable disability. No child who either returned home or was adopted had such a disability. The composite parent-child foster care picture suggests that low intelligence and physical disability were often associated with dependency and that Negroes were quite disproportionately represented; all these factors were major deterrents to adoption as well as to return home.

Psychological symptoms were recorded about as often for Brighton's children as for those in our other urban communities. But considering the age of the group and their multiple, long-term care experiences, Brighton's children in foster care manifested such symptoms less often than might have been expected. Perhaps, as in Jamestown, the more static social setting provided fewer challenges and thus fewer frustrations, so that the foster care status was, relatively, a less damaging one compared to other statuses in the community. However, symptoms definitely accrued after intake into care and were recorded much more frequently (in 42 percent of cases) on April 1 than as at the time of intake (in only 25 percent of the cases). And 61 percent of the children were recorded as being confused about their identity at the time we studied them. Children who returned home were less likely to give evidence of psychological symptoms, and none who was adopted had such symptoms. The children in foster care in Brighton seemed currently affectionate toward their foster father, their child welfare worker, and particularly, their schoolteacher. They were somewhat less affectionate with other children, but more of them seemed to get along with their peers than did not. But Brighton's children in foster care were no longer tied to their own parents, and only half of them were still affectionate with their brothers and sisters. Interestingly, the child who returned home could be profiled as a male child, ambivalent or withdrawn in his relationships with other children, quite confused about his identity, and slightly more tied to his own parents—but less affectionate with his brothers and sisters—than the child remaining in care. The child who returned home also, it will be recalled, was, on the average, two years younger than the average child who remained in care, and he stayed in care only one year. The profile suggests that lack of social adjustment in the care situation, combined with ingratiation with the elders who controlled his immediate destiny, may have been a major factor in a child's returning home.

In Brighton the majority of children in foster care were, to the same extent as in Jamestown, in a situation in which the rights of their parents had not been modified. For the most part, the legal tie remained. Only one in ten had been completely freed for adoption, and only Jamestown showed a smaller percentage than this. Thus, foster care proceeded to operate on a long-term basis in this New England community, with little thought apparently given to terminating parental rights and planning across the broad gulf that separated foster care from adoption. The responsibility of the whole community for the dependent was still demonstrated through formal care facilities. But where the dependent child's parents tended to be inadequate persons or social transgressors, the child also tended to carry these labels with him and to remain tied legally to the parents through whom he had received his ascribed status.

THE CHILDREN IN NINE COMMUNITIES

A major issue upon which our study focused was: What are the deterrents to movement into a permanent home for children who are in need of parents? We based our explorations on the premise that every child has a right to his own home. We can now summarize what we saw in nine communities across the U.S.A.

Placement Experiences

Most children in foster care were separated voluntarily from their parents. Where involuntary separation ran highest—in Summit—it involved marital and not economic problems and sometimes meant that a court ruling on final disposition of the children of a broken marriage was being deferred. Almost half, if not most, of the children in foster care in every community were separated because of neglect and abandonment, or death, illness, or economic hardship. As precipitators of parent-child separation, the less purely physical and more clearly psychological parental problems seemed to increase in importance with the complexity of the community and/or the professional character of the services provided.

Most of the children in foster care in our study were in foster families. In five of our communities foster family placement was clearly the preponderant type of placement used, while one community, King City, was in transition toward greater use of foster families. However, three of our communities were definitely "institution communities"—Norden, Summit, and Jamestown—and at least one out of six children in care in every community was in an institution. Most of the dependent children were first separated from their parents as preschoolers, although this pattern did not hold true for our three institution communities nor for rural Granger. Most of the children in six of our nine communities had had more than one placement—the predominant experience being two to three placements—though Summit, La Paz, and Jamestown had a preponderance of children with single placements only, and Brighton a preponderance with four or more placements. Moreover, most children were remaining in care from 2 to 5 years, the variations running from an average, for those in foster families, of 1.2 years in Summit to 8.0 years in Norden and, for those in institutions, of 1.1 years in Summit to 5.3 years in Centralia. And neither adoption nor return home was occurring to an encouraging degree for the children in care at the time of our study except, perhaps, in Summit, where about half of those in care on April 1 left care in the following six months. At the other extreme was Norden, where only 10 percent left care in the six months following April 1; in most of the other communities approximately 20 percent left care in a six- or nine-month follow-up period.[2]

Generally, the children who returned home were the children who had been dependent a much shorter time, on the average, than those remaining in care. Everywhere, except in Norden, the average period in care for the child returning home was two years or

---

[2] The follow-up on movement involved a nine-month period after April 1 in Centralia, Jamestown, and Brighton. In all other communities the period was six months.

less; in most communities returns home occurred in one year or less. Time was a most important factor in the movement of children out of care in every setting, for staying in care beyond a year and a half greatly increased a child's chances of not being adopted or returned home.

The Children's Families

A remarkable similarity appeared in each community in the percentage of children in care for whom parents had no clear-cut plans, whether for return home or for relinquishment for adoption. About half the children were in this situation, and in Norden the proportion ran to two-thirds. Most children were also in a situation in which neither one of their parents ever visited or had more than superficial contact with them.[3] Only in Summit and Brighton was this true for fewer than half the children. And in consistently fewer than one third (usually less than one fourth) of the cases did either father or mother have an adequate relationship with the agency responsible for the child. Payment for care was equally lacking.

The social characteristics of the parents of children in foster care were as varied, in some respects, as the communities in which they lived. There were Protestants and Catholics, whites and Negroes, Spanish- and Portuguese-Americans, their proportions depending upon the community, its economic and social conditions, its welfare services, and its perceptions of dependency. But consistently we found that the parents were not a highly transient group; agencies were dealing predominantly with families settled in a community. Most of these families had relatives or close friends living near-by. In age, the parents were an intermediate group; mothers ranged, on the average, from about thirty to thirty-eight years of age, and fathers from about thirty-five to forty-two years of age. Parents were usually in good physical health, of average intelligence, with at least an elementary school education and often a year or two of high school. However, most of the parents were no longer married

---

[3] Chapter 22 is concerned with the unvisited children in foster care.

to each other. Norden presented the largest proportion of parents still married to each other (30 percent), while Brighton and La Paz had the lowest percentages (10 percent). Both mothers and fathers tended to be currently living with a spouse, while mothers were more likely than fathers to be living with adults other than a spouse. But in 42 percent to 77 percent of the cases in all communities, parents' housing arrangements were such that there was either no space available for the child or he would have to share a room with an adult. It seemed, in all, a combination of social and psychological conditions rather than economic conditions *per se* that maintained the parent-child separation; for while the economic situations of parents were seldom comfortable, they were also not preponderantly situations of destitution in most communities, compared to the lot of other families in those communities. Perhaps La Paz would be the major exception to this statement, for unemployment was a major problem there when we visited. In most communities, however, the occupations of the fathers of most children in foster care were not far removed from the preponderant occupational level of most men in the community.

The Children and Adoption [4]

The adopted child of our study was, typically, under two years of age and had formed no relationships with natural parents or natural brothers and sisters. In most cases, he was born out of wedlock and moved into adoption at an early age, with equal facility from either an institution or a foster family placement. Adopted children were about equally distributed by sex (a preference for males was noted only in Brighton). The children were largely a healthy group and free of psychological symptoms or intellectual impairment. Natural parents of the adopted child were free of

[4] Much of this discussion is taken verbatim, with the permission of the authors, from Chapter VIII "Barriers to Adoption: a Study of Physical and Psychological Handicaps, Ethnicity, and Adoptive Parents' Expectations," by Ruth Baer, *et al.*, the report of a student group research project, done at the School of Social Welfare at the University of California at Berkeley in partial fulfillment of the requirements for the Master of Social Welfare degree, under the faculty supervision of Henry S. Maas.

genetic defect and physical incapacity. It was also found, generally, that the natural parents of the adopted child had lower socioeconomic status and education than the adoptive parents, so that, in effect, the adopted child experienced upward social mobility.

Cutting across this profile, however, there were some variations among the 187 children in adoptive homes in the nine communities. For example: 7 were of below average intelligence; 21 had some psychological or interpersonal problems; 33 had minor self-correcting physical handicaps (or handicaps correctable with limited time and expense); 4 had more serious physical disabilities, only two of which were irremediable; and 37 were of minority ethnicity. In a few cases, two or more of these characteristics appeared in the same child. In all, 42 percent of the adoptive children were children with barriers to adoption—many of them minor remediable physical disabilities. And, although a much larger proportion of children remaining in care than of those adopted had barriers, some children with barrier characteristics were, thus, in adoptive homes. A major finding of the study of barriers to adoption was that, generally, more adoptive parents, by their expressed attitudes at initial interviews, seemed willing to accept children with barriers than there were such children placed in adoption with them.[5]

The contrast, however, of the typical child in foster care with the typical adopted child was great.

The age factor was always a major differentiating element, for the children in foster care averaged across nine communities from 7.3 years of age in Summit to 14.0 years of age in Norden.[6] In addition, the child in foster care was more likely to have developed a relationship with his natural parents and siblings, and any relationship with siblings and natural parents was associated with lack of adoption. Also, the child in foster care was much more likely to ex-

[5] The study of barriers uncovered tolerances among the adoptive parents in expectations of age, physical condition, and emotional health that had not been tested by the placements made with them. *Ibid.*, pp. 219–20.

[6] Of the 187 children in adoptive homes, only 33 were aged two years or over. Of these 33, only 11 were aged six years or more. Finally note that 28 of the 33 children, including all of the 11 "oldest," were in the adoptive group with barriers.

hibit some psychological disturbance, although these symptoms did not appear more frequently at the time of our study than they had appeared at the intake of the children. It was found that children with psychological symptoms were often likely to have problems of self-identity and difficulties in interpersonal relationships, and the largest group of children with symptoms were those whose parents were markedly ambivalent about them. A circular process could be discerned in this situation. Ambivalent parents seldom relinquished their children for adoption. Thus the child remained in foster care, grew older, exhibited psychological symptoms, experienced many different placements because of these symptoms, his symptoms increased, and he became progressively less adoptable. It was found that symptomatic behavior in the children was positively associated, not with the length of time they spent in care, but with the number of different moves they had made in foster care.

It was also noted that a larger proportion of children in foster care than in adoption had natural parents who exhibited a genetic defect or were physically ill or handicapped. The child in foster care was more likely than the child in adoption to have one deceased parent; in fact, only one child of the 187 children in adoptive homes had one deceased parent. The child remaining in foster care was more likely to have a severe physical handicap which affected his social functioning, and he was more prone to be of dull-normal intelligence or mentally retarded.

Generally, too, the child of minority ethnicity was more likely to remain in foster care than to be adopted. Our minority child in foster care was either Negro, Spanish, American Indian, Portuguese, French-Canadian, or of mixed ethnicity. These children less frequently exhibited psychological disturbance and experienced fewer moves in care than the majority child. But since mothers of these children had less cooperative relationships with the agencies, and seemed to know less about the fathers of their children, we obtained less complete information on the backgrounds of children of minority ethnicity. However, no significant difference was found between the minority and majority group child with respect to his legal status, age at relinquishment, or manner of relinquishment, whether voluntary or involuntary. Voluntary parent-child separations in both groups had taken place for similar reasons with out-of-wedlock birth ranking first; however, a higher percentage of minority children were voluntarily separated because of illness and death, while more of the majority group children were separated ostensibly because of psychological crises in the parent group.

This was the profile, with its variations, of the child who was in foster care at the time of our study. Many such children seemed likely to grow up in agency homes with little sense of permanency.

VII. TWO SIDES TO THE PROBLEM

22. The Children Likely to Grow Up
in Foster Care

Of all the children we studied, better than half of them gave promise of living a major part of their childhood years in foster families and institutions. Among them were children likely to leave care only when they came of age, often after having had many homes —and none of their own—for ten or so years. Children who move through a series of families or are reared without close and continuing ties to a responsible adult have more than the usual problems in discovering who they are. These are the children who learn to develop shallow roots in relationships with others, who try to please but cannot trust, or who strike out before they can be let down. These are the children about whom we were most concerned.

We defined these children as those whose parents, we predicted, would not be taking them home again. Predictions on human behavior today always include sizable margins for errors—and we estimate ours to be quite broad, from 10 to 20 percent. Of course, if radical changes should occur in the child welfare field and its surrounding worlds the numbers of children in long-term care might be drastically reduced.

What were the bases used for defining the children likely to grow up in foster care? In our study, we used the frequency of, and feelings involved in, parents' visits with their children and the parents' plans, or lack of them, for the children's future. We thus combined three factors in our gross measure: parents' repeated behavior (visiting); parents' manifest feelings; and parents' expressed motives or goals—all associated with their performance and direction in the role of parent and in relation to a given child living in foster care. Variations in the combination of parental visiting and parental plans provided three quite distinct groups of children for study, described as "the unvisited," "the visited," and "the relinquished."

The first group of children were "the unvisited." They were children whose parents had no plans for them other than their remaining in long-term care and who never, or almost never, visited them. If "almost never," the parents also gave no other evidence of caring for the child, no evidence of involving emotions or relationship. These children were appropriately called "the unvisited."

The second group of children were "the visited." They were the children whose parents had, exactly like the parents of the unvisited, no plans for them other than long-term care but who had been visiting their children, often manifesting genuine concern for them, during at least the year preceding the time of our study.

The third group of children were "the relinquished." They were the children whose parents had either already relinquished their children for adoption or were desirous of, or committed to, doing so in the near future. In addition, none of these parents was visiting the children. Thus, unvisited, these children were also, in parental deed or desire, the relinquished.

The unvisited children seemed destined to remain on in long-term foster care unless adoption plans could be made for them. What were these children like? Were they like the children who were being visited or like those who had been relinquished for placement in adoptive homes? The visited children would stay on in care unless parents' plans and family conditions changed. How did these parents and children resemble or differ from the others? And was there a resemblance between the relinquished, those closest to, but not yet in, adoptive homes, and the children who had already been placed with adoptive parents? Our continuing study in contrasts led to the profiles of the three cases which fol-

low,[1] each representative of the children in one of our three groups
of those likely to grow up in foster care.

THE UNVISITED

Bobby Fallow, eleven and a half years old at the time of our study,
was the oldest of our three representative children. Moreover, since he
was almost six-and-a-half when the court first removed him, together with
his three older brothers, from the third story of a dilapidated little frame
house wedged behind another one on Possum Alley, Bobby was approaching his fifth anniversary of life in foster care. He had sound bases for
being an angry boy.

To the best of his knowledge, Bobby's parents were both living with
new mates—just where, nobody knew. There was no reason, however, to
believe that either of these unions was any better than the one in which
Bobby was born and irregularly cared for until he started school. The
agency had relationships with neither Mr. nor Mrs. Fallow, nor had there
ever been more than a few superficial interviews with them, enough to
indicate Mr. Fallow's indifference and Mrs. Fallow's resignation regarding
long-term care for the children.

Essentially, there were no current parental relationships between the
agency and four of every five families of the unvisited. Agency workers
either could not or did not keep up with these people. The possibilities
of changing their attitudes seemed remote; at least, current social work
knowledge and skill and high caseloads which allowed little time for most
clients gave scant support to agency workers' abortive efforts to help
thoroughly defeated parents like the Fallows develop some basic self-
respect.

The Fallow family way of life was of long standing. Very little mattered
to them, and, almost worst of all, they were beyond unhappiness or vital
concern about what seemed to them overwhelming odds. Moreover, regarding Bobby and his brothers, as in so many of America's metropolises,
the effects upon the children of their father's alcoholism and physical
brutality and their mother's complete ineffectualness had evoked no community action for some time. In fact, no action was forthcoming until
parental mistreatment had gone on for years and was finally recognized
at school, at first in one child's repeated absences. Where there existed

[1] Note that in all three groups there are no plans for the child's return to
family. The profiles are based on 132 children who were unvisited (and unrelinquished), on 139 children who were visited (and unrelinquished), and 141
children who were relinquished (and, of course, nòt visited).

only the germ of shared community sentiment and the silent concern of neighbors whose lot was little better, tolerances may have been broad, or else pity and anger did not often lead to calling on police or "the welfare."

When "the welfare" finally did arrive at the Fallows', Mr. Fallow, then aged thirty-eight and just having lost a new job as a laborer at the Navy base, was, as Mrs. Fallow said, "off on a holiday." She and the children were not eating adequately, since he had left no money in the house—and Mrs. Fallow could probably not have managed for long even if he had. Nor was this inability due to the fact she had never completed grade school. People with less education and intelligence have done better. There was just something blunted and dispirited about Mrs. Fallow which left her concerned but unable to function efficiently when it came to caring for the children. She seemed to need parental tending as much as they did. Her approach to their removal implied mixed feelings, but among them was relief from an overwhelming burden. The judge made the children wards of the court and referred them for placement until the Fallows could demonstrate their capacity adequately to feed, clothe, house, educate, and otherwise care for the boys. Two of Bobby's older brothers were already acquainted with the police.

Since leaving his parents, Bobby had lived in three different places—first at the old city orphanage, where on two occasions his mother visited the boys before she vanished. Bobby was then placed with his next older brother in a foster family; he was removed from there when it seemed that the two boys together were "too much" for the foster parents. Bobby's angry feelings toward his own parents, of whom he rarely talked, were now covered over. The child welfare worker who had known Bobby for two years and who seemed quite important to him—the one slim thread of continuity in an otherwise disjointed life—thought it best to leave the boy's present feelings toward his parents untouched. It is hard under the best of circumstances to help an early adolescent face up to the obvious fact that his parents are not sufficiently grown up themselves to provide him with an even minimally adequate home. Such parents are hardly suitable models for a boy in search of his own selfhood.

And yet, when one asks what enduring parental model Bobby might be offered—and the possibility of an adoptive home occurs—one wonders. At eleven and a half, Bobby still presented problems at school, was subject to unpredictable violent outbursts of anger at he knew not what, threatened repeatedly to run away he knew not where, and then became sulky-silent for days at a time. He was no longer the small, frightened wizen-faced child of six and a half, but was awkwardly growing by leaps and bounds in a way that confounded his confusion about who he was, or used to be, or would become. Where were the adoptive parents for the unvisited like Bobby Fallow? Too late for that? What then?

THE VISITED

Brendan O'Hara's story can be told more briefly. He was ten and a half, a year younger than Bobby at the time of our study. Brendan had been in care for three and a half years when we visited St. Mary's. But though his father quite regularly, and with a sad and muted concern for his children, came to see Brendan and the four others still at St. Mary's, Brendan remained, like Bobby, an outsider to family life.

The O'Hara children came originally from a, somewhat happier home than the Fallows. Mr. O'Hara was a steady worker, and Mrs. O'Hara, some high school education behind her, had become the hard-working mother of a large family until—no one was quite clear what happened, and Mr. O'Hara least of all—Mrs. O'Hara suddenly ran off with Mr. O'Hara's cousin. Mr. O'Hara began to act like a widower, and then, two years later, Mrs. O'Hara's death actually occurred. But from the time he had placed the children at St. Mary's, Mr. O'Hara had always spoken of the children's mother as though she were dead, and she might have been so far as he and the children were concerned. In this respect, the O'Hara children were not too different from most of the other visited ones, for fewer than one in four of this group were visited by both parents.

What was the future for Brendan, a silently troubled child with a bad stutter? His fate was obviously tied to his father. And while Mr. O'Hara saw the caseworker at Catholic Charities from time to time, and continued regularly to pay something toward the children's upkeep at St. Mary's (though less than half of what their board actually cost)—and Brendan himself had periodic visits with another caseworker—the die molding a future in foster care for Brendan seemed cast. At age forty-six, Mr. O'Hara lived not too discontentedly in a single room, alone.

THE RELINQUISHED

Quite different from both the unvisited and the visited was Margaret Mondina. Whether the probabilities of her being adopted were any better than theirs, however, seemed very doubtful. For since she had been relinquished for adoption, she was at least certain never to return to her parents—but still Margaret remained unadopted.

Margaret was born of an unwed Caucasian, Protestant mother and a Spanish-Indian father. Margaret's mother, then aged twenty-four, vacillated about keeping her daughter, took her home for six months, then placed her, then tried to care for her again, and finally gave up the child. Margaret was by that time two years and four months old. Timing seemed a crucial element in this case. When we made our study Margaret had been in care the longest of our three representative children—five and a half years. She was approaching her eighth birthday.

In addition to her age, of course, Margaret's ethnic background had made the finding of an adoptive home difficult. Fortunately, soon after she came into foster care, the agency placed Margaret in a foster family with whom she had stayed on. There is apparently a circular relationship between having a single, enduring place to live with parents and other children who form a family, and a child's emotional health. Thus, while it seemed unlikely that Margaret's lot would soon change any more than Bobby's or Brendan's, she was thus far, in terms of her own development as a young person, the best off of the three.

These, in profile, were the children most likely to stay on in long-term foster care. Further evidence of the unlikelihood that any of these children would return home, let alone be adopted, can be given in a more general contrast of the unvisited, the visited, and the relinquished.

In general, the unvisited were the involuntarily removed children of our least educated and most socially deviant and disorganized urban parents. While in 80 percent of the cases the parents were married to one another at the children's birth, most of these parents were now divorced or separated, though about half the mothers and half the fathers were living with new mates. In these cases neglect and abandonment of children were part of a larger syndrome of unremedied psychosocial incompetence. In most instances, parental rights over the children were modified.

In general, the visited were the children of slightly more rural and older parents whose family breakdown was more often (in a third of the cases) grounded in death, illness, or economic need, and to some extent in psychological problems, than in neglect *per se*. About half of these children were Catholic, and a sizable proportion were in institutional care in a locale where at least one parent lived near by. In half the cases full parental rights were retained; in half, parental rights were modified. It is notable that all our measures of these children's psychological adjustment indicated that proportionately as many of the visited as of the unvisited ones were disturbed—in both groups, well over half the children.

Parents of the relinquished were the youngest and most often unwed. In addition, in a subgroup of 22 percent of these cases, one parent was dead or, in a very rare case, both were—by far the largest such percentage among the three groups. Ethnically, by comparison with the 25 percent non-Caucasian composition of the unvisited and the visited, almost half of the relinquished (46 percent) were of minority ethnicity with a third (32 percent) being Negro or Spanish. Thus, in this group we locate the cast-offs, the doubly rejected, the children whose own parents could not or at least did not keep them. At the same time, these children were apparently not wanted by adoptive parents or at least had not been placed in adoption by the social agencies.

Many, if not most of the children among the unvisited, the visited, and the relinquished are going to grow up in foster care. Must all of them do so? Which ones need not? And for those for whom there are no preferable alternatives, can there be some creative community planning? More individual reviews on a child-by-child basis? Clearly, return home is most unlikely—and probably undesirable with parental conditions as we know them—for angry Bobby Fallow, half-orphaned and badly stuttering Brendan O'Hara, and legally relinquished Margaret Mondina. Did we see hope for permanent homes for such children in the world of adoptive parents we learned to know in the nine communities? This is another side to the problem, to which we turn in Chapter 23.

23. The Parents Who Adopted Children

Were older children who remained in foster care in our metropolitan areas likely to be taken into adoptive homes in our rural communities? Were adoptive parents' attitudes and expectations concerning the ethnic backgrounds of children more accepting of difference in our homogeneous or in our heterogeneous communities? Were children's physical or psychological deficiencies or temporary disabilities more acceptable to adoptive parents in the prosperous counties or in the economically more depressed ones? How did adoptive parents differ in the Old South's Jamestown and the New South's King City, or in New England's Brighton and the new West of Westport? These were the kinds of queries guiding our examination of the data on our adoptive parents. And underlying all such study was one basic question: Were children who seemed unadoptable in one part of the country likely to find adoptive parents in another part?

To find at least a partial answer to this question, we compared the adoptive parents in our study on a community-by-community basis. These were all couples with whom the agencies in our nine networks had chosen to place one or more adoptive children. What were the typical adoptive parents in each community like, how did they vary from community to community, and where there were more than a few parents in any community different from its most characteristic "type," what were these differences? Did they offer leads as to where children who were older or different might be placed in adoption?

We examined the groups of adoptive parents in each community along five dimensions. Each dimension seemed relevant to the characteristics of children whom agencies placed, or might have placed, in adoption. Thus we were interested in the parents: first, as biological organisms of given ages and degrees of health and reported capacity for having children of their own; second, as members of families of a certain size and residence; third, as members of ethnic, religious, and social class groups which in some measure, we assumed, determined their initial expectations and attitudes concerning children for adoption; fourth, as persons expressing certain expectations and attitudes regarding adoptive children; and fifth, as persons evidencing varying kinds of psychological reactions to their marriage, their childlessness, their plans for adoption, their own childhoods and their families of origin, as well as varying degrees of inner control in their expressions of feelings, ways of relating to other persons, and responses to the completion of tasks.[1]

THE REPRESENTATIVE COUPLE

For all the variations among our nine communities, in size and degree of urbanization, ethnic composition, economy, geography, and history, the profile of each community's adoptive couples is remarkably alike. (The few notable differences among them are elaborated in the next section of this chapter.) It is as though adoption standards in the child welfare field transcended in their potency any relevant differences among the nine community cultures.

Adoptive couple profiles in at least six, usually more and often all, of the nine communities coincided on each of the parental characteristics which make up the composite portrait of Jane and Harry Smith, the typical (modal) parents with whom adoptive placements in this study were made. Following this portrait, significant community variants from the Smiths are presented.

Jane and Harry Smith were both in their mid-thirties—Jane almost thirty-four, Harry thirty-seven—at the time of our study. Neither had ever been married before. Neither had any health problem which would in any way interfere with their being parents to an adoptive child, but the medical reports were clear that Jane could never conceive a child of her own.

The Smiths were approaching a tenth anniversary of childless married life when the baby was placed with them. For the preceding five years they had lived in Castle Gardens, a post war suburban development, where they were buying their home on a twenty-year G.I. loan. Their two-bedroom house on Strawberry Drive was compact and comfortable. What the Smiths had once called their "spare" room had in 1957 become

---

[1] The limitations in our approaches to the problem of studying adoptive parents are apparent. For example, to answer basic questions about parents who might adopt unadopted children we should probably have studied also the adoptive parent applicants with whom agencies did *not* place children. We should also ideally have used far more refined measures than some of the gross devices in our case schedules for assessing parental adjustment. For a first broad survey of the situation, however, our study techniques seemed appropriate.

the baby's. Valued at $12,500, the home was worth somewhat more than they had paid for it in 1952.

The Smiths were both white and Protestant, belonged to the same church, and were fairly active in it, according to their minister. In the course of growing up, their adopted child was likely to find religion taking on considerable but not an overwhelming meaning in his life. Education probably would be important for him too. The Smiths were both high school graduates for whom first the depression years and then the Second World War, they said, had variously affected their chances to undertake college studies. As a result, Mr. Smith thought he was not as far along in a career as he might otherwise have been. For eight years he had been working in the small advertising department at Atherton's, writing copy and doing layouts. His annual salary was "only $5,750," but Mr. Smith was expecting a Christmas bonus and then a raise starting with the new year. There were always new appliances and additional furnishings the Smiths thought their home needed. Still, they both showed good sense and some humor about money management, bills, and new acquisitions.

From the outset the Smiths were clear that they wanted only an infant for adoption. There was never any question either about their wanting the child to look, as much as possible, as though he belonged to them, and this probably meant his having, preferably, a similar nationality background. The interviews by the placing agency suggested that a minor remediable health problem in a child would not unduly upset the Smiths, but any evidence of psychological disturbance, certainly evidence of less than average intelligence, would make a child unacceptable to them. Education and getting ahead seemed almost too important. Matters of the mind which were different from the normal were mysteriously troublesome, though such deviation as out-of-wedlock birth, known by the Smiths to be the likely history of any child they could adopt, came within the realm of their understanding and tolerance.

There had, of course, been no occasion in the Smiths' lives for them to learn at firsthand about any kind of psychological problems. Both were quite stable and relatively comfortable people, markedly content with their own marriage, accepting of the impossibility of their having a child together and unquestioningly agreed that adoption was what they both wanted. Both looked back on their own childhood days and family life as happy. While Mrs. Smith's parents and two sisters lived half-way across the continent, weekly correspondence kept their relationship a close one. For Harry Smith, giving up the spare room to a baby meant some curtailment of his father's periodic visits from the city to Castle Gardens, but other arrangements could be made when Mr. Smith, Sr., wanted to visit.

All in all, both Jane and Harry Smith seemed psychologically well within the range of the normal in regard to how they expressed their feelings, related to other people, and accomplished tasks. If they were in any way different from our image of average Americans, it was in the tendency they both had to behave as though the inner controls of principle or conscience guided their action somewhat more than did the forces of external circumstance. Personal flexibility was not a notable trait for either of them. With Mr. Smith, the tendency toward self-restraint appeared more in how he handled emotions and himself in personal relations. With Mrs. Smith, imperatives were more in the sphere of tasks to be completed. But these psychological variations from "flexibility" were so slight as to be barely worth recording. On the other hand, the Smiths' capacities to weigh alternatives and act in response both to personal commitments and to social demands were amply illustrated in the manner they proceeded in adoption. Once they were decided about adopting a baby, they went about inquiring into community resources for adoption and then maintained an understanding acceptance of agency procedures leading up to the placement of the baby.

VARIATIONS FROM THE SMITHS

While most of the adoptive parents in most of our communities resembled Jane and Harry Smith, there were, of course, many couples who differed from them in significant ways. What was significant seemed related to our central question on the possibilities of adoptive placement for children who were somewhat older or different from the normal, white infant—a minor, remediable physical difficulty excepted—whom the Smiths were counting on receiving from an agency. Review of our data on both parental expectations and attitudes and on the characteristics of the adoptive children actually placed in each community—both "set" and behavior thus becoming the bases for generalization—led us to some interesting propositions.

Older children, that is, children beyond the age of five, were much more frequently acceptable to the adoptive parents in Norden, Summit, and King City than to the parents elsewhere. Also, only in these three communities was there any consistent evidence that children of dull-normal intelligence could be adopted. Examining the related facts about the adoptions in these three communities, we found, on the one hand, our largest proportions of farm owner or farm manager families among Norden (33 percent) and Summit (26 percent) adoptive couples and, on the other hand, our largest proportions of blue-collar and less skilled workers (53 percent) among the adoptive parents in King City. By contrast, older children were least acceptable, and least often placed, among the adoptive parents in Westport, Jamestown, Brighton, and Granger. Here too, and most clearly in Westport and Jamestown, no child with an I.Q. of less than 90 seemed likely to find adoptive parents. In these four communities, far more than in any of the others, the proportions of professional, managerial, proprietary, clerical, and other white-collar workers among the adoptive parents were highest (from 66 to 71 percent of all adoptive parents falling in these occupation categories). These were the parents who, like Jane and Harry Smith, wanted only an infant and valued education and getting ahead too much to be able knowingly to make a child whose intelligence was less than average a member of their family.

Liberal parental attitudes concerning the acceptance of children of mixed or minority ethnicity were most frequently expressed in four of the ethnically more homogeneous communities—Granger, Summit, Westport, and Centralia. Far fewer parents were so open-minded, and physical matching of child and parent seemed more often important in more segmented Jamestown, Brighton or King City, where, together with La Paz, ethnic differences were, in fact, most visible in the population at large and where the largest total proportions of ethnically different children in our study were actually placed in adoption, almost always with their own ethnic groups. The proposition pressed upon us was that more children of minority ethnicity might find ready adoptive parents in relatively homogeneous communities where ethnic difference was not so great a threat.

Clear-cut interpretation of our facts on physical handicap were not possible. Our adoptive parents did not seem to consider minor or remediable physical handicaps in children a barrier to their adoption, and we found no evidence, when we compared the numbers of children in foster care and in adoptive placements who had not-too-serious physical disabilities, that any but the most serious physical conditions *per se* kept many children out of adoptive homes. On the other hand, in our four most prosperous communities—Summit, Westport, Centralia and King City—we found large proportions of adoptive parents (25 to 44 percent of them) saying they would accept in adoption only a child who was physically perfect. In La Paz and Jamestown this factor rarely came up as an issue. Where we found the greatest wealth there seemed to be the most frequent insistence on childhood perfection in physical health. This is not to deny, however, that from a fifth to a half of the adoptive parents in these same four prosperous communities would have accepted a child with some minor physical anomaly.

Much more frequently rejected among our adoptive parents than the child with physical disabilities was the child with emotional disturbance. Evidence of a psychological problem among our children proved definitely a barrier to adoptive placement with the kinds of parents being reached by the agencies in this study. In only our two largest communities, Westport and King City, were as many as 25 percent of the parents willing to consider adoption of a child with psychological problems. In addition, in Summit 17 percent of parents would not have ruled out a child with such problems. But only 10 percent or fewer of the parents in Granger, Jamestown, La Paz, and Brighton remarked that they would be willing to adopt a child with symptoms of an emotional nature. Being older than two years of age, having an I.Q. of less than 90, or giving evidence of psychological upset was likely to bar a child from adoption with all but a very few of the adoptive parents under study—parents much like the Smiths who probably had never realized how children's psychological development is responsive to the kinds of certainty a home like theirs might offer.

Other patternable differences among the parents in our nine communities reflected on the adoptive placements made or not made with these couples. In our more rural counties—Granger, Norden, Summit, and La Paz—both mothers and fathers were somewhat younger than Jane and Harry Smith. In Summit, where mothers averaged thirty (by comparison with Jane Smith, who was thirty-three) and fathers averaged thirty-four (by comparison with Harry Smith, who was thirty-seven), tolerances for children who were different were generally far broader than in Jamestown or Brighton, where mothers averaged thirty-four to thirty-six in age, fathers thirty-eight to thirty-nine, and from more than a quarter to almost a half of all the fathers of newly placed babies were aged forty and over.

Evidence of sterility was presented for about half or more of the couples in only five of our nine communities—Norden, Granger, Summit, Westport, and Centralia. And only where we had both a high economic level in the community and high proportions of white-collar fathers—in Granger and in Westport—did we find many fathers reportedly involved in the deficiencies which kept the couples childless. Otherwise, as with Jane and Harry Smith, good health characterized almost all the adoptive parents.

The adoptive couples tended to be married a goodly number of years before a child was placed with them. While the Smiths were approaching a tenth wedding anniversary, parents in both Jamestown and Brighton not only tended to be older but also tended to have been married longer than couples elsewhere in our study— eleven or thirteen years on the average. The younger couples in Summit also averaged eleven years of marriage, but fewer there— only 13 percent of them—had been married as long as fifteen or more years, while in Brighton and Jamestown 33 and 21 percent respectively of the adoptive parents had been married 15 years or longer. For 10 percent of the Jamestown and Brighton parents, moreover, these were not first marriages, so the waits for children had been long ones. In both King City and La Paz more of the adoptive parents were remarried—about 20 percent—but the average length of current marriages was less than the Smiths, eight or nine years. The lowest average (median) was in Granger, seven years, where two of the six couples had been married less than five

years, as had as many as 15 to 20 percent of the parents in only two
other places, King City and Summit. On the whole, the parents of
our adoptive children were far from their first years of marriage. If
this fact promised continuation of the marital relationship, it probably brought, like residential stability, other elements into adoptive child-parent relationships about which we can only speculate.
On the surface, such time elements seemed to compound the differences in the familial situations of the Smiths' adoptive child
and of the children born to the family next door on Strawberry
Drive.

Family life among many of the couples we studied varied from
the Smiths' in certain ways, too. For one thing, it included other
children in the home much more often than we had expected.
While most couples, like the Smiths, had no children when the
baby was placed, there were one or more children (either adopted
or own children) in the adoptive homes of 44 percent of the Westport parents, 40 percent of the La Paz parents, 36 percent of King
City's, 26 percent of Jamestown's, 22 percent of Summit's, and in
a few of the homes (but less than 20 percent) in each of the four
remaining communities. Nevertheless, the three-person family was
the pattern in half or more of the adoptive living units everywhere
but in Norden. And like the Smiths, more than 80 percent of the
couples in seven of our nine communities (Granger and La Paz excepted) were home-owners. Single-family dwellings were the rule,
which almost always provided the adoptive child with a room of
his own. Moreover, it was a rare couple who became adoptive
parents when they had lived for fewer than four years in the counties we studied. If residential stability was necessary before an
agency would make a thorough adoption study, it must have acted
to some extent as a criterion for parent selection too, increasing
the likelihood, one might presume, of other kinds of stability in
these families. And only among the Granger and the Centralia
families were more of the homes located in urban rather than suburban environs; only among Norden families were most of the
homes in semirural or farm areas; for in all six remaining com-

munities more of the adoptive parents were housed like the Smiths in Castle Gardens than in city or country surroundings.

To live in such surroundings, adoptive fathers had to make much more than the average annual income in their communities. A significant finding was that while the range of median incomes for all our adoptive families was a relatively narrow one (the extremes of Granger and Westport excluded), the incomes of adoptive parents in the more depressed of our communities were regularly higher than the adoptive parents' income in our more prosperous communities! The lowest median income for the adoptive families, $5,400 (in 1957), appeared in Centralia, with the highest average U.S. Census-reported family income among our nine communities. La Paz's adoptive family median income of $5,750 was matched against far more prosperous Summit's median of $5,667. Brighton's was also $5,667 and Jamestown's $5,999—against far wealthier Centralia's $5,400. More adoptive parents in the poorer communities came from closer to the economic top of their communities than in more prosperous places like Centralia and King City, where blue-collar workers were a third of the adoptive parent groups. The one exception to this pattern was Westport. Westport's adoptive parent median income of $6,780 topped by about a thousand dollars King City's median, and in Westport, as in Jamestown, Brighton, and Granger with its high of $7,750, 66 to 71 percent of adoptive fathers were drawn from upper occupation positions. Across all of our nine communities but two (King City and La Paz), just about the majority of adoptive fathers were upper- or middle-level white-collar workers—and this included the two rural counties, Norden and Granger, and Summit too. But the white-collar counterparts of Harry Smith in King City were only 39 percent of the adoptive fathers there; an additional 7 percent were farmers, 32 percent were skilled workers, and 21 percent were semiskilled and unskilled workers.[2] In such occupa-

---

[2] More adoptive mothers who planned to work part time or full time appeared in King City than elsewhere (18 percent of the mothers, and mostly Negro), though there were one or more mothers planning to work in every community except Norden, Granger, and Brighton.

tional group membership facts we saw some of the bases for King City's greater apparent tolerance—certainly greater than that of Westport's parents—for children who were older and in some ways different from the average child.

Such a situation was not a function merely of differences in educational experiences among parents. High school graduation was the amazingly consistent educational median for both the Jane and the Harry Smiths right across our nine communities, including the most rural. And the husbands and wives having had some college or higher education were, in King City, 38 and 36 percent and in Westport 49 and 31 percent respectively of the adoptive fathers and mothers in each of these two big cities. It was true, however, that only in King City did as many as 8 percent of the adoptive fathers and 21 percent of the adoptive mothers have less than an elementary school education. (In Brighton, an equal 8 percent of the fathers had as little formal education, but none of the mothers there had completed less than eight years of school.) But, at least in our judgment, well over half of King City's adoptive parents showed a clear understanding of genetic forces which might operate detrimentally in adoption.

In regard to ethnic factors, not all parents were like the Smiths. Caucasian and nonethnic couples were involved in all the adoptive placements in Norden, Granger, Summit, and Centralia. But half of the couples in La Paz were Spanish, almost a third of King City's adoptive parents were of other than Caucasian or nonethnic backgrounds, about a fifth of Jamestown's adoptive couples were Negro, and a fifth of the Brighton adoptive couples were of minority national backgrounds, highly apparent in that New England city. In Westport, more than 91 and 94 percent respectively of the fathers and mothers were of the majority white group. But the lack of identical ethnic backgrounds in father and mother, suggested by Westport's percentages, was perhaps the rarest element in the whole ethnic-religious adoption situation, where "matching" has taken on such importance.

Parents' membership in the same church seems, by dint of the very few couples in our study who did not share such an affiliation, to have become, in the agency networks we studied, almost a *sine qua non* for an adoptive placement. Regarding religious factors at variance with the situation in Jane and Harry Smith's home, note that in La Paz most of the parents were Catholic and in Granger and Centralia half or more were Lutheran; that confirmation of church membership was obtained for fewer than half the parents in *only* two of our communities—Summit and Jamestown; and that religion had little or no expression in family life in only a very few of the homes in our study—a few in Summit and a few in Westport. In others, church tended to be as important as it was for Jane and Harry Smith.

Finally, our data do not suggest that all adoptive parents were, like the Smiths, psychologically adjusted on a base of rather strong inner controls, though this was clearly the predominant pattern. Relative contentment with themselves and their spouse in marriage was apparently an essential for an adoptive placement in just about every community, but in King City about 10 percent of the adoptive parents expressed some feelings of guilt, inadequacy, punitiveness, or resentment about their childlessness, and there were a few cases where one parent in a couple merely "went along" in the request for an adoptive child, clear that such a placement meant very much to the marital partner. In short, failure to show mutuality in the decision to adopt did not bar a couple from becoming adoptive parents in at least three of our communities. In a majority of cases in all communities except Granger both adoptive parents, like the Smiths, came from families that were free of psychosocial problems and recalled having had happy childhoods with parents and/or brothers and sisters with whom they still enjoyed satisfying relationships. Nevertheless, in every community there were adoptive parents, one or both of whom had not had such an ideal early family life. The frequency of adoptive couples with expressed difficulties in their own family experiences ran a range of percentages increasing from about 10 percent of the cases in Jamestown and Summit to somewhere about the 20s in Norden, Brighton, La Paz, and King City; to somewhere in the 30's in Westport and in Granger; to a high of about 40 percent in Centralia.

This is not to deny that in all but a very few of these cases whatever serious personal problems these early experiences might have generated, the adoptive parents had them well resolved by the time of their applications for a child. At the time of our study, personal modes of adaptation varied not too greatly. If more fathers tended to be inflexible about tasks in the predominantly upper occupational status adoptive families in Brighton, Westport, and Jamestown, and consistently more inflexible about the expression of feelings and personal relationships in more rural Summit and Norden or more blue-collar Centralia and King City, this seemed comprehensible. More of the mothers were freer than were inflexible in their emotions and in their behavior with others in rural Norden and half-Spanish, close-to-the-rural La Paz. But such variations were noted as but minor differences in an overwhelmingly homogeneous group of adults who, though living in nine quite diverse areas in the United States, bore a shockingly uniform similarity to Jane and Harry Smith.

PARENTS WHO ADOPTED CHILDREN WHO WERE DIFFERENT

Since one of our major goals was to shed light on the problem of adoptive placement for older children and children who were different, we could not stop our search after an essentially nonproductive analysis of regional differences among our nine groups of adoptive parents. We therefore tried a second and, as it turned out, somewhat more fruitful approach to our data—a comparative study of all the adoptive parents who had taken children who were different and all the remaining adoptive parents of completely normal youngsters. We found over all that in 42 percent of our adoptive cases the children involved were in some way different. About half of these children had some degree of physical disability. About 40 percent were of ethnic backgrounds unlike those of the majority. Less than a quarter of them gave evidence of some psychological problem. And exactly 8 percent of the children who were different (or 4 percent of the total children in adoptive placements) were judged to have below average intelligence. Some of the children had more than one of these disabilities.

For many reasons, only these four factors (and not age) were considered in defining the group of children who were different, but in effect almost all the children who were aged two years and over turned up in this special group. As a result, among the children whom we constituted as our normal group, 95 percent had not yet reached their second birthdays, and of the remaining 5 percent who were older, all were under the age of five! To this extent, then, our normal group was contaminated by the age factor! And all of our adoptive children with physical, ethnic, or psychological differences—including, incidentally, all the children in adoptions who were five years of age or older—made up the other group.

Who were the adoptive parents of this latter group of children? Mr. and Mrs. Judah Albert represent the couples who were adopting children who were in some way different. Mr. and Mrs. James Q. Holt speak for the couples who adopted only preschool normal children.

The Judah Alberts were slightly older than the James Q. Holts. The Alberts were also married a somewhat longer time. The key to major differences between families like the Alberts and the Holts, however, was that in many more of the former (about half of them) the fathers were skilled, semiskilled, or unskilled workers, while in about two thirds of the families like the Holts the fathers were in professional, managerial, or other white-collar occupations. Related facts then fell into place: more men like Mr. Holt had had some college education (almost 50 percent); more women like Mrs. Albert had gone no farther than elementary school (15 percent). Mr. Albert had been on his job longer than Mr. Holt, but twice as many fathers like Mr. Holt (about a third of them) had annual incomes, in 1957, as high as $7,000 or more. It was not surprising, then, that 15 percent of mothers like Mrs. Albert, after the placement of the child, planned to continue working, half of them full time and half of them part time, for the most part in white-collar jobs although some held skilled and service jobs. Only 2 percent of mothers like Mrs. Holt worked, all of them in white-collar jobs. Most of the working mothers were Negroes. About a fourth of the adoptive parents whose children were different were not members of the majority ethnic group in our society but included persons of all the visible minorities in the communities we studied.

With their newly adopted child, the Alberts were a family of four; the Holts were three. While 80 percent of families like the Alberts occupied single-dwelling units, as did 90 percent of families like the Holts, there were twice as many renters among the parents of children who were different. And the homes they owned were less expensive than the Holts'. A third of families like the Alberts lived in the city and another quarter in semirural and farm areas, while half of all families like the Holts lived in surburban communities. No matter, however, where either the Alberts or the Holts lived, they were to an equally high extent (80 to 90 percent) settled members of their home neighborhoods.

Also, they seemed with equally high frequency (in the 90 percents) to understand generally the place of heredity in a child's endowments. But twice as many families like the Alberts would accept a child of questionable background, and 33 percent (as against 14 percent of couples like the Holts) would consider adopting a child who was ethnically different from themselves.

Couples like the Alberts clearly wanted a child. Three quarters of them would not have let minor physical disabilities stand in their way, almost half would have considered a child with a mild emotional disturbance, though anything more serious would have been acceptable to only 10 percent of them. More than a quarter of these parents said they would take a child of between two and five years, and another quarter said they would accept an even older, school-aged child. Over half such parents were this receptive to children above the age of two years. Nor did the children have to be too carefully matched physically to the adoptive family to please these parents. In all these ways, the Alberts' tolerances far exceeded the Holts'.

With such attitudes, Judah Albert had understandably a different personality from Jim Holt's. For one thing, Judah was much less frequently than Jim reported to be a responsible party in the childlessness both couples had experienced. Moreover, Judah was more likely than Jim to seem like a patriarch, less open in his expression of feelings than Jim, though Jim was more likely to be stricter about work obligations around the house and elsewhere.

As though to counterbalance Judah and Jim, their wives, Mary and Helen, tended to reverse these differences, with Mary Albert being somewhat warmer when she was affectionate and angrier when she was angry than Helen Holt ever was. Mary Albert was also somewhat less formal in her personal relationships and somewhat less concerned about getting chores completed.

Finally, if the Holts considered their coming to the adoption agency a matter of self-referral, the Alberts got to it quite deviously, through a chain of secondary sources, encouraged along the way by others and, in this respect, most unlike, too, the quite fully self-propelled Jane and Harry Smith of Castle Gardens. But then, the Alberts had in the past known much more than the Holts or the Smiths of truly overwhelming experiences, during the depression years and at other times, so that if they showed less apparent initiative in reaching goals, they also evidenced more acceptance of who and where they were.

The adoptive parents of children who were different tended to live by standards which recognized and accepted human imperfection. These parents started with their own incompleteness and wanted to make a child in need of parents a member of their own family. They did not confuse the core of their desires for a child with surface matters of physical appearance or capacities related more to remote achievements of social position. To them the interchange of human feelings between nurturant parents and a child who cannot grow up without their continuing care was paramount.

VIII. NEXT STEPS

24. Action Called For—Recommendations
BY JOSEPH H. REID

The prime requisite for intelligent action in any situation is knowl-edge—knowledge of the facts, the circumstances which have pro-duced the facts, and, most important, awareness of those aspects of the situation which are still unknown or unclear. In this study, we have the most comprehensive and systematic evidence concerning children in foster care that has ever been available to the Ameri-can public and to the social workers and social agencies responsible for the care of over a quarter million children in this country.

It is evident to anyone reading the study that radical action is necessary if American communities are to protect adequately the children now living outside their own homes and the additional thousands of children in danger of losing their own homes. De-spite the enormous advances made by social welfare in caring for the dependent, neglected, and disturbed child, his lot, as revealed by this study, is an unhappy one, and more often than not he re-mains disadvantaged throughout his childhood.

This study, like any good research, has raised many questions which need further investigation. However, it has also provided major findings on which to base sound recommendations for ac-tion. The researchers have been careful to point out that this is a study of but nine American communities. Although it is probable that in no American community will the statistics of foster care vary widely from at least one of the nine communities studied, it is vital that every state, city, and rural area of the United States know the conditions of its children in foster care. Local studies comparable in method and scope to those reported in this volume should prove invaluable in focusing attention upon the shortcomings of any individual community in the care of its children and on the deterrents to such children's securing the same rights as any other American children. We recommend that communities review the methods for study presented in this report,[1] and, after adapting those which seem appropriate, repeat the study in their own communities. To obtain community action—and that is the prime purpose of this volume—we recommend that each community follow the procedure used in this study: namely, that of having a committee of influential lay citizens and agency representatives sponsor a study, examine its findings, and act upon them. Since legislators, county commissioners, the boards of United Funds and social agencies, and the general public in the final analysis determine the policies and provide the financing of child care programs, to do so intelligently they must understand the circumstances surrounding the lives of these children and their families.

The Child Welfare League of America believes that children will be best served by full reporting on the deficiencies as well as the achievements of child welfare programs. This study shows that some agencies and communities have developed imaginative child welfare programs, have placed the so-called "hard-to-place child," and have developed placement practices that are flexible. And undoubtedly there are many communities which have better and more imaginative records than those included in this survey. However, no one can read this material without coming to the conclusion that for a large number of children in foster care there are overwhelming deterrents to their becoming responsible, mature adults capable of being good parents. These children, for the most part, are denied the birthright of every American child—the right to a happy and secure childhood, enabling them to make full use of their inherent capacity.

The magnitude of the problem is seen in these statistics. There are 268,000 children in foster care in the United States; of these, 44,000 are in preadoptive homes, the remainder in institutions and foster family homes. In no more than 25 percent of the foster care

[1] See Appendix A.

cases in most of the nine communities studied was it probable that the child would return to his own home. Thus, if the nine communities reported upon in this study are representative of the rest of the country (although the authors of the study do not maintain that they are), we can only conclude that there are roughly 168,000 children today who are in danger of staying in foster care throughout their childhood years. And although in a third of the cases at least one parent did visit the child, in approximately half the parents visited infrequently or not at all.

What does the future hold for these "orphans of the living"? What is the most that we can do for them? Or beyond that, how could we begin to decrease their numbers in the future?

PREVENTIVE MEASURES

Despite tremendous advances that have been made toward preserving family life, there is still much to be done. As a nation we have sharply reduced the proportion of children in the United States who live outside their own homes. Advances in medical science, particularly the prevention of death of mothers in childbirth, reduction of industrial accidents, and the eradication of communicable diseases have sharply reduced the number of orphans in our country. As compared with 1920 there are less than one sixteenth as many orphans in the United States today. The Social Security Act, through its public assistance provision, has enabled thousands of children formerly placed in foster care to remain in their own home. Effective casework help for families by casework agencies has sharply decreased the length of time the children remain in care and in thousands of cases has prevented family breakdown.

But much foster placement is still associated with poor health, low income, and poor housing. In the three most uniformly prosperous of the nine communities, parents' economic hardship, illness, or death were "primary conditions" at the time of the child's separation in 12, 17, and 18 percent, respectively, of the foster care cases. In the other six communities, in from 24 to 40 percent of the foster care cases poor health and low income were "primary conditions" at separation. Moreover, housing of the parents of the children in foster care was such that there was either no space for the child or a room would have had to be shared with an adult in from 42 to 77 percent of the families in each of the communities studied. Only as the nation protects the earning capacity of families, particularly those of minority groups, can some foster placements be prevented.

By far, however, the single most important cause of foster placement of children is marital breakdown. Only about a fifth of the parents of children in foster care were married to each other at the time of our study. The largest group were divorced or separated. Rising illegitimacy rates also reflect a problem in society which cannot be corrected by changing social agency practices. Social agencies alone are helpless in combatting this situation. Strengthening family life, strengthening the morals and spiritual responsibility of American parents, can come about only as the churches, schools, and every other social institution improve the moral climate of America. The small nuclear American family, which is more often than not removed from the extended family group of grandmothers and uncles and cousins that formerly strengthened the ability of parents to carry out their parental responsibilities, needs far greater social protections than did the American family of fifty or even twenty years ago. In order to keep families intact, every community must provide a wide range of service, including financial assistance, marital counseling, psychiatric services, homemaker service, day care, and many other social services that are as necessary as a clean water supply in every American community. In the broader sense, the only preventive for children having to live unnecessarily in foster care is a healthy, economically prosperous, morally strong American family and a healthy, prosperous, and morally strong community.

It was not within the scope of this study to evaluate how many children now in foster care could have been prevented from entering such care had more adequate social services been available. We need not wait upon research to discover, however, how large a percentage of children would not be in care were basic services available in every community. Among the services most frequently absent in the American community are those designed to identify early the family that is in trouble and to bring services to it. In the elementary grades of public and parochial schools the first sign of family breakdown can be detected in the behavior of children, providing there are diagnostic services available in the school and providing these diagnostic services are correlated with casework services in which workers go to the homes of the parents and offer them help. Imaginative outreaching services are much needed. Such services provide help before it is too late. The study clearly indicates that by the time the family and child are known to the social agency, in a large percentage of cases family disintegration is already so great that remedial efforts are almost hopeless. Data on the rising numbers of illegitimate children found in foster care clearly indicate the necessity of providing more adequate services for unmarried mothers. Such services will only become available providing the community recognizes their essential nature and is willing to pay for them.

A particular word of caution is needed in regard to the statistics of the study. Communities can delude themselves by believing that because they have a smaller number of children in care than other communities in proportion to their population they are doing a better preventive job. But communities with the smallest number of children in foster care per thousand children in the population are not necessarily those with the best preventive services. In fact, the reverse may be true. In this study the two communities with the largest number of children in foster care also had the best preventive services—the "best" in most adequate and available preventive services. They had family services, protective services, trained court staff, and child guidance clinics, as well as the most adequately supported and professionally staffed child placement agencies. Communities such as Summit, which had the lowest proportionate number of children in foster care, tend to ignore the neglected child who requires services, and often the individuals responsible for administering the public welfare services, as well as the general community, delude themselves into believing that there is no such problem in their community. Paradoxically, those communities which had the best professional services also had some of the lowest rates of return of children to their own homes. However, it is probable that these communities also had a much lower incidence of children being returned home and then coming back into care. They had, moreover, higher rates of in-county adoption.

ADOPTION SERVICES

For only a fraction of children now in foster care is there a possibility of return to their own homes. For the rest, the alternative is either adoption or long-term foster care. It is this group of children, whose parents essentially have abandoned them, for whom action is urgently needed. In our opinion, a situation should not be permitted to exist wherein parents may essentially abandon their children in foster care and yet retain legal control over them. Certainly one of the first priorities is to clarify each child's legal status and to sever parental rights in all situations where it is obvious that the parents will never take responsibility for the child. Assuming that it is possible to free every child legally, adoption can, however, be the answer for only part of them. Only a very small percentage of these children are children who may now be considered "readily adoptable"—that is, children who are under five years of age, white, average or above in intelligence, with no irremediable physical disabilities and no serious personality problems. But experience has demonstrated that there are families who will adopt older children, children who are nonwhite, children of less than average intelligence, children who do have irremediable physical defects. There are families, also, who have the courage, love, and persistence to accept a troubled or problem child. Agencies need to locate these families and then whole communities need to support and accept the adoption of such children.

There are numerous measures that can be taken to promote the adoption of this group. This study indicates that many potential

adoptive couples are willing to take, for example, children with
greater physical difficulties than are placed with them. This suggests that many adoption agencies, or the workers in them, may
not have as much conviction about the satisfaction that can be obtained in the adoption of the child of less than average intelligence or serious physical defects or minority race as do adoptive
applicants. Conscious or unconscious attitudes on the part of caseworkers may well serve as a barrier to the placement of such children.

There is also evidence that suggests that adoption agencies do
not reach a large segment of the population that may well be the
greatest resource for the limited or the handicapped child. A
study by Fanshel of the adoption of Negro children [2] indicated
that the formalities of adoption agency procedure, fear of any
quasi-official agency, and a failure to effect communication may
well stand as a barrier to the work of the average social agency in
a Negro community. It is not unlikely that among the lower-
income groups, those with less education and less sophistication, the
services of adoption agencies are either unknown or distrusted.
In community after community studied in this investigation, it became clear that not only were some services not available, but in
some cases available services were not being used by certain segments of the public. This applies not only to adoption agencies
but to all types of social agencies. Typically, there were minority
group and social class variations in the use of adoption facilities.
In one community a Southern European group seemed to be making minimum use of the kinds of services which would help to
strengthen their family life and prevent the need for foster care
services. In another community that took pride in its child guidance clinic, it was quite clear that this facility was being used
primarily by professional families and not by the kinds of parents
whose children subsequently became those who needed foster care
services.

Since agencies frequently do not communicate with major segments of the public, they must study carefully why it is they do

[2] Fanshel, *A Study of Negro Adoption.*

not reach certain groups and develop methods and change procedure so that they can. Communities have the responsibility for supporting agencies so that they can provide needed services to the total community. Specifically, in the instance of adoption services, there are indications from this research that the families most likely to accept the child of average or less than average intelligence and the child with other handicaps are not being reached by agencies. There are also indications from other phenomena, such as the number of Korean or mixed-blood Korean children that are being adopted through non-social work organizations, that a large segment of the public is not reached by social agencies. Minor changes and procedures—for example, not requiring the filling out of questionnaires or the supplying of sterility information or coming to the agency for the first interview—have been found by some agencies to help bridge existing gaps between agencies and those segments of the population that are totally unreached. Seeking help from such organizations as labor unions, granges, specific nationality organizations, or clubs and identifying and overcoming the obstacles to the use of adoption agencies by certain groups within the general population can also be valuable. Churches, too, particularly those serving low-income groups and nationality groups, can be an invaluable avenue for reaching a better understanding with important segments of the population. Recent studies have indicated that broad publicity campaigns to recruit adoptive homes for difficult-to-place children, particularly those aimed at specific groups, are generally not so effective as face-to-face contact and word-of-mouth publicity. However, social agencies have proven that they can benefit greatly by persistent and consistent interpretations of their policies and regulations. An example of the sort of thing that might be successfully attacked in this manner is the common public belief that agencies place a premium on high-income families, or that there are other unusual requirements in respect to better than average housing, high school or college education. Another instance is the idea that formal church affiliation is an absolute requirement for adoption. For this, perhaps the agencies themselves are in some measure responsible, for, the study indicates, in practice a large percentage of agencies apparently placed children only with families having such an affiliation, despite the fact that many agencies do not stipulate it as a condition for becoming adoptive parents. The standards of the Child Welfare League of America that have been agreed to by all major church groups point out that the moral character of the family and not church affiliation *per se* should be the criterion for acceptance of adoptive applicants.

Many agencies have changed policies that used to restrict various segments of the population from becoming adoptive parents. Among them are such policies as requiring that the mother not be employed, or that there be a separate room available for each child. Particularly with some minority groups the policy that forbids placement of children with families in which the mother is employed would rule out a large part of such groups. Practices, too, have changed in adoption agencies. One found in many agencies, which should be extended, is the practice of placing children on a foster home basis with potential adoptive applicants. In other words, individuals who are willing to consider the adoption of a handicapped child, an older child, but who fear committing themselves without a period of trial, are accepted as foster parents and are paid a boarding fee by the social agency with the understanding that if the child's relationships with the parents develop satisfactorily, and vice versa, the home may become an adoptive home. Other agencies are paying for medical care for children adopted by families whose income will not permit them to defray such costs. A more radical suggestion, that should not be discarded without further exploration, is continued subsidy on a time-limited basis of families who cannot afford to adopt children—again, particularly, minority group families, whose income expectations are such that within a few years they will be able to take on the complete support of a child, though they cannot do so now. Still another practice, which can be found in a few agencies, and which also needs extension, is the placing of disturbed children with potential adoptive applicants on a foster care basis. Here the child continues to obtain therapy through referral either to a social agency or to a child guidance clinic or to a private psychiatrist. The plan implies that as the child is successfully treated, adoption will be considered by the foster parents.

The experience of some dozen states has proven that adoption resource exchanges are useful expedients in helping to place children with special needs. An adoption resource exchange is a simple device whereby a state-wide registry is established with which an agency that has a child for whom it cannot find a family may register the child, and with which agencies with families for whom they do not have a child may register the families. The resource exchange gets the two agencies together and many placements have been effected by this means. Every state should have such adoptive resource exchanges. When a majority of states have them, a national exchange should be established. The value of such an exchange seems self-evident. Prejudice toward minority groups varies regionally within the United States. For example, the Spanish-American Catholic child is more acceptable in the Midwest for adoption by non-Spanish families than he is in the Southwest. In certain cities there is prejudice against persons of Southern European nationality background which does not exist in other cities. Because of housing limitations it may be difficult to place families of several siblings for adoption in large cities, whereas in rural areas there may be a higher percentage of families who will consider adopting two, three, or more children of the same family.

The overwhelming number of children in this study were members of sibling groups, that is, they came from one large family in which many brothers and sisters were directly or indirectly affected by the family conditions which catapulted one or more of the children into foster care. It will be remembered that one finding of the study was that there are difficulties involved in finding homes for family groups. It should be noted that while about half of the children in foster care who were members of family groups were all living in foster care, in the other half of the cases some of the children were living with relatives. Basic research is needed to discover the extent to which relationships with siblings should be maintained as against the breaking up of a "family group"—which may often not be, in any psychological sense, a "family group"—so that one or more of the children might be provided with a permanent adoptive home. For which children is the need for siblings more important than the need for permanent parents? Here we need to weigh the meaning of sibling relationships against the meaning of permanent parents for many children who, on the basis of current assumptions and practice, are retained in the impermanence of foster care because they happen to have brothers or sisters.

More imaginative use needs to be made, too, of advertising and publicity through newspapers, radio, and television. Several experiments have proven successful whereby specific children available for adoption were "advertised." This was done by advertising in newspapers, by widely circulating brochures about an individual child or by interviewing children on television programs. Assumptions concerning confidentiality and what exploits or hurts children need to be carefully weighed against the possibilities of reaching potential adoptive families through publicity which makes a child real and alive.

LONG-TERM FOSTER CARE

It is not possible to overemphasize the importance of every child welfare agency's concentrating on the family as a whole and not the individual child in care. However, we must also face the fact that there are thousands of children in care for whom there is a family in name only and for whom the parents, because of their own irremediable inadequacies, will never be able to function fully. Therefore, for thousands of children foster care is preferable to their being in their own homes, for there simply is no own home and no possibility for one. Just as communities must make certain that there are adequate preventive services and services for work with parents, they must also make certain that they recognize the need for strong professional foster care services for those children unfortunate enough to be born to parents who can never fulfill their full parental responsibility. The need for foster care programs cannot be eliminated and communities should not blame themselves for this necessity.

We know that for many children in foster care adoption is not the answer. It will be remembered that the average age, that is the median age, of this group is about eleven years. For many older adolescents adoption is not feasible for psychological reasons. And unless there are radical changes in practice, in the attitudes of communities, and in the acceptance of handicapped children by the general public, it is most probable that a very large number of children will stay in foster care throughout their remaining childhood years. There is a large group of children, who may number over 60,000 in the country as a whole today, whose parents are content with their being in long-term care or present no other plans for them, but maintain relationships with their children and visit them frequently. Neither social attitudes nor laws permit the removal of such children from the legal control of their parents, nor, most importantly, would it be desirable psychologically for the children themselves. For these children communities or social agencies must face the fact that long-term foster care that protects the child's emotional health is required. A tremendous improvement must be made in our present foster care methods if this is to be accomplished.

The study reveals that most children experience re-placements during their period in foster care. Among the children studied, emotional disturbances was associated more with re-placement than with length of time in care. Extensive reevaluation of present assumptions as to what is the best form of foster care is needed. A reexamination of foster home care vis-à-vis institutional care, or at least some forms of group care, is highly overdue. Among the plans which require consideration is a more extensive use of group homes for long-term foster care. These are ordinary houses owned by a social agency in which groups of four to six children live with foster parents who are full-time employees of the agency. If the foster parents leave their employment, the child still has the security of knowing that at least the house in which he lives is his per-

manent home.   In certain large cities, also, the extreme shortage of
foster homes for minority groups, particularly Negroes, demands
exploration of practices other than the prevailing one of paying
foster parents a nominal sum that barely covers the cost of food
for a child.   For example, the average wage received by married
Negro women employed as domestics, factory workers, and so forth,
is low enough to make it feasible to consider their full-time em-
playment as foster mothers for one or two children.   The cost to
the community is still far less than that of the average institutional
care.   Shifts in institutional practices, such as the prevalent one
in which children are grouped according to age and sex, are also
overdue.   Some institutions, too, have long since passed the point
of experimentation with small cottages housing six or seven children of sibling groups, boys and girls of varied ages, particularly
for children who are likely to be in long-term foster care.

Basic research is needed as to what best insures the emotional
health of a child who is going to be in long-term foster care.   A
concerted effort is also needed to discover—in part through more intensive and systematic study and in part through better use of existing knowledge—the kinds of foster parents who are able to provide a relatively enduring family life for children with emotional
difficulties.   Identifying the motivation that makes of parents good
foster parents and then seeking out such families can do much to
reduce the numbers of re-placements in foster care which emotionally disturbed children are subjected to and the extent of disturbance among such children which is reinforced by their repeated
changes in homes.   We need to determine what services foster parents require in order to be more accepting of these children, including such mundane things as regular baby-sitting services financed
by the agency to enable foster parents to have sufficient freedom to
maintain their own emotional health.

In community after community it is clear from the data in the
study that unless children move out of care within the first year to
year and a half of their stay in care, the likelihood of their ever
moving out sharply decreases.   Early diagnosis and clear planning
are essential.   More than 70 percent of the fathers and mothers of

the children in this study either had no relationship with the agencies responsible for the care of their children or their relationship was erratic or untrusting. In many instances the agencies' resources were such that their staff's time was entirely consumed with the day-to-day job of caring for the children. They had no time for the kind of continuous work with the parents of the children which could effect the rehabilitation of the home. Frequently agencies fail to appreciate the dynamics of intrafamily relationships as a whole and work only with the child. Casework practices in such agencies need reexamination in the light of present knowledge of how all aspects of the total family affect each of the individual members.

The study indicates that where parental rights were modified by court action the chances of the child returning to his own home were also sharply decreased. Yet, not a few institutions have, for example, a policy that they will not accept children in care unless parental rights have been modified and they can control the visiting of parents. Such policies further weaken family relationships.

It is questionable whether the care and planning for the future of children should be left to individual agencies without some community control. In view of the fact that there are hundreds of children's agencies in the country without good professional services, it can be argued that central reporting to a responsible governmental agency is indicated. Most communities require that doctors report cases of communicable diseases to the Department of Public Health. Children who remain in foster care without visits from their parents—parents who have conflicting feelings about their children's return home or adoption—are in far greater danger than if they had contracted a communicable disease. If children's agencies were required to report to a responsible governmental agency every six months on their plans for children in care, as well as reporting cases where parents were failing in their parental responsibility, this would provide communities with information as to the incidence of such cases and would also serve as a stimulus for agency awareness of the children in their care. One state has already adopted such a system and has reported favorable results.

It is imperative that state licensing be strengthened so that child welfare agencies are permitted to operate only when they have adequately trained social service staff in sufficient numbers to insure consistent, competent, and continuous work with parents toward a permanent plan for their children. The parents—or their relatives—constitute the key that will either open the door for return to their own homes or free the children for placement in adoptive homes. When the parents of a child have no relationships with the social agency with whom their child is placed, obviously that child is in great danger of remaining in limbo.

Agencies need also to examine their practices carefully to make certain that they are helping to maintain a sense of responsibility and dignity in the parents of children under care. Nothing is more dangerous than agencies' assuming more responsibility than is necessary. Every parent needs to be encouraged and helped to remain as close to his child as possible and to take as much responsibility for him as possible even though the child cannot live in the parents' home. Supporting the child financially while in foster care, to the full ability of the parents, is of vital importance. This study reveals that on the average about two thirds of the parents paid nothing toward their children's care. It is very dangerous to relieve parents unnecessarily of their financial responsibility. Even small payments help to prevent parents from feeling so guilty about their failure to support their child that they drift away both from the agency and from their child. Encouraging parents to continue to take responsibility for such everyday matters as going shopping with their children to purchase clothing or school supplies, and paying for them, is also important, because they are very meaningful psychologically. Many parents do not realize their psychological importance to their child. They need to be helped to understand the meaning they have for their children, both through counseling and by recognizing the responsibility placed on them by the agency for the care of their children.

Communities need to examine laws relating to financial reimbursement of private agencies to make certain that they do not serve to weaken parental ties. For example, in some communities higher financial payments are available to the agencies providing the court has modified parental rights and assumed wardship. Not infrequently agencies will only accept children providing this modification has taken place.

The research findings indicate that parental ties are weakest where the child is placed in foster care in a location removed from the parents' place of residence. In other words, there tends to be a higher rate of return of children to their own homes and more parental visiting where the foster home or institution and the parents' home are in the same community. This finding bolsters the standard recommendation that wherever possible every community develop its own resources rather than rely upon large central resources for the placement of children. For example, institutions serving a whole state are not so desirable as a decentralized program of small institutions.

More demands and controls need to be exerted over parents at the time they place their children in care. Before accepting children for placement, agencies should reach a firm understanding with parents as to their responsibility for visiting their children, for payment of fees, provision of clothing, regular interviews with caseworkers, and reporting upon plans for the return of the child to his own home.

LEGAL PROBLEMS

Every community needs to examine carefully its legislation affecting children to make sure that the rights of both children and parents are protected. Laws should be codified and explicit, particularly in respect to provisions for guardianship and custody. It is also desirable to write into the statute law specific provisions which empower judges to terminate parental rights and make children available for adoption where there is clear evidence of the parents' abandonment of the child. New York State has recently passed such legislation, which permits social agencies to petition for termination of parental rights whenever parents have not visited their children for a period of one year and the agency can present evidence of their attempt to work cooperatively with parents. With such statutes judges have a clear mandate from the community to protect the rights of children and do not have to regard children as the property of parents. In many states common law rather than statute law governs the attitudes of courts toward parental rights. Frequently such law, following centuries-old precedents which regarded children solely as the property of their parents, controls present-day decisions to the detriment of the children. It is recommended that communities establish special committees of the local bar association (composed of both lawyers and social workers) to study not only legislation but also judicial decisions or judicial philosophies with respect to the interpretation of law. The study indicates that there are serious weaknesses in some communities in relationships between the courts, the bar, and social agencies. Sometimes there is mistrust and misunderstanding between the legal world and the world of the social agency. When such conditions exist, children, without a doubt, suffer. Community welfare councils and other community organization bodies have an important responsibility for bringing together the social welfare and legal interests of the community to make a common examination of the rights of children and their parents. Such activity can greatly clarify and strengthen the legal protection afforded children and can remove deterrents to effective action in behalf of children that now exist in many states.

Illegitimate children remain a group on whose behalf research and possible legal modification of their parents' rights is much needed. A significant percentage of children in long-term foster care are illegitimate. Many of these children are the offspring of unmarried mothers, who have a strong desire to keep their children and make a home for them. In many instances the mother may not be successful. It has been suggested by some that we adopt the German system of making every illegitimate child upon birth the ward of the state and of requiring the unmarried mother to show proof that she can provide a permanent home for her child. Such legislation in our opinion would never be acceptable to the American public and would be highly undesirable. However, research

needs to be conducted on what happens to the child and to the unmarried mother who retains her child. How successful is she in
providing a permanent home for her child? How many such children eventually find their way into foster care? Should there be a
time limit placed on unmarried mothers in respect to their making
a permanent home for their child? For example, the unmarried
mother who wishes to retain her child but must, of necessity, place
him in foster care after birth probably should not have an un-
limited amount of time to establish a permanent home for the
child. If within two years she is not able to care for the child herself, and has had some interpretation of what foster care might
mean for her child, should not the child be mandatorily relinquished for adoption? We should be reminded that effective counseling services to unmarried mothers during their pregnancy can
prevent many children from eventually returning for long-term
foster care.

AGENCIES AND THEIR COMMUNITIES

This study makes clear that communities must understand their
responsibility for their children who are in need of parents, and
assume it, for social agencies cannot, by any means, do the entire
job alone. They are but one small segment of a community.
Agencies can, however, do much to facilitate communication with
the larger community of which they are a part. Attitudes toward
dependency are integral to local ways of life and they vary from
community to community. Agencies must see as a vital part of
their responsibility the need to modify community attitudes where
those attitudes are detrimental to children. Variations of community attitudes toward dependent children are amply illustrated
in this report. In some communities there is a tendency to protect
or maintain the community-wide sense of well-being by ignoring
dependent children on the one hand or rejecting them on the
other. It is particularly evident that in many communities services for minority groups are much less available than for the majority group. Undoubtedly, such community attitudes affect the

kinds of foster parents or adoptive parents who are drawn into local child welfare programs.

People in general are ignorant of the facts concerning children in need of parents and the problems involved in their care. Typically, even the most well-informed do not know about children in foster care. Even the more informed and best-educated citizens usually think that children in foster care are orphans who need simply good food, shelter, and clothing. They do not know the background of these children and specifically what the problems are that have caused them to live in care. Communities frequently do not provide services because they have no awareness of their necessity.

Agencies must break their isolation from the community at large and reach the many people whose latent concern for children will provide the yeast for action. It is very important for agencies to learn—and then to make use of—the facts of composition of communities, so as to discover which groups in each community are the most likely to be responsive to the needs of dependent children and the most receptive to the human problems entrusted to them. The task of developing community values which support the sense that the children in need of parents are "ours" is not easily accomplished. But clearly child welfare agencies have a key part to play in any such community-oriented programs. The foundation such agencies have to build upon is the observation we have made that in none of the nine communities studied was there any lack of concern about children. Rather, too often there was lack of active concern; and active concern in a community is a necessity, for it results in public involvement in the selection of adoptive parents, foster parents, and social workers too, as well as in providing the financial resources to make good programs possible.

Child welfare services are woefully inadequately supported. Because services are starved for money, children are emotionally starved. The best-trained social worker cannot give adequate care to a case load of fifty to a hundred children. Yet this is not an uncommon load in the majority of public agencies, as well as in many private agencies, in the United States. The extreme shortage of well-trained social workers also reflects a lack of community concern and understanding of children's needs. Adequate care of children is not inexpensive. It is just as costly to mend a child emotionally crippled by disorganized family life as it is to cure the crippled leg of a child stricken with polio. For children in need of parents the community will pay the price sooner or later. The high incidence of mental disorders, criminality, or at best economic dependency among adults who as children had lived in the limbo of foster care, is clear evidence of this.

Children need what they need when they need it. Providing it "later" is always too late. Children cannot be their own spokesmen, their own lobbyists. Only as responsible adult citizens make clear to their legislators, to their directors of united funds and community chests, to their county commissioners, to their governors, what it is that children require, and what the price of fulfilling these requirements is, can we eliminate the tragedies of the "orphans of the living."

APPENDIX A: SOME NOTES ON THE METHODS
OF THE STUDY

1. Studying the Children and Their Parents

There were 4,281 children's cases that we studied extensively and 882 children's cases that we sampled for intensive case reading. (Details on numbers of children in the child populations and samples by community appear in Appendix C.) What was our definition of a case for study? How were the cases selected? What were the devices we used for collecting data on the children and their families? How reliable was the information obtained by field workers from agency case records?

A case for study was a child who had been separated from his own parents because of his dependency—but not because of his delinquency or illness—and placed in an agency-supervised family or institution for foster care or adoption. Having selected the nine communities according to the plan discussed in Section 4 of this appendix, and having discovered all the agencies in these communities (per Section 3 of this appendix) serving dependent children who either came from or were placed in the selected communities at the time of our study, we obtained from each of the agencies: a "white" roster card on every child who was in an agency-supervised foster family, institutional, or adoptive home placement on April 1, 1957, and a "blue" roster card on every child who had moved into an adoptive home or who had left foster care either to return home or for any other purposes during the six-month period between January 1 and June 30, 1957—that is, during the three months before or the three after our "as-of-date" of April 1.

Our research plan called for comparisons of children in foster care with those in adoptive homes and those who had returned home or had left care for other purposes. Blue card cases were needed to study the conditions of children returning home or leaving care for other purposes, and to increase the numbers of adoptive children for study.

The white roster cards, entitled "Child in Care April 1, 1957," called for identifying data on the age and sex of each child and completion of the following questions:

Date case opened (most recent intake):_____
Month   Year

On April 1, 1957, this child:

    Was living in:
    (*check one*)   foster family home_____adoptive home_____

                    institution (*specify by name*)_____

The blue roster cards, entitled "Child Leaving Care between January 1 and June 30, 1957," called for identifying data and completion of the following blanks:

Date case opened (most recent intake):_____
Month   Year

Date leaving foster care: _____
Month   Year

Child left foster care because: (*check one*)

    child returned to own home or relatives' home_____

    child entered adoptive home_____

    other reason (*specify*)_____

Any child who was in care for less than thirty days was arbitrarily eliminated from the study, since we were not concerned in this inquiry with the transient case. All other children were then classified in one of five categories: foster family, institution, adoptive home, returned home, or left care for other reasons. The children who were reported both on white cards, as being in foster care on April 1, and on blue cards, as having left care—between April 1 and June 30—were classified according to their blue-card categories. Thus, the term, "all the children in foster care," refers to all children who were in care on April 1 *and* who had not left foster family or institutional care by June 30—children who, in short, were in foster care for at least three months.

For each community, we then set up five separate rosters of children, listed alphabetically and regardless of supervising agency—one roster for all of the children in foster families, another for all children in institutional care, another for all children in adoptive homes (either there on April 1 or moved into such placement between January 1 and June 30), another for all returned home (between January 1 and June 30), and a fifth for all who had left care for other purposes (between January 1 and June 30). With the aim of obtaining a sample of a minimum of twenty-five cases in each category for each community, we chose our children from each of the five alphabetized rosters in each community using a table of random numbers. Where a community had twenty-five or fewer children in a category, we used a 100 percent sample. Table 32 in Appendix C presents population and sample figures on all the children under study. Table 33 concerns only the children in care on April 1.

Basic data on the children's age, sex, length of time in care, placement category, and movement out of care were available from the roster cards for our total population of children.   All other data were obtained by the four research staff members from agency case records in the field.   The research staff, traveling in two teams of two members each, a child welfare worker and a sociologist on each team, used a thirty-nine page schedule to record data on the children and their families for all the sampled cases.[1]

The case schedule for recording data was developed and pretested in two pilot projects, one in the San Francisco Bay Area and the other in a New England community during the year preceding the launching of the nine-communities study.   Reports of these two pilot projects appear in "Factors Associated with the Disposition of Children in Foster Care,"

Table 29

PERCENTAGES OF ITEM-BY-ITEM AGREEMENTS IN FOUR FIELD
WORKERS' INDEPENDENT USE OF CASE SCHEDULES ON
SAME CASES DURING PRE-FIELD WORK
TRAINING PERIOD

	Child Welfare Worker	
	Team 1	Team 2
Sociologist		
Team 1	83	77
Team 2	69	91

School of Social Welfare, University of California, Berkeley, available through university interlibrary loan service, and in Bernice Boehm's *Deterrents to the Adoption of Children in Foster Care,* published by the Child Welfare League of America.   The case schedule used in this study was further evolved by the research staff during a three-month period prior to the commencement of field work.   Agreements among field workers in a pretest use of the instrument are noted in Table 29.   From the data in Table 30, we infer that observed differences between the children in paired communities in regard to one of the more judgmental factors under study—psychological adjustment—were not at least differences between paired observers.   To this extent what was obtained from case records—and sometimes interviews with agency workers—would seem to reflect with reliability the basic facts we chose to study.

[1] Note that the same research team visited paired communities; thus observed differences between cases in, for example, Norden and Granger, or King City and Westport, are not likely to be functions of differences in observer bias.   Moreover, with two separate teams of case readers, similarities which cut across six or more of the nine communities cannot be functions only of uniform observer bias.

The complete framework for the thirty-nine page case schedule appears in Appendix B-1. The length of the schedule and the limits of space in this book preclude its publication here. At the time of this writing, it too is available, however, through university interlibrary loan service from the library of the University of California, Berkeley, in the appendix of a

Table 30

AGREEMENTS BETWEEN PAIRED FIELD WORKERS
IN PERCENTAGES OF CHILDREN JUDGED
ON PSYCHOLOGICAL FACTORS

	Team 1: in Norden, Granger, Centralia Only (197 cases)		Team 2: in La Paz, Summit, King City Only (293 cases)	
	Child Welfare Worker	Sociologist	Child Welfare Worker	Sociologist
Symptomatic behavior				
Symptom-free	50	52	65	62
Some symptoms	48	48	33	37
Unknown	2	—	2	1
Affectionate relationship with parents	14	6	32	29
Clear sense of self-identity	10	25	23	38

School of Social Welfare student report entitled "Barriers to Adoption: a Study of Physical and Psychological Handicaps, Ethnicity, and Adoptive Parents' Expectations." The case schedule should be made more readily available in a forthcoming Child Welfare League publication, a "census book" on the quantified case data in this study.

2. Studying the Legal System

The basic data from which comparisons of legal systems were made appear in Appendix D. These legal codes were compiled after a perusal of the laws of a state in an effort to draw together those sections of the codes that seemed relevant to the care of dependent children and their movement into adoption. At times such codes could be easily located, particularly if a recodification had recently occurred in the state. Usually they were scattered throughout various legal sections. Our presentation allows for some differences in specificity that did not always permit strict comparability. The legal material in Appendix D was submitted for review and correction by local authorities in each community.

In addition to drawing together certain relevant legal codes after the work in the field was completed, several sources of information available in the field were tapped. First, each case schedule on a child had a section for coding the child's legal status—whether and how parents' rights were modified—as well as one for designating the conditions of the child's separation from his parents—whether voluntary or involuntary and whether or not the court was involved in the separation process. After working on numerous cases, the researchers in the field began to see legal process as it operated in the cases of dependent children in the community. Also, at the time of interviews with staff members in each agency, a section of the agency schedule was filled out which asked for opinions from spokesmen in the agency on such questions as: Are there state laws clearly defining the responsibility of this agency regarding placement of children in foster care and adoption? Is it the belief of this agency that some existing laws are deterrents to the appropriate placement of children? What changes in state laws would the agency recommend? Are there judicial biases that, from your viewpoint, seem to interfere with appropriate foster care placement, release for adoption, or return of a child to his own home? Under what condition will the judge terminate parental rights in order to free a child for adoption?

Thus from many vantage points the researchers obtained opinions and locally expressed attitudes about the juvenile laws and about the judge who presided over the cases of dependent children. The judge's role, and his philosophy too, as perceived by others, then began to take form. The interview with the judge—sometimes at more than one session—was undertaken usually after a "feel" for the legal situation regarding the placement of children had been obtained. The judge was, at some point in the interviews, given an opportunity to discuss his situation and express his views in a relatively unstructured way. He was also asked specific questions like those above about the laws, his own practices, about the agency people he dealt with, and about the community in general. From the judge's statements, from statements of other people in the community who had to work with the law and the judge, and from the actual facts recorded on the legal situation in each child's case record, an outline of the interrelated elements of the legal system relating to child placement in each community was later filled in. The actual comparison of codes which appears in Appendix D came after the field interviewing and case coding.

3. Studying the Agencies

Selection of agencies for participation in our study was made to include all those placement agencies caring for the children in or from the community as of our study period. In many instances there were one or more other agencies available to the community, but since their resources were not being used at the time of our study they were not included in our agency networks.

Our aim was to understand the panoply of services for children in each community, as expressed by the network of agencies serving the children under study. In recording information on the children in care from agency records, the researchers began to get acquainted with agency practices. Then at several sessions with the executive, or his designated spokesman, a schedule on the agency was completed. In addition, several child welfare workers were briefly interviewed to uncover their responses to their work situations in the agency as it operated in the community. Finally, an agency board member for every major agency in our study in a community was also interviewed.

The basic instrument through which information on the agencies was obtained was the aforementioned schedule which was filled out for each agency in the study. For some smaller agencies this schedule was shortened by omitting items relating to perceptions of intra-agency conditions, but all agencies were asked about their relationships with other agencies. The schedule called for information on the following factors (some, matters of "fact" which were often obtained from a brochure, others, matters of opinion):

1. Agency auspices—source of policy-power and/or financial support
2. Historical background of the agency (including recent reorganization)
3. Agency services provided currently
4. Agency's eligibility criteria for clients served currently
5. Functions and responsibilities of the board, the executive, and the staff
6. Relevant legal guides to practice relating to placement of children
7. Budget of agency (including proportions utilized for various services and programs but emphasizing the perceptions of the executive and his board member of the "adequacy" of the budget)
8. Agency personnel—number, workload, training, turnover (mostly obtained from the personnel department)
9. Agency values and beliefs. In this section five "type situations" regarding the placement of children were presented, and the agency spokesman, usually the executive together with his child welfare supervisor, was asked to respond hypothetically to these situations. In this way, normal practice, conviction about permanent planning for children, and readiness to modify practice to meet challenging situations were explored.
10. Self-other percepts and morale. Questions relating to practice and to satisfaction and discontent were asked in this section. Included here

were the few questions directed to the individual workers interviewed as a particular case was discussed with a worker.

11. Agency communication pattern. Two situations, one requiring special care for a child and the other for an effort to change agency policy, were asked to be recalled out of the agency's recent history. Discussion of these cases, where they could be recalled, revealed something of flow of communication among board, executive, and staff levels in the agency.

12. Agency board. A listing of board members and their occupations (or husband's occupations) was obtained as an index to agency influence, position, and representation in the community.

13. Interagency relations. A series of questions uncovered an agency's perceptions of, and dealings with, other agencies in the community. Material from this section was found subsequently most useful in our summary analyses.

Some of the information obtained on agencies was not systematically analyzed for purposes of this report. The basic internal facts on history, services, number and training of staff, and eligibility requirements were all found useful. However, with the broad community-wide orientation of our study, it was decided to concentrate on interagency factors and to return to intra-agency material only as it seemed most relevant to determining the position and character of an agency in the complete network of agencies. Our sociometric diagrams were constructed after a careful reading of the material under number 13 in the list above (Section M in our schedule) so that agency dealings with one another were plotted from statements made by agency spokesmen. From this our very broad conceptualization of the "collaborative" or "noncollaborative" tendency was deduced to characterize a whole network of agencies in a community.

The index of collaboration, mentioned in Chapter 20, was derived as follows. Two factors were combined in the index: (1) Total possible collaborative relationships regarding cases and issues, counted separately and added together, were recorded for a given network; observed collaboration over cases and issues, subtracting for negative relationships, was recorded and the proportion of "observed" to "possible" was expressed as a fraction. (2) The weight of the case population in each network was obtained by multiplying cases in multiple-service facilities by weight "one," multiplying cases in dual-service facilities by weight "two," and multiplying cases in single-service facilities by weight "three." The average weight of the case load was obtained by dividing the weighted case total by the total number of cases. The fraction in (1), in which a whole number "one" would indicate perfect collaboration, was added to the fraction of one over the average weight obtained in (2), which would also be "one" if all cases were in a multiple-service facility. The total thus obtained was divided by two. Results (in which the first fraction in the numerator indicates observed over possible collaboration and the second fraction in the numerator indicates one over the case load weight) were:

Norden $\dfrac{\dfrac{2}{20} + \dfrac{1}{2.03}}{2} = .29$

Granger $\dfrac{\dfrac{6}{12} + \dfrac{1}{2.06}}{2} = .50$

Summit $\dfrac{\dfrac{0}{6} + \dfrac{1}{1.44}}{2} = .35$

La Paz $\dfrac{\dfrac{1}{2} + \dfrac{1}{2.12}}{2} = .49$

Jamestown $\dfrac{\dfrac{3}{156} + \dfrac{1}{2.64}}{2} = .20$

Centralia $\dfrac{\dfrac{25}{56} + \dfrac{1}{1.79}}{2} = .51$

King City $\dfrac{\dfrac{5}{30} + \dfrac{1}{1.12}}{2} = .53$

Westport $\dfrac{\dfrac{50}{90} + \dfrac{1}{1.74}}{2} = .56$

Brighton $\dfrac{\dfrac{3}{56} + \dfrac{1}{2.74}}{2} = .21$

Complete collaboration in a network where all cases are also in multiple-service agencies yields an index of 1.0, the highest score possible.

Complete collaboration in a network where all cases are in single-service agencies yields an index of .67.

No collaboration in a network where all cases are in multiple-service agencies yields an index of .50.

No collaboration in a network where all cases are in single-service agencies yields an index of .17, the lowest score possible.

4. Studying the Communities

Communities [1] were chosen because of their size and degree of urbanization, ethnic composition, economic level, and other factors related to family living and location. We made an effort to cover the different regions of the country. We wanted our "survey in depth" to span communities

[1] Except for the Greater Brighton Area, all communities were counties.

from rural to large urban in size and organization. We wished to sample the country so that differences in ethnic groups of the populations—especially Negro and Spanish-speaking—differences in levels of economy and in history and regionalism would be represented. Our final spread was such that a real diversity was obtained which we can only suggest as representative of some major "types" of community life in this country.[2]

As with any such venture for which no ready-made guideposts from past research are available, a number of "fits and starts" were made in pursuing relevant data and grouping such data. At first it was thought that all nine communities could be lined up on census dimensions indicative of degrees of urbanization and stratification, emphasis on family life ("familism"), and forms of formal community organization (power relations). But we felt a constant need to push back to comparable "basic realities" that could be related to forms and processes in the community "cultures" relevant to foster care and adoption. (The concepts used to make discrete community entities comparable when seen abstractly as cultures and social systems are presented briefly in Appendix B-4. The hard core of the basic community realities, obtained from the 1950 census, is presented in Appendix E.) These basic facts are all related to size and differentiation of the population in a given space, and to rate of change and movement (including evidence of socioeconomic levels attained) going on within that space. Some additional facts on history of community growth—form and process in the past—were obtained from encyclopedias and historical reports.

While we were in the field we also obtained material from Chambers of Commerce, e.g., maps on which our cases could be plotted and economic data. However, the 1950 census material, as a uniform source, remained the basis for community census facts reported in this book. No completely structured community schedule, comparable to the child schedule or the agency schedule, was taken into the field. Instead, an outline was followed which called for filling in information gaps in the areas mentioned above

---

[2] Our initial plan called for a pairing of equal-sized communities which were "matched" on all variables, presumably relevant to child placement, but one. Being clear that we wanted a pair of rural communities, a pair of small urban counties, a pair of metropolitan areas, and a pair of big cities, distributed across the country, by early 1957 we had collected and analyzed comparable census data on sixteen counties—among which were the finally selected nine communities included in this study. The census data gathered and analyzed on each of these communities had to do with (1) size and urbanization—1950 population, 1940–50 increase in population, and occupational breakdown; (2) ethnic composition; (3) familism—data on the marital status of females over age fourteen; and (4) economy—data on income. Final selection was made on these grounds. In our planning we eliminated two communities because we anticipated that the child welfare situation in them was, in 1957, a "touchy" one. No community which we approached, however, refused us entree for this study.

and listed representative groups in the community from whom someone should be interviewed. Remember that this was not a community study *per se* but a study of dependent children. Almost two hundred community interviews—of ministers, of other representatives of various denominations and ethnic groups, of physicians and lawyers and bankers, of labor and management spokesmen, *et al.*—in the nine communities explored "community attitudes" toward dependent children and their parents and toward adoption. The variations on the major theme of this book which came through in these informants' attitudes—depending upon who the respondent was, what his reference groups were, and how and where he was located in the social system—are presented in some detail in the body of this book. It must be said, too, that this interview material did much to fill out the dynamics of the community systems, the bare outlines of which were merely suggested by the initial census data gathered on each community.

APPENDIX B: FRAMEWORK OF CONCEPTS AND TERMS

1. The Children and Their Families

A. Information on the children was gathered in a case schedule constructed along several dimensions against which the children's foster care situations were analyzed.

1) *Biological characteristics.*—The basic conditions that characterized the child as an organism.

    (a) *Age*—recorded in years and months as of April 1 of the study year.

    (b) *Sex*—male or female.

    (c) *Physical disability*—referring to a physical anomaly (e.g., birth mark, supplementary digit, orthopedic defect, cleft palate, leukemia, etc.) that might be essentially self-correcting, remediable with effort, or irremediable, and which might affect primarily physical or social functioning or both.

    (d) *Physical health*—referring to acute illnesses or diseases not covered under 1) (c) above.

    (e) *Ethnicity*—see 3) (a) below.

    (f) *Intelligence*—see 2) (d) below.

2) *Psychological characteristics.*—Emotional, attitudinal, and intellectual characteristics of the child as a personality.

    (a) *Symptomatic behavior*—referring to developmental difficulties (e.g., in eating or speaking, in elimination, in sexual adjustment); school learning difficulties; aggressive or "acting-out" behavior; manipulative or "using-others" behavior; withdrawal or "turning-inward" behavior; difficulties in social adjustment other than those noted above; and psychiatric disturbances (e.g., being extremely anxious, showing extreme disturbances in expressing feelings, being bizarre in ideas or behavior). (Symptoms could be recorded multiply, and the most prominent symptom was given major emphasis. Also, symptoms were recorded for the child both at his intake into care and according to his behavior as of about April 1.)

(*b*) *Relationship patterns*—referring to feelings and attitudes toward other persons in the child's world. The child was located in a matrix of his own feelings and attitudes ranging from neutrality or indifference, to affection, to ambivalence or conflict, to open hostility. He was related in this way to (1) his biological parents, (2) his brothers and sisters, (3) his foster or adoptive mother, (4) his foster or adoptive father, (5) his child welfare worker, (6) his school teacher, (7) his cottage parents, and (8) other children who were his peers.

(*c*) *Self-concept*—referring to the child's perception of himself. We attempted to infer whether the child was relatively clear or confused about his worth and identity as a person, where he belonged, and where he was going.

(*d*) *Intelligence*—referring to an evaluation of the child's learning and problem-solving capabilities, from a test or estimate.

3) *Group memberships.*—The more specifically social names and labels placed upon the child in his culture. (It should be noted that age and sex could also be considered group membership items.)

(*a*) *Ethnicity*—referring to any visible racial or nationality group which a given community treated as discrete.

(*b*) *Religion*—referring to the church preference designated for the child by his parent or to the preference recognized by the agency for the child.

(*c*) *Membership in family group*—referring to the presence or absence of brothers or sisters in the natural family, and the number of such siblings.

4) *Legal status.*—The legal situation of the child, involving the court-sanctioned rights of others in regard to him. We considered whether the child was fully tied to his parents legally, whether his parents' rights had been modified, whether he was completely free for adoption, or whether his legal status was considered unclear.

5) *Placement history.*—Major conditions in the child's experience at separation from his own parents and during his time in care.

(a) *Separation experience*—

(1) Age at last separation from own parents or relatives.

(2) Voluntary or involuntary nature of separation.

(3) Precipitating cause for separation.

(4) Parental participation at time of first placement.

(5) Number of separations from own family prior to current separation.

(*b*) *Placement pattern*—

(1) Kinds of placement child has had.

(2) Child's age at time of each placement.
(3) Sequence of placements.
(4) Numbers of each kind of placement child had.
(5) Number of years of each placement.
(6) Length of current placement.
(7) Relationship of agency to placement.
(8) Concomitant conditions of replacement.
(9) Six- or nine-month follow-up placement of children in care on April 1.
(c) *Social work activities in regard to case in care:*
(1) Nature and extent of worker activities at intake.
(2) Intensity and area of worker activity, following intake, with child, parents, substitute parents, and other persons close to child.
(3) Evidence of agency review of casework plan for child during previous twelve-month period.

B. Information on the child's biological parents was also gathered in the case schedule along several dimensions relevant to the child's foster care situation.

1) *Biological characteristics.*—Organic factors affecting ability to serve as parent to the child.
(a) *Age*—of each, as of April 1 of the study year.
(b) *Genetic physical or mental disease or defect* (for each or both)—referring to anomalies or illnesses for which at least a tendency is inherited and might be passed on to children.
(c) *Physical incapacity* (for each or both)—referring to illness, injury or defect that affects the person's ability to operate as a parent (could be the same condition noted in (b)).

2) *Marital status.*—Factors relating to home situation between parents that affect ability to serve as parent to the child.
(a) *Marital relationship between parents on April 1*—referring to whether parents were married to each other, separated, divorced, unwed (never married), one widowed and one deceased, or both deceased.
(b) *Marital status of parents at birth of child*—referring to whether parents were married to each other, unmarried to each other but one or both married to someone else, or both unmarried at time of child's birth.
(c) *Father's and mother's individual living arrangements on April 1*—referring to with whom or in what family setting each mate was living.

3) *Socioeconomic and other group memberships.*—These items both out-

lined the physical capabilities of the parents to maintain a home for the child and patterned a social group (or class) membership for them against the norms of their community and its cultural definitions.

(a) *Ethnicity*—recorded similarly as for the child.

(b) *Religion*—recorded similarly as for the child.

(c) *Education*—referring to school attainment of each parent.

(d) *Occupation*—recorded by census categories for each parent.

(e) *Economic status*—gleaned from rent paid or value of home, and from management of funds so that a poor, adequate, or comfortable condition was inferred which would or would not be worsened by the presence of the child.

(f) *Residence and housing*—referring to how settled parents were in a community, where members of extended family were, type of housing, sleeping space for child, and proximity of parent to the child for visits.

4) *Psychological and psychosocial adjustment.*—These items were related to reasons that, given the personality and the personal feelings and attitudes of each parent, the child and parents remained separated.

(a) *Intelligence*—recorded for each, similarly as for the child.

(b) *Current psychosocial condition* (of each parent)—referring to the personal situation (whether in jail or institution, etc.), antisocial attitudes or behavior (either involving the child directly or not), marital conflict (divorce, separation, etc.), or personal conflict in motivation to serve as parent.

(c) *Contact with child*—referring to whether either or both parents visit child, how frequently and regularly, and with what degree of emotional involvement.

(d) *Payment for care*—referring to monetary payment for the child's care.

(e) *Relationship with agency*—referring to existence, extent, and nature of contact maintained by each parent with the agency.

C. Information on foster or house parents was recorded as it seemed relevant to the child's situation. Only ethnicity of foster parents, occupation of the foster father, attitudes of foster parents toward natural parents, attitudes toward the agency, and the agency's perception of the foster home—and use of it—were recorded.

D. Information on adoptive parents (for those children who were adopted) also was recorded as it seemed relevant to movement into adoption situations.

1) *Biological characteristics.*—Organic factors relating to adoptive parenthood.

(a) Age.

    (*b*) Fertility and source of deficiency.

    (*c*) Physical health.

2) *Marital status.*—The factors relating to the home and family situation of the adoptive parents.   Such items as:

    (*a*) Previous marriage.

    (*b*) Present marital status.

    (*c*) Previous natural or adopted children (whether living or not).

    (*d*) Number of years married.

3) *Socioeconomic and other group memberships.*—These items located the adoptive parents socioculturally in their community, and defined agency perceptions of these adoptive families.

    (*a*) Ethnicity.

    (*b*) Religion and religious climate or emphasis in the home.

    (*c*) Educational attainment.

    (*d*) Occupation of each parent (and occupational stability of the father).

    (*e*) Income of the family and number of people to be supported by it.

    (*f*) Rent or value of home.

    (*g*) Stability, type, and location of residence, and sleeping space for the adopted child.

4) *Psychosocial characteristics.*—These items were all related to the attitudes of parents toward one another, toward their family situation, and toward adoption.   Included were beliefs and feelings about:

    (*a*) Age of a child.

    (*b*) Legitimacy of child.

    (*c*) Hereditary factors.

    (*d*) Ethnicity of child.

    (*e*) Physical health of child.

    (*f*) Emotional health of child.

    (*g*) Intelligence of child.

    (*h*) Appearance of a child wanted for adoption.

In addition:

    (*i*) Their acceptance of childlessness.

    (*j*) Mutuality of decision to adopt.

    (*k*) Satisfactions in their own childhood family relationships.

    (*l*) Degree of personal rigidity or flexibility in expression of affection, relationships with others, and tasks.

    (*m*) Attitude toward the agency, and source of referral to it.

2. The Legal System

The legal codes relating to child care in each community, together with an analysis of the roles of the judge and of those who dealt with him, were studied with several concepts in mind.

A. Role.—Our basic approach to the judge in each community was to determine what attitudes and behavior seemed formally prescribed for the person occupying the position of juvenile judge, how the person in the position interpreted social expectations for it and expressed that interpretation in his attitudes, and how others dealing with him expressed, through their attitudes, their expectations of the behavior of the juvenile judge. Thus the "legal role," and not the personality of the judge (although personality influenced interpretation of role) was the element we focused upon.

B. Child's rights or parents' rights orientation.—These tendencies were placed at opposite ends of a continuum conceived to express the predominant emphasis of the codes and statutes, and the attitudes of the judge and of others involved in the legal process, relating to the separation of children and parents in a community. No legal system completely exemplified one tendency or the other; however, it seemed that a tendency could be discerned either toward greater protection of children in their right to an adequate home or toward greater protection of parents in their rights to their own children.

3. The Interagency Network

Networks of agencies were studied, primarily, through a sociometric orientation, i.e., each agency was located in a pattern which included all the agencies serving the children of our study in a given community, and the existence or absence of dealings over cases or issues was plotted for each agency in relationship to all the others. Factors conceived to affect an agency's participation in the network were:

A. History.—A brief chronology on the development of each agency and of its auspices and major reorganizations.

B. Services.—The kinds of placement programs offered by each agency—and whether an agency offered a single service, dual services, or multiple (foster family, institution, and adoptive care) services, as well as the clients —children and families—to whom it might restrict its services.

C. *Extent of professionalization of agency.*—This term referred mainly to the proportion of all child welfare workers in a given agency who had one or more years of professional graduate education in social work. No attempt at evaluation of quality was made. Values and agency plans were noted. (Our efforts, for purposes of this study, to refine and operational-ize the concept of professionalization further—to include, for example, the factor of worker's case load—failed because of what seemed to us to be an overwhelming number of elements related to the quality of services an agency gives.)

D. *Spatial factors.*—The location of each agency was determined, as was the geographical area which its program covered. Distances between agency units and physical focus of program also seemed relevant.

E. *Collaboration or Noncollaboration.*—From agency interview schedules it was determined which agencies had dealings over cases and issues with each other. A general tendency was inferred from each network pattern-ing, locating a network along a continuum running from two poles: one at the extreme where all agencies had dealings with each other over cases and issues; the other at the extreme where no agencies dealt with each other over either cases or issues.

4. The Community

The study concentrated its major comparisons of general patterns of child care upon whole community units, each of which was given a pseudonym. A community was the basic physical, spatial, geographic area—inhabited by given numbers of people and having legal boundaries—in which foster care and adoption were observed. These areas were compared in the light of three basic realities: their size and extension, including numbers and kinds of people, and space and space usage (economic aspects); their history of growth; and their current rates of population change (indicating the pace of movement within them). From these basic facts conceptual ways of looking at form and process in each setting were derived. Three directing conceptions underlay the basic orientation:

A. *Culture.*—This concept indicated that each community was a field of symbols—an arena of names and definitions—through which the shared meanings and values of phenomena relevant to our study were prescribed for participants.

B. *Social system.*—This concept indicated that each community was an arena in which the participating persons and groups—with their values—were interrelated. The character of the community—like the predispositions of a personality—could be discerned when the interrelatedness of the parts was determined. A community's predominant tendencies in reacting to dependency were patterned by the way in which those involved in the drama of dependency were interrelated in that drama.

C. *Role*.—This was the basic unit of our analysis. It represented the crystallization in a person or group of certain consistent attitudes and values. Persons and groups expressed different attitudes and acted differently, and these attitudes and behaviors were expected of them by others, depending upon their position in the social system and the way they were involved in the drama of dependency in the system.

Other concepts were derived to fill out a matrix of form and process against this backdrop of *culture, system,* and *role*.

1) *Forms of social differentiation*.—This referred to the basic clusterings of difference, determining how roles were defined and reacted to, in a sociocultural system.

   (a) *Homogeneity-segmentation-heterogeneity*.—Along this continuum we indicated tendencies toward sameness, toward well-defined major clusterings of difference, and toward multiplicity of difference in role configurations.

   (b) *Nonstratification-stratification*.—Along this continuum we indicated evidence of a special case of differentiation, coincident with (a), in which social definitions implied class layers so that some role configurations were given higher value and others lower value.

   (c) *Private-public*.—Along this continuum we further noted whether, and how, differentiated roles were confined to a more informal and intimate context or placed in a more formal and less intimate context.

2) *Processes of social interaction and cultural value orientation*.—This referred to the basic preference (or predisposition) tendencies inherent in the prescribed roles of a sociocultural system having certain forms of differentiation.

   (a) *Ascribed-achieved emphasis*.—Along this continuum we noted in a system: whether the tendency was to define and prescribe roles in terms of qualities attributed to the person or group by reason of past place, position, or situation; or whether the tendency was to define and prescribe roles in terms of qualities attained by present efforts and future strivings.

   (b) *Separateness-interdependence emphasis*.—Along this continuum we noted in a system: whether the tendency was toward independent separation of the differentiated parts—each primarily responsible to self and to own group; or whether the tendency was toward reciprocal interdependence of the parts—each responsible to the other and to the whole.

(*c*) *Personal-impersonal (and contractual) emphasis.*—Along this continuum we noted in a system: whether the tendency was toward "whole," face-to-face, and more informal relationships; or whether the tendency was toward specialized, formal, and fragmented relationships between persons.

3) *Orientations to dependency as deviation.*—We made a final effort, in looking across the total matrix, to infer: whether the tendency was toward exclusion and rejection of the dependent child—relegation to the "they"; or whether the tendency was toward inclusion and acceptance of the dependent child—drawing him into the "we."

APPENDIX C: BASIC PLACEMENT DATA
ON THE CHILDREN

In Table 31, the U.S. Children's Bureau provides us with a nation-wide and territorial estimate of the numbers of children in foster care and adoptive homes at about the time of the "as-of-date" for this study, April 1, 1957 (plus and minus three months).

In Tables 32 and 33, the numbers of children by community in the populations and samples of this study, and the numbers by placement on April 1, are presented.

The length of time children were in care and the number of moves they made while in care are presented in Tables 34 through 36 as two important kinds of data available from our review of the children's placement histories.

Finally, data on the children likely to stay in foster care because of their parents' plans for and/or lack of visits with them appear in Table 37.

A complete report of our quantitative data on the children's placement experiences, on the children's families, on the characteristics of the children themselves, and on other facets of the case material is to appear as a "census book," available through the Child Welfare League of America, Inc., 345 East 46th Street, New York 17, New York.

Table 31

ESTIMATED NUMBER OF CHILDREN IN FOSTER CARE IN THE
CONTINENTAL UNITED STATES AND TERRITORIES
MARCH 31, 1957 [a]

		Children in Foster Family Homes			Children in Institutions for Dependent and Neglected Children [b]
Auspices	*Total*	*Total*	*Boarding Homes*	*Adoptive Homes*	*Free, Wage, or Work Homes*	
Total	254,000	179,000	131,000	40,000	8,000	75,000 [c]
Public	140,000	124,000	97,000	21,000	6,000	16,000
Voluntary	114,000	55,000	34,000	19,000	2,000	59,000

[a] From Department of Health, Education, and Welfare, Social Security Administration, Children's Bureau, Division of Research, January 21, 1959.

[b] Exclusive of those for delinquent youth.

[c] Increased to 83,697, as of November, 1958.

Table 32

TOTAL CHILDREN UNDER STUDY BY CHILD POPULATION
AND SAMPLE PER COUNTY

| | | Children in Foster Care | | | Children Who Left Foster Care | | | |
		(1) In Foster Families	(2) In Institutions	(3) Total (columns 1 and 2)	(4) In Adoptive Homes	(5) Returned to Own Family	(6) Left for Other Reasons	Total (columns 3, 4, 5, 6)
Norden County (Abbotsford)	Population	18 (23%)	49 (63%)	67 (86%)	6 (8%)	3 (4%)	2 (3%)	78
	Sample	18	26	44	6	3	2	55
Granger County (Daleville)	Population	20 (62%)	5 (16%)	25 (78%)	6 (19%)	1 (3%)	– (0%)	32
	Sample	20	5	25	6	1	–	32
Rural Communities	Population	38	54	92	12	4	2	110
	Sample	38	31	69	12	4	2	87
Pine County (Summit)	Population	9 (4%)	85 (38%)	94 (42%)	89 (40%)	39 (18%)	– (0%)	222
	Sample	9	41	50	23	21	–	94
Santa Ana County (La Paz)	Population	73 (65%)	13 (11%)	86 (76%)	10 (9%)	14 (12%)	3 (3%)	113
	Sample	36	13	49	10	14	3	76
Small Urban Counties	Population	82	98	180	99	53	3	335
	Sample	45	54	99	33	35	3	170

		Children in Foster Care			Children Who Left Foster Care			
		(1) In Foster Families	(2) In Institutions	(3) Total (columns 1 and 2)	(4) In Adoptive Homes	(5) Returned to Own Family	(6) Left for Other Reasons	Total (columns 3,4,5,6)
James County (Jamestown)	Population	80 (22%)	189 (51%)	269 (73%)	45 (12%)	51 (14%)	7 (2%)	372
	Sample	42	31	73	27	27	4	131
Lake County (Centralia)	Population	147 (51%)	50 (17%)	197 (68%)	74 (25%)	11 (4%)	6 (2%)	288
	Sample	55	19	74	28	5	3	110
Greater Brighton Area (Brighton)	Population	131 (49%)	75 (28%)	206 (77%)	27 (10%)	29 (11%)	4 (2%)	266
	Sample	46	28	74	27	16	2	119
Metropolitan Areas	Population	358	314	672	146	91	17	926
	Sample	143	78	221	82	48	9	360
Stark County (King City)	Population	446 (41%)	244 (22%)	690 (63%)	236 (21%)	155 (14%)	18 (2%)	1,099
	Sample	46	25	71	28	17	7	123
Makah County (Westport)	Population	907 (50%)	201 (11%)	1,108 (61%)	478 (26%)	184 (10%)	41 (2%)	1,811
	Sample	62	29	91	32	14	5	142
Big Cities	Population	1,353	445	1,798	714	339	59	2,910
	Sample	108	54	162	60	31	12	265
Total	Population	1,831	911	2,742	971	487	81	4,281
	Sample	334	217	551	187	118	26	882

Table 33

CHILDREN IN CARE ON APRIL 1, 1957, BY PLACEMENT CATEGORY

	Total Number on April 1	Percentage in Foster Families	Percentage in Institutional Care	Percentage in Adoptive Homes
Rural Communities				
Norden County (Abbotsford)	76	25	67	8
Granger County (Daleville)	30	67	17	17
Small Urban Counties				
Pine County (Summit)	193	6	55	39
Santa Ana County (La Paz)	107	77	16	7
Metropolitan Areas				
James County (Jamestown)	339	30	64	6
Lake County (Centralia)	272	58	20	22
Greater Brighton Area				
(Brighton)	254	58	37	6
Big Cities				
Stark County (King City)	963	51	31	18
Makah County (Westport)	1,621	62	17	21

Table 34

LENGTH OF TIME CHILDREN WERE IN FOSTER CARE IN EACH OF NINE COMMUNITIES

(Based on all children in foster care)

	Total Years in Care (in percentages of children) at Time of Study			Average Years in Care (median) at Time of Study	
	Up to 1½ Years	From 1½ to 5½ Years	More Than 5½ Years	Children in Foster Families	Children in Institutional Care
Rural Communities					
Norden County (Abbotsford)	14	46	40	8.0	4.5
Granger County (Daleville)	32	48	20	3.0	1.3
Small Urban Counties					
Pine County (Summit)	72	21	7	1.2	1.1
Santa Ana County (La Paz)	23	43	33	3.0	3.0
Metropolitan Areas					
James County (Jamestown)	35	36	28	1.5	2.6
Lake County (Centralia)	22	44	34	2.3	5.3
Greater Brighton Area (Brighton)	28	26	46	7.6	2.7
Big Cities					
Stark County (King City)	27	46	27	3.7	2.9
Makah County (Westport)	35	44	21	3.1	2.0
Mid-mark	28	44	28	3.0	2.7
Range	14–72	21–48	7–46	1.2–8.0	1.1–5.3

Table 35

LENGTH OF TIME CHILDREN WHO LEFT FOSTER CARE HAD BEEN IN CARE

(Based on children in leaving-care categories)

	Children in Adoptive Homes			Children Returning Home			Children Leaving for Other Purposes		
	Percent in Care Up to 1½ Years	Percent in Care Over 5½ Years	Average Years (median)	Percent in Care Up to 1½ Years	Percent in Care Over 5½ Years	Average Years (median)	Percent in Care Up to 1½ Years	Percent in Care Over 5½ Years	Average Years (median)
Rural Communities									
Norden County (Abbotsford)	67	17	1.0	33	33	4.0	—	50	6.0
Granger County (Daleville)	50	—	2.0	100	—	0.2	—	—	—
Small Urban Counties									
Pine County (Summit)	78	4	1.0	95	—	0.7	—	—	—
Santa Ana County (La Paz)	80	—	1.0	64	—	0.8	33	67	11.0
Metropolitan Areas									
James County (Jamestown)	78	—	1.1	41	7	1.8	25	50	4.2
Lake County (Centralia)	61	4	1.2	40	—	2.0	33	67	11.2
Greater Brighton Area (Brighton)	67	—	1.3	69	12	1.0	—	100	12.7
Big Cities									
Stark County (King City)	68	—	1.3	71	6	1.0	29	57	10.8
Makah County (Westport)	87	3	1.2	50	7	1.8	60	20	1.2
Mid-mark	68	—	1.2[a]	64	6	1.0[a]	25	50	6.0[a]
Range	50–87	0–17	1.0–2.0	33–100	0–33	0.2–4.0	0–60	0–100	0–12.7

[a] Apparently, staying in care beyond a year and a half greatly increases a child's chances of "growing up" in care.

Children who are placed in adoption or return home tend to be those who have been in care a relatively short time.

Table 36

NUMBER OF MOVES OF CHILDREN IN FOSTER CARE
(By percentage of children in foster care in each of nine communities)

	One	Two or Three	Four or More [a]
Rural Communities			
Norden County (Abbotsford)	12	57	32
Granger County (Daleville)	32	36	32
Small Urban Counties			
Pine County (Summit)	77	20	3
Santa Ana County (La Paz)	54	32	14
Metropolitan Areas			
James County (Jamestown)	55	36	9
Lake County (Centralia)	25	51	25
Greater Brighton Area (Brighton)	34	28	38
Big Cities			
Stark County (King City)	24	49	27
Makah County (Westport)	22	48	30
Mid-mark	32	36	27
Range	12–77	20–57	3–38

[a] Instability in relationships fosters personality disturbances. In six of our nine communities a quarter or more of the children in foster care had had four or more placements by the time of our study.

Table 37
CHILDREN LIKELY TO STAY IN FOSTER CARE
(By percentage of children in foster care in each of nine communities)

	Children whose parents were content with their being in long-term care or presented no other plans for them—and both of whose parents never or very infrequently visited them [a]	Children whose parents were content with their being in long-term care or presented no other plans for them—and at least one of whose parents did visit them more than infrequently [b]	Children whose parents had relinquished them or expressed an interest in doing so—and whose parents never visited them [c]
Rural Communities			
Norden County (Abbotsford)	23	36	16
Granger County (Daleville)	24	20	32
Small Urban Counties			
Pine County (Summit)	22	16	24
Santa Ana County (La Paz)	22	35	35
Metropolitan Areas			
James County (Jamestown)	36	21	23
Lake County (Centralia)	32	22	23
Greater Brighton Area (Brighton)	15	31	20
Big Cities			
Stark County (King City)	21	23	32
Makah County (Westport)	20	25	27

[a] These children are likely to stay in long-term foster care unless adoptive plans can be made for them.

[b] These children are likely to stay in long-term foster care unless parents' plans for them change.

[c] These children are ready, or almost ready, for adoptive placement, provided adoptive homes can be found for them.

See Chapter 22 for profiles of the children in each of these three types of situation.

APPENDIX D: LEGAL DATA

A Condensation of Comparable Codes and Statutes Affecting the Placement of Dependent Children

1. In Two Rural Counties

Norden County (Abbotsford)

Child may be removed temporarily if:

destitute, homeless or abandoned
dependent on the public for support without proper parental care or guardianship
habitually begs or receives alms
under ten, entertains in public for pay
living in house of ill fame or with vicious or disreputable persons
living in unfit home, living with someone with serious infectious disease endangering child's health, or under other unfit conditions within the spirit of this chapter

Placement after removal restricted by:

requirement of placement in same religion as far as practicable
uses specified of funds for placement:

Aid to Dependent Children not available for foster care except in home of relatives
state shares or pays full cost of placement in state institution, depending on parent's veterans status
county pays full cost of foster home or private institution placement;

Granger County (Daleville)

Child may be removed temporarily if:

parent or guardian neglects or refuses, when able to do so, to provide support, education, medical and other necessary care
abandoned by parent, guardian or other custodian or is otherwise without proper custody or guardianship
home is unfit by reason of parental depravity, open and notorious fornication, habitual drunkenness (for one year), or in relation to child, cruelty, desertion (more than six months), neglect, or contributing to delinquency

Placement after removal restricted by:

requirement of placement in same religion (required without qualification in one section governing placement in general; required "as far as practicable" in section dealing with placement after termination of parental rights)
No comparable restrictions on use of funds for foster care

amount paid to individual payee
published monthly
additional fund for destitute orphans and neglected children
authorized (but rarely collected)

Permanent removal (termination of
parental rights):

No specific provision for termination
of parental rights, but:

placement in state institution for
dependent children terminates
control by parent or committing
court
juvenile court may remove child
from custody of parents at hearing separate from adoption proceeding and commit to adoption
agency

Adoption:

Relinquishment to adoption agency
permitted without court action
Permanent custody of child may be
released only to licensed agency or
on court order (but attorneys do
not consider this section as pro-
hibitive of nonagency adoptions)
Permitted without parental consent
if:

parent dead, hopelessly insane, imprisoned for felony, inmate or
keeper of house of ill fame
parents not married (of parents not
having custody)
parents have released to agency
parents have been deprived of custody because of unfitness to be
guardian
child in state institution

Permanent removal (termination of
parental rights) permitted if:

child abandoned
child substantially and continuously
neglected when parents able to give
parental care and protection
parents are not fit and proper, according to section permitting temporary removal, and court finds
parent's conduct likely to be detrimental to child's health, morals,
or well-being

Adoption:

Relinquishment to adoption agency
permitted only through termination of parental rights in juvenile
court
Permitted without parental consent
if:

child abandoned for five years
parent cannot be found
parent insane or incompetent
parent has lost custody of child in
divorce proceeding
father of illegitimate child
parental rights have been terminated

2. In Two Small Urban Counties

Pine County (Summit)
Temporary removal of child (as dependent) permitted if:
destitute and homeless orphan

Santa Ana County (La Paz)
Temporary removal of child (as dependent) permitted if:
destitute, homeless, or abandoned

abandoned by parents and dependent on public for support

parents or guardian have willfully neglected for six months to take reasonable care

parents because of mental incompetency, physical disability, slothfulness, drunkenness or habitual use of narcotics, or other dissipation or immoral practices or standards are failing and will probably continue to fail to care and provide for

in care and custody of depraved or habitually vicious, immoral, corrupt, drunken, cruel, or indigent parents, guardians, or custodians

constantly or frequently subjected to or surrounded by vicious, corrupt, or immoral influences

habitually permitted or required to frequent public places to beg or secure alms or to consort with reputed thieves or prostitutes, alone or with parents or custodians

permitted or required to play musical instrument or sing for hire in pool halls or on streets or public highways

parents are confined in penal, charitable, or state educational institution in state for more than six months and child is left without reasonable care and protection from lawful guardian or next of kin

dependent on public for support

without proper parental care or guardianship

found begging or soliciting or receiving alms

found in house of prostitution

found living with vicious or disreputable person

without responsible parent or guardian

home is unfit by reason of parents' or guardians' or custodians' neglect, abuse, mistreatment, cruelty, depravity

Restrictions on placement after removal:

Child may be committed to care of reputable person of good moral character or suitable institution or a child care or adoption society

No restriction on placement based on religion

Dependent child shall, when practicable, be placed in suitable and approved family home and become a member of a home and family by adoption or otherwise

Restrictions on placement after removal:

Child found dependent and neglected may be placed under care and control of individual or association for care, custody, and control of orphans or dependent and neglected children

Orphan or abandoned child may be committed to charitable institution if court is satisfied that there is no proper and suitable person willing to adopt or assume care or provide support of child; court to have due regard to commit to institution which will not proselytize or interfere with child's religious belief

Permanent removal:

No provision for separate legal proceeding for terminating parental rights

Removal as dependent child transfers all parental rights to the person, institution, or society to whom child is committed by court unless court specifies otherwise, but adoption order under such commitment cannot be made for three- to six-month period specified by court and parents may, if court orders, reclaim child during this period

Adoption:

Child may be relinquished to agency for adoption

Permitted without parental consent (living parents of legitimate child, mother of illegitimate child) if:

parent deprived of civil rights

parent adjudged guilty of adultery or cruelty and divorced for this cause

parent deprived of child's custody because of cruelty or neglect

Permitted with consent of mother or certain persons other than parents if:

child abandoned by parent or parents

father has unlawfully ceased support

Permanent removal:

No provision for court termination of parental rights but court may permit child found dependent or neglected to be adopted without consent of parent or guardian

Adoption law provides for separate hearing to determine need for consent of parent or guardian to child's adoption

Adoption:

No provision for relinquishment to agency for adoption without court action

Permitted without parental consent (parents of child born in wedlock, mother for child born out of wedlock) if:

parent has been deprived of custody through divorce or legal separation

parent has been deprived of custody under proceedings governing temporary removal as a dependent and neglected child (or similar proceedings)

court-appointed guardian has given consent

name or whereabouts of parent or guardian is unknown and cannot be ascertained

parent or guardian when obligated and financially able to do so has willfully failed to maintain and support child

parent or guardian guilty of such cruelty, depravity, abuse, or gross neglect toward child that child should be removed from custody of parent or guardian

3. In Two Metropolitan Areas

James County (Jamestown)

Temporary removal of child (as neglected or dependent) permitted as follows:

A neglected child is one under sixteen in a Domestic Relations Court, under eighteen in a Juvenile Domestic Relations Court (James County's is a Domestic Relations Court):

(a) who is without proper guardianship

(b) who has been abandoned or deserted by either or both of its parents or any other person lawfully charged with its care and custody

(c) whose parent or guardian or the person with whom the child lives, by reason of cruelty, mental incapacity, immorality, or depravity is unfit properly to care for such child

(d) whose parent or guardian has been sentenced to imprisonment for crime

(e) who is under unlawful or improper supervision, care, custody, or restraint by any person

(f) who wanders about without lawful occupation

(g) whose parent, guardian, or custodian neglects or refuses, when able to do so, to provide necessary medical, surgical, institutional, or hospital care for such child

(h) who is found in any place the maintenance of which is in violation of law, or

(i) who is in such condition of want or suffering or is under such improper guardianship or control as to injure or en-

Lake County (Centralia)

Temporary removal of child (as neglected or dependent) permitted if:

abandoned by parent, guardian, or legal custodian

without proper parental care because of fault or habits or disability of parent, guardian, or legal custodian

without necessary subsistence, education, or other necessary care, or the special care required by child's condition because parent, guardian, or legal custodian neglects or refuses to provide it

child's occupation, behavior, condition, environment, or associations would endanger his or others' welfare

in home requiring license and license has been refused by licensing agency

in home for adoption and court approval is required but has been refused

in custody of person whose petition to adopt him has been denied and case transferred to juvenile court for this reason

child comes within provisions of the section dealing with delinquent children but this conduct results wholly or partly from parental neglect

without parent or guardian

in need of special care and treatment because of condition and parents' guardian, or legal custodian unable to provide it

parent or legal custodian for good cause desires to be relieved of his legal custody

danger the morals or health
of himself or others

Placement restrictions:

If removed from home, child may be
placed in care of:

relative or other fit person
suitable public institution
association, agency, society, or institution, including any orphan
home, hospital, or private home
approved by court
any officer, board, or department
authorized to receive children as
public charges

Religious restrictions:

Child must be placed as far as
practicable in care of institution
of person of same religious faith
of parents, unless placement is
in state institution

Financial restrictions:

ADC given only in home of relative. DPW manual says children in church homes or orphanages are not eligible for
assistance according to state and
federal law
State funds available for foster
home care by state regulation
Child in county charge when placed
in institution, foster home, etc.
Reports may be required by court
from agency or instittuion to
which child is committed
Authority of institution is same as
that of parent or guardian as to
person of child
Child may be deeded by parents

Placement restrictions:

If removed from own home, child
may be placed in:
foster home
legal custody of:

relative
agency, which may contract for
care by private agency
licensed child welfare agency
State Department of Public Welfare, which may contract for
care by private agency

Commitment must be for specified
time, and annual reports to court
or person holding legal custody required

Religious restrictions:

State and county welfare departments and child welfare agencies
must provide for moral and religious training according to religious belief of child or parents
Adoptive placement where practicable shall be in same religion
as natural parents of child

Use of funds for foster care:

County pays full cost of child committed to or placed by county
in private institutions; County
Board of Supervisors sets maximum payment for such children
ADC funds (one third supplied by
state) may be used for foster
home care if child *placed by
county agency* ("placed by county
agency" is interpreted to include
children eligible for ADC funds
being served by voluntary agencies; state share of cost is paid
to foster home rather than to
agency)
Special local funds and some Federal Child Welfare Service funds
available for foster home care
and other needs of children not
eligible for ADC funds
If child is committed to SDPW,

county pays state $5 a week for child regardless of type of placement

Permanent removal (termination of parental rights):

No provision for termination of parental rights, except by parental consent to adoption

Permanent removal (termination of parental rights) permitted if:

parents consent in writing to termination

parents have abandoned

parents have substantially and continuously or repeatedly refused to give minor necessary care and protection

parents, though financially able, have substantially and continuously neglected to provide child with necessary subsistence, education, or other necessary care, or have neglected to pay for these when child's legal custody with others

parents are unfit because of debauchery, habitual use of intoxicating liquor or narcotic drugs, or repeated lewd and lascivious behavior, and their conduct is found detrimental to health, morals, or well-being of child, if legal custody has been removed from parents for one year by court and not returned during that period

parents found mentally deficient and are and will continue to be unable to give child proper parental care and protection

parents found mentally ill and one of first four other reasons for permanent removal existed before finding of mental illness

After termination of parental rights, guardianship (including right to consent to adoption [1]) shall be given to:

county welfare department of county with population over 500,000 (a figure which limits this provision to one county of state; does not include Lake County)

licensed child welfare agency

[1] But adoption may be granted without guardian's consent if court finds refusal to consent as arbitrary, capricious, or not based on substantial evidence.

State Department of Public Welfare

individual in whose home minor has resided one year prior to termination of parental rights

Adoption:

Requires consent of parents, guardian, or custodian but does not specify procedure for giving consent except that these persons must be made parties to adoption proceeding

No specified waiting period between adoptive placement and completion of adoption

Provision for agency adoption procedure:

Children's Services authorized to place for adoption and as guardian of children committed to its care consent to adoption

If orphan or foundling home has custody of child, petitioners for adoption may file and do not need to prove child's parentage

Guardian *ad litem* must be appointed before adoption hearing can be held

Investigation to be made by probation officer, but this is not mandatory

Adoption order may be revoked at any time by the judge for cause

Illegitimate child may not be adopted if parents were unmarried unless parents could have married legally in state (not always enforced)

Public welfare department bases adoption program on its legal authority as welfare agency of the state. Legal authority for private agencies' adoption programs through their charters

Adoption:

No provision for setting aside adoption order

Relinquishment of child to agency authorized only in connection with termination of parental rights in court

Permitted without parental consent (both living parents of legitimate child, mother of illegitimate child) if parental rights have been terminated

Court approval of adoptive placement required, unless made by licensed or authorized adoption agency; court approval must include investigation by public or private child welfare agency

Residence of six months in adoptive home required between filing of petition and granting of adoptions, but court may waive this requirement

Other laws:

Provision for licensing of agencies and institutions by State Department of Public Welfare but all religious and certain public institutions and agencies are exempt by law

Other laws which may influence placement:

Service to unmarried mothers:

On notice to State Department of Public Welfare of admission to hospital of unmarried pregnant woman state department must

Separate institutional facilities for each race

take steps to protect child's interest

ADC given to any mother six months before or six months after birth

Federal child welfare service funds and special local funds available for temporary care of unmarried mother or her child

4. In Two Big Cities

Stark County (King City)

Temporary removal of child (as dependent or neglected) permitted if:

dependent upon the public for support

destitute

homeless

abandoned

does not have proper parental care or guardianship

habitually begs or receives alms

is found living in any house of ill fame or with vicious or disreputable person

child's home is unfit because of neglect, cruelty, or depravity of parents, guardian, or custodian

parents or guardian permit child to use intoxicating liquor (except for medicinal purposes) or become addicted to use of liquors or permit child in or about any place where intoxicating liquors sold

Makah County (Westport)

Temporary removal of child (as dependent [1]) permitted if:

found begging, peddling, selling, playing musical instrument for gain or entertaining publicly, or aiding anyone so doing, unless for regularly organized school or society

vagrant, or wanders in nighttime without lawful business or occupation

without parent or guardian exercising proper parental control

destitute

home is unfit because of neglect, cruelty, or depravity of parent, guardian, or custodian

parent or custodian is habitual drunkard or does not provide properly for child and child is destitute or in danger of being brought up to lead idle, dissolute, or immoral life

for any cause, in danger of growing up to lead idle, dissolute, or immoral life

frequents billiard or pool room or place where liquor is sold or given

---

1 Courts differ in interpretation of dependent and delinquent: State Department of Public Welfare is not permitted to accept delinquent children for placement and many children who have committed delinquent acts are referred to State Department of Public Welfare as dependent or dependent-delinquent because of limitations on placement of delinquent children.

away or company of reputed criminals, vagrants, or prostitutes or is found living in house of prostitution

incorrigible

habitual truant according to state law

uses intoxicating liquor as a beverage

uses tobacco, or narcotics without physician's direction

and court finds that parent or guardian is incapable or has failed or neglected to provide proper maintenance, training, and education for child, or that the welfare of child requires that custody be taken from parent or guardian

Placement restrictions after removal:

Court may turn child over to care and custody of any suitable person or any suitable institution in the county or state organized for purpose of caring for "dependent children" and which is willing and able to care for the child

Child becomes a ward and is subject to the guardianship of the individual or institution. Such individual or institution has authority to place child in a suitable family home, the head of such family being responsible for maintenance and education of child

Once a child is adjudged dependent or neglected such parents or guardians shall have no right over or to the custody, services, or earnings of said child except on such conditions as the court may impose

Dependent or neglected child from infancy to sixteen years of age may be committed by a judge to the State Home for Dependent and Neglected Children for the child's minority. Child may be placed in a foster home if the superintendent deems it advantageous, but no more than twenty may be boarded at any one time

2 Not used for dependent children.

Placement restrictions after removal:

Court may commit child to:

probation officer for placement in suitable family home

suitable institution for care of delinquent or dependent children

association for care of neglected, delinquent, and dependent children

reputable citizen of good moral character

State Department of Public Welfare must accept custody of children committed to it and provide care for children in need of protective services but must use approved private agency services for child care as far as available

Financial restrictions:

ADC funds limited to placement with relatives of designated degree

Court may order support by county up to $12 a month for six months at a time if parent, guardian, or custodian unable to pay 2

State Department of Public Welfare must pay at a reasonable rate established by the department for children accepted as eligible for support

Financial restrictions:

ADC funds not available for foster care

No restriction as to religion or color in foster care

Court may require reports at any time

Permanent removal of child (termination of parental rights) permitted, and is a separate proceeding from adoption proceeding:

Court uses same section of law as applies to temporary removal of child as dependent and neglected; court must specify that order includes right to consent to adoption

Adoption:

Relinquishment to agency authorized, and further consent of parents then not necessary

Permitted without parental (mother only if child born out of wedlock) consent if:

living parent or parents voluntarily abandon and desert child for two years and child is left to care of other persons

living parent or parents fail to contribute substantially to child's support commensurate with financial ability, for two years

(Juvenile Court judge may consent)

Consent need not include adoptive parents by name

No white child may be adopted by a Negro person, or a Negro child by a white person

No religious restrictions on placement

No report to court required after placement [3]

Permanent removal of child (termination of parental rights):

No specific provision for terminating parental rights, but under law governing adoption:

court may deprive parent of custody, after notice to parent, so that parent's consent to adoption is not necessary

court may commit permanently to child care association, suitable institution, or reputable citizen and may give association the right to place for adoption

Adoption:

For adoption, parental consent is ordinarily required and would be given as part of the adoption proceeding, but the need for consent might be eliminated in the following ways:

a. relinquishment (with court approval) by the parent to an adoption agency

b. permanent commitment to an agency with the right to place for adoption

c. court hearing, separate from adoption proceedings, at which, if circumstances warranted, parents' consent might be found not necessary for adoption

Permitted without parental consent (both living parents of legitimate child, mother of illegitimate child) if there is a court hearing and court finds that:

parent has been deprived of civil

[3] But customarily submitted.

rights for reasons which would warrant permanent deprivation of parental rights for child's welfare

parent has been deprived of child's custody by court, but not merely in connection with divorce, annulment, separate maintenance

parent has been adjudged mentally ill or incompetent for a year and not restored to competency and court finds best interests of child served by depriving parent of custody

parent found by court to have deserted or abandoned child under circumstances showing willful substantial lack of regard for parental obligations

Adoptive placement and relinquishment to adoption agency must be with prior approval of court

Other laws which might affect placement of children:

ADC limitations:
Maximum amount of individual grant
Child must be citizen to be eligible
Provisions for unmarried mothers:
Maternity homes must report to local health officer birth of child within twenty-four hours
No state funds available to pay for foster care
County probation department may use county funds to purchase care from private agency

Other laws which might affect placement of children:

Licensing law:
SDPW licenses children's institutions and child-placing agencies, except those not operated for profit and operated under adequate local control by established board of laymen or by a church organization
SDPW in providing for the care of children in need of protective services must follow policy of using only properly approved private agencies [4]

Services for unmarried mothers:
No specific legal provisions

[4] This section is used in lieu of a more inclusive licensing law, but an agency or institution exempt from licensing and not requesting public funds would not require license or approval.

5. In the Greater Brighton Area

Temporary removal permitted if:

Department of Public Welfare considers child in need of foster care, based on application of parent or guardian or one acting on behalf of child

child voluntarily surrendered to public welfare department by parents for consent to adoption

child for whom Department of Public Welfare has been given temporary or permanent guardianship, not including the right to consent to adoption unless expressly included in the court order

child committed by Juvenile Court, Juvenile session of district court, or any superior court as in need of care and protection; reasons for petition to start such a proceeding given as:

child without necessary and proper physical, educational, or moral care and discipline

child is growing up under conditions or circumstances damaging to a child's sound character development

child lacks proper attention of parent, guardian with care and custody, or custodian and whose parents or guardian are unwilling, incompetent, or unavailable to provide such care

child under fourteen left any place and seemingly without parent or legal guardian (temporary and such lawful provision as seems in best interests of such child to be arranged by Department of Public Welfare)

child in independent (nonagency) foster home and after investigation public welfare department judges welfare of child or its protection from neglect so requires

Restrictions on placement if removed from own home:

Court may commit child in need of care and protection to Department of Public Welfare until twenty-one years of age or until in opinion of Department of Public Welfare the object of his commitment has been accomplished, or make any other appropriate order for care and custody as may conduce to his best interests; no provision for further order of court once child is committed to Department of Public Welfare, except in connection with support orders

Court may arrange a placement with a private agency willing to receive the child and usually continues the case for the duration of the placement. Unless the parent can support, the private agency would finance the case

In case of appeal, which may be by child, parent, guardian, person appearing in child's behalf, or department, case will be heard anew, and child may be committed to custody of department or placed in care of some suitable person or licensed children's foster care agency pending appeal decision

Court may commit child, or department may transfer committed child in need of care and protection, to board of public welfare of child's settlement if board requests, and boards may transfer such children to department

No legal restriction on department or boards of public welfare in purchasing foster family or institutional care from private agencies. This is done at discretion of public agencies. Because of lack of clarity on respective responsibilities of these two public agencies for financing foster care of settled dependent children, boards of public welfare rarely purchase care but leave with the department responsibility for making placements. When foster care is purchased, the private agency sets the rate and the public agency decides whether or not to make the purchase

Department may use public or private institution or school only if child found to be in need of special care, treatment, or education and must enter reason for such placement in records; otherwise must place in private families

No child to be denied free exercise of religion of parents, surviving parent, or deceased parents; department, board, or agency caring for child in family home must use home of same religious faith (if Protestant denomination, "same religious faith" includes any other denomination of the same religion) as child's unless sufficient reason precludes, and if so, reason must be part of record of child's care

Probate court may order department, board, public or private institution, person, association caring for child to permit parent, guardian, or next-of-kin to visit child if his welfare and public interest will not be injured

Permanent removal (termination of parental rights):

No specific provision for termination of parental rights, but adoption law provides for hearing (separate from adoption proceeding) to determine need of consent for adoption

Adoption:

Permitted without parental consent (parents of legitimate child, mother of illegitimate child) after separate hearing if:

parent hopelessly insane

parent imprisoned in penal institution in state with term of three years remaining at time of adoption petition

parent willfully deserted or neglected to provide proper care and maintenance

parent has suffered child to be supported for more than one year continuously prior to adoption petition by an incorporated charitable institution or by a town or by the state

parent convicted of drunkenness for third time in year and neglects to provide proper care and maintenance for such child

parent has been convicted of being a common nightwalker or lewd, wanton, and lascivious person, and neglects to provide proper care and maintenance for such child

Written surrender of child for adoption to department or agency is equivalent of consent to adoption subsequently approved by department or agency

Public welfare department takes steps to secure guardianship of child after voluntary release is signed by parent

Adoption order must give custody when practicable only to persons of same religious faith as child or must include facts which impelled any other disposition

All petitions for adoption must be approved in writing by Department of Public Welfare or by an agency authorized by department

Appeal may be made by petitioners to the department's Advisory Board if aggrieved by arbitrary refusal of department or agency to approve petition. Advisory Board would make findings known to court, which has final responsibility for final determination as to approval of the petition

APPENDIX E: BASIC COMMUNITY CENSUS DATA [1]

1. Social Differentiation

We looked at differentiation in our communities in several ways. One basis for differentiation was contained in census figures on ethnicity, which are detailed in Table 38. In communities like Norden and Summit initial,

Table 38
ETHNIC GROUPS IN EACH OF NINE COMMUNITIES
(By percentage of population in 1950)

	Native White	Foreign-born White	Negro	Spanish Surname [a]	Predominant Origins of Foreign-born Whites
Rural Communities					
Norden County (Abbotsford)	97	3	—	—	Germany
Granger County (Daleville)	92	8	—	—	Norway, Germany, Sweden
Small Urban Counties					
Pine County (Summit)	96	3	—	—	Canada, England and Wales
Santa Ana County (La Paz)	94	2	—	60	Mexico
Metropolitan Areas					
James County (Jamestown)	57	1	41	—	————
Lake County (Centralia)	88	10	2	—	Denmark, Germany
Greater Brighton Area					
(Brighton)	77	21	2	—	"Other Europe," England and Wales, French-Canada, Poland
Big Cities					
Stark County (King City)	79	3	18	5	————
Makah County (Westport)	85	11	2	—	Canada, Norway, Sweden

[a] Persons with Spanish surname are included in native white figures but are also recorded separately from a special census count for Southwestern states.

[1] All data in tables in this appendix were derived from the 1950 U.S. Census.

"ascribed" homogeneity was apparent, while in Santa Ana, James, and
Stark counties large, visible native-born ethnic categories of a racial or
quasi-racial nature persisted.   In Granger, Lake, and Makah counties
nationality differences existed but were tending to be washed out by historical social processes.   Finally, in Brighton, segmented differences remained, as multiplicity of difference coalesced into social class strata, but
did not persist as two or three major categories.   Percentages of foreign-
born did not indicate the continuing extent of ethnic differentiation in a
community since second or third generations of native-born whites might
be more or less assimilated depending on initial differences of their fore-
bears and subsequent movement processes in the cultures.

Another view of differentiation in our nine communities was obtained
by looking at their occupation and income breakdowns—perhaps a secondary or more "achieved" basis for differentiation—which are presented in
Tables 39 and 40.   From such data we obtained further pictures of crystal-
lizations of social differentiation.   Some communities, like Summit, Centralia, and Westport, tended toward homogeneity at a comparatively high
socioeconomic level; others, like the two rural communities of Norden and
Granger, were at an understandably lower level.   Communities like La

Table 39

OCCUPATIONAL STRATA IN EACH OF NINE COMMUNITIES
(By percentage of population in 1950)

	Farmers and Farm Managers	Professional and White-Collar Workers	Skilled Workers	Semiskilled, Service Workers, and Laborers
Rural Communities				
Norden County (Abbotsford)	27	25	9	37
Granger County (Daleville)	32	28	9	31
Small Urban Counties				
Pine County (Summit)	7	50	15	27
Santa Ana County (La Paz)	4	45	15	33
Metropolitan Areas				
James County (Jamestown)	2	35	15	46
Negroes only	3	8	6	81
Lake County (Centralia)	3	35	19	42 (25% "operatives")
Greater Brighton Area				
(Brighton)	1	28	13	58 (38% "operatives")
Big Cities				
Stark County (King City)	1	44	16	38
Negroes only	—	11	5	83
Makah County (Westport)	1	50	17	31

Table 40

ANNUAL FAMILY [a] INCOME IN EACH OF NINE COMMUNITIES

(By percentage of population in 1950)

	Under $500		Median		$10,000 and Over	
Rural Communities						
Norden County (Abbotsford)	13		$2,277		1	
Granger County (Daleville)	12		2,071		1	
Small Urban Communities						
Pine County (Summit)	10		2,877		2	
Santa Ana County (La Paz)	15		2,329 (Spanish [b] $1,400)		3	
Metropolitan Areas						
James County (Jamestown)	19		1,701		1	
Negroes only		32		$839		0.1
Lake County (Centralia)	7		3,598		3	
Greater Brighton Area						
(Brighton)	11		2,580		2	
Big Cities						
Stark County (King City)	9		3,078 (Spanish [b] $1,134)		3	
Negroes only		15		$1,681		0.2
Makah County (Westport)	9		3,222		3	

[a] For families and unrelated individuals.

[b] All figures on "Spanish" are based on state-wide figures for "urban, Spanish-surname" populations and are merely representative of the specific communities.

Paz, Jamestown, and King City were typified by socioeconomic disparities or by the existence of visibly "depressed" population segments.

2. Social Change and Movement

Table 41 provides basic data on population change and other factors relevant to social dynamics and child welfare services in our nine communities. Rural Granger and highly urban Brighton both showed the slowest rate of population increase. Brighton added to this the highest median age of population while Granger had youth but reflected a loss of persons in the young-parent age group (20–44). King City and Westport, our two largest communities, were growing the fastest, with Summit just behind; but Westport retained an older population while King City had the highest proportion of young adults in its population. La Paz, followed by Jamestown, had, proportionately, the most children and a young median age, but these children came in large numbers from a depressed segment of the population. Physical mobility figures showed Brighton most "inert," with Summit, King City, and Westport the most active. Summit had the most movement into the community from outside while King City and Westport had the most movement from house to house within the community—perhaps evidence of growing suburbs, which also appeared in Jamestown.

Table 41

POPULATION CHANGE, AGE DISTRIBUTION, AND EDUCATION
IN EACH OF NINE COMMUNITIES [a]

(By percentage of population in 1950)

	Population Change			Age Distribution			Education	
	Population Increase 1940-50	Internal Mobility (in different house) 1949-50	Mobility from Outside County 1949-50	Under Age 15 (children)	Ages 20-44 (young parents)	Median Years of Age	Of Persons 14-17, Those in School	Median School Years Completed (persons 25 and over)
Rural Communities								
Norden County (Abbotsford)	5.3	9.3	7.6	24.5	33.5	30.5	91.1	8.8
Granger County (Daleville)	−5.2	8.7	6.7	30.6	33.2	29.0	85.2	8.9
Small Urban Counties								
Pine County (Summit)	40.2	16.0	12.0	28.9	38.0	29.9	90.1	12.0
Santa Ana County (La Paz)	23.8	11.0	11.0	35.2	36.1	23.4	85.8	9.5 (Spanish [b] 7.5)
Metropolitan Areas								
James County (Jamestown)	36.1	15.5	5.5	32.9	40.3	24.5	78.9	8.7 (Negro 4.9)
Lake County (Centralia)	16.5	10.8	4.0	25.8	37.1	31.4	87.7	9.2
Greater Brighton Area (Brighton)	2.3	6.4	2.3	22.7	37.0	34.0	76.0	8.3
Big Cities								
Stark County (King City)	52.5	19.3	7.1	27.4	44.2	28.8	83.2	10.4 (Spanish [b] 5.2; Negro 7.6)
Makah County (Westport)	45.2	16.9	7.3	24.2	39.6	32.5	91.4	12.1

[a] It should be noted that over-all median figures on communities like La Paz, Jamestown, and King City (with sizable depressed segments) are greatly depressed. Similarly, low median population ages in La Paz and Jamestown represent the influence of large groups of young children in Spanish and Negro families.

[b] All figures on "Spanish" are based on state-wide figures for "urban, Spanish-surname" populations and are merely representative of the specific communities.

BIBLIOGRAPHY

Abbott, Grace. *The Child and the State*. Vols. I and II. Chicago: University of Chicago Press, 1938.

Barriers to Adoption: a Study of Physical and Psychological Handicaps, Ethnicity, and Adoptive Parents' Expectations. A Group Research Project, by Ruth Baer, Alma Dalmasso, Wilbur A. Finch, Jr., Dorothy E. Howard, Nancy E. Jehl, R. Warren Jones, Nancy Nason, Rama Thursby, and Marie Walsh. Under the faculty supervision of Henry S. Maas, School of Social Welfare, University of California, Berkeley, June, 1959.

Bendix, Reinhard, and Seymour Martin Lipset (eds.). *Class, Status and Power: a Reader in Social Stratification*. Glencoe, Illinois: The Free Press, 1953.

Board Member of a Social Agency: Responsibilities and Functions. New York: Child Welfare League of America, Inc., 1957.

Boehm, Bernice. *Deterrents to the Adoption of Children in Foster Care*. New York: Child Welfare League of America, Inc., 1958.

Bowlby, John. *Maternal Care and Mental Health*. 2d ed. Geneva: World Health Organization, 1954.

Bridwell, Mable M. *A Study of Hard-to-Place Children*. Part III: Children under Jackson County Juvenile Court Jurisdiction. Publication 111. Kansas City, Missouri: Community Studies, Inc., 1957.

Broom, Leonard, and Philip Selznick. *Sociology*. Evanston, Illinois: Row, Peterson and Company, 1955.

Burma, John H. *Spanish Speaking Groups in the United States*. Durham, North Carolina: Duke University Press, 1954.

Charnley, Jean. *The Art of Child Placement*. Minneapolis: University of Minnesota Press, 1955.

Citizens Committee on Adoption of Children in California. *1953 Final Report*. Los Angeles, 1953.

Close, Kathryn. *Transplanted Children: a History*. New York: U.S. Committee for the Care of European Children, Inc., 1953.

Cohen, Albert K. *Delinquent Boys: the Culture of the Gang*. Glencoe, Illinois: The Free Press, 1955.

Committee on Adoption and Services to Unmarried Mothers. *Children Deprived of Adoption*. New York: Welfare and Health Council of New York City, 1955.

Committee on Adoption Standards, Child Welfare League of America, Inc., New York. Working Draft, 1956. Final version published New York, 1958, by the League as *Standards for Adoption Service.*

Committee on Standards for Foster Family Care, Child Welfare League of America, Inc., New York. Working Draft, 1956.

Committee on Standards for Group Care, Child Welfare League of America, Inc., New York. Working Draft, 1957.

Community Organization of Child Welfare Services: a Study of Casework Policies and Procedures as They Affect Community Relations and Their Impact on Service to Clients. New York: Child Welfare League of America, Inc., 1955.

Dai, Bingham. "Some Problems of Personality Development among Negro Children," in *Personality in Nature, Society, and Culture,* Clyde Kluckhohn, Henry A. Murray, and David Schneider (eds.). New York: Alfred A. Knopf, 1953.

Davis, Allison. *Children of Bondage: the Personality Development of Negro Youth in the Urban South.* Washington, D.C.: American Council on Education, 1940.

Dollard, John. *Caste and Class in a Southern Town.* New Haven: Yale University Press, 1937.

Drake, St. Clair, and Horace R. Cayton. *Black Metropolis: a Study of Negro Life in a Northern City.* New York: Harcourt, Brace and Company, 1945.

Erikson, Erik. *Childhood and Society.* New York: Norton and Company, 1950.

Factors Associated with the Disposition of Children in Foster Care. A Group Research Project by Betsy Cogburn, Lorraine G. Corden, Lily L. Jean, Yoshiko J. Mukai, Margaret E. Purvine, Alma H. Savedra, Herbert R. Smith, and Maida G. M. Thomas. Under the faculty supervision of Henry S. Maas, School of Social Welfare, University of California, Berkeley, June, 1957.

Fanshel, David. *A Study in Negro Adoption.* New York: Child Welfare League of America, Inc., 1957.

Frazier, E. Franklin. "Ethnic Family Patterns: the Negro Family in the United States," *American Journal of Sociology,* Vol. LIII, No. 6, 1948.

Freud, Anna, and Dorothy T. Burlingham. *War and Children.* New York: Medical War Books, 1943.

Glickman, Esther. *Child Placement through Clinically Oriented Casework.* New York: Columbia University Press, 1957.

Gordon, Henrietta L. *Casework Services for Children.* Boston: Houghton Mifflin Company, 1956.

Hagan, Helen R. *Distinctive Aspects of Child Welfare.* New York: Child Welfare League of America, Inc., 1957.

—— *Relationships between Child Care Agencies.* New York: Child Welfare League of America, Inc., 1955.

—— *The Institution as a Casework Agency.* New York: Child Welfare League of America, Inc., 1958.

Hayes, Ruth B., and Muriel F. Steevers. "Allowances in Foster Care," *Children,* Vol. II, No. 3, 1955.

Hunter, Floyd, Ruth Conner Schaffer, and Cecil G. Sheps. *Community Organization: Action and Inaction.* Chapel Hill: University of North Carolina Press, 1956.

Josselyn, Irene M. *Psychosocial Development of Children.* New York: Family Service Association of America, 1948.

Kahn, Alfred J. "Sociology and Social Work: Challenge and Invitation," *Social Problems,* Vol. IV, No. 3, 1957.

Kaufman, Irving. *The Contribution of Protective Services.* New York: Child Welfare League of America, Inc., 1957.

Leavy, Morton L. *The Law of Adoption.* 2d ed. New York: Oceana Publications, 1954.

Lindesmith, Alfred R., and Anselm L. Strauss. *Social Psychology.* Rev. ed. New York: The Dryden Press, 1956.

Littner, Ner. *Some Traumatic Effects of Separation and Placement.* New York: Child Welfare League of America, Inc., 1956.

—— *The Strains and Stresses on the Child Welfare Worker.* New York: Child Welfare League of America, Inc., 1957.

Maas, Henry S., *et al.* "Socio-Cultural Factors in Psychiatric Clinic Services for Children," *Smith College Studies in Social Work,* Vol. XXV, No. 2, 1955.

Maas, Henry S., and Martin Wolins. "Concepts and Methods in Social Work Research," in *New Directions in Social Work,* Cora Kasius (ed.). New York: Harper and Brothers, 1954.

MacDonald, Mary E. "Children Placed by the Jewish Children's Bureau of Chicago in 1939 and in 1950–52," *Social Service Review,* Vol. XXVIII, No. 3, 1954.

MacIver, R. M., and Charles H. Page. *Society.* New York: Rinehart and Company, Inc., 1949.

Merton, Robert K. *Social Theory and Social Structure.* Glencoe, Illinois: The Free Press, 1957.

Metropolitan Communities: a Bibliography with Special Emphasis upon Government and Politics. Prepared by Government Affairs Foundation, Inc. Chicago: Public Administration Service, 1956.

Mills, C. Wright. *White Collar: the American Middle Classes.* New York: Oxford University Press, 1953.

Mulford, Robert M., Victor B. Wylegala, and Elwood F. Melson. *Caseworker and Judge in Neglect Cases.* New York: Child Welfare League of America, Inc., 1956.

Mussen, Paul H., and John J. Conger. *Child Development and Personality.* New York: Harper and Brothers, 1956.

Myrdal, Gunnar. *An American Dilemma.* New York: Harper and Brothers, 1944.

Parsons, Talcott. *The Social System.* Glencoe, Illinois: The Free Press, 1951.

Parsons, Talcott, and Edward A. Shils (eds.). *Toward a General Theory of Action.* Cambridge, Mass.: Harvard University Press, 1952.

Polansky, Grace Hilford. Meeting Needs of Children in Placement. Master's thesis, School of Applied Social Sciences, Western Reserve University, 1949.

Policy and Strategy in Social Welfare: Report to the Churches. New York: Department of Social Welfare, National Council of Churches, 1957.

Polier, Justine Wise. *Parental Rights: the Need for Law and Social Action.* New York: Child Welfare League of America, Inc., June, 1958.

Proceedings of the Conference on Research in the Children's Field—Chicago, April 4–7, 1956. New York: National Association of Social Workers, 1956.

Reid, Joseph H. "Principles, Values, and Assumptions Underlying Adoption Practice," *Social Work,* Vol. II, No. 1, 1957.

Reid, Joseph H., and Helen R. Hagan. *Residential Treatment of Emotionally Disturbed Children: a Descriptive Study.* New York: Child Welfare League of America, Inc., 1952.

Riesman, David. *The Lonely Crowd.* New Haven: Yale University Press, 1953.

Sandusky, Annie Lee. *Public Welfare Services to Children in Their Own Homes.* New York: Child Welfare League of America, Inc., 1957.

Saunders, Lyle. *Cultural Difference and Medical Care: La Gente De La Raza.* Philadelphia: Wm. F. Fell Company, Printers, 1954.

Schapiro, Michael. *A Study of Adoption Practice.* Vols. I, II, and III. New York: Child Welfare League of America, Inc., 1956.

Schulze, Susanne, *et al. Distinctive Knowledge and Skills in Child Welfare: a Symposium on Developing Generic and Specific Knowledge through the Study of Children's Services.* New York: Child Welfare League of America, Inc., 1955.

Schwartz, Morris S., and Charlotte Green Schwartz. "Problems in Participant Observation," *American Journal of Sociology,* Vol. LX, No. 4, 1955.

Seeley, John R., R. Alexander Sim, and Elizabeth W. Loosley. *Crestwood Heights: a Study of the Culture of Suburban Life.* New York: Basic Books, Inc., 1956.

Selvin, Hanan C. "A Critique of Tests of Significance in Survey Research," *American Sociological Review,* Vol. XXII, No. 5, 1957.

—— "Durkheim's Suicide and Problems of Empirical Research," *American Journal of Sociology,* Vol. LXIII, No. 6, 1958.

Shevky, Eshref, and Wendell Bell. *Social Area Analysis.* Stanford Sociological Series No. 1. Stanford, California: Stanford University Press, 1955.

Socio-cultural Elements in Casework: a Case Book of Seven Ethnic Case Studies. New York: Council on Social Work Education, undated.

Stanton, Howard R. "Mother Love in Foster Homes," *Marriage and Family Living,* Vol. XVIII, No. 4, 1956.

Stone, L. Joseph, and Joseph Church. *Childhood and Adolescence: a Psychology of the Growing Person.* New York: Random House, 1957.

Talbert, Robert H. *Spanish-Name People in the Southwest and West.* Fort Worth, Texas: Leo Potishman Foundation, Texas Christian University, 1955.

Taylor, Hasseltine Byrd. *Law of Guardian and Ward.* Social Service Monographs No. 35. Chicago: University of Chicago Press, 1935.

United Community Funds and Councils of America, Inc. Expenditures for Health and Welfare Services, by Field of Service and Auspices, and Receipts by Source of Funds, Table No. 11 in *Expenditures for Community Health and Welfare, 1955: Summary Report.* Bulletin 192. New York, 1955.

United States Bureau of the Census. *Census of Population: 1950.* Vol. II: *Characteristics of the Population.* Washington, D.C.: U.S. Government Printing Office, 1953.

—— *Census of Population: 1950. Special Reports: Institutional Population.* Population Census Report P-E No. 2C. Preprint of Vol. IV, Part 2, Chapter C. Washington, D.C.: U.S. Government Printing Office, 1953.

United States Children's Bureau. *Adoptions in the United States and Its Territories, 1955.* Statistical Series No. 39. Washington, D.C.: U.S. Government Printing Office, 1957.

—— *Children Receiving Child Welfare Casework Service from Public Welfare Agencies, March 31, 1956.* Washington, D.C.: U.S. Government Printing Office, 1956.

—— *Children Served by Public Child Welfare Programs, 1957 with Trend Data 1946–57.* Statistical Series No. 45. Washington, D.C.: U.S. Government Printing Office, 1958.

—— *Essentials of Adoption Law and Procedures.* Publication No. 331. Washington, D.C.: U.S. Government Printing Office, 1949.

—— *Financing Public Child Welfare Services, 1956.* Statistical Series No. 46. Washington, D.C.: U.S. Government Printing Office, 1958.

—— *Foster Care 1956.* Child Welfare Reports No. 8. Washington, D.C.: U.S. Government Printing Office, 1957.

—— *Protecting Children in Adoption.* Report of a Conference Held in Washington, June 27 and 28, 1955. Publication No. 354. Washington, D.C.: U.S. Government Printing Office, 1955.

—— *A Research Program for the Children's Bureau.* Washington, D.C.: U.S. Government Printing Office, 1953.

—— *Standards for Specialized Courts Dealing with Children.* Publication No. 346. Washington, D.C.: U.S. Government Printing Office, 1954.

Vincent, Clark E. "The Unwed Mother and Sampling Bias," *American Sociological Review,* Vol. XIX, No. 5, 1954.

Warner, W. Lloyd, and Paul S. Lunt. *The Social System of a Modern Community.* New Haven: Yale University Press, 1941.

Weissman, Irving. *Guardianship: a Way of Fulfilling Public Responsibility for Children.* U.S. Children's Bureau Publication No. 330. Washington, D.C.: U.S. Government Printing Office, 1949.

Whyte, William H. *The Organization Man.* Garden City, New York: Doubleday Anchor Books, 1957.

Williams, Robin M., Jr. *American Society.* New York: Alfred A. Knopf, 1951.

Witmer, Helen Leland. *Social Work: an Analysis of a Social Institution.* New York: Rinehart and Company, Inc., 1942.

Wolins, Martin. "Social Science and Social Work: an Appraisal of Interdependence," *Child Welfare,* Vol. XXXV, No. 2, 1956.

INDEX

303, 337, 338, 343, 347–49; adoption in, 297(*tab.*), 298, 303(*tab.*)–5, 308, 314, 337, 344, 346–47, 349; Community Council, 299, 301, 341; United Fund, 300, 302; Society for the Prevention of Cruelty to Children (SPCC), 300, 303, 318, 319, 320, 321; St. James Orphanage, 300, 319, 335, 341; return home in, 303(*tab.*), 314, 344, 347, 348; legal roles in, 318–22; Welfare Department, 318–22, 335, 337, 338, 339; Family and Children's Welfare Society, 319, 338, 339, 340–41; placement pattern of, 333–34(*tab.*); *agency network in:* 335–42; diagram, 335(*fig.*); characteristics, 336(*tab.*); history of services in, 337–38; Children's Friend Society, 337, 338, 341; St. Benedict's School, 339, 341; children and parents in, 342–49; population of dependent children under study in, 419(*tab.*); codes and statutes of, 436–37

Caliveri, Judge Manuel, of Brighton, 318–22
Callen, Bobby Jo, case history of, 214–15
Cape Verdians, 299, 300, 305
Case histories, in rural areas, 10–14, 24, 69–72; in small urban areas, 74–79, 82, 85, 94, 140–42; in metropolitan areas, 145–48, 212; in big cities, 214–17, 284–86; of children likely to grow up in foster care, 358–61; of adoptive parents, 364–66, 375–77
Case records, selection of, 398–99; percentages of item-by-item agreements in study of, 400(*tab.*); agreements in judgment of psychological factors in, 401(*tab.*); framework for collecting data in, 408–12; numbers in study, 418–19
Caste and Class in a Southern Town (Dollard), 150*n*.2
Castillo, Tita, case history of, 77–78, 94
Catholics, adoption of, 14, 28, 66, 67, 92, 98, 165, 207, 238, 281, 284, 285, 373; social patterns and, 17*n*.6, 18, 81, 86, 93, 96–97, 152*n*.5, 166, 224, 227, 231, 232–33, 293, 300, 301, 346,

387; foster care and, 63, 65, 132, 134, 138–39, 202, 205, 208, 210, 275, 276, 345, 361; agencies for, 71, 108, 125, 185, 186, 187, 189, 191, 195, 229, 235, 237, 241, 243, 256, 258, 261, 262, 265, 266, 267, 268, 319, 335, 339
Centralia, population of dependent children under study in, 144, 419(*tab.*); Welfare Department, 146, 162, 193; Catholic Children's Agency, 147; adoption in, 147, 148, 162, 163(*tab.*), 165–67, 176–77, 181, 196, 198, 200, 206, 207–208, 210, 274, 291, 307(*tab.*), 308, 313(*tab.*), 329(*tab.*), 330(*tab.*); placement, length of care and separation ages of children in, 148; foster care in, 148(*tab.*), 160–62, 180, 181, 191, 196–98, 199–206, 210–11, 331(*tab.*), 332(*tab.*), 333(*tab.*), 343, 350; population of, 151*n*.4; economy of, 151–52, 167; social patterns of, 151–56, 287, 288; education in, 152*n*.5; median income in, 152*n*.5, 294, 440(*tab.*); occupations in, 152*n*.6; return home in, 162, 163(*tab.*), 172, 179, 180, 181, 196, 200, 203–4, 205, 312, 313(*tab.*); St. Vincent de Paul Society, 166; legal roles in, 171–74, 315(*tab.*); codes and statutes of, 174–78, 315(*tab.*), 428–32; institutional care in, 176, 195, 197, 199–200, 273, 274, 332(*tab.*), 343; legal issues in, 178–81, 194; *agency network in:* 189–97; diagram, 190(*fig.*); characteristics, 191–92(*tab.*), 326, 327, 328; history of services in, 193–94, 325; Graham Home, 195; children and parents in, 198–206
Charles, Rex, case history of, 147
Child guidance clinics, 44, 45, 193, 382, 384, 387
Children, dependent, sense of self-identity of, 1, 22, 68, 139, 146, 147, 209, 214, 215, 283–84, 348, 354; method of study, 2, 10, 398–401, 408–12; problems of, 7–8, 24, 59, 378–80 (*see also* Psychological symptoms, behavior problems and); relinquished, 11, 14, 64, 139, 147, 204, 214, 360–62; visited, 13, 360, 361–62; unvisited, 64, 131–32, 146, 204, 357–60, 362; interpersonal relations of,